'A clarion call to make tomorrow much better for our children, offering evidence, ideas and practical steps that need to be taken urgently. Politicians of all stripes should have this book and the actions on top of their to-do list!'
**Professor Sir Michael Marmot CH,
Director, UCL Institute of Health Equity
and author of THE HEALTH GAP**

'Makes a compelling case that strong, healthy, confident children are the essence of a thriving nation … a shot in the arm for all who believe this generation holds the key to a better future.'
Lisa Nandy MP

'Deeply practical, a route map of where we have gone wrong and what we can put right. It should be required reading for the next government.'
Brendan Cox, founder of the Together coalition

'Children are 20% of our population, 100% of our future. This book comprehensively shows how failure to acknowledge that is the biggest missed opportunity.'
**Tim Loughton MP, former Children's
Minister and co-Chair of the All-Party
Parliamentary Group for Children**

'A society's top priority must be to protect the well-being of all its children. I know as my childhood was stolen from me. This book shows how it can be done.'
**Emmanuel Jal, former child soldier, singer
and songwriter, peace activist**

'Brings together an astonishing group of experts to paint a picture of how and why we should make our country a better place to be a child. Through data, stories, metaphors and essays, Paul Lindley has created a vision offering radical and challenging ideas for the changes necessary for generations of children to thrive. It all deserves serious consideration.'
Naomi Eisenstadt, first Director of Sure Start and formerly Deputy Chair of the Poverty and Inequality Commission for Scotland

'Mandela said, "Our children are … our greatest asset as a nation." Paul Lindley uses this to set out the vital regeneration of our children's future: a brilliant, exciting manifesto for change, a real gift to any political party with vision.'
Baroness Helena Kennedy KC

'Paul Lindley combines new insight, essays and stories in a compelling agenda for change. Like Thomas Coram 300 years ago, he challenges the great injustices for the next generation and calls upon us all to build a better future for our nation. Reflective, expansive and inspiring.'
Carol Homden CBE, CEO of Coram

'The right book at the right time … full of fresh ideas. It should be required reading for all policy makers in national and local government.'
Andy Burnham, Mayor of Greater Manchester

'A powerful and inspiring account of why and how we can make this the best country for children to grow up in. A must-read for policy makers of all political parties.'
Claire Ainsley, Director of the Project on Center-Left Renewal at the Progressive Policy Institute and former Labour Party Executive Director of Policy

RAISING THE NATION

How to Build a Better Future for Our Children
(and Everyone Else)

Paul Lindley

Foreword by
Helle Thorning-Schmidt

Dear Chris,
May you find an
ally and inspiration
in the pages of this
book.
merry christmas !!
Love,
Heather,
Max & Arlo

First published in Great Britain in 2024 by

Policy Press, an imprint of
Bristol University Press
University of Bristol
1-9 Old Park Hill
Bristol
BS2 8BB
UK
t: +44 (0)117 374 6645
e: bup-info@bristol.ac.uk

Details of international sales and distribution partners are available at
policy.bristoluniversitypress.co.uk

British Library Cataloguing in Publication Data
A catalogue record for this book is available from the British Library

ISBN 978-1-4473-6647-8 paperback
ISBN 978-1-4473-6648-5 ePub
ISBN 978-1-4473-6649-2 ePdf

Cover design: Jamie Keenan

Photograph from Chapter 9 © Sesame Workshop
Photographer: Ryan Donnell
Photographs from Chapter 10 © Nancy Richards Farese

Bristol University Press and Policy Press use environmentally
responsible print partners.

Printed and bound in Great Britain by CPI Group (UK) Ltd,
Croydon, CR0 4YY

FSC
www.fsc.org
MIX
Paper | Supporting
responsible forestry
FSC® C013604

For Alison, Ella, Patrick, Sheila and Vic.

Thank you for giving me the confidence
to use my voice, the privilege of a variety
of positive life experiences, and the love
that underpins my well-being.

Contents

Essay contributors

Chapter 2: How did we get here?

Sophie Howe, first Future Generations Commissioner for Wales

Helle Thorning-Schmidt, former Prime Minister of Denmark and
    ex-CEO of Save the Children International

James Kirkup, journalist, columnist at *The Times* and Director at the
    Social Market Foundation

Chapter 3: The early years

Nicole Green, founder and CEO of Catch Communications

June O'Sullivan MBE, founder and CEO of London Early Years
    Foundation (LEYF)

Chapter 4: Play

Paul Ramchandani, Professor of Play in Education, Development and
    Learning, University of Cambridge

Sophia Giblin, play therapist, founder of Clear Sky and of
    Treasure Time

Bo Stjerne Thomsen, Vice-President and Chair of Learning through
    Play at The LEGO Foundation

Samira Musse, community activist and co-founder of the Barton Hill
    Activity Club

Chapter 5: Local spaces

Tim Gill, scholar, writer, consultant on childhood and campaigner for
    children's play and mobility

Alice Ferguson and Ingrid Skeels, co-founders and Co-Directors of
    Playing Out

Rachel Toms, Director of Urbanism at Sustrans

Chapter 6: Education

Anita Okunde, student

Valerie Hannon, ex-teacher, founder of the Innovation Unit, senior education consultant and author

Sophie Maxwell, founder and CEO of The Really NEET Project and of Escape Assessments

Rt Hon Alan Milburn, former Minister of Health, ex-Chair of the Social Mobility Commission and Chair of the Social Mobility Foundation

Chapter 7: Health

Corinna Hawkes, Professor of Food Systems and Director of the Division of Food Systems and Food Safety at the FAO

Nick Wilkie, Chair of the Parent–Infant Foundation, UK Director of Save the Children and policy adviser to the Cabinet Office and HM Treasury

Ellen O'Donoghue, CEO at James' Place

Rt Hon Sadiq Khan, Mayor of London and former Government Minister

Chapter 8: Digital

Amy Jordan, Professor and Chair in the Department of Journalism and Media Studies, Rutgers University and *Ellen Helsper*, Professor of Digital Inequalities in the Department of Media and Communications, London School of Economics and Political Science

Mike Adams OBE, campaigner for disability rights and founder and CEO of Purple

Henry Warren and Oli Barrett MBE, entrepreneurs and co-founders of the TOTS campaign

Michael Preston, Executive Director at the Joan Ganz Cooney Center and commissioner in the UK's Digital Futures Commission, *Zaza Kabayadondo*, designer and researcher in EdTech and *Stacy Galiatsos*, consultant in digital learning systems

Chapter 9: Children society fails most
Jemeillia, young person in the care system
Graham Handscomb, Professor of Education and ex-local authority
  Director of Education
Sherrie Westin, President of Sesame Workshop
Anne Longfield CBE, campaigner, Chair of the Commission on Young
  Lives and former Children's Commissioner for England

Chapter 10: Democracy
David Runciman, Professor of Politics, University of Cambridge and
  host of the Talking Politics podcast
Nell Miles, undergraduate student and environmental activist
Nancy Richards Farese, photographer
Yasmin Waljee OBE, Pro Bono Lawyer and Partner at Hogan Lovells
  with *Haylea Campbell*, Associate at Hogan Lovells

Chapter 11: Voice
Sir Anthony Seldon, headteacher, ex-university vice-chancellor,
  author, political commentator, historian and educator
Charlotte Church, singer, songwriter and founder of The Awen
  Project
Kerry Kennedy, human rights lawyer and President of Robert F.
  Kennedy Human Rights

Chapter 12: Variety
Ndidi Okezie OBE, CEO of UK Youth
Jon Yates, Executive Director of the Youth Endowment Fund and
  author
Janice Allen, headteacher

Chapter 13: Well-being
Ruth Luzmore, former headteacher
Kirsty McNeill, Executive Director for Policy, Advocacy and
  Campaigns at Save the Children UK
David Gregson, founder of #BeeWell, co-founder of Phoenix Equity
  Partners, Executive Committee Member of the Institute for Fiscal
  Studies and Director of the Barclays Women's Super League

Acknowledgements

This book exists because my ripple of an idea that has become *Raising the Nation* has been given energy and momentum from hundreds of others' own ripples of support. Together, collectively, we have created a wave that is potentially powerful. That potential could now begin to break down barriers to building a better future for children (and for everyone else).

Each ripple maker has been invaluable to causing *Raising the Nation*'s wave to roll. To each, my gratitude for their energy, time, expertise, patience, kindness and support is immeasurable. Thank you.

My greatest thanks are offered to Ruth Luzmore and Katherine Trebeck: for over a year you were my sisters, advisers, collaborators, inspirers, friends, critics, colleagues and believers. From the first capital letter to the final full stop, you invested in the idea and helped me hone my final manuscript with your research, stories, advice, logic and humour. My life is enriched by our experience, as is this book.

I am wholly indebted to all the essayists whose expertise, ideas and calls to action bring added depth and credibility to the book and website (www.raisingthenation.co.uk). Each of you has lent your name and knowledge to this project with generosity and friendship, and without ego.

Thank you to the whole team at Policy Press. Alison Shaw, you bought into the concept of where my imagination had gone without hesitation, and that support has unlocked all that followed. Ginny Mills, you are a superb editor, knowing how to both push and support me to find the final manuscript. Grace, Rebecca, Kathryn, Dawn and Jess, you each have created your own unique ripples that are part of our wave. Thank you also to the anonymous and non-anonymous reviewers whose feedback on my initial manuscript has shaped a significantly improved final offering.

There are many people whose – probably long forgotten – small words of hope, kind introductions, own imaginations, advice and encouragement are mini-ripples in themselves. Claire Ainsley, Chris Brown, JP Cherrington, Peter Docker, John Goodwin, John Heffernan, Sonny Leong, Dennis Marcus, Michael Marmot, Lisa Nandy and Rachel Reeves are among such early pebble throwers.

Thank you Alison, my wife and my rock, you have always supported me with my crazy ideas. This project is no different. Your countless ripples have helped it morph from imagination and ideas to structure and reality. I love you.

My gratitude would be incomplete without a private thank you to two people whose humanity, vision and impact have, for decades, been giant waves transporting me through my life: Nelson and Bobby. I'm proud to include your legacies in *Raising the Nation*.

Finally, my thanks to *you* for reading this book. The real power of its wave, to break down barriers of resistance and carry hope for a better future, is now in your hands.

Foreword

Helle Thorning-Schmidt

Former Prime Minister of Denmark
and ex-CEO of Save the Children International

When I was very young, one of my first social actions was to write a triumphant essay celebrating the Danish government's abolition of the right for parents to use corporal punishment. I started anti-bullying activities in school when I was ten.

Later, as a mother of two young children, I experienced the intense desire for wanting their lives to be full of hope, and the world they inherit to be a place where they could thrive and shape their future – feelings universally shared by parents throughout history.

And later still, as Prime Minister of Denmark, I knew that all my challenges – economic growth, climate change, inequality, conflict – were always innately about the world we pass on to our children and how we equip them to solve the challenges they will face.

After my time in government I was proud to lead Save the Children, because I have always believed that if you can improve the lives and futures of children, you can transform the world for the better. After all, the children of today will one day be making decisions in their workplaces, communities, government and across the international community. The perspectives, experiences, beliefs, knowledge, skills and attitudes that will determine how they carry out those tasks almost always have their roots in childhood.

The Geneva Declaration of the Rights of the Child states that 'Mankind owes to the child the best it has to offer' (League of Nations, 1924). It is also a truth that the fate of the world is truly determined by the lives of its children.

When Paul Lindley approached me about this book, I had no hesitation in offering my support. He has gathered an impressive array of experts who share his passion and belief that building a child-centred future is exactly what is needed now. From scalable local pilots to top-down legislation, and from political frameworks to community actions, this book contains many fantastic ideas and proposals, which, when considered together, make a powerful argument for change that is hard to resist. His concept of a National Children's Service is a place from which to build a brighter future.

This book is a challenge to us all: whether we are in positions of policy influence, are parents, or are hoping to have children or work with children in a professional or voluntary capacity. It challenges us to demand change and to make changes. It is a call to action to demonstrate in deeds, not just words, that we understand that our society's children will be our society's future. We need to reset and raise our measures of success for our children, focusing on providing them with a voice to shape their lives, a variety of experiences and choices in living their lives, and protecting their well-being so that they may thrive.

I have enjoyed reading the ideas of my fellow contributors, and have been inspired by their policy ideas. More so, I applaud the way Paul has brought together the learnings and proposals from other academic, campaigning and lived experiences, and woven them into his own tapestry that offers a focus on which to build our society in the coming decades – and to measure its success. I am uplifted by his ambition for creating a transformative agenda for the next decade. I hope that you will be too.

One of the contributing essays in the book introduces us to Ariadne's thread – a golden silk thread that helped Theseus find his way out of a giant maze and escape the Minotaur in Greek mythology. Today we use the term for the ability to problem solve out of situations where all can appear lost, because there are golden threads all around us – we just need to know how to look for them. This book shows us how.

Our world will be shaped by our children. So let's all help them thrive and create our brightest future.

Copenhagen, March 2023

Preface

In May and June 1995, South Africa hosted the third Rugby World Cup – the first major sporting event to be held in the country since the end of apartheid. The tournament would end with victory for the home team and the remarkable sight of their recently elected president, Nelson Mandela, presenting the trophy dressed in the controversial Springbok shirt and cap, sporting colours that had, under apartheid, only been awarded to White athletes. This moment created an iconic image, showing the world what Mandela had to say, without him saying a single word.

In those same months, Mandela used the power of actual words to cast light on another big challenge. Two speeches in particular cut deep into my moral imagination. For nearly three decades I have cultivated them, de-weeded their soil, and seen them germinate and grow into the green shoots that are the genesis of this book and the philosophy that it proposes.

In May 1995, Mandela said,

> There can be no keener revelation of a society's soul than the way in which it treats its children. ... As we set about building a new South Africa, one of our highest priorities must therefore be our children. The vision of a new society that guides us should already be manifest in the steps we take to address the wrong done to our youth and to prepare for their future. Our actions and policies, and the institutions we create, should be eloquent with care, respect and love.
>
> This is essentially a national task. The primary responsibility is that of government, institutions and organised sectors of civil society. But at the same time we are all of us, as individuals, called upon to give direction and impetus to the changes that must come.

Our actions should declare, in a practical and exemplary way, the importance and the urgency of the matter.[1]

And in June he added: 'Our children are the rock on which our future will be built, our greatest asset as a nation. They will be the leaders of our country, the creators of our national wealth who care for and protect our people.'[2]

The gauntlet Mandela threw down is: if we really want the best possible future for our country, we must nurture, develop and equip our children – our greatest asset as a nation – to thrive in it. That is the core challenge this book sets out to meet.

Raising the Nation seeks to build a compelling case for *why* the future strength of our communities, environment and economy fundamentally depend on our ability to nurture smart, strong and kind children. In its chapters I have drawn together ideas, activities and evidence to reach conclusions and propose actions to set out *how* we can achieve this possible future. Consequently, it illustrates that building a child-centred future will earn political, economic and societal dividends that can bring real and lasting systemic improvements to the way we all live. It also implies that if our government doesn't prioritise this vision, we should demand that it does.

I have written *Raising the Nation* partially to offer political parties the impetus to develop child-led policies, equipping them to deliver on pledges to build a better future. I also wanted to share a glimpse of the plethora of ideas and opportunities that exist to create a coherent, compelling and practical pathway to that better future. This book presents only a tiny fraction of the ideas and actions already being implemented – at small scale or in different lands – in the world today. I've shared these to inspire rather than to be prescriptive and exhaustive. Finally, I hope its conclusions might provide a spark that creates energy to propel campaigners to organise the latent political power that families possess, and so generate the momentum to deliver the proposed changes.

This book is published approximately ten years after I sold Ella's Kitchen, the company I founded, and the UK's biggest baby food company. Named after my daughter, that business, and my entrepreneurial journey within it, showed me that, to steal a quote from Muhammad Ali, 'impossible is nothing'. Since then, I have explored something of a 'plural' career as I try to use my experience, passions and networks to create positive change for children and their future opportunities in adulthood. I have learned so much over the last three decades from the impressive experts with whom I have worked.

From Sesame Workshop I learned how critical social-emotional learning is in early childhood development; from Robert F. Kennedy Human Rights, it's been the power young people have when they feel confident to speak truth to power; from London's Child Obesity Taskforce I saw first-hand the reality of health inequalities and the complexities of the causal issues affecting so many children's lives; from Nickelodeon I came to understand the power of having a voice, as well as the opportunities presented by tech and the media to help children's lives; from Ella's Kitchen I learned how to create change from nothing, and to leverage the power of business to be a force for good in society; from my extraordinary position as chancellor of the University of Reading I have seen how a culture of curiosity, coupled with access to knowledge and expertise, can equip people to challenge the status quo; and from *Little Wins*, my first book, I saw how the power of a narrative can inspire an audience to reassess how they think about things.

Each experience has deepened my understanding of the issues children face, and has helped me develop solutions to improve their lives. These experiences have allowed me to build friendships and relationships with people who deeply care about the welfare of children. They have given me an insight into how we, as a society, treat our children. When coupled with my curious mindset, I realised I had a rare opportunity to draw together ideas I've seen over the years that respond to the perennial problems we face as a society. I could ask questions that are too often unasked, rethink possibilities for the future, draw on trusted relationships and reach out to new people – all helping develop a changed mindset as to what we regard as 'success' in our country.

And so, the quest for a child-centred future began. It developed from an idea based on little more than an aspiration for the future to a project I hope will leave you, the reader, with a deep sense of possibility. At its core is a vision for how our country can not only be better tomorrow than it was yesterday, but also be the best place for children to grow up in, to become the people they each have the potential to be, thereby creating the best possible future society. This quest concludes with my vision for a National Children's Service: a policy-making framework concept and programmatic ideas to ensure children can thrive and we can build a better future for everyone. While this idea is still in its infancy, I am beginning a debate, to assist young people to participate in its development and to create an enabling environment for its realisation.

My conclusions and proposed actions are informed and supported by fellow thinkers, creators, activists, artists and agitators who have generously penned short essays sharing their expertise and insight that help build my case. Each brings a deep understanding of a core aspect of what a child-centred future needs to be. I asked each to reflect on what they have learned and, in their essay, to challenge our government to address a failing, correct an oversight and/or create an opportunity with respect to children's lives. I have been humbled and astounded that so many responded positively and offered an insight into what they have seen and learned, and what they propose for action. The folks whose ideas you will read have a broad array of expertise, from academic, professional, campaigning and lived experiences, with ages ranging from 16 to 86. They cover aspects of childhood that reflect the wide range and diverse talents of our society.

I realised early on in this project's development that I would have too many essays to include in the limited number of printed pages available, and cheerfully ignored this problem for a while. The challenge didn't become real until I started receiving the drafts and realised that the quality of ideas, and relevance of experience, was both broad and deep. This demanded that I rethink how to present such a repository of inspiring material. I realise now that I responded in the same way I did with any business challenge − by rethinking the offer and creating something new. That resulted in reimagining what a book is and how it is read. And so this book not only includes the physical, digital or audio version that you purchased, but also a companion website − www.raisingthenation.co.uk − which hosts additional content including more essays, and I hope, over time, a deep reservoir of community conversations and perspectives based on the ideas at the heart of *Raising the Nation*. The additional essays are linked to QR codes at the end of the printed version of the relevant chapters and are embedded in live URL links in the e-book. Like its subject matter, this project's structure aims to transform the established way of thinking.

Building a child-centred future is critical for a nation to flourish. This is true not just because today's children will inherit the stewardship of society and, if they thrive as children, they are likely to do so as adults and be best placed to be excellent stewards. It is also true because with such future stewardship, today's adults will have a better chance of thriving in their older age. But that is not all. Children also matter in their own right, in the here and now; in their imaginations, love and energy; and in the hope, perspective and balance they bring to broader society. *Raising the Nation* is a concept that plays to the heart of our humanness in the context of how we live together, value each other and aspire to create a hopeful future.

Only time will tell if this vision for a new kind of society works for you, whether the ideas, evidence and touchpoints it presents, and the way it makes you feel, are impactful enough to cause you to question how we measure 'success' and why we currently prioritise other things over our children's opportunities to thrive. On closing the book, will its arguments have given you sufficient capability, opportunity and motivation to change individual and collective behaviours, and will enough of us insist that our government governs in our name, with the principles of a child-centred future at its core? In short, can this book – and each of us who reads it – live up to Mandela's challenge from 1995 to reveal our society's true soul?

The book's accompanying website is at
www.raisingthenation.co.uk

1

Introduction

Every generation inherits a world it never made; and, as it does so, it automatically becomes the trustee of that world for those who come after.

Robert F. Kennedy[1]

We've all been one. Many of us have them. The word 'child'[*] evokes emotions from the very personal to the broadly cultural, from intense memories to generic, but engaged, observations. Those who are parents[†] almost uniformly make the commitment: 'I will do anything my child'. Feelings about childhood, universal across cultures and generations, conjure up juxtaposed images of wonder and longing; imagination and order; certainty and confusion; excitement and terror. Perhaps such feelings are just about being human, but if so, they're vibrant human, unlimited human, pure human. There is a reason why some of the most iconic images associated with war feature children in distress. They induce our most essential humanity and empathy.

Emotive, visceral, and so often affected by the actions of others, children are a political cause of enormous importance and – above all – potential, if only we are willing to grasp it.

There are 8 million dependent children in the UK,[2] each a future steward of our country's well-being. There are 14 million parents

---

[*] Throughout this book I use 'child' or 'children', the definition adopted by the United Nations Convention on the Rights of the Child (UNCRC), for any person under the age of 18.

[†] Throughout this book I use 'parent/s' as the definition for all those who undertake parenting and caring duties for children.

(of children under 18)[3] and another 14 million grandparents.[4] Tens of millions more people have a wider relationship with children. The vast majority care deeply for the welfare of, and opportunities afforded to, these children. And they all talk. What impacts a child's life, and therefore their support networks' lives, is news that is shared.

The compelling nature of causes involving children is regularly apparent in eye-catching political responses: from universal free school education, Sure Start and childhood immunisation to paid paternity leave. Marcus Rashford demonstrated this in 2020 when the England footballer became a social justice campaigner. Single-handedly raising public awareness of children in England going hungry during school holidays, he mobilised widespread public support and secured a U-turn from the UK government in its stance on food voucher support for families in need. Rashford was just 22 years old at the time.

Yet, despite this widespread concern, the nation's children are facing more precarious lives than they have for decades: 31 per cent of British children live in poverty, a figure higher than any other age group,[5] and all children's relationships, education, mental health and life prospects have since been disproportionately impacted by the COVID-19 pandemic.[6] Be they moral, political or economic, the arguments to implement bold new ideas are as indisputable in logic as they are in terms of raw emotion.

To focus on children would be about much more than potential political power. The future strength of our economy, communities and environment depends on raising smart, strong and kind children from each and every walk of life.

While significant strides in improving opportunities for children have undoubtedly been taken by UK governments over the decades, they have rarely been made with a children's or family strategy as the cornerstone underpinning their central philosophy or agenda. The significant exception was the New Labour government that came to power in 1997. It truly did aim to rebalance the needs of citizens across all age ranges, and placed huge emphasis on prioritising children's opportunities, often seen as being at the expense of others.[7] Many remember Tony Blair's campaigning mantra of 'education, education, education',[8] but in addition, his party's approach to reducing child poverty, increasing early years development and providing child protection, and access to resources, was also deliberate, strategic and largely successful. Examples of policies from this government, and evidence of their impact, pepper this book. A drift, followed by an active turn away from this focus, occurred following the 2010 General Election.

Over a decade later, no political party in the UK now truly lives and talks the language of children as its central message. This book sets out the case to change that. It invites all political parties to take up the mantle and build their vision with an emphasis on prioritising children. Any political party needs an anchor if it is to advocate a vision for the future. A child-centred future offers such an anchor, an imaginative, evidence-based, policy-grounded and story-led concept.

A VUCA world

The history of this century to date is of an increasingly volatile, uncertain, complex and ambiguous world, something that scholars have termed 'VUCA'. It's a world where there is:

- volatility, through the increasing pace of change;
- uncertainty, because of the increased unpredictability of the future;
- complexity, with the increasingly interconnected nature of organisations, industries, markets and geographies;
- ambiguity, with multiple plausible interpretations of why situations are ever more confusing.[9]

The complexity of people, institutions and technologies is deepening, such that the idea that 'everything is connected' is more apt than ever. For example, the financial crisis of 2008 spread around the world from unlikely causal origins in predatory lending techniques targeting low-income homebuyers in the backwoods of the American Midwest. But, having germinated there, it was able to bring down global financial institutions and set the table for a decade of austerity right across the developed world.

Cacophony has been the soundtrack to the entire lives of everyone under 30 years old in the UK. They have known nothing other than a VUCA world. To them it is normal to be swept from one unpredictable crisis to the next. They are a generation that has, so far, been disempowered from being able to truly steer, or even plan, the direction of their lives. Circumstances and speed have made redundant the support systems, resources, skills and environment that previous generations have relied on to meet the challenges of their changing world.

Previous crises have invariably sparked new thinking that stems from a determination that tomorrow will be better than yesterday. But this century's challenges have been so numerous, so deep and so swift that society has not yet found the time and space to truly collectively do this. That's not to say there aren't incredible activities, inspiring programmes and effective energy being spent on tackling individual current challenges. No, it's a relative lack of collective leadership and vision for transformational, coordinated and connected responses across the plethora of all those challenges that is lacking now. This book takes a step into that chasm, proposing a holistic frame for public policy and political manifestos that meets the challenge of thriving in our VUCA decades.

For those under 30, the VUCA events that have dominated their youth are likely to dominate their worldview as young adults and for the rest of their lives. Such events encompass:

- an environmental crisis due to current patterns of human production and consumption;
- a social justice crisis that exposes an unforgivable widening of inequalities;
- the global financial crisis of 2008 that saw the banking system collapse;
- the consequential economic crisis that brought a decade of austerity, stagnated markets and flat-lined standards of living;
- a political crisis manifested in Brexit and populist politics;
- the public health crisis of COVID-19 that has disproportionately affected this generation's education, social development and job opportunities;
- a personal health crisis of fragile mental health exacerbated by the impact on children's anxiety in the face of the other crises;

- a technology crisis, with the ubiquitous and dangerous presence of always-on social media in teenagers' lives; meanwhile governments try to play catch up against constantly evolving forms of cyber-hacks and ransomware;
- the terrorism crisis manifested in 9/11, 7/7, the London and Manchester Bombings and other atrocities;
- a geo-political crisis evidenced by the consequences of Russia's invasion of Ukraine and escalating tensions between China and the USA.

How can we ensure that the next generation of children are raised in a society that better supports them so that each can develop the skills, confidence and opportunities to thrive in the context of ongoing volatility, uncertainty, complexity and ambiguity? And are those older generations, especially those who hold more of the decision making and political and economic power today, willing to fundamentally reprioritise our public policy and aim for new measures of national wealth and cultural success to do this?

Making the case for change

The concept of a future super-charged by the benefits realised after children grow up having become the people they had the potential to be is something I've been discussing and developing for three decades. Over that time, I've evolved from pondering questions of why, as a society, we prioritise the things we do, to examining why we don't even do the things we could do. In speaking to experts over the years, I've untangled three threads that are common to virtually every conversation I've had and every piece of evidence I've seen. They are present in the common themes embedded in the essays that form a core part of this book, and they are equally to be found in the evidence presented in the following pages, irrespective of whether from academic research, practical actions or lived experience. They emerge from the stories the numbers tell, precedents history bequests and in the data patterns that can be analysed when things have gone wrong. The threads show that children best succeed when:

- they and their families have agency, a voice, to shape their lives;
- their childhood is full of varied positive experiences;
- their well-being is prioritised.

My conclusion is that if we orient public policy, interventions, assessment and measurement of success under a framework of increased voice, variety and well-being for children, we will individually and collectively thrive in the face of the VUCA future. Chapters 2 to 10 share many such contributions, from which you may draw out these threads. In Chapters 11 to 13 they are specifically and explicitly highlighted and drawn together to support my bold concept of a National Children's Service, which is then shared in Chapter 14.

The threads keep emerging because one or more of them is invariably broken by society's decisions and actions, and the consequences tell us, with crystal clarity, what we ought not to ignore. As we start to pick up the threads, I'll guide you to an inescapable conclusion: that child-centred approaches to public policy should matter to us all, irrespective of whether we have children or not, because it is our best route to a better future.

Our VUCA world presents complex challenges that leaders have struggled to come to terms with. People, especially young people and children, have, however, responded with rapidly shifting and unique perspectives on the world around them.

Contrary to some assumptions, Darwinian evolution is not about natural selection causing the biggest to survive, or the fastest or quickest to learn. It shows that it is those who can *adapt* to changing environments who thrive. Each time society normalises the priority of a motorist driving to work over a child walking safely to school we lose a fragment of that ability to adapt. Each time the incentives to chase profits from selling high fat, salt or sugar foods results in them being marketed directly at children means we lose another. When a troubled child is excluded from school because, in the short term, it is easier than to better support them at school, another is lost. Together with endless other fragments, society fails to adapt to the changing environment that has become, through just these three examples, more polluted, obesogenic and siloed.

Why children matter

Before we turn to understanding what needs to be done differently to build a better future, let's first head off some of the arguments people might make against a focus on children.

First, some people instinctively challenge the basis that today's children aren't thriving, arguing that today's younger generations 'have never had it so good'. In a sweeping dismissal, such people allege they are a 'snowflake' generation that can't cope with the realities of life that have been an inherent part of existence since our nomad ancestors. They say there's nothing unique about the 21st century or about childhoods today, except that parenting and affluence have brought expectations, entitlement and a lack of resilience, grit and determination to our children. While I utterly disagree, even if there was some substance to these dubious claims, their argument would, in fact, re-double the need for change. For if today's children really do lack resilience, determination and an ability to cope with the real meaning of life's challenges, then we really are in deep trouble.

Others argue that it's ridiculous to even suggest that this generation of children, in this country at least, are struggling. They would likely point out that:

- children are better educated;[10]
- life expectancy has never been higher;[11]
- child mortality in the UK trends lower year-on-year;[12]
- as the fifth richest nation in the world in 2020,[13] with the highest GDP it has ever recorded,[14] our whole society, including our children, is wealthier than ever.

All of which may be true as a whole, but these factors do not constitute the definition of 'thriving'. They ignore the other data points – human ones – that are needed to make longer, richer, more educated lives fulfilling. Critically they are inflicted by the 'tyranny of averages': the breadth of spread from the 'average' child to those children experiencing abject poverty or extreme wealth. As we shall see, it is the widening of the gap between the opportunities, access and networks available to different groups of children to which people making 'on the whole' arguments are blind.

Others contend that we can't possibly believe that today's generation of British children are thriving less than other generations in our history. They cite the grandparents of today who grew up during a period of food rationing after war and for some, evacuation from their homes and communities during it. Or the two generations before them, having the misfortune to be children working in factories from nine years old under the harsh realities of Victorian work laws. Others will compare the privilege children enjoy in the UK and juxtapose it with those displaced in the refugee camps of the Middle East, or those starving in Yemen, or those with no education or access to decent health services in climate-ruined, war-ravaged or economically desperate regions right across the world – and say, 'get real'.

Of course, there is some basis for these comparisons; those times and those childhoods are incomparable to life in the UK today. But there is no merit in comparing our daily lives to those centuries ago: inequality and inequity are here, right now, and children compare themselves with *each other*. And make no mistake, there are children today who are as sick or as abused as any in history in absolute terms: the names of high-profile cases such as Baby Peter and Victoria Climbié are etched on recent British memories.

Reducing debates to such 'whataboutery' is irrelevant to our challenge let alone to a government charged with delivering manifesto promises, accountable to an electorate who have been sold a promise of why their lives will be better in the future. It is important to recognise that we haven't yet got it right, and to present a compelling case to ensure we can do so for this generation and the next.

Members of Parliament must face the evidence of what is happening to families in their constituencies and be informed by hearing stories of their lived experiences – evidence showing that a million antidepressant prescriptions were issued to the UK's children between 2015 and 2018;[15] and stories revealing acute overcrowding experiences, like that of a father who shares his two-bedroom flat with his wife and four children and says the only place he can go to let off steam is the bathroom.[16]

It is important to acknowledge exactly why children thriving matters to us all. Everyone wins when all children have a chance to find their own unique purpose, and each can best find theirs by having more voice, variety of experience and well-being in their childhoods. Here are three reasons why:

- *We need a thriving society to meet the unprecedented pace of change.* If society is to thrive, humankind must come together now more than ever. Take this example: experts believe that the COVID-19 pandemic will not be truly over until 70 per cent of the world's population is fully vaccinated.[17] Another example is the government's 'levelling up' agenda in the UK, which each major party has now realised is critical to national success, and which is seen as the master key to unlocking the talents of people in every part of the country.
- *Adult society is simply what happens when children grow up.* In 30 years time, the people who will make the goods and services we will consume, the leaders of our institutions and the carers who will look after us in our old age, they are all children right now. We need thriving children today to deliver a thriving society tomorrow.
- *Children are more than simply tomorrow's adults.* They have ideas, ambitions, compassion, opinions, questions, morals and values that *right now* are as much a part of our collective humanity as are those of anyone else, perhaps more so in that for so many adults, children are a conduit for our primal emotions. Children have influenced world events: Malala Yousafzai was 15 years old when she was shot for speaking up for her right to go to school in Pakistan, and from then began challenging the whole world to educate more girls. Louis Braille was the same age when he completed his alphabet of raised dots that brought the world a way for the blind to read. And Anne Frank was just 13 years old when she first penned her diary, which has proven to be a timeless reminder of the horrors of war and hate.

It's not just the ideas and direct actions of children that have nudged the world forward. Adults have evolved to be 'hard-wired' to protect children in distress. Millions remember how they felt when they first saw Alan Kurdi. He was just three years old in 2015, when his parents dressed him in his blue shorts and a red t-shirt and sought to give him a better life, but the next day little Alan had drowned, his body washed up on a Greek beach. His lifeless body was photographed and shared around the world as a visceral image of the unfairness of the lottery of birth and circumstance.

More happily, each and every day the sound of children's laughter, the sight of them at play and their learning in overcoming new challenges brings immeasurable joy and a sense of perspective to millions of adults. As Brendan Boyle, a partner at the design agency IDEO and play expert, said to me:

> Wouldn't it be so cool and transformative if we piped kids' laughter into work offices. Just think of any playground, where you hear the kids running around and laughing. I think there's more joy in that playground than there is in the whole of Las Vegas. Wouldn't you like to go back to the simple pleasure and joy of those years?[18]

Action built on statistics *and* stories

As public health champion Victor Sidel once remarked, 'statistics are people with tears washed away'.[19] Numbers and data can be used to tell stories, reveal patterns and predict outcomes, and they are often rightly core to political decision-making processes. However, statistics alone don't tell a story in the round. They ignore the humans behind the numbers and often disguise the people they pertain to. The abstract magnitude of statistics can undermine their connection to actual lives. Russian dictator Joseph Stalin knew this psychology well, and reportedly observed, 'if only one man dies of hunger, that's a tragedy. If millions die, that's only statistics.'[20]

Statistics are vital to design public policy and to allocation of resources, but, in isolation, they don't always motivate us to act, or to act in the best way for the most people. There are two dangers to an empirical, data-heavy reliance in designing public policy.

First, it can lead to a 'dictatorship of the majority', when resources are allocated to where the majority use them and the minority completely misses out. Disability justice campaigners face this all the time when their opportunities for equity of opportunity are ignored under cost versus benefit analysis. Hence, for example, the exclusive use of touchscreen technology to access public services is challenging for people with numerous types of disability. It is worth remembering that children are a (voteless) minority too.

The second danger is that decision making becomes reduced to 'quantity', logical analysis, rather than 'quality', humanitarian provision. Sometimes the reason to do something is because it's the right thing to do. Nothing more, nothing less. This is especially true of policy around children. If society believes that all children deserve a great childhood, just because we value great childhoods, irrespective of what that means to the potential of future adults, then policies to enhance childhood experiences should be designed as such. Rationalisation, in the absence of humanity, at an extreme has delivered unthinkable historical outcomes.

To plan a better future for our society, it is essential to understand the array of evidence and statistics in personal human context, because ultimately policy is not about budgets, efficiencies, legislation, regulation or services; policy is about the people it impacts and how they live their lives.

In formulating possible solutions to build that better future, it is also vital to understand the framework of government and democratic powers across the UK. The UK government must command support from a majority of MPs in the Westminster Parliament and secure a mandate from the British electorate at a general election. It has powers over 'reserved matters'[21] across the UK and 'devolved matters' for England. Devolved matters for the other three UK nations are the responsibilities of the Scottish and Welsh Parliaments and the Northern Ireland Assembly, each of which is directly and separately elected by each nation's electorate. Each Parliament/Assembly in turn devolves some democratic decisions and delivery of a range of services to elected metropolitan mayors and local authorities. Devolved powers vary across the nations, but generally include education, housing, environment, social care and health.

Conclusions

Across the coming chapters I will explore ideas and propose solutions to help give voice, variety and well-being opportunities to children and families in this decade, so we can drag our institutions, bureaucracy, government and democracy to a place where they can best serve us by helping our children thrive. That place is where my concept of a National Children's Service can be built.

Each chapter will delve deep into a specific aspect of childhood, and will:

- share what's not working, to hopefully provide the motivation and desire for readers to *want to act*;
- highlight a better way by showing how we can overcome barriers to change and give policy makers, children and parents alike the ability to believe that they *can act*;
- seed ideas of interventions to drive specific responses and fire up those who want change to occur with the determination that they *will act*.

In creating such actions, my goal is not to present a prescriptive set of instructions, but simply to begin the debate. Neither is my goal to present a complete set of issues, or solutions, across the whole breadth of childhood experiences or societal failings to its children. Indeed, I appreciate that the necessary editing process has resulted in some seriously relevant and challenging aspects to some children's childhoods being under-discussed and potentially under-acknowledged. I'm especially aware of serious issues like youth justice, domestic violence, child protection and sexuality and identity. I do, however, believe that the book's concluding ideas offer a systemic solution to structurally tackle all endemic childhood issues.

Nor, finally, am I naive enough to think that this book in itself will tilt the way society sees itself, but I do believe it could create a small ripple that, with others, and over time, will hopefully contribute to building a wave of change to a better future for us all.

To start us off, and to set the debate in context, the next chapter looks at how the concept of childhood has evolved to where it is today, and what's different for this generation of children.

2

How did we get here?

We cannot always build the future for our youth, but we can build our youth for the future.

Franklin D. Roosevelt[1]

Elizabeth was six years old when she had her first job, a 'doffer' in the garment industry: ensuring that the machines ran to maximum efficiency. From 7am to 6pm, six days a week, for the rest of her childhood, she was on her feet all day. She was given 40 minutes for lunch, beaten with a strap if she was slow, and fined an hour's pay if she was 15 minutes late for work.

Emmanuel was seven years old when war came to his town and his father sent him away to be safe. Unfortunately, where he was sent wasn't the education camp they imagined – it was a war camp; he wasn't given a pencil to write, but a gun to fire. By the time he was ten he had fought in three brutal battles. He had no idea if he had killed anyone because he only knew how to fire indiscriminately. In order to survive he killed snails and birds: it was eat them or eat the body of the boy who had died of starvation after they had escaped from the camp together.

Two true stories of brutal childhoods. Are they from the past or present day? From the UK or elsewhere?

Elizabeth Bentley was born in 1808 and worked in a flax mill in Leeds throughout her childhood. We know this because she gave evidence, aged 23, to a parliamentary Commission that contributed to the introduction of the first child labour laws.[2]

Emmanuel Jal was born 172 years later, in 1980. He was a child soldier, fighting in Sudan and Ethiopia. We know this because he is the author of *War Child*.[3] He is now an international hip hop artist and peace activist.

Researching for this book, I came across an extremely sobering statistic: half of all humans have died before their 16th birthday.[4] For those who didn't survive beyond 16, their whole lives, everything they ever knew, was as a child. Further to this, one-quarter of all humans who have ever lived died before their first birthday.[5] They had no memories, and never really knew what it was to be alive.

To properly understand *human* history, we need to understand the history of childhood.

A brief history of childhood

Some experts argue that today's notion of childhood emerged during the Enlightenment of the 17th and 18th centuries, before which children were considered to be mini-adults, and were treated as such.[6] Others challenge this and argue that childhood has always been recognised as a distinct phase of life, as evidenced throughout European history.[7] This argument is based on sources including religious laws, which stated that children's moral responsibility began at the age of 12, and secular laws, which exempted children from adult punishment until they were in their teens. Its proposition is that parents today will relate to parents in mediaeval times, whose young children were also taught nursery rhymes, fed porridge, shod in soft slippers, given 'badges' to chew, wooden frames to learn to walk, sweet treats to enjoy and toys to play with, many of which would be still recognised in computer games today![8]

Throughout the Middle Ages, 'education' – in the sense of training, as opposed to the classroom – existed, but until the 19th century, for the vast majority of children it was the exclusive function of families. The exceptions were aristocratic boys and those destined for priesthood, who went to schools and universities from the Middle Ages.

During the 17th century there was a shift in philosophical and social attitudes towards children.[9] English philosopher John Locke was particularly influential in defining this new attitude. His philosophy, *tabula rasa*,[10] was the idea that at birth the mind is a 'blank slate' without rules for processing data, and that information is added and rules for processing are formed solely by sensory experiences as children grow into adults. The implication of this thinking was that it is the duty of parents to 'imbue the child with correct notions'. Locke emphasised the importance of providing children with 'easy pleasant books' to develop their minds rather than using force to compel them, as 'children may be cozened into a knowledge of the letters; be taught to read, without perceiving it to be anything but a sport, and play themselves into that which others are whipped for'.[11]

During this period, ideas about the values and norms of the 'ideal' family centred round the upbringing of children. It became widely recognised that children possess rights on their own behalf. This included the rights of poor children to sustenance, membership of a community, education in spiritual matters and job training. The Poor Relief Act of 1601 put on each local parish a responsibility for all the poor children in their area.[12]

Jean-Jacques Rousseau developed the 'Romantic' attitude towards children in his famous 1762 novel *Emile, or On Education*, describing childhood as a brief period of sanctuary before encountering the perils and hardships of adulthood. The Romantics' views contrasted with the culturally dominant, stridently moralistic, Calvinist views of infant depravity – the belief that children were born with original sin and were prone to sin in childhood, and that it was a parent's job to reform them.[13]

With the onset of industrialisation, the reality for many children was exploitation in the workplace. Although child labour was common in pre-industrial times, children would generally help their parents with family farming or cottage crafts. By the late 18th century, however, children were employed in factories and mines and as chimney sweeps,[14] often working long hours in dangerous jobs for low pay.[15] For example, in England and Scotland in 1788, two-thirds of workers in water-powered cotton mills were said to be children.[16]

As the 19th century wore on, the contradiction between the conditions on the ground for children of the poor and the middle-class notion of childhood as a time of innocence led to the first campaigns for the legal protection of children. From the 1830s, reformers attacked child labour, bolstered by Charles Dickens' descriptions of horrific London street life.[17] The campaign that led to the Factory Acts began a slow culmination of restrictions on child labour – from 1833, when the first limits were set so children working in the cotton and woollen industries must be aged nine or more, right through to the Factory and Workshop Act 1901, where the permissible child labour age was raised to 12. Progress was slow.

The latter half of the 19th century saw the introduction of compulsory state schooling for children across Europe, which began to remove children from the workplace and place them in schools. Taxes funded universal free schools and the training of teachers, just as they do today.

Play, a crucial and central part of being a child since antiquity, also began to be recognised and encouraged more formally by the beginning of the 20th century, with factory-made toys (such as dolls and dolls' houses) becoming accessible to almost all children. Along with this came the growth of the advertising industry that targeted both parents and children. Sports activities began to be organised for boys, and the Boy Scouts was founded in 1908, providing young boys with outdoor activities aimed at developing character, citizenship and personal fitness.[18]

By the 1940s, led by the middle and upper classes, and eventually adopted by working-class families, parents' perceptions of their 'reward' for parenthood had changed. By then, they had effectively swapped the earned income and domestic labour streams of previous generations by having large numbers of children for the cost burden of childrearing and the love, smiles and emotional satisfaction anticipated from their (fewer) children.

Childhood rights and protections continued to expand across the second half of the 20th and into the 21st century. For example, in 1947 the minimum school leaving age in England was raised to 15, in 1972 to 16,[19] and from 2015 all under-18-year-olds now have to be in education or employment with training.[20] The age of criminal responsibility in England and Wales was raised from 8 to 10 in 1968, where it remains, which is extremely young considering that children are not considered mature enough to serve on a jury, and is the lowest in Europe.[21,22]

Laws protecting vulnerable children have also been significantly overhauled in recent decades. The Children Act 1989 brought together and simplified existing legislation relating to the care of children. Within family law, it shifted the legislative focus towards keeping families together, and valuing children as individuals with their own interests and rights. Indeed, it codified the principle that protecting the welfare of a child could justify a parent's rights being overridden for the first time. The Act was pretty revolutionary in a number of ways, including defining parental rights versus parental responsibilities, the use of orders concerning who a child should live with, and imposing significant and additional responsibilities on local authorities to contribute to the care of children in need.

The Children's Act 2004 extended the responsibility for promoting the welfare and well-being of children and created the roles of a children's commissioner and director of children's services within a local authority. The Children and Young Persons Act 2008 and the Children and Social Work Act 2017 have added to the suite, and represent a significant response to protect vulnerable children's childhoods.

But perhaps the high-water mark in this journey of childhood has been the United Nations Convention on the Rights of the Child (UNCRC), which, in 1989, codified the legal rights of children. It was ratified by the UK Parliament in 1991.[23] You will meet the UNCRC many times throughout this book.

This brief history illustrates that the 21st-century conceptualisation of childhood is a relatively modern one and, for all its advances and development, remains imperfect, contradictory and evolving. For example, as James McNeal observed of the USA in the 1980s, there are:

> persistently baffling contradictions between the private sentimentalisation of our own children and the collective indifference to other people's children. Contrast four-to-twelve-year olds' almost five billion dollars of private annual income in the form of allowances, gifts from parents or relatives, and payments for household chores and odd jobs spent mostly on discretionary expenses with the stinginess of a public pocketbook that reduces a fourth of the nation's children to poverty (McNeal, 1987, p 32).[24]

In recounting this often-bleak history of childhood, I wanted to illustrate the emergence of a recognition, followed by actions, that children need specific protections, training and education, and that they thrive when they experience supported childhoods.

An example to counter such history with future-facing optimism came in 2016, in Wales, when a quiet revolution saw Sophie Howe become Wales' first, indeed, the world's first, future generations commissioner. The commissioner is the legal guardian of the interests of future generations, providing guidance and advice to the Welsh government and public bodies. In my mind her role represents the interests of today's and tomorrow's children and adults. Sophie completed her term in 2023, and wrote this essay for us shortly beforehand.

On being the world's first future generations commissioner
Sophie Howe, first Future Generations Commissioner for Wales

As the Future Generations Commissioner for Wales, I often get asked: 'How can you know what future generations will want?' And I can't know for sure. But what I do know is that I wish our ancestors had thought about my generation and the problems we may face. Perhaps if they had, we wouldn't be living in a world that allows the poor to get poorer, our planet to get hotter, and our communities to be separated by hate.

Our generation doesn't need to have the same legacy; we can be good ancestors. We can use the knowledge we have to make sure our Earth is habitable for those who come after us. My educated guess is that our children, and grandchildren, and their children, will want a world in which they can thrive.

That future is in the hands of today's generations. We must have a fundamental change in the way we think and act if we are to deliver on this legacy. Currently, systems of governments around the world do not enshrine the rights of future generations. Our leaders are continuing to make decisions that put profit and politicians before our people and planet.

In Wales, things are not perfect, but we are starting to make big structural decisions to create real change 50, 100 and even 250 years down the line. We are the first of only two countries in the world that has legislated to protect the interests of people yet to be born, and the only country in the world with an independent future generations commissioner to hold our government to account to today's children *and* their children and beyond.

How does it work?

The Well-being of Future Generations (Wales) Act 2015 makes it a legal duty for our government and public bodies to achieve seven connected, sustainable well-being goals: to make our nation healthier, more equal, resilient and prosperous; as well as a responsibility to the globe and the communities and cultures within it.

The Act also tasks us with working in specific ways to improve decision making. Our decisions must involve our communities and be a collaborative effort between sectors. That's why, for example, we have doctors working with museum directors to tackle loneliness and isolation. It asks us to shift our mindset to preventative decision making, rather than acute, reactive efforts alone. It means we must be holistic in our thinking, seeing the connections between the present and the future and between issues. The Sustainable Development Principle from the Act requires our government and national institutions to demonstrate how they are making decisions that meet today's needs without compromising the ability of future generations to meet their own. The Act also gave me one incredible job: 'the guardian of future generations', responsible for holding those under the Act to account.

The Act in action

One of the best examples of the Act in action, and a moment that has given me tremendous pride, is the victory of persuading the Welsh government to cancel plans to build a 13-mile stretch of additional M4 motorway. The road, which would have run through environmentally sensitive wetlands, was considered to be a done deal. It was an economy versus environment argument, and in those situations, the economy generally wins. Yet the framework of the new Act bound politicians to make the decision in favour of communities and the environment instead. Wales now has a new transport strategy that places active travel, such as walking, cycling and public transport, at the top of the travel hierarchy and the car at the bottom. So far, 55 road schemes that were being considered have been halted in line with the Act to explore more sustainable options, and record sums of money have been invested in active travel and public transport. Additionally, transport must be considered an issue of equality, especially for our children and young people. Currently, one in four young people said travel costs were a barrier to attending job interviews, and two in five said poor public transport was a barrier to getting a decent job.[25] We also know that children from low-income families have fewer opportunities for extra-curricular activities and fewer options for education because of high travel costs.[26] The Act requires us to see the connections between issues, and understand that improved transport is not just good for the environment, but for tackling inequalities in our society, too.

The introduction of a Basic Income pilot scheme for those leaving care is another great example of the Act helping our children in the present, and those in the future, and is a promising step towards a Universal Basic Income (UBI) in the near future. Research shows that a UBI would decrease overall poverty rates in Wales by 50 per cent and child poverty would decrease by 64 per cent, bringing it to a rate of under 10 per cent in Wales, where it is currently the worst in the UK.[27]

We know that we will not achieve societal change by passing legislation alone, and nor will we achieve it by simply changing processes and bureaucracy. What is needed is to win the hearts and minds of the people, to make the future generations' agenda part of the very essence of how things are done.

Building momentum
In getting there, such an agenda faces three types of people, who I call:

- *Frustrated Champions*, who believe in the Act, but who are often bound by the structures and institutions around them that are unwilling to change;
- *Passive Procrastinators*, who leave it up to others;
- *Abominable 'No'-men*, who are ingrained in the systems of old, and who put up barriers at every turn, making change slow and arduous.

To change the culture, we need Abominable 'No'-men to become Passive Procrastinators, the Passive Procrastinators to become Frustrated Champions, and the Frustrated Champions to become significantly less frustrated. That will be the tipping point for future generations thinking. When this happens, the voice of the people will be too loud to ignore.

What more needs to change?
So where do we go from here? I know that Wales is on the right track, but to have global impact, there is a need to get others on board.

'Futures thinking' is already popping up around the globe. The Network of Institutions for Future Generations now has representatives from the Netherlands, Hungary, Gibraltar, Canada and Israel. Closer to home, the Scottish and UK Parliaments are working on their own future generations' legislation. Most promisingly for the globe, the United Nations (UN) has announced its support for the establishment of a UN Special Envoy for Future Generations, and is planning a Futures Summit as well as a UN Declaration for Future Generations.[28] I would like to see every country in the world demonstrating how their decision making is accounting for the interests of future generations. In this, the UN embedding global commitments could be a game changer.

The future generations agenda is not perfect, but it constitutes cause for hope. Hope for a future where our children are not crippled by anxiety in our polluted planet, but are free to be children. A world where we have hope again.

Children and realpolitik

Despite obvious pockets of real progress in recent years, political realities (aka realpolitik) generally mean political objectives tend to trump what children need. The result is that successive governments have effectively de-prioritised investment in children's long-term opportunities, and have focused instead on the shorter-term policy promises of economic growth, lower taxes, 'triple-lock' pensions and the establishment of a national identity. Perhaps it's a consequence of the UK's form of democracy, but the mechanisms around policy choices seem to encourage a particular focus on delivering the supposed needs of core and swing voters. It is, of course, difficult to untangle the cause and effect of actions in a complex society, and the dynamics of the drivers of democratic decision making, and I certainly make no claim to try to do so definitively. I do, however, keenly observe that governments tend to commit disproportionately low investment in children compared to their population size and benefits in terms of future fiscal savings, let alone moral or social justice rationales. It is possible that relative under-investment is correlated to a perceived lack of the immediacy of return within the electoral cycle, the fact that children don't vote, or the legal framework of their rights and status as children is not sufficiently embedded in statute. It is possibly all three!

Perhaps the cruellest example of realpolitik versus children is when they become collateral or manipulated pawns in an adult's game of national defence or offence, extreme populism or ideological dogma: through war.

In wars, children are the last group of people to be thought about yet the first to face the consequences of a particularly acute manifestation of the breakdown of human relations. Helle Thorning-Schmidt, a former politician and former Prime Minister of Denmark, has written an essay for us on this subject.

Our greatest failure: children in armed conflict

Helle Thorning-Schmidt, former Prime Minister of Denmark and ex-CEO of Save the Children International

Bergen Belsen, 1945: a 15-year-old girl dies in a concentration camp less than two months before its liberation, leaving behind a diary of a life lived in hiding. Her name was Anne Frank.

Soweto, 1976: a dying 13-year-old boy is carried away from a student protest having been shot by the police force of apartheid South Africa. His name was Hector Pieterson.

Ukraine, 2022: a photograph of a smiling 10-year-old girl with pink hair appears on screens around the world as one of the first child victims of the Russian invasion. Her name was Polina Kudrin.

These are just three of the many children we recognise as icons of the horror of conflict and war. Their suffering provokes our deepest shock and outrage, making a mockery of that eternal idea that through the eyes of a child you will see the world as it should be.

Indeed, for more than a century, the international community has recognised this, and developed legislation intended to protect children in conflict zones.

Codifying the rights of children

In 1919, in the shadow of the First World War, when around 5 million children were starving in central and eastern Europe and rates of child mortality were at record highs, a British woman and social reformer, Eglantyne Jebb, proclaimed that, 'All wars are waged against children' and began campaigning to support such children.[29]

Against considerable resistance from those who believed that Britain should help its own rather than its recent enemies' children, she built a broad coalition of supporters to establish the first children's charity with an international focus, Save the Children. It drafted the first ever Declaration of Children's Rights, which was adopted by the League of Nations in 1924.[30] The United Nations (UN) adopted an expanded version of this declaration, which was to inspire the most wide-ranging expression of the principle that all children, and not just 'our children', have the same inalienable rights: the 1989 UN Convention on the Rights of the Child (UNCRC).[31] It enshrines key principles such as: the best interests of the child; non-discrimination; the child's right to be heard and to take part in decision making; and the child's right to life, survival and development.

In 1996, a ground-breaking report for the UN on the impact of armed conflict on children[32] led to the creation of a UN Special Representative for Children and Armed Conflict to monitor and report violations, and in 2005, the UN Security Council established a mechanism to monitor and report on six grave violations against children in conflict zones.[33]

Where we are now

So, for more than a century, the profound importance of protecting children when adults resort to military violence has been recognised. Yet in 2014 an estimated 230 million children were living in countries affected by armed conflict,[34] and a 'staggering' average of 71 verified grave violations a day are committed against children.[35]

Tragically, another war on European soil is again reminding its leaders of the urgent moral and strategic imperative for the international community to protect children from the horrors of armed conflict. As Graça Machel has said, 'It is unforgivable that children are assaulted, violated, murdered and yet the world's conscience is not revolted, nor our sense of dignity challenged.'[36]

How can it be that we are not more outraged by the fact that a baby just a month old is tortured? That girls as young as six are being raped? That boys aged ten are forced to become child soldiers? That children die of their wounds because hospitals have been bombed?

These all-too-common violations and threats to children are horrific enough, but they exist on top of the incredibly difficult circumstances in which children affected by armed conflict already live: destroyed communities, increased hunger and disease, homelessness, the absence of schooling, the breakdown of every part of society.

And long after those physical scars have healed, the psychological effects of exposure to conflict and violence continue to destroy the lives of children. If a child feels abandoned by their family, community and the world, what does that tell them about the world?

Whether they become our leaders of tomorrow or members of society, it is our responsibility to ensure that the world's children will be able to play their unique role defined not by the violence and suffering inflicted on them, but by their potential and character.

What the conflict in Ukraine can teach us

During my time as Prime Minister and as CEO of Save the Children International, I was closely briefed on conflicts worldwide where the tactics of war had become more brutal and inhumane, violating children's rights. As I, and others, advocated for supporting children from these countries, we faced populist arguments in many European nations that expounded the pervasive belief that these children were not 'our children' and therefore not 'our' responsibility.

In the UK specifically, government unwillingness to rise to its moral and legal responsibilities during these conflicts created a disconnect between a natural human compassion towards those – including children – driven from their homes, and a willingness to act. We can see a clear pathway between attitudes around immigration inflamed during the Brexit debate, the militarised patrols in the English Channel, the increasing use of language that criminalises those seeking sanctuary and, most recently, the policy to transport people seeking asylum in the UK directly to Rwanda and be processed for settlement there.

However, the war in Ukraine has jolted many European people, and some of their governments, out of their complacency. Within the first month of Russia's attack on Ukraine more than half of its children had been displaced.[37] As I write in August 2022, over 6.6 million refugees have fled the country,[38] the vast majority being women and children. The UK, which only permits entry to those who navigate a complex visa application, has received just over 115,000 people, of which about one-third are children.[39]

The UK government's shamefully slow and bureaucratic initial response was inadequate, yet its 'Homes for Ukrainians' scheme is popular with its citizens who have generously and voluntarily welcomed refugees to live with them. It knows that it needs to actively facilitate and support the partnerships between local councils, voluntary organisations and citizens that its policy necessitated, but which it has failed to sufficiently do. This is not history. This is our present. And how the UK government learns will define our future.

My call to action

The UK government can and must do better for this and future conflict responses. Slow bureaucracy, inadequate coordination and a lack of leadership as well as simple inaction have consequences. It, like governments everywhere, must ask itself the simple question: how are we contributing to end the age of impunity, where schools and hospitals get bombed and no one is asked to take responsibility? And it, like all governments, must commit to ending all violence against children, whether abroad or at home. Violence against children in war zones, sexual exploitation and abuse of children, child marriage and the abduction of children are each inhuman practices that every government needs to face with moral leadership and have a plan to tackle. Now.

Because, as in the poignant words of the child victim of war, whose story and diary opened this essay, 'How wonderful it is that nobody need wait a single moment before starting to improve the world.'[40]

Why is change critical now?

While certainly existing, the sparks needed to ignite a drive to a future propelled by meeting children's needs have never quite caught alight. Economic cycles, realpolitik, system architecture, national priorities, a lack of political bravery or vision and other factors have ostensibly extinguished the sparks. Whatever the dampeners are, the power of the state's engine to drive such transformational change has thus far not been unleashed.

So why do I believe that the sparks could ignite now?

At its simplest, the speed of change across multiple aspects of the way we live individually, and as communities, has altered. The dynamics in society across a suite of areas are transformationally different than they have ever been. Recent governments have not sufficiently evolved our institutions to cope with such change. We see it in lagging responses to things that unexpectedly accelerate, for example adequate safeguarding protections against the ubiquity of social media in young people's lives, or the delayed economic action to counter the rampant inflation of 2022. We also see it in the absence of responses to things that unexpectedly rapidly slow down, such as addressing flat-lining industrial productivity or stubbornly slow crime reduction. Most political leaders tend not to be confident enough, or perhaps brave enough, to take the necessary steps quickly enough to address these challenges. Every generation sees change, no society stands still, and if our leaders don't move nimbly to keep up with changes in culture, technology, dominant philosophies and individual opportunity, they essentially move backwards.

In the last century those inflection points – the consequential moments when seismic events unleashed new ideas, actions or rights – delivered transformational momentum and changed our social structures. For example, in the first decade of the 20th century the response to endemic poverty brought the introduction of state pensions, free secondary school places for all children and basic welfare provision. The response to the Great Depression and the Second World War brought the Beveridge Report and the establishment of the National Health Service (NHS) and welfare state, as well as measures designed to protect security, such as the formation of supra-national institutions like the United Nations, Bretton Woods system and the North Atlantic Treaty Organization (NATO).

In this century, Tony Blair and David Cameron's governments began to transform the civil and social rights of increasingly diverse groups of people (for example same-sex marriage), while Gordon Brown's government made serious attempts at reducing inequality with substantial changes to the pension system and tax credits. However, reforms have struggled to be future-proofed against the dizzying speed of social and economic change society has experienced, and particularly how our children have experienced it.

We now have a moment to begin to change all that. Four core aspects to our modern-day lives have been transformed in this century, and form a quartet of overlapping reasons why we must act now. They are:

- the VUCA global context;
- short-termism as the dominant driver of decision making;
- digital technology;
- structural demographic changes.

Each of these impacts the infrastructure, public services and culture of society. And for each, society is inadequately prepared.

The VUCA global context

The Center on the Developing Child at Harvard University has undertaken and collated extensive research on the biology of stress to show that healthy child development can be derailed by excessive or prolonged activation of stress response systems in the body and brain. A VUCA world is one where such derailing is commonplace, and today's children are likely to have seen parents stressed and powerless as they are buffeted by pandemics, economic crashes, public discord and climate and ecological emergencies. The uncertainty is the narrative for their whole childhood, whether they are protected by supportive relationships or, as is the case for many children, not. This means that, in a world where caring adults are impacted by events beyond their control and the state does not sufficiently deliver support, children's physiological and psychological development suffers, often irreparably.

Research shows that communities that are flexible and individuals who are open to change are those that can flourish with new experiences.[41] Given that a VUCA world, and an environment that causes toxic stress, is unlikely to recede anytime soon, society must find ways to accelerate its collective and pooled coping responses, and support and teach children to be open to change. If it does, a VUCA future can eventually be tamed to be a future in which children thrive.

Short-termism

Children and young people in the UK are growing up in a world where everything they *think* they may want is available instantly. As author Simon Sinek observed:

> You want to buy something, you go on Amazon and it arrives the next day. You want to watch a movie, log on and watch a movie. You don't check movie times. You want to watch a TV show, binge. You don't even have to wait week-to-week. ... Instant gratification. You want to go on a date? ... Swipe right – bang – done![42]

On top of this are the increasing powers of business, marketing and the ubiquitous social media platforms to amplify that desire for immediacy. Consider, for example, the explosive growth in the number of social media influencers who operate in an unregulated sector that can now target children. They act as hidden persuaders, using what appears to be organic content creation to market to those least able to distinguish advertising.[43] The influencer marketing industry has a global market worth US$16.4 billion.[44] Being an influencer is now an aspirational, serious career goal for many children. Business marketing's dominant narrative implies our default state is unhappy unless we consume now. Invariably these pressures on consumers encourage borrowing, with instant credit enabling this. I don't think it unreasonable to conclude that experiencing this type of world will have knock-on effects, beyond the well-documented impact on children's self-esteem, to the development of patience and resilience, as well as perceptions of what constitutes a 'good' life.

But it's not just consumption. Our children live in a world where the short-term pressure of public exams, coupled with fewer skilled job opportunities and wider competition for such jobs, encourages most families to passively prioritise the short term, where exam results are seen as the golden ticket for future opportunity, against long-term well-being such as developing non-academic skills and protecting mental health. This, in turn, encourages those who set the school curricula to give active prioritisation to short-term exams. And so the cycle becomes ever more entrenched.

The economy has also morphed to prioritise short-term financial returns rather than building a longer-term foundation of broad-based wealth. The consequences of such emphasis include a growth in inequality, a systemic obsession with unsustainable economic growth and a reduction in transparent public reporting.

Finally, we see short-termism in politics, where it is arguably especially concerning. The nature of the electoral cycle in the UK means that representatives are, on average, 2.5 years away from an election when they will need to account for results. This naturally tends to compel actions targeting short-term and visible impact, at the expense of the long-term societal goals and investment in the contexts that underpin them. In the last decade this has appeared to have accelerated beyond recognition with the advent of successful populist manifesto promises to win elections. The number of populist leaders in, or recently in, power has more than doubled since the early 2000s.[45] Critics of populism warn that its leaders say whatever they think their electoral base wants to hear – truth or lie, benign or malignant – to secure power. This risks translating into divide-and-rule strategies as, once elected, populist politicians focus on delivering benefits for those who helped them secure power, which usually means only a minority of the voters, and never primarily children.

Children are growing up buffeted by the fall-out. There are few handrails to help navigate their way through, as seemingly every institution has adopted a short-term focus, whether in terms of educational, political or investment return.

Digital technology

Children in the 21st century are obviously avid users of digital technology and are growing up as 'digital natives'. Equally obviously, most children of the 20th century, like me, were not. Most children in the UK now use at least one form of digital technology every day, with more than one in five saying they spend seven or more hours a day online at the weekend and almost half spending over three hours online on a school day.[46]

And it's not just teenagers; research suggests that pre-schoolers become familiar with digital devices before they are exposed to books.[47] Increased ownership of personal devices such as smartphones, tablets and laptops has also affected how children of all ages use technology, with concerns raised that their usage is becoming more private and harder for parents to monitor. Internet safety, safeguarding, cyberbullying, use of social media and screentime addictions are new challenges. Government and business need to ensure that the net impact of technology is positive on children and is in service of their ability to thrive. (Chapter 8 examines this in detail.)

Deep demographic changes

The demography of the UK has fundamentally changed in my lifetime, yet our institutions, systems, bureaucracies and democracy have not adapted to serve the population as a whole, and children in particular.

I was born in 1966. In that year:

- The birth rate was 17.47 births per 1,000 people. By 2022 it had shrunk to 11.32 (a fall of over 35 per cent), and by 2100 it is forecast to be as low as 9.5.[48]
- Women in England and Wales had an average of 2.75 children; in 2022 it was 1.65, over one child less for every woman.[49] In addition, access to fertility technology, and the flexibility of choice that comes with that access, has also changed. A consequence is children experience less similar childhoods in comparison with their parents than they did back in 1966.
- Parents also have a more diverse set of experiences influencing their parenting approach. For example, many of today's children benefit from a significantly more involved parenting role by their fathers than children in 1966 would have experienced. Yet in 2018, over 20 per cent of children were growing up in a single-mother household[50] compared to 6 per cent of children in the 1960s and 1970s.[51]
- Life expectancy was 71.44 years, but rose to 81.65 years in 2022, and is forecast to reach 90.76 years in 2100.[52]
- There were about 400,000 people over 85 years old, whereas in 2016 there were 3.2 million, and this group is forecast to reach 5.1 million by 2066.[53]
- Those under 16 represented nearly 24 per cent of the UK population, while in 2022 that group was less than 19 per cent, and is forecast to be just 17 per cent by 2066.[54]
- The over-65s comprised less than 12 per cent of the population; in 2016 they represented 18 per cent, and are forecast to be over 26 per cent by 2066.[55]

As children comprise a declining proportion of the population in countries like the UK, there is a risk that their voice, already insufficiently heard, will be further corroded. One element of this is already apparent: voting. By 2066 almost 32 per cent of the predicted electorate will be over 65, double the number when I was born.[56] At the same time, those under 16 years old in 2066, whatever their actual numbers, and even if the voting franchise is reduced to 16 years old, will still represent zero per cent of the electorate.

The conclusion of these generational shifts is that the odds are increasingly stacked against children due to their declining absolute and relative numbers. As David Runciman has noted: 'Our growing social conformity is not simply because the old are aping the habits of the young. It is because in any society where the middle-aged and elderly are the dominant economic and political blocs, their interests predominate.'[57]

In the context of these facts, the ability, and desire, of state institutions to allocate sufficient resources to support children's general well-being is questionable. James Kirkup tackles this assertion head on in this essay for us.

The politics of children: Britain's choices and priorities

James Kirkup, journalist, columnist at *The Times* and Director at the Social Market Foundation

The two years of Britain's pandemic experience revealed a lot about our nation's priorities. Some aspects were encouraging: we showed ourselves able to take selfless collective action in the face of a wider threat. But some were dismaying.

The foremost conclusion I drew was that this country doesn't think children are very important. How else can one explain the decisions taken on lockdowns, school closures and other COVID-19 mitigations? The blunt facts are that COVID-19 is primarily a threat to older people. Yet many of the measures put in place to contain it imposed the greatest costs on the young.

Noting this reality isn't rejecting or even criticising those measures: I have no ideological opposition to lockdowns, and I make no claim to have had better ideas for how to respond to the virus. But my point is more specific: Britain responded by doing things that fundamentally disrupted the lives of children, often without even acknowledging that damage. I think the lack of attention that politicians paid to the impact on children was culpable, and is illustrated by recent acknowledgement by some that closing schools may have been unjustified.

The COVID-19 cohort not only missed out on learning and development opportunities, but rates of obesity are significantly higher; they are more likely to experience mental health problems; and, perhaps most troubling of all, some simply disappeared – more than 100,000 children went missing from the English school system in 2020 and 2021.

The national neglect of children during the pandemic is likely to entrench inequalities that too often have their roots in childhood. It is a sad fact of British life that economically disadvantaged children are likely to grow up to be economically disadvantaged adults, and unhealthy children become unhealthy adults.

In particular, the rise in childhood obesity may yet come to be seen as the most baleful consequence of a policy decision that saw even playground gates locked. Without a significant shift in our approach to obesity, children struggling with excess weight are likely to lead shorter lives than they would otherwise have had. Childhood obesity must be seen as both a national scandal and a national priority.

Why don't we make children a greater priority? Part of the answer comes down to numbers. Many of the demographic changes underway in Britain have positive origins: on aggregate, we are leading healthier lives with better healthcare, meaning we are living longer. The trend towards greater life expectancy is arguably one of humanity's greatest achievements over the last couple of centuries, more recently matched by declines in infant mortality.

But one consequence of rising life expectancy is a larger cohort of older people, who – naturally and reasonably – expect the state to meet their needs. Since this is a world of scarce resources, meeting those needs means trade-offs: as every new economics student learns in their first lesson, a pound spent on butter cannot be spent on guns. And a pound spent on healthcare – which largely, but not exclusively, benefits the old – cannot be spent on education – which largely benefits the young.

Demographic change helps explain what strikes me as one of the most important and revealing facts about British public spending over the last generation. Thirty years ago, health and education both consumed roughly 12 per cent of all government spending. Today health gets around 20 per cent of spending, and education barely 10 per cent. That gap will only widen as the demands on health and care services grow with an ageing population.

Numbers underpin politics. Older people vote, and politicians want to make them happy, allocating resources accordingly. For a sobering glimpse of where the interaction of demographics and politics leads, look at Florida. One of the wealthiest American states has some of the most underfunded state schools, because an electorate that includes an outsized group of retirees expects its representatives to prioritise that which directly serves them, not wider society.

The British demographic picture is not so stark. There are around 14 million people aged 60 and over in the UK, and around 13 million aged under 19. The young are not outnumbered, yet their interests are often deprioritised in policy making.

The best explanation I can offer for that is a wider problem with British politics and government: short-termism. We are woefully bad at making choices whose benefits are measured in decades. Instead, our leaders too often focus on the things that can be gauged over limited years or just months, often with one eye on the clock counting down to the next election.

Consider the case for significantly improving support for children in their early years. The combined weight of evidence and advocacy on better early years provision is enormous. But when will the nation get a return on the resources required today to expand a two-year-old's cognitive and social development? Certainly not before the next election.

It is a cliché to point out that children are the future, but it's a cliché that's most important to recall in an economic context. The happy story of global economic growth means that an advanced economy such as the UK can only hope to retain its vital comparative advantage if its population has the skills and abilities needed for that work. Failing to properly support the current generation of children risks condemning Britain to long-term decline, something that should worry even the most calculating of resource-allocating policy makers.

But children are not just future productive units for economic gain. They are humanity's purpose: there is surely nothing more important for us to do than try to make sure that those who come after us lead better, happier lives than our own. And on that fundamental point, I worry that Britain is too often failing.

I've run the Social Market Foundation for over six years now, overseeing research into many areas of public policy and national life. But few findings have troubled me as much as the work we did in 2021 with teenagers and young adults, exploring their attitudes and expectations for the future. We found that young people today are more pessimistic about their prospects than their peers were in the wake of the global financial crisis of 2007–08. Half of our respondents said they had given up on ambitions they held when they were younger, with particular concerns about the long-term implications of their disrupted education, their ability to compete in a tough job market and to own their own home. Many doubted they'd ever start a family of their own. The grim bottom line of that research: at an age when they should be full of hope for the future, too many youngsters have already given up on their dreams.

It doesn't have to be this way. As I've tried to explain here, this all comes down to choices and priorities. We can choose to make children, their experiences and their futures, more important. The first step towards that choice is proper analysis, discussion and debate, which is why I'm pleased to be playing a small part in this collection. It really couldn't be more important.

James's essay pinpoints with absolute clarity the case for how generational shifts have diminished the priority afforded to children's well-being. But things are getting worse for children in other aspects of demography too. Let's look at relative affluence and where the benefits of rising prosperity accrue:

- In 1966, 15 per cent of children in the UK were living in relative poverty.[58] By 2019/20 it was over 31 per cent.[59] So in my lifetime, the proportion of children living in poverty has doubled.
- In 1966, 37 per cent of people over 65 were living in relative poverty.[60] In 2020 that number, thankfully, had reduced to 18 per cent,[61] a halving of relative poverty experiences for that demographic.

There is also a fundamental change, and speed of change, happening in the cultural and heritage tapestry of the British population. In 1966, the UK population included 886,000 people who identified as being from a 'minority ethnic group',[62] representing 1.5 per cent of the population. By 2021 that proportion (in England and Wales) had increased to over 18 per cent.[63]

The broadening of the collective experiences and diversity of the British population over my lifetime has brought untold economic, social and educational benefits.[64] However, the ability of state institutions to allocate resources and reflect cultures, demographics and population needs is not currently set up to ensure all its children in the coming decades can thrive. Simple examples include the way history is taught to capture events of cultural relevance, or in the clear under-representation of non-White teachers in classrooms[65] or systemic biases in the youth justice system.[66]

Conclusions

In reviewing the history of childhood and the fundamental changes in the context in which it is now lived, this chapter has set the scene for those that follow.

The 'norm' of childhood today is transformationally different to that of previous generations. The new norm is one in which public system structures, civic support and government legislation have been too slow to support adequately. The consequence is children and their families have less of a voice in shaping their lives. This reduced agency is further impacted by the fact that childhood is increasingly experienced from siloed, unvaried environments and in VUCA circumstances. In this context, preserving children's well-being can get lost by the fast pace of living and endemic short-termism.

What is no different to previous generations is the fact that the opportunity for children to thrive remains dependent on national choices and priorities, which we will now start to explore.

3

The early years

It is easier to build strong children than to repair broken men.
Misattributed to Frederick Douglass[1]

Chloe was born in May 2020, in the middle of the first COVID-19 lockdown – one of 1.2 million babies born in England and Wales during the pandemic.[2] Her mum, Juliette, found the experience incredibly hard. Juliette is one of over 200 new mothers who have told their stories in the book *Born in Lockdown*.[3] The experience, shared by nearly all these mothers, was one of both stress and loneliness. As one mother wrote:

> It takes a village to raise a baby, I read somewhere. Where's my village, I wondered? Feeling so removed from everything today. Even your baby giggles can't penetrate a certain greyness. ... I wonder how many other mums are out there, like me at the moment. ...
>
> As the second lockdown was announced my heart sank. The small trusted support network I'd managed to build would no longer be able to help me at home and I feared my mental health would spiral again.[4]

Babies born during lockdown represent more than 2 per cent of all people in England. Their parents share a unique experience of isolation, declining mental health, bonding challenges and reduced health visitor support. During lockdowns, their babies may have met no one else, seen their grandparents only at a distance or online, and interacted with no other babies whatsoever, at the very time when their brains were doubling in size.[5] The social distancing and closure of childcare they experienced is also likely to have long-term impacts on their language development, sleep patterns and cognitive functions.[6]

Such lockdown experiences highlight an uncomfortable fact: despite babies being among the most vulnerable in society, and the most dependent on nurturing care and stimulation, they almost always bear the brunt of decisions where their needs are not centre stage.

Early years are the most critical years of life given their impact on capacity to thrive in later years. Yet society tends to afford them scant value, consistently foregoing a golden opportunity to make the future better. We have an opportunity to change this.

The idea of early childhood development

Sitting on New York's Fifth Avenue, on the edge of Central Park, is a building as striking on the outside as it is inside. The Guggenheim Museum of modern and contemporary art was conceived as a 'temple of the spirit' by its famous designer, Frank Lloyd Wright. Opened in 1959 its design was controversial then, but it is now revered. It is no accident that it looks a bit like a young child's toy. Within its vast collection are hundreds of modern art paintings depicting cylinders, cubes and spheres. Every day thousands are in awe and yes, a few people might be less impressed, believing that a toddler could have created them. Some have argued that those people aren't entirely wrong as the genesis of much modern art and architecture lies in how artists and architects played when they were toddlers.[7]

Lloyd Wright and his fellow modernists were the first generation whose toddler years were influenced by the work of Friedrich Froebel. Children today have been similarly influenced, for Froebel revolutionised understanding of early childhood development and created a new space for it to bloom: the kindergarten. Froebel's ideas were considered radical when he first presented them in the 1850s, but his principles have since become part of mainstream early years practice. His six principles

– unity and connectedness; autonomous learning; the value of childhood in its own right; relationships matter; creativity and the power of symbols; and the central importance of play[8] – are still aspirational today. Yet, despite the evidence, many governments and state agencies seem to struggle with the bottom-up ideas and principles Froebel set out.

Froebel considered the health, physical development, environmental conditions, emotional well-being, mental ability, social relationships and spiritual aspects of development critically important. He learned about young children by simply watching them, especially at play.[9]

'Serve and return' interactions

The most used piece of sports kit in our house is the table tennis table. At parties, it is often the scene of endless knockabouts, fierce competitions, beer pong or simple a relaxing pat back and forth while having a chat. Our usual game – which we call 'Around the World' – involves everyone running around the table, taking it in turns to return a shot, until someone misses and is knocked out, when it restarts again, and eventually there is just one person left. It lasts for ages and is the best fun when everyone is still serving, running round and returning. Oddly, it's also a great analogy for human brain development!

The foundations of each human brain are built from before birth through to those first five or so years of a child's life. Our brains are made up of neurons: specialised cells that send messages to the rest of the body to function in particular ways and manage our emotional and social capacities, as well as physical functions. Between the neurons are neural connections. These are pathways on which lightning-fast messages are sent. In the first few years of life, it is estimated that more than a million new neural connections form every second in a child's brain.[10] Basic skills first – hearing and vision – followed by language and speech, and then higher cognitive functions. This foundation-laying begins to reduce around the age of five through a process that allows circuits to become more efficient. Neural connections can keep forming throughout life, but early connections are the ones giving strong foundations for later connections.[11]

So how can we help infants create strong foundations? Here's where the table tennis comes in. What it has in common with early childhood is the concept of *serve and return*. 'Serve and return' interactions (a phrase coined by Harvard researchers)[12] help to shape and strengthen neural connections.

Imagine you're watching an adult interacting with a baby. The baby babbles, the adult looks them in the eye and babbles back; the adult covers their eyes for a quick game of peek-a-boo, the baby laughs, the adult smiles, and this goes on. This is serve and return in action. The caregiver can support this by looking out for the 'serve' when a child initiates – perhaps they are pointing or making a little sound and then the caregiver 'returns', maybe by saying 'I see!' or bringing an object closer or nodding. Then the caregiver keeps the interaction going by taking turns, creating that all important back and forth rally.

All serve and return requires is that there is a caregiver–child relationship that is reliable, caring and responsive.[13] Sadly, research shows us that a breakdown in these types of interactions, or a presence of interactions that are not appropriate, will have a negative impact on the formation of neural connections.[14] Living in an environment where caregivers are suffering from chronic or 'toxic' stress, for example due to poverty, repeated abuse, maternal depression or a COVID-19 lockdown, can also negatively impact the development of healthy neural foundations.[15]

That said, not all stress is chronic or toxic: some positive stress is part of healthy development. Take, for example, stress that might increase the heart rate or bring a mild elevation of hormones – perhaps for a young child, the first experience on a slide or a soft play ball pit. Another form of stress essential for healthy development is what researchers term 'tolerable stress' – the type that manifests from serious, but temporary, stressful experiences such as the loss of a loved one or an injury. This type of stress is not harmful to a child if mediated by the presence of supportive adults who can help the child adapt.[16]

However, scans of neural connections in a brain impacted by toxic stress show that the neurons are damaged and there are fewer connections.[17] Weaker neural connections can lead to lifelong problems in learning, behaviour and physical and mental health.

The Healthy Child Programme

In 2009, the Healthy Child Programme (HCP) was introduced in the UK for families with children between conception and the age of five years old. It has since been extended to families with children aged up to 19. It aims to be a universal prevention and early intervention programme comprising screening, immunisation, health and development checks at key ages,★ alongside advice on health, well-being and parenting. The check at two-and-a-half years old is, however, the last mandated review before school nurses are expected to pick up on any needs at primary school, around two years later.

A 2020 survey found a disturbing picture: one in five children do not actually have this check.[18] Indeed, in some (predominantly poorer) areas, 65 per cent of children have *not* had it. This means that local authorities in such areas are unsure about the needs of children who miss their checks. Are they vulnerable? Do they have specific needs? Due to the difficulty of data sharing across teams, local authorities have no idea if the children are known to other services (such as the NHS, Department for Work and Pensions or social care).

All information from HCP reviews is literally handwritten in the 'Personal Child Health Record' (aka, the 'Redbook') that each family keeps. Anecdotally, if they lose this book, it is notoriously hard to replace. The Redbook can't therefore be used for large-scale population analysis to show the true state of the development of our nation's youngest children, or to predict – and therefore be used – to implement preventative measures from data science. Despite technological revolutions, the Redbook has not fundamentally changed in over 25 years.[19]

Just think what problems would be prevented from early anticipatory, and data science-led, well-being interventions right across childhood if the HCP was truly prioritised, updated and funded.

★ The HCP checks include weight, height, sight, hearing, speech, movement, behaviour and social skills, as well as making sure vaccinations are up to date.

Parenting and mental health

Crucial to the development of healthy young children are parents who are skilled, confident and healthy enough to support their child in their early development. The perinatal period (from the beginning of pregnancy to the baby's first birthday) brings significant risk to a mother's mental health, with one in five women suffering from some form of mental health issue, from mild anxiety to even psychosis.[20] There are a multitude of factors that shape mental health generally, including systemic factors such as environment, our society's cultural failings and the impacts of poverty. Here are just three such factors.

Feeling judged and not seeking help

Lots of people find the job of parenting stressful. This can affect their relationship with, and development of, their baby.[21] Research shows many mothers are more likely to put their child's health before their own, and feel more comfortable seeking help for their child than for themselves, for example in relation to food, sleep, play and social interaction. Many feel judged for the behaviour of their child or how they handle this in public. Lots of us have been there: our child is having a meltdown in the middle of a supermarket, screaming and refusing to move, staging a sit-down protest.

New parents' networks

Since time immemorial we have known of the importance of informal networks for new parents, and how much family members, friends and neighbours become part of their daily routine, provide valuable assistance and help manage the fear of feeling judged. Accessing such networks has changed as young people increasingly have moved away from families and as urban and suburban populations have grown. The new network structures are, however, often less personal and less supportive.

Some of the more successful programmes available to soon-to-be parents offer training and support through a trusted network of equals. For example, the National Childbirth Trust (NCT) brings together soon-to-be-parents via 17 hours of classes learning about childbirth and early parenthood. These classes are an opportunity to make friends with people facing similar experiences, and many of the 70,000 who attend each year make friends for life.[22] The NHS also provides free antenatal classes. Such programmes are a base on which to build even better, and more integrated, clinical, educative, social and mental health support in a child-led way.

Breastfeeding

I hesitated before writing this section. Breastfeeding is perhaps one of the most emotive topics I cover in this book. My knowledge on the subject comes from founding and running a baby food company, having been a father of babies, chairing London's Child Obesity Taskforce and researching this book. However, I obviously have no lived experience of breastfeeding.

The World Health Organization (WHO) recommends exclusive breastfeeding for the first six months of life.[23] In the UK there is a minimum age at which baby foods can be marketed (four months) as well as restrictions on marketing[24] by formula milk providers.

The role of government is to provide knowledge and support to mothers and collect data to ensure that the best decisions can be made by both families and regulators. Strong evidence shows that peer-to-peer support groups can help with knowledge sharing and support. For example, breastfeeding peer support networks have a positive effect on breastfeeding duration rates,[25] and help mothers feel more confident and less vulnerable to self-doubt.[26]

Breastfeeding has been shown to have a positive effect on the mental well-being of both mother and baby, when it goes well. Research suggests it decreases inflammation on the mother's body, when depression has an inflammatory effect,[27] and that it releases oxytocin, which opposes cortisol and lowers the stress response, reducing the mother's blood pressure and anxiety.[28] There is also some evidence that it may aid the development of secure attachment between mother and baby.[29] When breastfeeding is not going well, it can cause toxic stress to both mother and baby, which is especially acute if the mother feels isolated and helpless, such as without peer support or information to make informed choices.[30]

Breastfeeding data is not currently robust enough to enable policy makers to support the best family-level decisions. Local authorities have the responsibility for, and must carry the cost of, data collection, and yet are not empowered or resourced to do anything with the findings. Because of this, they tend not to prioritise the data collection and analysis needed to inform policy. Collecting such data is so important that the motivational dynamics must change.

Finally, there is strong evidence that in countries where the government guarantees paid maternity leave for at least six months, rates of exclusive breastfeeding are 9 per cent higher.[31]

Childcare and early education

The Organisation for Economic Co-operation and Development (OECD) gathers data comparing social policies between countries. It has found huge differences in the rates of children attending formal childcare.* Several factors can explain this: parental preference and cultural norms, availability of extended family members to take on informal care and take-up of parental leave. Use of childcare in the UK is relatively low. For example, in 2016 73 per cent of children over three years old attended childcare (the 26th lowest out of 31 OECD countries) and only 29 per cent of under-three-year-olds attended (19th out of 31).[32] The reason is down to cost: the UK has among the highest childcare costs in the OECD.[33] The charity Pregnant Then Screwed found that two-thirds of families are paying the same or more on childcare than on their mortgage or rent.[34]

There are many studies that show why professional, quality, affordable, universal and accessible childcare is a critical measure of how much a nation prioritises children. Pre-schools and nurseries especially can play an important part in combating social exclusion and promoting inclusion by offering disadvantaged children, in particular, a better start to primary school. One of the most comprehensive studies was undertaken by the Effective Provision of Pre-School Education (EPPE) project back in 2004, which

---

* Formal, or registered, early years childcare includes childminders, nannies, day nurseries, pre-schools and nursery classes in schools.

was the first major European longitudinal study of a national sample of young children's development. It demonstrated the positive effects of high-quality pre-school provision on children's intellectual and social behavioural development.[35] What matters is both the *quality* of the pre-school setting experience as well as the *quantity* (attending consistently over months, rather than increasing hours). The case is so compelling to me that if I had my last public pound to spend it would be in quality, universal childcare opportunities.

Nicole Green feels the same way. She is a mum with experience of navigating the childcare system. She is also an entrepreneur and an employer of many parents of young children at the company she co-founded, Catch Communications. She has written this essay for us.

Childcare: a public investment, not cost

Nicole Green, founder and CEO of Catch Communications

In late 2019, I temporarily left the communications agency I'd started, placed it in the good hands of my business partner, and embarked on a very different type of start-up journey: becoming a mum.

I returned to work much earlier than I intended, to accommodate my husband's loss in earnings due to the pandemic, while he took over full-time childcare. While heart-wrenching, there were two silver linings. My husband got valuable time as primary caregiver for our son, and we delayed the battle and expense of the English childcare system by over a year. We'd relocated 150 miles to be near my family support network. This set-up saves us around £500 per month on childcare.

I know I write this piece from a place of privilege. Both my husband and I earn healthy salaries and, with some flexibility on working hours, we can split childcare, the domestic load and our lives evenly. But I'm also an employer of mostly freelance consultants, a large proportion of whom are women. While I seek to accommodate their needs, no amount of flexibility in their working life has made up for the shortcomings of the childcare system. Most work fewer hours than they would like to because of access and cost of childcare, and others, like me, have relocated to be nearer to family for help.

Parents have had to make crippling decisions about having a career, covering their household costs, and providing safe and nurturing care for their child.

The problems with childcare in the UK come down to three things: availability, affordability and quality.

Let's start with availability. I've lost count of the number of friends who, when pregnant, are told that the waiting list for nurseries is three years long. Apparently, we need the gift of foresight to plan childcare. Nearly half of all councils say they don't have enough childcare for the children under two in their communities.[36] As of March 2022 there were 4,000 fewer childcare providers in the UK than April 2021.[37] This is because, thanks to chronic underfunding, providers literally can't manage to keep the lights on, but increasing costs to parents isn't an option as they just can't afford to pay either.

Which brings me to affordability. Trades Union Congress analysis shows that the average annual nursery bill for a family with a child under two has increased by 44 per cent in the 12 years since 2010, from £4,992 to £7,212.[38] Nor are the current government-'funded' free nursery hours enough: the Early Years Alliance[39] claims that there is a financial shortfall of 32 per cent for nursery places for two-year-olds.

Finally, there is the issue of quality: some nursery workers and childcare professionals are paid less than the average minimum wage in the UK, as they are apprentices or are in the younger pay bracket.[40] One in two childcare workers are claiming benefits because their pay is so low. A sector defined by low pay, low morale, high staff turnover and a lack of respect or esteem impacts quality of provision. What message does it send that we allow the professionals who care for our children during vital stages of their development to be treated so poorly?

When it doesn't pay to work, and the availability and quality of childcare is decreasing rapidly, emotional and practical pressures converge, and many parents (nearly exclusively women) decide that working is just not worth it. In March 2022, Pregnant Then Screwed research showed that almost half of working mothers were considering leaving their jobs, and 40 per cent were working fewer hours than they wanted to because childcare fees were unaffordable.[41]

A better way of doing things is possible.

Take Finland, where 70 per cent of pre-school children attend publicly run, subsidised early childhood education (rather than 'day care'),* delivered by university-educated teachers.[42] Or Sweden, where childcare workers can earn the national average salary.[43] Or Iceland, which tops the United Nations

---

* 'Day care' does not necessarily provide early childhood education, but provides a simpler service of care or oversight, looking after children while their parents are at work.

Children's Fund's (UNICEF) rankings for childcare quality,[44] and Icelandic couples spend just 5 per cent of their income on childcare (and single parents even less).[45]

Our leaders need to explain why the Finns, Swedes and Icelanders can manage this, but the English cannot.

An investment in our future

The New Economics Foundation calculated that for every £1 a childcare worker is paid, they will generate £7 of value (by releasing parents' earnings), and a further £9.50 of value in terms of the contribution made to children's early development.[46]

So here's my idea: government spending on childcare should be removed from the current budget and reclassified as investment. Just like high-speed rail, roads and hospitals, childcare is a vital piece of our social and economic infrastructure. It is wrong and misguided for childcare to be treated as a cost when investing in early years education is one of the best investments the state can make.

By classifying childcare as an investment, we could also maximise the impact of 'free childcare' (rarely acknowledged in societal or economic terms). Annually women in the UK provide 23.2 billion hours of unpaid childcare care, worth an estimated £382 billion, while men provide 9.7 billion hours, worth £160 billion,[47] and grandparents more than 1.7 billion hours, at £3.9 billion.[48] A greater investment in the community-based infrastructure, such as high-quality and free-to-access support groups, activities and playgroups, will enable children and parents to thrive.

A 2019 government review found that the UK economy could be boosted by £250 billion and 1.1 million more businesses if more was done to close the gender gap in British entrepreneurship.[49] Investing in childcare will nurture a flourishing entrepreneurial community of female founders. Politicians from all parties have long paid lip service to supporting British start-ups and scale-ups, promoting entrepreneurship and building an ecosystem that makes Britain the best place in the world to found and scale high-growth companies. Fixing childcare is a key part of the puzzle and makes it easier for parents – women in particular – to return to work and reach their full potential.

Changing how we approach childcare will set the tone for a fundamental rethinking of how we deliver and value early years care and education – not simply because it pays today, but because of the dividends it will pay in the future.

Funding and culturally seeing childcare through the lens of long-term investment must be a core part of the answer towards a better future – for children and for society at large. In her essay, Nicole notes that there are significant government funds and various credits available to all working parents, but understanding and accessing them can be confusing. Financial support comes from an array of government departments, while some entitlements require families to pay and then reclaim. Entitlements in England include:

- tax-free childcare;
- tax credits available for low-income working families;
- Universal Credit for low-income families;
- childcare vouchers;
- a universal right to 15 hours per week for all three- to four-year-olds of working parents,* extended to 30 hours for some less affluent families.

As well as a complicated system of funding to navigate, what parents are entitled to falls short of what they need. Providers must therefore work out how to bridge the shortfall themselves or risk closure. Some offer additional paid-for services: for example charging £16 for lunch and snacks a day, with parents understanding that this is to try and make up the shortfall.[50] The lack of public investment has led to some nurseries being bought by private equity-owned chains (modelled on the debt-laden care home takeover models),[51] while others are closing their doors for good; there were 17 per cent fewer nurseries in 2021 than in 2015.[52]

Finally, the cost versus investment point in Nicole's essay echoes a 2016 UK Women's Budget Group report, which showed that twice as many jobs and tax receipts could be created from investment in care industries (child and elderly care) than the same investment currently generates in the construction industry.[53]

---

* The UK government's 2023 Budget committed to an extension of the entitlement to 30 weeks of childcare provision for all under-five-year-olds of working parents from September 2025.

There are other economic models under which early years education could be structured. June O'Sullivan founded and operates a group of nurseries under one such alternative. She has written an essay for us on why government should adopt a social enterprise model as the way we 'do' early years education.

A social enterprise approach to childcare

June O'Sullivan MBE, founder and CEO of London Early Years Foundation (LEYF)

When I was a young single parent, I worked as a nurse. I searched for childcare and eventually found a small private nursery in southeast London. I turned up and found an unwelcoming environment, where parents were not allowed to settle their children. On day two, with my child still very upset, I was told that they could have given his place to a doctor's child. I never went back! I did, however, vow to develop a high-quality nursery model accessible to all children, especially those in need. All children would be welcomed and we would build a community of networks and relationships to foster cooperation, shared values and trust. Twenty years later, after a career as a psychiatric nurse, an under-eights social worker, an 'early years child-minding lead', a nursery group operations manager and a trainer, I designed the London Early Years Foundation (LEYF).

Why early years education and care?
Every society should take great care of its children, including educating its youngest members, because generally, what is good for the child is good for society. Too many children from disadvantaged communities cannot access high-quality early years education and care. Nearly a third of children do not reach a good level of development by the time they reach five years, and already children from disadvantaged backgrounds are 4.6 months behind their peers by the end of their first year at school.[54] In the words of economist and philosopher Amartya Sen, there is 'clearly remediable injustice' when disadvantaged children are not provided with educational opportunities.[55]

Why a social enterprise model?
Currently, in the UK, the provision of early childhood education and care is primarily through the open market with some state input. How can

outsourced services ensure not only the quality of education, but also that disadvantaged families are given the same access to quality education as the more affluent?[56]

I was keen to develop a social enterprise model, a business model that combines commercial viability with social outcomes. In our case, it enabled some cross-subsidy so we could provide at least one-third of our places to children from disadvantaged families.

How London Early Years Foundation makes a change

A childcare social enterprise must have a specifically designed 'social' pedagogy where the teaching and learning is designed to deliver inclusion and overcome social injustice. LEYF's goal is for all children to be educated together, to build trust and social capital, and reduce social segregation and prepare for a globally connected world.

LEYF provides inclusive, equitable opportunities, recognising that a child's development can only be understood by taking account of the complex system of relationships of their immediate and wider world. Our staff are offered a range of training from their arrival as apprentices right through to the LEYF degree. Training and professional development opportunities are underpinned by research and the interests and enthusiasm of staff. Staff must know the child and their unique ways, and understand their own role in helping children make friends, find their place in the nursery and their community and value their thinking and independence. Children need their voices heard to retain some control over their own learning and development and to understand their role in the world. Our approach includes literacy and numeracy, but also life skills, such as the ability to manage their emotions, make well-balanced decisions, resolve conflicts constructively, develop healthy lifestyles, good social relationships and responsibility, critical thinking, creative talents and other abilities that give children the tools they need to pursue their lifelong potential.

At LEYF, the cultural capital gap is directly linked to children's access to an abundance of rich language. Language not only consists of words, sentences and stories; it incorporates art, dance, drama (including pretend play), mathematics, movements, rhythm, music and Makaton. Play is the best vehicle for children's learning. Play is how they express strong feelings, rehearse experiences and interact socially, often with great enjoyment.

Many children from disadvantaged neighbourhoods attend nurseries either hungry or undernourished. Children cannot learn if they are hungry, and therefore it's imperative we address this as a matter of course. Children attending a social enterprise nursery need to be provided with a healthy, well-balanced diet with varied menus using fresh seasonal foods and simple ingredients. LEYF has created the first Early Years Chef Academy to train chefs to source, prepare, cook and present food that is nutritious while procured in a way that supports the Green LEYF sustainability approach.

Social enterprise nurseries recognise the power of the community. We weave weekly outings into parts of the community that may seem closed to children, like parks, galleries, theatres, markets, restaurants and local interest sites, as well as building relations with elderly homes, local charities, food kitchens, youth programmes and wherever there is room for a relationship that will build social capital.

Summary
Children have no time to wait for us to ponder, debate, cogitate and ruminate. A good social entrepreneur can leverage the power of the market to build a socially purposeful childcare business. Many social entrepreneurs, including myself, are driven by a persistent, almost unshakable, optimism, persevering because of the belief that they will succeed in spite of messages to the contrary. We need the government to act to support the creation of a network of social enterprise nurseries that are part of the early years infrastructure so it's not just the lucky few who can access this provision.

June's essay taps into how business models and motivations matter, as do the way staff are supported, rewarded and motivated. The dominant operating models for early years education in the UK (ranging from 'state-funded' to 'private equity-owned') has resulted in inadequate funding, which directly impacts on the workforce. There is also a lack of investment in training and no clear progression paths.

In addition, the lack of respect afforded to those working in the profession impacts recruitment. The OECD has picked up on this, citing that many see it as an 'easy career', before experiencing it as harder than expected.[57] All of this has led to a sector suffering from a recruitment and retention crisis. Dr Kate Hardy of the University of Leeds, on leading a review into the experience of childcare workers during the COVID-19 pandemic, observed: 'To think that the staff are being paid poverty wages while we pay more on childcare than our mortgage is really upsetting.'[58]

We (society at large) undervalue the skills, professionalism and dedication of the people who look after our youngest people, our most vulnerable citizens, at the very time of their lives when their development is at its most sensitive. It's hard to imagine a crueller paradox.

Sure Start

The 1997 General Election was seismic in many ways – one of which was that for the first time a major party (Labour, which won by a landslide) built its manifesto around a focus on children. Another was that Labour promised that its new chancellor would, if they won, be responsible for aspects of social domestic policy as well as the public purse. The result of this approach was a transformation programme called Sure Start: a highly impactful, successful, targeted investment that shook up the way government thought about early years.

After consulting with 13 different government departments (a rare example of cross-department co-creation in itself!) Sure Start brought together a raft of services 'to support the complex and varied physical, developmental and emotional needs of young children and families'. The original intent of the programme design was to focus on the 20 per cent most deprived areas.[59]

Sure Start's services included childcare, primary healthcare, early education and play and support for families. The goal was that its services would 'be easily accessible, ideally within "pram pushing distance"', and backed up by outreach to offer support in the home.[60] Any services not already freely provided to all were free to low-income families and at a fair cost to better-off families. Sure Start centres were the hubs of this provision, and sought to promote the physical, intellectual and social development of children. Services were developed in consultation with parents, and therefore reflected local needs. Pretty revolutionary.

An independent evaluation concluded that after 10 years 'this investment utterly transformed early-year services while representing a relatively small contribution from the perspective of the Treasury – just 0.05 per cent of public expenditure'.[61] In 2011, the Allen Report found that the positive impact of Sure Start lasted throughout childhood and beyond.[62] For example, at their peak, Sure Start centres prevented 13,000 hospitalisations a year among 11- to 15-year-olds.[63] A Department for Education (DfE)-commissioned review identified economic benefits across numerous aspects of society: increased health, reduced crime, increased parental earnings and better educational attainment. Crucially, these effects continued over the long term.[64]

The Sure Start programme grew to over 4,000 centres by 2010,[65] but as it scaled, it began to lose some of its radicalism. Its first director, Naomi Eisenstadt, noted that it lost the magic ingredient of parental empowerment, voice and meaningful governance. Decisions were moved to local authorities and then to Whitehall.[66] It also became skewed towards educational performance and evaluation, and had been widened to reach all children, not just the disadvantaged.

And then austerity came. It was a political response to the global economic crisis of 2008, and the Sure Start programme was, somewhat quietly, wound down – up to 1,000 local centres closed between 2010 and 2019.[67] Although 1.8 million children (many living in poverty) were still using the Sure Start programme in 2018,[68] its impact and presence was a fraction of what it once was. In its first five years the number of British children in poverty fell by 600,000.* Since Sure Start has been wound down, and cuts to public services and social security have been implemented, child poverty has risen back to the 4.28 million it was in 1998.[69] In essence, political choice has reversed a quarter of a century of gains, and this chance to deliver a child-centred future has been a missed opportunity.

The economic case for early years investment

Disadvantage at a younger age can disproportionately impact a child's life. On average, 40 per cent of the overall development gap between disadvantaged 16-year-olds and their peers has already emerged by the age of five.[70]

---

* It is worth re-emphasising here that other parts of the strategy that will have contributed to the economic impact included changes to social security and labour market dynamics. The reduction in poverty was not exclusively related to the impact of Sure Start.

The godfather of early years economics, James Heckman, a Nobel prize-winning economist, developed a model to understand this dynamic:

$$\text{Invest} + \text{Develop} + \text{Sustain} = \text{Gain}$$

- *Invest* in educational and developmental resources for disadvantaged families to provide equal access to successful early human development.
- *Develop* and nurture early development of cognitive and social skills in children from birth to age five.
- *Sustain* early development with effective education through to adulthood.
- *Gain* a more capable, productive and valuable workforce that pays dividends for generations to come.[71]

Heckman best summarised his thinking in his paper 'The economics of inequality':

> We can invest early to close disparities and prevent achievement gaps, or we can pay to remediate disparities when they are harder and more expensive to close. Either way we are going to pay. ... Investing early allows us to shape the future; investing later chains us to fixing the missed opportunities of the past.[72]

The empirical evidence is pretty convincing:

- Heckman took longitudinal evidence to show that high-quality investments in early years result in stronger families and multi-generation outcomes, and can break the cycle of poverty.[73]
- He took multiple sources to calculate that the rate of return on investment for quality early years programmes is 13 per cent.[74]
- He also showed that skills developed through quality early childhood education last a lifetime.[75]

There is a plethora of evidence from a wide variety of gold star sources that reinforce his message. Steve Brine MP, Chair of the All-Party Parliamentary Group for Childcare and Early Education, highlighted that in the UK £1 invested in early education has the same societal impact as investing £7 in education for adolescents.[76] In 2015, US President Barack Obama's Executive Office reported on the effects of investing in early years learning programmes, concluding that for every $1 invested, society benefited by roughly $8.60.[77]

It's time for government to embrace Heckman's model to underwrite radical early years policies.

Insights from around the world

The case for intergenerational care

In 2017, the UK's first intergenerational co-located care home and nursery opened in South London. Co-founder Judith Ish-Horowicz had felt the absence of her grandparents, who were murdered at Auschwitz, but when she married, she found a wonderful surrogate in her husband's grandmother. Judith explained, 'grandparents can provide an unconditional love for their grandchildren. Parents may have worries, judgements, but grandparents can just adore.'[78] Judith, who also founded, and still runs, her Apples and Honey nursery school, started taking babies and toddlers to Nightingale House, the nearest elderly care home. In 2014 she teamed up with it to develop a proposal for a co-located nursery–elderly care home. Not only are the residents supportive of the partnership, but there is strong buy-in from local families. One said,

> By bringing the two generations together, they share common physical challenges (eg manipulating tools such as scissors), hands and fingers are strengthened by playing with playdough, and other challenges are offered for hand and eye coordination. To see them working collaboratively to complete tasks is warming. There is mutual respect and enjoyment being in each other's company. The elderly get to have the joy of children visiting them with the laughter and quirky moods and behaviours. Children enjoy the patience from people who are not in a rush.[79]

Lorraine George, who works for Torbay Council in England, visited intergenerational settings in the USA and found many benefits to young children, including improvement in language development, increased reading and literacy skills, greater self-esteem and confidence among vulnerable children and the development of empathy and kindness.[80] Torbay Council now operates 20 care homes that partner with early years providers.

Intergenerational care has international precedent. Its origins are from Tokyo when, in 1976, Shimada Masaharu opened the first care home and childcare centre on the same site. The success was such that, by 1998, there were 16 intergenerational facilities in the city.[81] Providence Mount St Vincent Center in Seattle is probably the most globally recognised. Describing itself as a 'vibrant living care community', it has 400 residents and 125 places for children aged between six weeks and six years. All visits between residents and children are planned and supervised by teachers who work with therapists to coordinate activities such as art, music, exercise and games, as well as small group activities.[82]

Intergenerational care is a win–win. It supports those who are ageing, those who are young, paves the way for social cohesion and, from an economic point of view, is efficient to run.

Jamaica's early childhood stimulation intervention

The early childhood stimulation intervention was a two-year home-based intervention that began in Kingston, Jamaica, in the 1980s with two aims: to improve nutrition and to improve mother–child interactions. The target group were physically underdeveloped children, and the programme consisted of weekly home visits from a community-based public health practitioner (whose training included toy making!). A major focus was improving interaction between mother and child – those serve and return interactions discussed earlier. The health visitors taught the mothers how to make simple toys using readily available materials, and the mothers were encouraged to play with their children, with the homemade toy.[83] Three decades on, 37 per cent of those who participated as toddlers had higher earnings than a control group.[84]

Cuba: childcare nirvana?

In 2016, 99.5 per cent of under–six–year–olds in Cuba attended an early childhood education programme or institution.[85] Cuba has a holistic approach to early childhood development (ECD): services are delivered universally across the country, but specific attention is paid to access for the most vulnerable. Prioritising ECD within the national development strategy has been a constant in Cuba for over 60 years. What is particularly impressive is that its ECD is an integrated system across traditional government silos, it encourages active family and community participation, and it is staffed by highly qualified people.

Conclusions

The range of factors influencing how young children develop in their early years is enormous. These cover every aspect of their lives, at the most important time of their lives, setting the trajectory for the rest of their lives. The diversity of the areas and types of intervention a government could make is therefore also enormous. Prioritising the most impact and ensuring integration across different aspects of life (and, most importantly, different government departments) is therefore of critical importance in pursuit of a child–centred future. Early years is *the* area where economic return on investment is highest, where political argument should be easiest and where the science is crystal clear. The opportunity to build a cohesive, coordinated, cross-department commitment to world-beating childcare, educational development, health monitoring and serve and return simulation is clear.

Four additional essays, containing more proposals for government, are hosted at www.raisingthenation.co.uk:

- Sally Hogg is a Senior Policy Fellow at the Faculty of Education at the University of Cambridge, and, until 2022, was Deputy CEO of the Parent–Infant Foundation. She has written on how parent–child relationships must be a key target for public policy given their critical role in a range of important outcomes.

- Leslee Udwin is a renowned film producer and director, who founded her education charity Think Equal in response to the traumatic themes emerging from many of her documentaries. She has written with a practical adoption of Professor Heckman's equation for government to consider.

- Duncan Fraser is a therapeutic coach and founder of the Useful & Kind charity and the Mindful Leadership Foundation. He has written on providing relationship programmes for teenagers that embed the benefits of 'attachment theory' between parent and baby well before people become parents of young children themselves.

- Mark Cuddigan is CEO of Ella's Kitchen, the company I founded. He is also an entrepreneur and a leader in the B Corporation movement. He has written on incorporating sensory food education, through play, in early years curricula.

4

Play

When children play, they're working. For them play is both a serious and necessary business.

Mister Rogers[1]

Recently I found myself distracted by a video on my Twitter feed of some juvenile pandas using a toddler-sized slide. They were clearly having fun and I found myself thinking 'they are so human-like, just kids at play'. I'm not alone; videos like this have millions of views – a sign, I suspect, that people find them strangely uplifting.

All mammals play – particularly when they are young – but why? If we think about wild animals' need to survive, playtime uses up vital and hard-earned calories that could otherwise help them get through the hardships of winter and support them becoming fertile and having more offspring. Play can be dangerous, too. Rough and tumble play makes animals more susceptible to injury and increases the risk of a predator attack when they are distracted. So if it seems purposeless and risky, why do mammals do it?

The hypothesis is that play increases animals' evolutionary fitness. It develops physical attributes such as motor skills, strength and endurance, supports social bonding within groups, reduces acts of aggression and establishes hierarchy. Finally, it seems that play trains animals to deal with the unexpected in life, and is a way of coping with stress.[2] Indeed, as noted by the incomparable Fred Rogers, creator and host of the iconic pre-school television series *Mister Rogers' Neighborhood*, 'when children play, they're working'.[3]

I, like so many parents the world over, enjoyed joining in with my children's play. Led by them, I've 'grown down' with gusto to help create the physical incarnation of their imaginations. There I was, a chief executive of a large company, gladly pouring imaginary cups of tea for dolls and preparing bowls of food for imaginary pet dogs, and loving it.

What is childhood play?

Let's start by agreeing what play is. The *Concise Oxford English Dictionary* defines it as: 'to engage in activity for enjoyment and recreation rather than a serious or practical purpose'.[4] Play has no clear purpose, and yet it is highly meaningful and crucial for development. It's pointless, yet essential. It's got no goal, yet it teaches us so much. Perhaps its paradoxical nature means that cultures, societies and public services largely fail to find a place for play.

To be considered play, rather than games or sports, it seems that an activity needs to meet the following criteria: be voluntary rather than organised, relaxed, have no clear purpose or function other than enjoyment or recreation, and have elements that are exaggerated or unplanned.

Play starts at a young age, before we can talk or walk, and as the seminal work of Jean Piaget explained, it follows four stages: from functional to constructive to symbolic (or fantasy) to rules-based. Piaget explained that play hones and develops cognitive, social, physical and emotional skills.[5] It is a vital part of well-being throughout life, but must start in early childhood. It is important to recognise, therefore, that as play is vital throughout childhood, this chapter is not simply about play for the very young, but for children of all ages.

Babies start playing with objects around the age of four months. You'll see them exploring with all their senses: putting things in their mouths, reaching for objects or filling up and emptying out containers. Their play progresses from exploring 'what does this object do?' to stimulating their imagination: 'what can I do with this object?' They will build and then inevitably knock things down, trying again, using different items. Objects might be used to solve challenges, for example, becoming a tool in pretend play.[6]

Pretend play is unique to humans. It begins around age two and includes language, self-awareness and development of representational activities such as mirroring 'real life' with dolls. Child psychologist Lev Vygotsky argued that pretend play helps children because it promotes their capacity for social understanding, self-regulation and cooperation, and helps them understand symbolic representation in language and objects.[7] Pretend play happens everywhere, but circumstances and cultural norms may influence how much it is encouraged.

Take play fighting, which is both physical and pretend play. It is a vital stage for children and peaks at about eight years old, before it develops into rule-based games. Adults often try to prevent rough play because of a general lack of understanding of its playful nature, the misconception that all rough play includes intent to harm and concern for accidents.[8] Often associated with boys, 'rough and tumble' may develop skills for survival for mammals in the wild, but it can be helpful for learning to manage and regulate aggressive feelings. Rough play is known to help the development of socio-emotional skills such as reading facial expressions, inferring another person's intent and understanding social boundaries. Perhaps we need to educate adults about rough play?

In all its forms play is critical to the creation of a child-centred future. Yet how do we encourage it in our children, where do we have spaces and opportunities to play, and how can we improve where we fall short? What, indeed, can government do to promote play?

The proactive power of play

In Chapter 3 I discussed the negative impact of toxic stress on early childhood development. However, during times of stress, children of all ages benefit from using play as a way of expressing their feelings and dealing with the cognitive and emotional conflict they are experiencing.

The protective power of play has been witnessed in the highly stressful context of war. For example, one study looked at the agency play gave to children growing up in the Gaza Strip, where play helped the perception of normality arise out of the stress of the conflict. As 11-year-old Yousef explained: 'After the war, you couldn't even tell where the street we used to play on had gone. ... My friends and I went back there to play. I remember those streets, narrow and a bit dirty, we loved to play there. We met on the rubble.'[9]

Research from The LEGO Foundation has shown the role play has in coping with childhood adversity.[10] There is a promising link between play facilitation, or interventions, and children's ability to understand and cope with the demands of their environment and respond with self-regulation to better manage anxiety in stressful situations.

Being able to self-regulate is important for positive outcomes in childhood, such as school readiness,[11] academic success[12] and being able to adapt to social situations. Difficulties developing self-regulation may contribute to behavioural and emotional problems in adolescence.[13] It has also been suggested that pretend play contributes to younger children's development of self-regulation.[14] Think of a time when you've seen young children playing at superheroes and tell me this isn't complex work you're witnessing! At speed they negotiate and mediate who is the hero, villain or victim. They distinguish their own emotions from that of their assigned role. They plan, adapt and evolve plots using language and objects at hand to control their play. Increasing spaces and opportunities for quality play in children's daily lives and contexts – at home, in school and in public areas – provides them with ways to channel negative emotions and practice strategies to overcome stress.

At a time when children's toxic stress levels are rising, play can be an important antidote. There are lots of opportunities to ensure that local environments create spaces to play (see Chapter 5), while play-rich programmes, such as summer holiday camps or Sure Start centres, are obvious response provisions too, as is the specific use of play as a therapy to address toxic stress.

Paul Ramchandani has an enviable job title: Professor of Play. In this essay he shares his insight and ideas about what governments need to do to ensure there are more physical and time spaces for children to play.

Making space for play

Paul Ramchandani, Professor of Play in Education, Development and Learning, University of Cambridge

Play is a central part of childhood, and a key part of most children's day. Play is the main way in which children (particularly younger children) explore, experiment and build an understanding of the world.[15] This starts from the earliest point of life – in playful relationships with parents and carers, where young babies begin to learn both directly from those carers, but also in the way that carers and others react to them. Children begin to understand that what they do has an effect on the world.[16] This 'agency' is one of the most powerful driving forces behind children's development. It starts with little things, like a child knocking over a toy in a game. When a parent reacts and says something like 'look what happened, you knocked over the toy', the child begins to associate their action with an effect, and so begins to learn about their agency.

Agency is only one benefit of play. In playing with friends and siblings, children learn about taking turns, managing difficult feelings when they lose, and reforming friendships when something has gone wrong. In addition, physical play allows children to develop strength and physical health.

I've seen the benefits of play for children's health and development throughout my career working as a doctor in the NHS – and I've seen the harmful effects on children's physical and mental health when they have been deprived of opportunities to flourish. Play is too often an overlooked and neglected part of childhood. In my role now, as Professor of Play at the University of Cambridge, I am privileged to get to better understand play.

When we value play, we show that we are valuing childhood – not just as a period of life that is preparation for adulthood, but as a critical time of life and development in itself. Children need to explore and to learn. If we don't allow this, if we constantly push children, dictate their entire day, remove space and time for play, exploration and fun, we damage their development – the opposite of what we surely intend.

Children know the importance of play too![17] In a recent national survey of children's views undertaken by the Children's Commissioner for England, play was the most commonly mentioned word.[18]

For most of the last 50 years, the UK has done well on many, although not all, markers of childhood. Markers of core health, such as infant mortality, or overall child health, such as rates of infectious diseases, have all moved in a positive direction.[19] However, over the past decade, as inequalities have widened and rates of poverty have increased, outcomes for important areas of health, mental health, children's quality of life and equity of life chances have decreased.[20] Our children are doing less well than they should. We are moving in the wrong direction.

Some of this has been exacerbated by COVID-19, and the disruption to children's schooling and social relationships. Children's mental health has been adversely affected by this.[21] However, we should not overlook the fact that worrying trends were there before the pandemic began.

Over recent years, children's opportunities to play have diminished. They have less time for breaks and play during the school day,[22] less space for play and sport and less freedom to roam and explore, perhaps particularly in cities.[23]

What needs to happen?

A reduction in opportunities to play isn't the only factor driving increased rates of health problems and diminishing quality of life. Other factors, such as increased poverty and inequality and worries about schooling and future job opportunities, have a large role as well.

This is surely a time to stop and ask ourselves, why are we as a nation reducing children's opportunities for play and activity? What are the effects of this now and in the longer term? What should we do about this? And what should we expect those running the country to do about this?

As a general overarching policy shift, we should require that all policy considerations put the needs and requirements of children at the centre. This means having someone representing children and the future, wherever decisions are made, including in national and local government. Beyond that, there are three areas of action that should be taken in relation to play.

First, we need to offer children the space to play – both physical spaces, but also time in their days. Spaces to play offer children greater opportunities and can reduce the inequality of space available to children from urban backgrounds, where gardens are less available. Supporting children in play, with strong supportive playful interactions with caregivers, can lead to better cognitive and behavioural development, right from the start of life. In one example from my own team's work, children whose fathers engaged with them playfully when they were three months old went on to have lower levels of behavioural problems at age one year[24] and higher scores on cognitive tests at age two.[25]

Second, we must ensure that planning decisions, in the long and short term, consider children and their ability to roam from home and access space to play. This does not mean one small, manicured play area in each housing development. Spaces to play can take many shapes and include rough land. It must include consideration of how children can safely move around an area, so they aren't reliant on parents taking them to friends or local activities. Additional benefits would be making routes to school and spaces around them safe wherever possible. There are social as well as physical health benefits when this happens.

Finally, we need to ensure that time for play and activity is built into the school day, so that children (especially younger ones) have the chance to run around, talk and recharge between lessons. Being outdoors is important, and school is one place where we can ensure equity so that all children have safe access to outdoor time to play.

Conclusion

Opportunities for children to play have reduced over recent years. This reduces children's opportunities to exercise, interact with friends face-to-face and learn important physical and social skills. It means they miss out on the benefits of play for all aspects of development. It is time that we put children more at the centre of our planning and thinking in all areas of policy as the best way of ensuring the best outcome for all of us. Play can be a powerful force for opportunity for children; we should harness its benefits for children now and for their futures.

Play as therapy

Given that young children's verbal abilities are not fully developed, they are often better able to communicate complex issues and emotions through play than through words. Play therapy is a counselling intervention for young children,[26] especially those who have encountered adverse childhood experiences (ACEs) and who may go into new relationships or situations feeling unsafe. A trained play therapist can use playtime to observe and gain insights into a child's problems, help them explore emotions and deal with unresolved trauma.

The impact of play therapy is impressive, not only in terms of outcomes for the child, but also economically. Play Therapy UK has evidence that between 74 per cent and 83 per cent of children receiving play therapy show a positive change.[27] They estimate that the average cost of using play and creative arts therapies is £693 per child, and that a notional return to society is at least

£5,267 in the long term (using Heckman's equation as evidence). In addition, they cite better academic results and less stress for teachers, more successful fostering placements and faster response to medical treatment. They also claim that there are significant benefits for children with additional needs, such as those with physical disabilities, those with reduced sight or hearing, as well as those who are neurodivergent.

Sophia Giblin, a trained play therapist with a Master's in Play Therapy, believes that government can embrace the opportunities for play, which she shares in this essay.

Let the children (and parents!) play
Sophia Giblin, play therapist, founder of Clear Sky and of Treasure Time

I was 15 years old when my mum was diagnosed with an aggressive form of stomach cancer. She passed away just three months later. I went from a bright, engaged and creative teenager to one whose entire world was shattered. I struggled through my late teenage milestones into early adulthood, and it became clear that I'd lacked crucial appropriate support to help me process the trauma of losing my mum.

I felt inspired to help children and young people who had experienced trauma, to give them the help they needed, at the time they needed it the most. So, at the age of 23, I set up Clear Sky children's charity[28] having discovered that play therapy was a hugely effective way of helping young people process their feelings, and went on to study a Master's in play therapy.

After several years of study, practice and research I noticed a common pattern in my work with children: when parents were on board and receptive to bringing some play therapy skills and principles into their home, children made much better progress. They needed fewer therapy sessions and were less likely to be re-referred to another therapist. The parent–child relationship is the foundation of good mental health for children, and we can nurture these relationships through play.

How is play linked to happiness?
Children's happiness has been on the decline since The Children's Society started collecting data in 2009.[29] Concurrently there has been a worrying demise of child-led play and an increase of psychopathology in children.[30]

The studies show children experiencing increased levels of depression, anxiety and hopelessness. These concerning symptoms are convincingly linked with the reduction in levels of child-led play.

Parents and play

Children will naturally 'play out' their experiences, and playing gives them a safe and controlled environment to make sense of the world.[31] It allows them to explore their interests, express joy and process their fears and disappointments.

The sensitivity of their parents is shown to play a large part in a child's emotional development, and can be measured by the parent's responsiveness, positive affect and acceptance.[32] High parental sensitivity is also known to predict attachment security, which is shown to have a protective effect on children's mental health across their whole lives.[33] On average, securely attached children show more curiosity, independence and self-reliance, which tends to result in higher levels of competence and resilience as adults.[34]

Yet in today's world there are a number of things that can get in the way of the development of secure attachment, with many parents experiencing social disadvantage, poor mental health and lack of social support, plus work–life stress[35] and constant access to technology.[36] Research indicates that parents who have a lot of stress in their lives may struggle to practice some of the necessary skills that help children develop secure attachment.[37]

To develop a secure attachment with their caregivers, children need time and attention. Play provides the perfect vehicle for helping parents to tune into their children and support the development of secure attachment.

Parent–child play has three core benefits:

- building secure attachment between parent and child;
- helping children develop creativity, imagination and problem-solving skills;
- the development of empathy and social skills.

These benefit children, but because of the social, cultural and economic implications that come with a lack of secure attachment and poor mental health, they matter to everyone. Bringing parent–child play into the family home as part of the normal routine requires us to give parents time, support and resources.

Promoting play: the Treasure Time programme

I developed a six-step programme for parents and carers showing positive improvements in the attachment between caregivers and children through easy-to-deliver playtimes.

Treasure Time has been designed to increase the quality of the time children and adults spend together playing. The programme has been created to help children develop a secure 'attachment' to their grown-up, who learns responsive, consistent and predictable responses to the child through weekly therapeutic play times. The ingredients of Treasure Time are: 20–30 minutes of dedicated playtime each week, a box of simple toys, a timer, a 'Do not disturb' sign and some key skills and tools for the adults to use when playing with their child.

What the government needs to do

I see a clear way that the government can support the introduction of parent–child play.

My idea is a National Play at Home Scheme. When children start school they would take home boxes of toys, and parents and carers would be able to learn from short, interactive videos to help them deliver child-led play sessions. Parents would follow a six-session guide, for 20–30 minutes of uninterrupted time each week dedicated to play, where they would learn how to communicate using play through delivering the sessions. This time would be designed to give parents the skills necessary to support children's transition to school by giving children a regular outlet to explore and express their feelings in a safe space, through play. Once core skills have been learned by the parent, the playtimes would ideally continue weekly throughout the child's time at school, to provide ongoing positive benefits to both the child and parent.

Evidence to support a National Play at Home Scheme can be found in similar schemes that promote reading at home, where children take books home from school to practise reading with a parent, which show excellent benefits for children's development.[38]

I believe we can build on this work with a National Play at Home Scheme to teach parents and children how to play together in a way that supports the development of secure attachment, empathy, social skills, creativity, imagination and problem-solving skills.

The evidence shows that parent–child playtimes are an essential part of children growing up healthy, happy and securely attached. My idea would provide a solution that helps our next generation to develop the capability, emotional literacy and resilience needed to tackle some of the challenges that the next generation will face.

Learning through play

In their paper 'Why Play = Learning'[39] Roberta Golinkoff, Kathy Hirsh-Pasek and Dorothy Singer collated convincing research that play supports both socio-emotional and academic learning outcomes. They explain that:

- five- to 11-year-olds who have free play at school are more attentive to their work in the classroom;
- guided play helps with self-regulation: during play children learn to 'subordinate their desires to social rules';
- pretend play is a predictor of language and reading readiness;
- four- and five-year-olds build foundational mathematical concepts during free play, for example patterns and shapes, comparisons of size and linking numbers with physical objects.

Their findings have been confirmed through a recent University of Cambridge meta-analysis,[40] and the implication from the research is clear: play and guided play offer strong support for academic and social learning.

Given the findings linking play and learning, is play promoted? No. The British Children's Play Survey of 2020[41] shows that children aged 5 to 11 played for just over three hours each day, with the majority of that happening at home or outside in home gardens, rather than in nature or in the community.

It's shocking that play has been so devalued in western culture that it is increasingly downplayed in policy initiatives. Take school, for example, where children spend significant portions of their time and therefore offer the most opportunity for ensuring play is a priority. In the USA 30,000 schools have dropped recess (breaktime) to make more room for academic learning, while from 1997 to 2003 children's time in outdoor play fell by 50 per cent.[42] Consequently, in the last 20 years, American children have lost over eight hours of discretionary playtime per week.

There's a similar pattern in the UK. In 2019 a UCL study found five- to seven-year-olds had 45 minutes less breaktime per week at primary school than children of the same age did in 1995, while secondary pupils aged 11–16 had lost 65 minutes.[43]

One obvious solution to counter this reduction in playtime would be to simply reintroduce it! A more innovative and perhaps more impactful solution would be to ensure that play is formally incorporated as a 'strategy' within class time; and to ensure effectiveness, make sure that teachers are trained in utilising play as a learning method. Bo Stjerne Thomsen is Chair of Learning through Play at The LEGO Foundation and has used this essay to share his experiences of changing the way teachers are trained in Denmark.

Reforming teacher education towards playful learning

Bo Stjerne Thomsen, Vice-President and Chair of Learning through Play at The LEGO Foundation

As the needs and structure of the economy and job market face rapid changes, the existing education system needs to adapt equally rapidly so that children grow up as creative, engaged and lifelong learners, with appropriate skills to thrive. Recent international reports[44,45,46] reveal a need to redesign the education system so it is more equitable and aligned with future needs.

The LEGO Foundation exists to redefine play and reimagine learning, inspired by the evidence on 'learning through play'.[47] This essay shows how such reimagining is already happening in Denmark, and how children's learning has been shifted by embedding playfulness into teacher training.

Past assumptions about what 'quality education' looks like cannot be used to inform the future of education. 'Traditional' approaches to instruction, the role of the classroom, assessments and community engagement have failed our children and exhausted our education workforce. But hope is to be found in Denmark, which has started to reform the teacher training system by embedding 'playful learning' at its very heart.

A growing pressure on schools
Over recent years there has been growing pressure on schools' performance, from both governments and parents.

Most governments now recognise that measures of students' success should not be limited to standardised academic achievements, but should include students' aptitude more broadly.[48] Our work in Denmark shows that these skills are best nurtured via motivation to keep learning throughout life,[49] and with a strong attention to the *voice* of children.[50] However, schools struggle to get the resources for supporting a broader set of holistic skills (like play skills).

Parents also expect innovative teaching and 'equity' to be advanced in schools. Schools are also expected to support the culture of, and links to, their community.[51]

Training and support currently provided to teachers in most parts of the world is inadequate to deliver a 21st-century personalised learning system. Teacher training has evolved into a rigid and theoretical model, with no significant basis in the science of learning or practical training in navigating a modern, complex classroom. It has taken away the excitement and motivation for innovative teaching. It dissuades and demotivates teachers *and* fails to set children up to thrive in this modern world.

Denmark's education system: nurturing a joy of learning

One measure of students' success and growth remains unchanged: a genuine joy of learning. Joy and curiosity are core determinants of overall life satisfaction and predict people's capacity to grow, adapt and thrive throughout life.[52] Thankfully there is an opportunity to nurture joy through playful experiences, and the Danish government has taken it.

While children are flexible in learning new skills, this flexibility declines as we grow older. This matters because:[53]

- a significant part of sparking creativity relates to challenging – and being able to adjust – your mindset;
- adults need to remain engaged in learning, play and creativity to thrive in life. Curiosity, confidence and emotional regulation are critical for successful careers and when facing new challenges.

During the COVID-19 pandemic The LEGO Foundation worked with the Danish teacher colleges and broad education stakeholders to implement, and then evaluate, more flexible teacher training practices. This included training in why play is fundamental for learning, how children play, and how to teach and provide playful learning in the classroom. The evaluation of this work shows that not only did teachers and students increase well-being, but teachers also found new ways to improve educational outcomes.[54] The teacher training system is being reformed to include a more solid understanding of the science of learning through hands-on practical activities (that is, play). Teacher training colleges are now equipped with play labs, physical materials and technology, because the government has come to recognise that the core skill of a teacher is their ability to invent new and playful activities.

Three things we can learn from Danish teacher training

1. *Support broader outcomes of success:* A critical metric for assessing the performance of a school should be evidence of a sustained focus on teaching holistic skills. Denmark has several measures of student success regarding whether children holistically thrive in schools. It is possible.

2. *Reform teacher training with playful learning:* In Denmark, all teacher training colleges now focus on embedding playful learning as an integrated part of their courses,[55] with the relational practices between teachers, students and materials the core component. School leaders and teachers balance the more classical instructional approaches with the use of guided play and open-ended opportunities.[56]

3. *Enable access to broader materials and experiences:* The teaching methods that best prepare children for the future need to be innovative, where teachers nurture playful, creative and hands-on learning approaches based on real-life problems. Government should fund the use of hands-on (play) materials, a broader range of teacher training experiences and new technology to widen the opportunities for teachers to contribute better to curriculum and teaching development.

Across The LEGO Foundation work we can see that building teachers' skills through giving them training on the science and practices of children's learning through play, alongside broadening the measures of success, can bring innovation to the education system. Other governments can adopt the policies shown to work in Denmark. Playful learning is the key to ensuring our children's skills match those a modern world requires, and that they are set up to thrive in life.

Playing outside

Bo explained how governments can support teachers to be better at supporting their students' play. What else influences whether children get the play they need?

A wide range of contextual, socio-demographic and economic factors predicts children's play, including the availability of, and proximity to, safe spaces. In 2020, the Intergenerational Foundation estimated that there were around 1.73 million children in England living in homes officially deemed to be overcrowded.[57] They already had evidence of an overlap between living in an overcrowded household, economic deprivation and having access to a private garden, and so concluded it was highly likely that most of these children were reliant on *public* spaces to not only get away from what could be a challenging living environment at home, but also, to play. The good news is their survey found that 95 per cent of the population lived within a 15-minute walk to a green public space (park or playing field). But children are more likely to play in a private garden – possibly because parents feel there would be significantly reduced risk from injury, traffic or strangers. The fact that one in eight households has no garden space is a problem, and this is particularly true for younger, minority ethnic and economically deprived families in urban areas.[58]

Samira Musse is a parent and community activist living in a tower block in Bristol. She has written this essay for us about the realities for children and families on her estate, and what she wants the government to do.

Find your village: play, community and changing things in a tower block community

Samira Musse, community activist and co-founder of the Barton Hill Activity Club

Home

Children in Somalia, from the moment they wake up until they go to bed, play outside. Adults are also outside most of the time – they gather and talk – everyone knows each other. People pretty much only sleep indoors – life is mainly lived outside!

Since the civil war in the 1990s, Somali families have been coming to the UK and have mainly been put in tower blocks – the total opposite to life at home, where tower blocks are hotels or offices. Can you imagine? High up, crammed into small spaces, indoors all the time, not knowing anyone. Nowhere to meet, and nowhere to go.

Because of this, life can feel very stressful and isolated. Not surprisingly, you see people going in and out who seem depressed and downcast. I've lived on the 14th floor with my children for 12 years now. And do you know there are five doors – five! – between entering the block and getting into my flat. That's five layers to get through in order to see people or go outside. People get very anxious in the little communal spaces between doors, worrying about crime, fire and being trapped. It's meant to make people feel safe, but we don't.

Being trapped in these small boxes has a massive impact on children's lives: not seeing friends or being active, on screens a lot, young children with speech delayed, very young children without space to crawl or toddle and other children with anxieties and poor health.

Lockdowns shone a light on how hard life is in big blocks of flats with little outside space. But what people maybe don't know is that in some ways, lockdown was not that different to everyday life for us. There's always a kind of lockdown for a lot of people.

So my first policy ask is this: all families with young children, from any background, should not be housed in high-rise flats. Only houses, or low-rise blocks.

Space

Children should be allowed to be children. To be free and have fun, not to be restricted, like during schooltime. Children need space to play: green space, parks, other spaces.

The space available for children in our housing block is a tiny play park. This was always used by dog owners, so when children would play football there, we'd have to wash dog poo from their shoes, clothes and even their skin. Adults have no outside sheltered space where we can gather.

Our nearby parks are run-down and only have equipment for very young children. Older children need play, too. When adults see older groups of young people, especially boys, they think 'here comes trouble!' and treat them differently, but often they just want to play together.

If we want children to be happy and healthy, we have to find ways to give them the safe space they need to play! But people with less money have less access to space where children can play. We need to make things much, much fairer.

Locally we have tried to help. We called for our green space to be fenced off from dogs – it now is! We helped with a plan for new developments. My motivation to do a 'Play Street' was also part of this, to open up safe space right on the doorstep, so people could come together. And it was wonderful! Children chatting, playing, chalking, running, kicking a ball and even singing. They had a real sense of 'our space' and wanted to do it in other places too!

So this is my next policy ask: all housing should have enough green and other space for children who live there to play in. Children and people of all ages should be able to get to parks that are maintained.

The village

It is important that we don't forget about supporting older children and teenagers in this. It's the crucial age for connection. But this is when they start to become disconnected from the outside world: just school, home, school, home.

It's also the age when children are most influenced by what's around them, so it's important to have positive influences so they grow up healthier, more into their education, happier, seeing friends, playing, connecting, doing sport and exploring life. This makes a huge difference and prevents a lot of problems later on.

There are many barriers to this where I live. There are lots of drug users, and it doesn't feel safe to let children out alone. Racism is also a problem. Some people are angry at us for being here and simply for who we are, some are afraid of difference, while others are struggling in their own lives and just see us as someone to blame. A racist experience can make you feel you cannot go to that space again, and that is terrible.

And yet, so much could be done to make all this better, starting with bringing children and people together so they understand and respect differences.

This is why we set up the Barton Hill Activity Club, to find a way for our children to be active and outside together. We started meeting informally after school, and now there are more than 40 parents with children involved. That's new friends, a community, trusted adults and role models. You come outside, talk to neighbours, there are people all around, children playing. It's like being back in Somalia!

Women from older immigrant communities nearby – Irish and West Indian – say to me: things would have been different for my children growing up if they'd had this. Their children experienced drug use (including overdoses), mental health problems and constant juvenile detention. There was no 'village' to help them.

So policies must change for 'the village' to exist; spaces for people to come together, including provision of activities for older children.

Changing things: 'not for me, but with me'

Lots of people feel they have no power to change things. Authority can be intimidating – council, police, housing management – and they are afraid to speak up or feel there's no point. But if you don't speak up, nothing will ever change. I always say, just start with something small, like we did.

But for most people on a low income, living in overcrowded homes and dealing with so much, the last thing they can do is take on more. And we don't need more consultation forms either – just come and hear us! And let's see what can be done together.

I see many policies or rules written by people who are not affected by them and so they don't make sense, or they do harm. For example, during COVID-19 our school offered laptops to families – but only if they signed an agreement that if it got damaged, they would pay for them. Would people without any money feel safe signing such an agreement?

So my final policy ask: check local and national policies, rules and processes with those who have lived experience. And this approach will empower and support children, too, as they grow up, because they will feel included and that their voices are heard.

A home, a safe space to play together, community and a voice. Beyond education, isn't that what we all want for our children?

Playing safely

As Samira makes clear, access to green space to play in is not enough: safety – or more accurately, parental perceptions of safety – also matters. While lower-income families may have relatively better access to a park,[59] those parks are likely to be more crowded,[60] and parents have more concerns regarding crime, safety and danger when a child is in a public space rather than a private garden. In 2020 Professor Helen Dodd and colleagues published evidence that the average age at which parents allow their children to play unsupervised outside was nearly 11 years old, two years older than those parents themselves recall being allowed.[61]

It seems that parents have become more wary of their children playing outside. Why might this be? A good place to start would be in misplaced good intentions. The new(ish) concept of 'helicopter parenting' epitomises these: where parents constantly oversee their child's activities and environments to swoop down to pick the child up if they perceive 'risk'. Some are even moving from helicopter parenting to 'snow plough parenting', where they actively move any difficulty or potential risk out of their child's way. These approaches – deliberate or not – beg a question: if we shield children from all risk, how will they learn safe limits? You don't need to look far to see how prevailing parental culture soon translates into legal precedent with calls for banning conker fights,[62] imposing fines for climbing trees and flying kites,[63] and even in the USA a lawsuit against parents who allowed their children to walk home unaccompanied.[64] Knowing what we now know about the holistic value of play, isn't this all just so self-defeating?

Play™

A final aspect of play that has been transformed over the last generation or so, and which continues, is in its commercialisation. As academic Stephen Kline points out,[65] starting with the modest advertising of toys in a few magazines in the 1900s, playthings have become intimately bound to the expanding global reach of children's promotional industries. He suggests that the progressive transformation of children's commercial media into outlets for the 'merchants of playthings' is an unstoppable global trend, estimating that 80 per cent of children's play is designed, produced and sold by only 12 leading multinational corporations, mostly Japanese and American. Kline concludes that the commodification of play over the 20th century marks a profound transformation of play cultures.

I recognise this as I reflect on how the generic Action Man and buckets of LEGO® of my childhood, where my play was largely directed by my imagination, have been replaced by Power Rangers dolls and Harry Potter-branded LEGO® sets for my children's play. Today virtual games feature franchised, characterised toys, where play is mostly directed by algorithms and coding of the brand owners.

Playing inclusively

Accompanying the growth in the commercialisation of play, and a shift in control of play from the imaginations of children to marketeers and product designers, are challenges over inclusivity. The opportunity for all children to be able to play with toys or in games that relate to their experience of life and who they are is important for their development. The market largely fails to deliver here, either because non-dominant groups are too small a demographic for financial returns, or because the executives making decisions fail to include diverse experiences, cultures or interests. That lack of diversity is particularly evident, but not exclusive, to dolls, books and digital games.

For example, the Centre for Literacy in Primary Education charity found that 9,115 children's books were published in the UK in 2017, but only 391 (4 per cent) featured a non-White character. In addition, the character from a minority ethnic background was the main character in only 1 per cent of these books.[66] Its 2021 survey found the 1 per cent has increased to 8 per cent, but given that 32 per cent of school children in England come from non-White backgrounds, most of the books read still aren't properly representing children in the UK.[67]

In 2020, Professor Toni Sturdivant recreated a famous experiment from the 1940s that had been significant in bringing racial integration in US schools, through the landmark *Brown v The Board of Education* Supreme Court ruling in 1954. Doing so was part of her research to understand how Black children see 'race' today. Back in the 1940s Kenneth and Mamie Clark – a husband-and-wife team of psychology researchers – used dolls to investigate how young Black children viewed their racial identities. The Clarks found that given a choice between Black dolls and White dolls, most Black children preferred to play with White dolls. They ascribed positive characteristics to the White dolls, but negative characteristics to the Black ones. Some of the children became 'emotionally upset at having to identify with the doll that they had rejected'. The Clarks concluded that Black children – as a result of living in a racist society – had come to see themselves in a negative light.[68] Sturdivant discovered that not much had changed in 2020: young Black girls had a strong preference for playing with non-Black dolls, and repeatedly rejected the Black dolls. She showed that these findings have 'significant implications for early childhood teachers and how they anticipate notions or misconceptions children have about race, structure discussions and activities around race and racism, and scaffold children's development of their racial identity'.[69]

Some tentative progress to include 'minority identities' is being made: Playmobil's toy accessibility school welcomes students with a range of physical abilities, the Fashionista range of Barbie dolls includes four body shapes, seven skin tones and a doll with a prosthetic leg, and Selma's Dolls has Annie, a soft, cuddly doll who happens to have Down syndrome.

Another aspect of inclusion with respect to play is socio-economic circumstance, which is often overlooked as a barrier to inclusive play. After all, isn't the outdoors free? It's not. Curious School of the Wild[70] reminds us about a range of barriers to participation in outdoor play and activities, such as the cost of food, kit, outdoor knowledge and literacy and formal 'inclusive' clubs or programmes – such as the Duke of Edinburgh Award scheme.

Another prevalent barrier to inclusive play is genderisation – think princesses for girls and soldiers for boys – during early childhood, meaning that gender-typed toy play can result in gender differentiation in children's skills and abilities.[71]

Building on good news from the bottom up

The genderisation issue has been taken up by Let Toys Be Toys, a grassroots campaign that started a decade ago from an internet discussion group that asked the toy and publishing industries to stop limiting children's interests by promoting some toys and books as only suitable for girls and others only for boys. They clearly hit a nerve: they claim that after the first three years of campaigning, 14 retailers removed gender signs from stores.

In her book *The Dear Wild Place*,[72] Emily Cutts recounts her community's successful David versus Goliath bottom-up approach against a housing development in Glasgow's North Kelvin Meadow, a place now known as 'The Children's Wood'.

In the late 1990s the area was an abandoned sports ground and had become a drugs den. Emily and other local residents started to transform the wasteland by sowing grass seed and planting trees. Over the coming years, Mother Nature and the wider community chipped in. But as they did so, developers were making plans to build on the site. By 2008 a campaign had been formalised to fight these plans and protect the community green space. Residents started to fix the abandoned brick building. They installed compost bins, flowers, bat boxes and raised beds. In 2011 Emily and her fellow residents formed an official children's playgroup in the Meadow, and started bringing schools to the land and hosting regular public family events. Forest schools and after-school clubs followed. The residents linked with the University of Glasgow's Psychology Department to examine children's attention span after spending time in different locations. They found concentration levels were best after spending time in a natural environment.[73] The Children's Wood that Emily and her neighbours created is a tangible example of the benefits of a child-centred future. It illustrates what can happen if priorities are rebalanced. And it shows the – often latent – power of determined parents.

A similarly inspiring bottom-up example of efforts to prioritise children's play can be found in Cardiff. Since 2021 Cardiff Council has been implementing a 'Play Lanes' pilot initiative. In the Grangetown neighbourhood they sought to transform a number of lanes into child-friendly spaces by empowering residents and improving community cohesion through intergenerational action. Together they aim to make access to play more equal across Cardiff by ensuring all children have more safe spaces to play in.[74]

Conclusions

Play is vital to human development: children learn so many vital skills from it, it is the 'work of the child' and it is a core component of a thriving childhood. So often play is undervalued by policy makers and educators and is sometimes misunderstood by parents. There seems to be a paradox in that play can mean everything, but is defined as being nothing of consequence. Perhaps this is at the heart of the challenge?

We have seen how play is best, most effective and beneficial when it is free of rules and adult interventions and is child-led. In cases where play *has* been prioritised, children and communities have thrived as a result.

Play is also most beneficial when its access is fair. That level of fairness reflects society's values. For example, perhaps attitudes to ethnic equity in play is a key litmus test as to society's overall progress towards racial equality, not in terms of diversity in the number of products, but in the play they stimulate.

The importance of play is underscored by the fact that access to it is a defined right under Article 31 of the UNCRC. As I explain later in Chapter 10, incorporation into UK law would ensure the principle is legally enforceable and upheld.

Such a transformational recognition of the importance of play would build on the work of a previous administration. In 2008, the Department for Children, Schools and Families published its *Play Strategy*, which stated that 'time and space to play safely is integral to our ambition to make England the best country in the world for children and young people to grow up – it is vital to children's physical, emotional, social and educational development'.[75] Every local authority was charged to deliver on this vision, targeting children most in need of improved play opportunities, and £235 million was invested.

The 2008 Play Strategy was a radical, children-centred goal, yet political choices in the age of austerity took hold and led to its early demise. It is time to rebuild that radicalism with prioritisation to safe, playful spaces, teaching teachers to play, ensuring school days have plentiful playtime and the raft of other ideas this chapter has explored in aiming to create thriving childhoods and a thriving nation.

One additional essay, containing another proposal for government, is hosted at www.raisingthenation.co.uk:

- Esther Marshall is a girls' rights campaigner and former Global Lead for Gender Diversity and Inclusion at Unilever. She has written on policies government could adopt to de-genderify play.

5

Local spaces

Let's design a city where kids have great early stories.
Erion Veliaj[1]

My childhood memories are coloured by the events and culture of the 1970s and 1980s, with music being a particular pull back to the past. Among the artists who provided the soundtrack to my youth was Cat Stevens (now known as Yusuf Islam). Many of his songs address themes of childhood, but one in particular still resonates. It shares powerful environmental messages, prompted by the apparent 'advances' of urbanisation, consumerism, the primacy of adults' needs and reliance on fossil fuels. It poses a rhetorical question in its title, 'Where do the children play?' That question is at the heart of this chapter.

Many public and private spaces have become the exclusive use of certain sections of society.[2] They have become unavailable or unwelcoming to others, especially children.

This chapter focuses on five aspects of local spaces where it has become harder for many children to access or navigate over the last generation: play spaces, their homes, transport, air quality and the advertising that permeates so many neighbourhoods.

Buzz off

We've all seen them. Groups of 'youth' hanging around in the park, street or outside shops. A sight that may prompt an emotional response: recollection of one's own youth, anger that they're not doing something more worthy with their time, or concern that there's going to be trouble.

For some residents, business owners and even public services, gatherings of young people in 'their' area is something to be controlled. And some have found a way of simply getting rid of young people: a 'Mosquito'. Also known as an anti-loitering (or by the media, an 'anti-child')[3] device, the Mosquito is a small box that emits a high-pitched ultrasonic sound only people aged 25 or younger can hear. One teenager described it as a 'prolonged beep akin to tinnitus'.[4] Despite calls from the United Nations (UN),[5] the Council of Europe[6] and continued debate in Parliament,[7] these devices have not been banned or even regulated in the UK.

There is much about them that disturbs me. Their impact is both discriminatory (in that it affects only the young) and indiscriminatory (in so far as it impacts on any young person who is not causing any harm or distress to anyone). You could be walking along with your child or grandchild and have no idea they are in distress, because you cannot hear it. Can you imagine the outcry if, for example, all retired people were targeted with a device that made it unpleasant for all of them to drive, because younger people were irritated that some drove too slowly?

The use of Mosquitos is outrageous, and especially shocking is that so few are scandalised by the indiscriminate hostility towards the only group in society who can't vote (and can't sue), especially given that they have every right to be in shared public spaces. The wider implications have been picked up by the UN, who recommended that the UK take 'urgent measures to address the "intolerance of childhood" and general negative public attitude towards children, especially adolescents, within society'.[8] This recommendation and concern is quite a big deal. The position adopted by the Mosquito device proponents that they are perfectly legal speaks to a deeper question around local spaces that incorporate public places, transport and housing: just who is this space for?

Children's local spaces

Perhaps another way of looking at the existence of an item like the Mosquito is to explore spaces that children and young people need and can access. Why is it that children currently gather in public spaces that are not designed for socialising? Where can children spend time outside their home, a place that is free or affordable to access, somewhere safe and where they can influence what it offers?

In the past, the answer may have been youth clubs, a critical part of the youth space ecosystem for over a century. But funding cuts have resulted in a 51 per cent drop in the number of youth centres supported by English local authorities since 2011.[9] Young people now have fewer places to go and socialise together than previous generations enjoyed.

The impact of this was recognised with the government promising a 'National Youth Guarantee' by 2025, whereby every young person would have access to regular clubs and activities, including opportunities to volunteer. It remains to be seen whether the earmarked £560 million will be forthcoming.[10]

There has also been a reduction in the number of dedicated public spaces for younger children in recent years. Between 2014 and 2016 local authorities across England closed over 200 children's playgrounds, with plans to close 234 more.[11]

Perhaps, against the backdrop of cuts in investment in dedicated local spaces for children, it's not surprising that some end up gathering in places adults claim for themselves. The opportunity for reducing antisocial behaviour is clear, but not through deterrence via devices such as the Mosquito in public spaces; it is through offering safe spaces for children of all ages. This requires a shift in mindset in how society values children, and their respective rights and needs. Local spaces should be built around the needs of the most vulnerable, rather than efficiency, economic priorities or the most influential lobby groups.

Tim Gill is a renowned scholar, writer and campaigner for children's play and mobility. His essay calls for a 'children's lens' in planning policy, as a powerful catalyst for healthier, more sustainable neighbourhoods for people of all ages.

Children: an indicator species for towns and cities

Tim Gill, scholar, writer, consultant on childhood and campaigner for
children's play and mobility

The way we build towns and cities is not serving children and young people.
Too few places have enough welcoming outdoor spaces where children can
play, socialise and relax. Too many neighbourhoods are dominated by cars
and blighted by traffic danger and air pollution. As a result, children are not
only less healthy, but are also less able to gradually get to grips with the world
around them, weakening their connection with nature, local communities
and the wider world.[12]

There is strong evidence of the health benefits of outdoor play and active
mobility for children. Some of these benefits arise from the fact that in play
– and, to some extent, in active travel – children are exercising a degree of
independence and self-control, and in doing so learning how to self-regulate,
make decisions and choices and respond to uncertainty. Hence play and
independent mobility create learning and developmental experiences that
go beyond those offered in more structured activities.[13]

Child-friendly urban planning

Over the last decade or so, my work as an independent scholar and global
advocate has focused on how the built form of neighbourhoods can be
improved for children, their families and communities and the planet. My
solution – set out in my 2021 book *Urban Playground: How Child-Friendly
Planning and Design Can Save Cities*[14] – is to look at towns and cities through
a 'children's lens': to see children not just as one section of the population,
but as a group who inspire us to think harder about our collective, long-term
future, and about what healthy human habitats look and feel like.

'Child-friendly urban planning' is partly a matter of involving children,
but it is more than mere participation. Insights from public health, child
development and participatory planning all suggest there are two dimensions
of what makes cities work for children. The first dimension is choice and
variety in places to go and things to do, including space for outdoor play.
The second is mobility: making it easy for children to get around easily and
safely, whether on foot, by bike or scooter.

The connections between child-friendly urban planning and children's
health and well-being are intuitively obvious and supported by empirical
research. UNICEF studies across over 15 countries show a strong and
consistent link between the time children spend playing outside and their

subjective well-being.[15] Other international studies show similar links between children's independent mobility and their overall health and well-being.[16] What is more, the approach also maps neatly onto what children around the world tell us they like and do not like about where they are growing up. Whenever we take the trouble to ask children for their views, no matter where they live, their demand for spatial choice and freedom comes through loud and clear.[17]

One real-life example of a child-friendly neighbourhood is Vauban, a planned eco-suburb of some 5,500 people, on the outskirts of Freiburg in Germany. The entire district is designed for car-free living. Cars are allowed, but the street network and design ensure that drivers go slowly. What is more, cars can only park in one of three peripheral long-term car parks. Great walking and cycling networks and efficient public transport mean that very few families feel the need for car ownership. As a result, almost all of the space between buildings is available for public use: for play, recreation and active travel. This child-friendliness is not just a side-effect: it was an explicit part of Vauban's rationale and vision, informed by landmark sociological research on children's play and mobility back in the 1990s.[18]

There has been a steady growth in interest from urbanists and designers in children's lives in the city. Some of the most innovative, strategic projects have been supported by the Bernard van Leer Foundation, a global non-governmental organisation (NGO) whose focus is early childhood development. Its Urban95 initiative invites adults to see cities from a height of 95cm – the average height of a healthy three-year-old – and to ask what they would do differently. Since its launch in 2016, Urban95 has invested more than £20 million in over 75 cities around the world.

Another prominent global programme is the Child-Friendly Cities Initiative (CFCI) run by UNICEF. This rights-based municipal accreditation scheme – with thousands of participating cities – has a longstanding focus on participation. In 2018 it introduced substantive outcomes that city leaders should consider, including explicit goals around both public space and mobility.

Child-friendly urban planning can make a real difference, as Urban95 and UNICEF's CFCI are showing. A child's lens can be a catalyst for a compelling urban vision, and can shape ambitious programmes to improve public space, increase active travel and transform neighbourhoods.[19] Barcelona is another example, with its post-pandemic 'school streets' programme, which aimed to reclaim street space outside over 150 schools by 2022.[20] This comes on top of longstanding commitments around active travel, public space, urban reforestation and children's play.

Here in the UK, too, interest is growing. Cardiff and Leeds have signed up to UNICEF's CFCI and have taken forward projects focusing on public space. In Cambridge, a new mixed-use district will lead to thousands of new homes. The masterplan puts inclusive, active travel and attractive public space – and children and families – centre-stage, with cars literally and figuratively marginalised.

The truth is that our human habitats are not just failing children. Decades of car-centric, business-as-usual urban planning means that sedentary, unhealthy lifestyles and environmental degradation are baked into many neighbourhoods, even those developments billed as sustainable.[21] This creates huge challenges in making the shift to the low carbon economy that the planet needs.[22]

Conclusion

One of the challenges in transforming the built form of cities is the sheer complexity of the issue with different points, scales and types of intervention, diverse change agents and competing, if not conflicting, interest groups.[23] Navigating this complexity means building a shared, long-term strategic vision that helps to overcome narrow vested interests.

Child-friendly urban planning pulls together insights from sustainable planning and healthy child development in a way that makes these goals both more real and more ambitious. It is a catalyst for change at every level of decision making, but especially for city leaders who are searching for a positive vision. The key levers for change lie at the local level, and local authorities already have most of the powers they need. What is missing is national leadership and direction. One catalytic change at the national level would be to ensure an explicit focus on children in transport planning, for example through a strategic push to boost walking and cycling to school, underpinned by major investment. The launch in 2022 of Active Travel England (ATE) could create a rare opportunity for such a move; ATE head Chris Boardman has stated that new cycling schemes 'must be usable and want to be used by a competent 12-year-old'.[24]

Enrique Peñalosa, a former Mayor of Bogotá whose progressive transport and public space programmes transformed that troubled city, famously said that children are an 'indicator species' for neighbourhoods. This is not just a snappy maxim. The presence of children of different ages being active and visible throughout the streets and public spaces of towns and cities, with and without their parents or carers, is a sign of the health of human habitats, just like the presence of salmon swimming in a river.

Tim puts together a powerful case for change, but is it possible? It is. With political will and focus it has been implemented across public spaces in perhaps one of the most unlikely cities in Europe.

Tirana: a city redesigned for its children

When Erion Veliaj became Mayor of Tirana, capital city of Albania, in 2015, he knew he had a challenge on his hands. The city had swollen in population since the fall of communism in 1991. After living under centralised control planning, people found themselves with a new power to take individual decisions. This led to a race to build informal houses and buildings. Car ownership, once the preserve of the few, exploded to the point where Tirana was one of the most polluted cities in Europe.[25] While the country had a young population, its overcrowded, underinvested and polluted capital city was not a desirable place to raise children.

Veliaj won his election campaign with a pledge to make the city a place where children would thrive, with the rallying call: 'let's design a city where kids can have great early stories'.[26] On assuming office, however, he found there was a mountain to climb. Distrust of politicians meant that, as Veliaj recalls, 'the biggest and the most difficult infrastructure project [we faced] was only 10 centimetres long. ... Mental infrastructure.'[27]

Veliaj saw that in order to transform people's thinking about the city, he would need children on his side. One example neatly illustrates how he achieved this. Play space had long been privatised in Tirana. The lack of planning and the sprawl of illegal buildings meant that spaces for children to play came with a cost attached: fenced-off areas attached to cafes and bars. This meant people needed to be able to afford to pay for coffee or beer in order for their children to play. The Mayor chose to tackle this, starting with Tirana's iconic Skanderbeg Square. The piazza, once a fully pedestrianised area, had become nothing more than Europe's biggest roundabout. Veliaj organised a day when this area would be shut to traffic and instead used as a free play space for children and families. Car users complained, but the children loved it, and Veliaj had the political bravery to grab hold of the children's enthusiasm to influence parents and grandparents and extend the experiment. The one-off no-car day became a monthly event, and then more frequent, until it was part of citizens' 'mental infrastructure'. It is now fully pedestrianised. Emboldened, Veliaj authorised the city to reclaim land that had been illegally built on. He created new free-to-access neighbourhood playgrounds, funded by support and input from both government and the private sector.[28]

Veliaj also has made use of an old cultural habit from communist times, that of surveillance. But he turned the tables by creating an app so citizens can report vandalism or mounting rubbish. Residents send in a photo of the problem and receive a message when it is solved by City Hall. Such visible responsiveness has brought confidence and pride for residents, and vandalism rates have plummeted as enthusiasm for the concept of putting children into the heart of neighbourhood life has soared.

In 2023, Veliaj remains Mayor and Tirana was named the official European Youth Capital. His zeal of reinventing his city for children continues apace:

- three major city parks have been 'reinvented';
- 500,000 new trees have been planted, including many under a scheme where children are invited to plant a tree on their birthday;[29]
- cycle lanes have opened across the city and bicycle riding lessons are taught in kindergartens;
- 70 new playgrounds have been built or are pledged, with a commitment to open one each month.[30]

In implementing the transformation of their city, Veliaj's team collaborated closely with organisations like 8 80 Cities – who believe that if everything done in cities is great for an eight-year-old *and* an 80-year-old, then it will be great for all people – and with the Urban95 initiative that Tim Gill wrote about.

In the UK, Alice Ferguson and Ingrid Skeels have taken a 'ground-up' approach to change. They have written this essay for us calling on government to ensure children get access to their fair share of public space near their homes.

Why 'playing out' matters for children

Alice Ferguson and Ingrid Skeels, co-founders and Co-Directors of
Playing Out

Dump your school bag and grab a snack. Out the front door, knock for your friend and get them out to play. Find where the other kids are. Kick a ball about, show off your tricks, make up a new game. When you're older, start to explore the neighbourhood, go to the skate park, plan a bike ride.

All of this, simply having the freedom to play out and get around independently near home, was a completely normal part of British childhoods until recently. It didn't need money, a destination, transport or parental supervision. It was simply the result of children's free, democratic access to public space close to home. The dramatic loss of this over the past 50 years has had a huge impact on children's lives, health and development – yet has gone almost completely unnoticed and unchallenged.

Just ask any adult who grew up with this sense of freedom and they will list a whole range of positive social and personal outcomes: friendships forged across all ages and backgrounds; skills developed and confidence increased; a deep connection built with your neighbourhood; the pure enjoyment of physicality, free play and self-determination. And all this was on top of the more obvious, functional benefits for children's health that come from being outdoors, active and social.

A dramatic loss

Back in 2009, as parents of young children living in the city (Bristol), we were concerned at how much things had changed compared to our own childhoods. Our children were spending far too much time indoors, inactive and isolated. In one generation, the physical and social environment had changed to the extent that it no longer felt safe or acceptable to let your children simply 'play out' on the street or near home, as we had done. Unwilling to accept the status quo we decided to try and push back. Alice and her neighbour, artist Amy Rose, devised the simple, resident-led 'temporary play street' model, closing their street to cars for a couple of hours after school. It was a 'light bulb moment'; simply removing through-traffic opened up the space for large numbers of children to come out and play.

Seeing an appetite from other parents to take similar action, our small group then set up Playing Out as a national movement aimed at restoring this essential part of life for all children. Since then, the organisation has driven the growth of play streets across the UK and beyond. As of early 2023, over

1,500 street communities across all walks of life have regularly opened their streets for play, directly benefiting 45,000 children and enabling over 1 million 'play hours'. Building on our pioneering work with Bristol City Council, over 90 local authorities have now implemented play street policies. Interest in the model has spread globally.

This temporary model demonstrates what is needed longer term: safer streets and spaces, more connected communities and children's needs being recognised and prioritised.

It has become increasingly clear that our own parental concerns reflect a wider and worsening modern reality: children everywhere have lost the freedom they once had to play out near home. Children's time spent outdoors,[31] outdoor play,[32] 'roaming range' and independent mobility[33] have all massively reduced over a few decades.

Even pre-pandemic, 80 per cent of children were not getting the basic hour per day of physical activity they need to be healthy and well,[34] suggesting that organised sports have not compensated for the loss of freedom to simply be outside: walking, cycling and playing. One in four children now leave primary school clinically obese,[35] and children's mental health is at crisis point.[36] The loss of access to free (in all senses) outdoor play in shared space has impacted children from the most disadvantaged communities the hardest.

What needs to change?
We need to look at what is fundamentally wrong with children's lives and change that. Outdoor play may not be a silver bullet, but restoring the freedom to play out near home could go a long way to ensuring all children, regardless of background or circumstance, are happy, healthy and part of their communities.

Screens, indoor technology and lazy parenting are often blamed as the cause of children's sedentary behaviour. But the reality – demonstrated clearly by play streets – is that when children are given time and permission to play out with others in a safe space on their doorstep, they leap at the opportunity and are naturally physically active. So what is stopping them from doing this?

Undoubtedly, the biggest barrier to children's freedom is traffic dominance – children have been pushed out of residential streets that were once a shared space for play and community. Parents consistently say that the very real danger posed by cars is the main thing preventing them from letting their children play out near home or roaming further afield.[37]

Outdoor space within housing estates has also become increasingly off-bounds for children. Adults' right to 'quiet enjoyment' of outdoor space is often a condition of tenancy agreements whereas children's right to play is not. Play bans are all too often implemented by housing providers in response to a single complaint. Patches of green and other informal space are being sold off or built on, seemingly without regard to their play value for local children.

So what can be done? The success of play streets suggests that the answer is in some ways very simple. To play out, be physically active and socially connected, children essentially need two things: easy access to safe space on their doorstep and permission to use it. Seeing others playing out and normalising this is another important factor for both children and parents.

Play streets are a quick, simple and low-cost way for communities to start to build these conditions, but policy changes are also needed. Residential streets that are safe for play; housing estates that welcome children playing outside; easy access to local parks, playgrounds, green spaces and other public spaces; safe routes so children can get to these places independently on foot or wheels; more connected communities that support children's right to play out near home.

National policies that could help create these conditions include:

- children's right to play outside their homes established in law, and housing policy requiring that outdoor space is accessible, safe and welcoming to children;
- a child 'lens' applied to all policies regarding streets and other public spaces;
- public health and physical activity strategies prioritising children's outdoor play and freedom;
- a 'child MPH' speed limit on residential streets, supported by low-cost physical measures.[38]

No one set out to erode children's freedom or to take away all that it gave them; it's just what happened while people were making decisions about other things, and because children were so little considered in those decisions. But the vicious cycle can be reversed – temporarily through play streets, and longer term through policy measures. If children are out and about in their streets and neighbourhoods, they will be 'seen and heard' in society, making it much harder to ignore their needs. Through feeling valued and connected in their communities, they will gain a sense of citizenship, agency and responsibility for the world around them. If we want current and future generations of children to grow up happy, healthy, caring and empowered, we need to first restore their freedom to be outside.

So far, we've read about uplifting examples of actions that have transformed public spaces so children are not only welcome, but where planning prioritises children. Ensuring that children thrive in the private space of home is equally important.

A house is a home

My children are in their early twenties and forging their own lives. They pop back to us often, however, and still think of our house as home, a place of refuge. But sadly, many children do not grow up with the comfort that such stability offers, and the harsh truth is that where a child lives directly impacts on their ability to thrive. The location of a home determines much of our opportunity and experience, including the school we will attend, the friends we will make and where we will play. The physical quality of the home is also vital – housing is a social determinant of health and well-being.[39]

When researching this book, I discovered one striking finding in regard to housing: that the statutory 'overcrowding standard', conceived in Victorian times,[40] has not been updated since 1935.[41] In other words, although our understanding of the need for space and privacy has come a long way since Victorian times, official thinking and action has lagged behind.

The National Housing Federation found that one in five children are living in unsuitable housing, with overcrowding the most common issue, affecting 1.1 million children.[42] Recent government data from England has found that overcrowding is at its highest rate in the social rented sector (9 per cent) and in the private rented market (7 per cent), which contrasts with a stable level of 1 per cent in private ownership.[43] Similarly to the findings around access to green space, households from minority ethnic groups are more likely to be overcrowded than White British ones.[44] A recent National Housing Federation survey of those living in overcrowded conditions found that a quarter of parents were sleeping in corridors, bathrooms or kitchens, that overcrowding was impacting parental mental health and causing family arguments, and that most children didn't want to come home.[45]

Children in overcrowded houses are not only indirectly impacted by growing up in homes with adult stress, but they are also far more likely to be at risk of infections and respiratory problems due to poor quality housing.[46] One study found that children living in damp homes were 32 per cent more likely to be at risk of a wheezing illness such as asthma.[47] In November 2022, the coroner at the inquest into his tragic death found that two-year-old Awaab Ishak had died as a direct 'result of exposure to mould', endemic in his damp-ridden council house in Rochdale.[48] Children growing up in poor quality housing are also exposed to long-term consequences, not only with the increased risk of respiratory disease,[49] but also through higher risk of depression in adulthood.[50] Overcrowded conditions invariably mean that for children there is less space to play, less space to study,[51] and an increased likelihood of absences from school due to medical reasons.[52]

The impact is even more challenging for children growing up without a stable home. Homelessness does not just mean those who are sleeping rough: it includes those living in temporary, insecure or inadequate accommodation. Numbers are growing, with Shelter estimating that on Christmas Day in 2017, 128,000 British children were homeless, a number that has risen every Christmas since 2011. Recent economic circumstances, including the cost-of-living crisis, have meant that families who are not 'yet' homeless, but living in private rented accommodation, are now more at risk of eviction.

The impact of insecure housing on children is profound. In 2017 Shelter interviewed British teachers about what they noticed in children experiencing homelessness.[53] Social isolation emerged as a concern for children often unable to access basic hygiene facilities, with reports of young people needing to use showers at the local gym to wash.[54] Teachers also reported a lack of sleep, which, in turn, leads to isolation. Children often have to share rooms (where different sleep patterns collide), leaving them tired and anxious. Another longitudinal study similarly found that even after having been rehoused, children's mental health issues and development delays remained significant. Children who have experienced homelessness are also more likely to be absent from school, and are more likely to have to move schools as part of rehousing.[55]

During COVID-19 lockdowns, emergency powers were granted to cease all evictions from private and social housing.[56] This was a sensible measure, but it also tells us that it is perfectly possible for the law to protect those at risk of eviction. Shelter estimated that in the last three months of 2021, when the no-eviction rule had been removed, 55,000 children were, with their families, evicted or made homeless.[57] Surely, as a country that claims safeguarding children is a national priority,[58] we could devise a safety net system that ensures that children being made homeless is exceptionally rare?

In addition to moral obligations there are good economic reasons to ensure families live in decent houses, epitomised by the concept of 'failure demand'. 'Failure demand' was first used by occupational psychologist and author Jon Seddon in 1989 to describe the increase in demand for a service being a reflection of a problem rather than a sign of success.[59] Translated to social policy, considerable state spending in direct and indirect payments and support for homeless and poorly housed families has consistently increased over the years. This is money spent as a reaction to the current set-up, and barely questions the root causes of the homelessness issue.[60]

Transport: going the distance

I have so many vivid memories of leaving the school gates as a 1980s boy (complete with dodgy mullet!). I took two buses across Sheffield to visit my nan and get my fill of the fizzy drink Dandelion and Burdock. I especially remember that, for years, the journey cost just 2p, and that you popped your money into a machine that basically imprinted your 2p coin on your ticket. I thought it was the coolest thing ever – that, and the fact that the city subsidised local journeys for children so that they could be independent and travel across the city to be spoiled by their grandmothers, without struggling with the cost.

Transport is an enabler – and the lack of it is a blocker – to an ability to thrive, perhaps particularly so for children. Sustrans, a charity that makes it easier for people to walk and cycle, aims to connect people and places, create liveable neighbourhoods, transform the school run and deliver a happier, healthier commute. Its insight provides evidence that transport connects young people to opportunities, be they in education or employment, and provides chances to develop skills or time to build relationships.[61] So what transport systems do children use? Are they working for all, and what's changing or in need of change? Research by Sustrans shows that:

- getting a lift by car constitutes over half of journeys for under-17-year-olds, although the use of buses does increase as children get older;
- the average length of journeys that 11- to 16-year-olds take has increased in recent years, meaning more car use and less walking;
- young people are making fewer trips in total than they did 20 years ago, with cost cited as a major influencer in this decline;
- young people are critical of the quality of transport and would rather go by car;
- cars are still seen as a key to freedom, but children in urban centres express more positive attitudes towards walking, cycling and public transport than those in rural areas.[62]

Children growing up in rural areas have particular challenges as investment in local public transport has significantly declined (many routes lack profitability for private companies, while local authorities are underfunded and subsidies hard to finance). One answer is that public transport should not be expected to break even or return a surplus. Instead, the focus should be on the benefits of inclusion, health, opportunity, education and work that deliver a societal dividend in other ways. In addition, innovation in on-demand bus services in rural areas using demand-responsive transport apps (where buses alter their routes and destinations on demand, rather than using fixed timetables and journeys), and other technology, has the potential to significantly reduce childhood transport poverty. In 2021 the Department for Transport invested £20 million in 17 regional pilots, to evaluate the public service benefits such innovation could bring.[63] We wait to see what impact this has had on rural children's mobility.

Available, affordable, ubiquitous public transport has been a passion of the Mayor of Greater Manchester, Andy Burnham, for years. He sees its value squarely in the 'enabling' argument, especially for young people, and began work to deliver his vision as soon as he was elected.

In 2019 Greater Manchester launched its Our Pass scheme, giving free public transport annual passes to all 16- to 18-year-olds, and to all 18- to 21-year-olds leaving the care system. The pass also grants discounts and access to numerous educational, entertainment and cultural activities in the region. In its first three years, over 100,000 young people have been issued with a card, and over 18 million journeys have been taken.[64]

In 2022, Burnham announced a £1.2 billion investment over five years to integrate the region's public transport services (bus, tram, train, cycle). Operations were taken back into public control and the services offered to the public as a single service accessible for a single subsidised fare of £2 per adult and £1 per child (whatever the journey across Manchester's Beeline network).

Transport for London (TfL) operates all London's public transport networks. Since 2005, it has similarly offered (to registered Oyster Card holders) free travel across the whole network for under-11-year-olds, and free bus and tram travel for 11- to 18-year-olds. In 2020, as part of the first COVID-19 emergency funding deal for TfL, the government required the suspension of such free travel. Shortly afterwards, an Early Day Motion in Parliament raised concerns about the effect on low-income households, in a city where 37 per cent of all children are living in poverty. The Motion recognised that the decision would reverse the significant benefits of free travel: greater social inclusion, reduced car use and reduced road casualties. It further recognised opposition to the change among London's young people, including a petition by Joshua Brown-Smith, which had, by then, gathered 185,000 signatures, along with opposition from the Child Poverty Action Group in their #DontZapTheZip campaign.[65] In October 2020 free travel was protected as part of a second COVID-19 emergency funding deal.

Manchester and London's models are fully integrated networks providing child-led, forward-looking visions that central government and other regions need to emulate.

Air quality: a right to clean air

There has been a huge increase in cars over the last two generations. In 1971 just over 50 per cent of households owned a car;[66] by 2018 this had leapt to just under 80 per cent of households.[67] The explosion in the number of cars makes roads more dangerous for children (and everyone else). They are less able to play, cycle or scoot, and the air quality in many places has deteriorated so much that it has become lethal.

In a 2017 joint investigation, Greenpeace and *The Guardian* revealed that thousands of schools in England and Wales were in locations with illegal levels of nitrogen dioxide – a pollutant produced by diesel vehicles.[68] In 2021, Global Action Plan, an environmental charity, commissioned research that found that more than a quarter of British schools, from nurseries to sixth form colleges, were in locations with high levels of small particle pollution. This means an estimated 3.4 million children are learning in unhealthy environments.[69]

A more visceral example came in December 2021, when a coroner in London made legal history by ruling that air pollution was a cause of the death of a nine-year-old girl, Ella Adoo Kissi Debrah in February 2013.[70] He concluded that her death had been caused by acute respiratory failure, severe asthma and air pollution exposure. She had been exposed to nitrogen dioxide and particulate matter pollution in excess of World Health Organization (WHO) guidelines, and the legal limit set at both European Union (EU) and UK level. The principal source was traffic emissions. The state's failure to reduce pollution levels to legal limits possibly contributed to her death, as did the failure to provide Ella's mother with information about the potential for air pollution to exacerbate asthma. It's an awful, tragic, yet landmark case.

It is also no coincidence that Ella lived in an area of social deprivation. Air pollution is more prevalent in such areas: 66 per cent of man-made carcinogens are emitted in the 10 per cent most deprived English city wards.[71] These communities are also likely to have less access to green spaces, which improve air quality, and receive less spending on public transport necessary to reduce overall vehicular traffic.[72] Indeed, children with asthma who live close to a green space present fewer asthma symptoms than those who live further away.[73] Lung disease is also strongly linked to social deprivation and health inequalities, accounting for 11 per cent of deaths in children under 15, and around 9 per cent of all child hospital admissions.[74]

In February 2019, a joint survey by UNICEF UK and the Royal College of Paediatrics and Child Health found that 92 per cent of child health experts believe the public should be more concerned about the negative impact of air pollution on children's health.[75] A similar number warned that toxic air is already causing health problems for children, and called for government to prioritise tackling this. The joint report came less than a month after UNICEF UK had criticised the UK government's Clean Air Strategy for missing the opportunity to commit to legally binding targets to reduce air pollution and prioritise measures to protect children.

Given current government plans, air pollution in the UK is expected to remain at dangerous levels for at least another 10 years.[76] The estimated cost to health and social care services is upwards of a staggering £2 billion, as a result of its impact on heart disease, stroke, lung cancer and childhood asthma – another example of failure demand in action.[77]

Former UNICEF UK Executive Director Mike Penrose succinctly summarised the issue:

> Children have a fundamental right to grow up in a clean and safe environment that gives them the best possible start in life. The persistent, illegal breaches of air pollution limits across the UK are an unacceptable violation of this. … The UK is home to more children suffering from respiratory conditions than anywhere else in Europe.[78]

UNICEF UK proposed three actions to address this issue:

- legally binding targets for air quality;
- a cross-governmental action plan for healthy air for children;
- a Little Lungs Fund 'to pay for measures that specifically reduce children's exposure to toxic air'.[79]

Rachel Toms, an expert in healthy urban design, has written an essay for us that holds the key to a holistic approach to car use, travel and the wider local environment.

Regime change is needed in our public spaces

Rachel Toms, Director of Urbanism at Sustrans

The environments we grow up in

When I was 12, my sister and I had fun playing tennis in the street – when we saw a car coming, we'd stop to let it pass. We'd go up the road to meet our friend Ali and go to the local shop on our bikes or put on our roller boots and see who could go fastest down the next street, which was on a hill.

Now, after many years of practice in the built environment, transport and health, I understand how lucky I was to be able to go out without an adult, ride a bike in the street and play outside, without fear. Living in a leafy suburb helped make this possible – but at the same time the nearby dual carriageway and a six-lane ring road meant that it was too dangerous for us to cycle into town or to our school, even though both were less than three miles away, a bikeable distance.

In almost all urban areas, the streets, parks and other outdoor spaces are a still a mixed bag. Some children can walk from home to a park where there are all kinds of fun things to do. Others are surrounded by litter-strewn streets and underpasses, with nowhere safe close by to run off steam. Kids on some housing estates have well-cared for areas to play and meet up with pals in, but on others, youngsters must navigate alleyways that smell of pee, overflowing bins and plentiful dog poo. Far too many kids live on streets lined with cars and with no space for play.

The reality is that the quality of the outdoor environment matters. The more pleasant the environment, the higher the property prices – and typically the richer the residents. And the more unpleasant the environment, the cheaper the homes and the less affluent the families.

None of this is 'fair'. So what can we do to make systemic changes to our communal space – our 'public realm' – to make it so? How can we make things like walking, cycling, playing and socialising safer, more convenient and pleasant for more children? As your inner five-year-old knows, this stuff needs to be easy and fun.

Two solvable problems

The fundamental weaknesses of the public realm in supporting the well-being of children come from two main problems. By addressing both we can achieve transformative change that benefits everyone.

The first is the dominance of motor traffic:[80,81] the volume and speed of vehicles and the proportion of outdoor spaces taken up by parked cars. Over the last 70 years, we have wrongly ploughed huge resources into enabling travel by private motor vehicle. Despite ever-growing evidence that investing in walking and cycling yields greater economic benefits,[82,83,84] we've built more roads and have wedged more and more vehicle lanes and parking spaces into our towns, cities and villages. The resulting motor journeys and car-dependency have contributed to a host of societal, economic and environmental problems: air pollution, obesity, traffic noise, congestion and carbon emissions.[85]

The second is the way that the public realm is funded and governed. In local government, statutory responsibilities and budgets for transport, highways, waste collection, spatial planning and parks are typically separated, with car-based mobility being given undue priority in policy making, budget setting and decision making. As a result, efforts to improve the public realm to increase well-being fall drastically short.

Transforming streets and spaces

Recognising that many streets and public spaces were not conducive to (child or adult) well-being, leaders in cities across Europe have taken bold action to dramatically upgrade them. In the Netherlands, they've been making streets safer for walking and cycling since the 1970s, so nearly 75 per cent of children now go to school by bike. In Ljubljana, the entire city centre is now car-free, making streets safer and more fun for families, resulting in 92 per cent of residents now happy with the quality of life in the city. In Paris, they've created a 'new aesthetic' in their city streets, putting in play areas, more trees, water fountains and cycle lanes, thereby transforming neighbourhoods into family-friendly environments. Barcelona's Superblocks programme is drastically improving quality of life and reducing air pollution and noise, as every third or fourth street has been converted into a haven for playing, walking, cycling and chatting. All of these schemes faced initial resistance from some residents and businesses, but all have ended up being strongly supported once the transformation is complete.

Regime change opportunity in the UK

If UK towns and cities are to transform their streets and public spaces to reap such rewards for citizens – young and old – regime change is needed in how our public realm is funded and governed. I propose a new approach where local authorities continue to manage streets and spaces, but through a much stronger mechanism, encompassing:

1. Political and technical leadership from the top, with a government minister and a chief public realm official appointed to together drive progress in policy, funding and standards.
2. A single statutory public realm function in local government, with an elected member and a chief officer leading action to improve neighbourhood spaces: covering streets, trees and parks, outdoor play and sport, urban transport, markets and outdoor events.
3. A locally held combined budget for the public realm, with funding coming from existing revenue sources such as council tax, business rates, road tax, infrastructure grants, developer contributions and parking permits.
4. Reformed accountability, meaning all decisions contribute to clearly defined outcomes for residents and businesses. People of all ages and interests, including children, steer decisions and hold local authorities to account.
5. A duty to meet specific standards, for example, providing a play space for toddlers close to homes or keeping streets and spaces clean and 'playable'.
6. Powers to resolve problems such as obsolete phone boxes and advertising totems getting in people's way. Currently private companies can block their removal.

Will this cost more money? Certainly not in the long term. As with the state education system, we would invest upfront to enable the next generation to live in a modern economy and thrive as individuals. Or, in the case of the public realm, to live in a place where your environment makes it fun to be alive.

Advertising

One aspect of 21st-century living that has been quietly revolutionised is the commercialisation of people's personal space: a land grab of any apparent opportunity to sell stuff.

Whereas in the 1970s the average consumer in the USA saw about 500 adverts a day, today the estimate is 10 times more, at 5,000.[86] Advertising generally targets young people, and they generally consume digital content more than other age groups.[87] I look specifically at the impact of the digital revolution on children's lives in Chapter 8, but digital content is not the only culprit in the expansion of advertising into more corners of children's lives than ever before. As a society we have commercialised parts of our physical local spaces, be that through the sponsorship of village roundabouts or local sports teams' kit, to the actual names of the venues in which we go to see sports and cultural events.

In 2019, London's Child Obesity Taskforce (which I chaired) argued that parents should be able to take their children to sports, leisure, public and cultural activities and shops that are free from uninvited promotion of unhealthy food.[88] We noted that children do not generally earn incomes, they do not easily have legal recourse, and many do not have the experience or sophistication to differentiate between advertising and objective information. Yet they are often exposed to advertising and sophisticated promotional techniques that influence their behaviour. We know that regulating advertising has a tangible impact. When the Mayor of London Sadiq Khan restricted the advertising of high fat, salt and sugar foods on the entire TfL network, families reduced their consumption by 1,000 calories a week.[89] There is an opportunity to go further, in London and across the country, by extending such restrictions to all outdoor spaces. National government could give local authorities the powers to make such child-focused, forward-thinking choices.

Conclusions

The calls for government action offered in this chapter focus on separate aspects of where children live their lives. It is worth noting that city mayors have been at the centre of designing and implementing solutions to improve the local environments in which children grow up. Perhaps the biggest opportunity, however, comes from a bigger cultural and legal framework: one that acknowledges that if something is good for an eight-year-old and an 80-year-old, it is going to be good for everyone.

One additional essay, containing another proposal for government, is hosted at www.raisingthenation.co.uk:

- Sir David Bell, a university vice-chancellor, Chair of Karbon Homes and former Permanent Secretary at the Department for the Environment, has written a powerful case for a change in government policy on housing.

6

Education

Education is not the filling of a pail, but the lighting of a fire.
Misattributed to W.B. Yeats[1,2]

Last summer, I listened to a young man who had just finished his A Levels talk passionately about the experiences his state secondary school had provided. Supported by a talented and committed teaching staff, he had succeeded, both academically and pastorally. He raved about the opportunities to develop 'a diverse understanding of the world', for example a month-long cultural exchange to India. He said his school helped its students discover, and then nourish, lifelong passions – in his case, organising and participating in musical productions. At 18 he was articulate, intelligent and reflective – attributes I see in so many young people and which fill me with hope.

But what he went on to say bothered me. He described a printout he'd been given to share with a higher education body or potential employer, a simple list of his subjects and his predicted grades – a narrow and crude summary of his rich and fulfilling school life. It offered no reflection on his character, his wider experiences, or the abilities his school had nurtured.

Having been an employer, I know such a piece of paper is rather useless: it is at best a one-dimensional record of attendance and expected performance in course assessment. It illustrates nothing of the person's passions, potential and how they think and approach problems.

Anita Okunde is another promising young person. She's grown up with so many disadvantages but has a fierce resolve to make an imperfect system work for her. A young activist, she recently achieved three A*s and an A in her A Levels. She's written an essay outlining the obstacles she encountered at school and how she is determined to change them.

Transforming a rigged education system

Anita Okunde, student

As a Black, working-class immigrant who happens to be a woman, my experience of society differs from that of many of my peers. Although I am only 18 years old, I have racked up an extensive list of titles: youth activist, campaigner, youth commissioner of a bill through Parliament, a University of Oxford offer holder, and so on. But I sometimes feel that my need to overcompensate with my titles is due to insecurity about my self-worth. I have come to believe that my value is only my accomplishments.

And I can't help feeling that one of the reasons for this lies in the education system. Many of my school experiences were not designed or delivered in a way that supported me to succeed. The curriculum was not made for me. My experience is not unique: a little over a quarter of pupils eligible for free school meals (FSM) went to university in 2017–18 compared with almost half of those who did not receive FSM.[3]

A rigged system

The education system is rigged on the basis of class, race and gender.[4] The curriculum also does not sufficiently engage with the big problems of today, such as climate change, racial inequality and gender inequity.

Although my high school was not known for its grades, I went to school with bright people prepared to put in the work. Our learning environment was not built for us to succeed. With access to better facilities and more support, we would've been a lot better off.

My work as an activist allowed me to link different problems to find their root cause, and every problem I start from always leads me back to what we are taught at school. The goal must be liberation of structural inequalities perpetuated by schools so that all students are given the same support to succeed. The potential is to build an education system to address these issues, and in the long term, prevent them.

Instead, my experience has been of schools as competition, where success is measured by grades rather than the whole self. The attitudes towards productivity in adults are fostered in young people through schooling. This leads to a range of problems, not least mental health services dealing with the impact this culture in schools has on my fellow pupils.[5]

'Occupational crowding' is a term I learned in A Level economics. It describes a systematic approach of pushing certain groups into specific jobs, in turn meaning those groups are overrepresented in these jobs, contributing to wage discrimination linked to discrimination against these groups. For example, despite being so proficient at maths that I participated in competitions, and being clear I wanted to work in politics, I was pushed to follow careers of nursing or care. Even earlier in my life, I was taught to minimise my thoughts, be less 'bossy'; it wasn't until I had the grades and was deemed 'capable' that my ideas were taken seriously.

We can do schools better

I do believe that with even slight changes we can see a better education system, not only for future generations, but in time, for the current one too.

The work I have done through Girl Up Manchester to educate girls about their periods and their uteruses has been a defining part of my activism. Being able to give back to my community in a way that can be passed down to others created a ripple effect, with more girls feeling comfortable about their periods, and knowing about the more sustainable alternatives to disposable period products. Educating girls on eco-friendly alternatives, and giving them out for free, would see a massive reduction in plastic pollution and improve girls' ability to manage their periods. If a four-week Girl Up pilot with 20 girls had such an impact on its own, imagine what could be achieved if something similar was part of the school curriculum for all girls.

Another example that illustrates the potential for schools to be springboards for everyone's success, not just for a few, is seen in my experience of applying for university. As a first-generation immigrant with no one in my family having applied for university before me, support from groups like Target Oxbridge and Zero Gravity filled in the gap. They work to ensure low-income students and students from minority ethnic groups have support that mirrors that of selective schools. They show work to reform the education system and its gaping inequalities has started. All those who want to succeed, when given the right tools and programmes like these, will be able to.

My ask of government

We often tend to forget that youth activists are young people, mostly children, trying to fix the world's biggest problems while balancing school, social lives and family, when changing the world shouldn't be their burden. But young activists such as me don't want praise for their tenacity with a pat on the back or some slight acknowledgement; we need change and actions to match politicians' flowery words.

The curriculum needs to be more relevant to all children's experiences and life circumstances by engaging with the big problems of today, those that touch the lived experiences of so many students. The system fails unless all children have an equal chance to reach their ambitions – even those not born into a heritage of university attendance, or those whose access to school does not relate to their home circumstances, or those who are pigeonholed by occupational crowding. At present those children are failed. The government should review the National Curriculum against this goal, and de-rig the bias it holds against those students not of the empowered class, race or gender.

Listening to young people's experience of our education system has certainly challenged my thinking. The organisation, States of Mind, recently hit the headlines with their participatory research project 'Breaking the silence',[6] which challenged the school inspection body Ofsted over their negative impact not only on school staff, but also on the students themselves.[7] Their powerful open letter and accompanying documentary[8] is a beacon of what young minds and voices can shine a light on when they are given the opportunity to voice their concerns, and to share their knowledge and experiences of education.

Let's begin thinking about how to improve the education system by seeking to answer the surprisingly difficult question: what is the purpose of education? Valerie Hannon, a highly experienced education consultant and author,[9] has written an essay for us on this very question.

A new narrative for a different future

Valerie Hannon, ex-teacher, founder of the Innovation Unit, senior education consultant and author

What have we done?

I have reached the point where, although deeply implicated in the current education system all my life, I am now utterly committed to a profound change in how we go about the most important job we, as a species, must do. It is strange to look back on a 40-year career in education, working in the UK and internationally, serving in senior roles in schools, local and central government and research, and finding oneself asking: how did we get to this? What have we done? But that is what I now find myself thinking.

Elsewhere in this book, the world our children and grandchildren face is described as 'VUCA' (volatile, uncertain, complex and ambiguous). Others have described it as the 'Age of Hyperchange and Disruption'.[10] I reflect with a growing sense of anxiety on the gap between the learning experiences offered to our children in schools and what they need in terms of responding to the gravity (and indeed, opportunity) of what lies before them and what they need to *shape that world*. Instead of obsessing about the frankly trivial blips in pass rates at GCSE or A Level, we should be thinking about levels of mental ill health in young people (currently at record levels);[11] the obesity epidemic;[12] misogyny and the use of pornography;[13] and the difficulty many young people have in distinguishing fact from opinion.[14]

How many educators share this perception, and how many of them also feel constrained by existing 'systems' – of regulation and prescription – to continue with the old paradigm? Parents are starting to feel this way too.[15] And many people – including learners themselves – are calling for change, not just a superficial twiddling with the system. Practitioners in schools have been trialling and innovating hopeful new practices, but they are at the margins, trying to justify themselves against a set of criteria and metrics that are no longer fit for purpose. The question really is: what is holding us back?

The problem: an underlying and outdated narrative

We will not get the kind of empowering, enabling system of education we urgently need unless we understand that the current system is held in place by a narrative about learning that is out of date and very damaging. Everything begins with the story we tell ourselves about ourselves. And this particular story is so taken-for-granted, so widely understood to be 'just common sense', that it eludes scrutiny and debate. The story is about *what education is for*.

I believe we have to haul this narrative out into the daylight and subject it to tough interrogation. Is it what we really believe? And if not, what do we want our narrative to be? What is the prevailing story about education? At its heart, it is economistic and competitive, and it says:

- education makes nations more prosperous because it increases growth;
- education is the route to the best jobs;
- education is the route to social mobility;

- success in education is getting qualifications;
- subject-based academic qualifications are the qualifications that really matter;
- getting into university is a key success indicator; without a degree, you are a second-class citizen.

The first point to note is that the uber-goal – economic growth, especially as defined by GDP – is an increasingly dubious objective. Of course we all want prosperity and a decent standard of living. But now we can see that infinite growth on a planet with finite resources is an impossibility. Moreover, growing numbers of economists and others are redefining what our goals in this field should be.[16]

Individualistic though the current model of education is, it fails on even its own terms. The qualification base of the current system is criticised by employers and labour market experts as 'unfit for purpose'. Neither school leavers nor graduates are well prepared for work. The high stakes testing system is too narrow, too shallow and causes real stress and harm to young people.[17] Yet, we persevere with it. And despite around half of the population not going to university, the education system is still geared to degrees, too often writing off the potential of the other half.

In order to free ourselves from the stultifying effect of these assumptions that hold such a powerful grip over our education public policy, we have to ask the question: *what is education for?* We have to ask this afresh, in the light of our real current circumstances and the 'Age of Hyperchange and Disruption', the most profound effects of which our children will encounter.

It is time to create a new story.

What new narrative?

Young people themselves must be empowered to design and create the kind of future they want. So it would be strange to prescribe here the shape of that in detail. We do, however, have a responsibility to begin the debate, to assist young people to participate in it, and to create the enabling environment for its realisation. We need a new and different public discourse to help that happen.

Suppose we propose that the purpose of education should be learning to thrive in a transforming world. Not succeed, but *thrive*. Immediately one is forced to ask: what does it mean to thrive? Getting and spending, consuming, winning. ... They are leading to our destruction, and young people increasingly know it.

Thriving happens on four levels:

- *Planetary:* if the planet does not thrive, we are toast.
- *Societal:* if our societies are dysfunctional, we cannot extract ourselves to be safe.
- *Interpersonal:* strong, healthy relationships are the basis of a thriving life.[18]
- And finally, thriving *intrapersonally:* having a secure identity, good mental health, personal purpose – this is the foundation for everything else.

Notice this throws up not an individualistic agenda, but rather a highly collective one. It will give the proper foundations for the changes in curriculum, in pedagogy and in assessment that are urgently needed. And it will set the direction for a change in how we design schools to be organisations fit for the future.[19]

That is the kind of debate that I believe we need to be having. If we hold that debate, and if we engage young people in it authentically, we will create the conditions for change that all the contributors to this book long for. I fear that without it, we will remain stuck, and our descendants will pay the price.

Too narrow a goal

The history and debate surrounding how we've ended up with our current education system and the underpinning narrative that Valerie describes is complex, contested and worthy of its own dedicated book, but it's generally agreed that the beginnings of our current education model can be traced to the Industrial Revolution.[20] Success of a country is invariably measured and compared by governments through its GDP, a measure that Senator Robert F. Kennedy famously remarked:

> does not allow for the health of our children, the quality of their education or the joy of their play. It does not include … our wisdom nor our learning; neither our compassion nor our devotion to our country; it measures everything, in short, except that which makes life worthwhile.[21]

With such a compass for a country, is it little wonder that narrow goals shape thinking in education?

The idea that a good life is one that is based on income and consumption is not without foundation: ours is not a safe world to face on a low income. Access to so many of the basics of life – decent housing, transport, even food – often comes with a price tag beyond the reach of many. Graduates earn on average £10,000 more annually than non-graduates,[22] so it makes sense for families, schools and society to aim for higher numbers going to university. In turn, entry to higher education is supposedly based on academic grades, so focusing on academic outcomes seems logical. Schools that produce better grades are thus more likely to be more popular with parents.

Two issues concern me in this – and I say this as chancellor of a leading British university. First, a system that focuses on academic qualifications as the pinnacle is one that has incomplete goals. Of course we want society to be knowledgeable, literate and numerate, but we also want to develop the skills and attitudes needed to thrive in a VUCA world, such as caring for the environment, wise decision making, collaboration, respect for diversity and managing to achieve a reasonable level of well-being despite living in a post-truth world. Surely, as a basic starting point, we need to design an education system that empowers its students to contribute towards positive societal progress?

Second, I worry about the failure in the system to recognise that economic status tends to impact on academic outcomes in the first place. For example, those who come from economically disadvantaged backgrounds and become graduates earn less than their counterparts.[23] In fact, the Institute for Fiscal Studies found that despite decades of targeted intervention and investment in England, the academic gap between those receiving FSM (a [flawed] proxy for living in poverty) and other children has not narrowed,[24] suggesting that education alone is not a pathway to economic security.

A complex and competitive system

When I think about the multiple actors in the English education system, I'm reminded of a particular being from Greek mythology:

Cerberus, the multi-headed dog who guards the entrance to the Underworld. These 'heads' are often snapping away at one another, be it for funding or for influence. Here are some of the main heads of our education Cerberus and their basic functions in the system, with parents and children the least powerful actors.

Regulatory bodies include:

- DfE (Department for Education), led by a secretary of state, and responsible for providing children's services and education in England;
- Ofsted, a non-ministerial agency that inspects services providing education to all ages;
- Ofqual, which regulates qualifications, examinations and assessments.

Professional bodies include:

- Chartered College of Teaching;
- teaching unions, with multiple unions representing different sectors with differing aims.

Providers include:

- local authorities, whose statutory duties include ensuring all children have school places, safeguarding responsibilities and oversight for all state-funded schools;
- multi-academy trusts (MATs), not-for-profit trusts that operate more than one academy school (see below); local authorities have no control over MATs; some are large and influence education policy;
- teacher training providers – there are currently ten different routes into teaching in England, with varied training experiences;
- universities, which are involved with delivery of higher education, education research and some teacher training;
- assessment and qualification bodies, including five different boards that award secondary qualifications and a DfE-funded body that writes all statutory assessments for children up to age 11;

- state-funded schools, including:
  - community (maintained) schools, run by local authorities, and which follow the National Curriculum
  - foundation or voluntary schools, run by local authorities, but with more freedoms in the curriculum and admissions; often linked to religious groups
  - academies and free schools, run by not-for-profit trusts; they have freedom over their curriculum as well as teachers' salaries
  - grammar schools, which can be any of the above, but are academically selective for entry
- independent schools, also known as 'private' or, confusingly, 'public' schools; these are fee-charging schools that are free of many of the regulations applied to state schools; many benefit from charitable status.

Other stakeholders include:

- business interests, which will have contracts with schools to provide things such as catering, curriculum delivery, tuition, supply agencies for teacher absence, recruitment consultants, school improvement consultants, and so on;
- charities, which support and represent various interest groups in education;
- governing bodies, the group responsible for the strategic running of a school; some are employees of the school, trust or local authority, and others are volunteers from the parent body or local community;
- school staff, who work in a school with statutory duties under codes of professional conduct;
- parents, who can express preference over which state school to send their child to within their catchment area; if they have the resources, they can choose to send their child to a fee-paying private school or to 'homeschool';
- children, mandated to attend school after they turn five until the July of the school year they turn 16; after this they must do one of the following:
  - stay in full-time education, for example at school or sixth form college

- start an apprenticeship or traineeship
- spend 20 hours or more a week working or volunteering while also doing part-time education or training.

Running through these numerous intertwined interests is an economic motivation for educational achievement. This is then translated into economic solutions applied to the delivery of education. By this I mean that improvement to the education system is invariably seen as best obtained via competition and the application of market-like principles. It can be seen in the public ranking of schools, where the academic performance of children determines the school's position in annual local and national league tables. It can also be seen in the grading of schools by Ofsted, where schools are inspected and graded according to a snapshot in time of the school's performance over one or two days.

Without doubt, schools do vary and fluctuate in quality of provision. However, rather than a supportive process working alongside schools to help them improve, the political solution has been 'competition' to force improvement, with pupils effectively becoming marketised as finished products (or, more accurately, their exam results are), rather than constantly developing human beings with potential.

We need to remember that this market approach is exacerbated by parental preference since pupil numbers directly impact school budgets, with each child bringing an annual monetary budget. Introduced in 1988, parental preference means that in England, a parent applies to the local authority with a ranked top three or four schools they would prefer their child attends. A school with fewer pupils has less funding, giving school leaders less possibility for improvement (and fewer opportunities for the pupils). Therefore, it is in the school's best interests to attract families and pupils. This leads to diminished opportunities for those in less well-funded schools. Looked at from a national scale this is a zero-sum game with a self-perpetuating cycle; and from a local level, it reinforces inequity and inequality.

Even more economic bias is built into this system. We know that pupils receiving FSM are less likely to achieve as well as their peers, so schools in disadvantaged areas are less likely to attain top Ofsted assessments or student exam results. The same is true for schools that are more inclusive and take in higher numbers of pupils with special educational needs and disabilities (SEND).

Finally, let's also not forget the impact of location: house prices are higher near in-demand schools, which pushes out families on lower incomes.[25] Children in rural areas have fewer, if any, options to choose from in the first place. With the removal of local authority control (with over half of all pupils attending academy schools), politicians have raised concerns that schools are now less transparent and accountable to the community they serve.[26]

The education system is built on a market approach. As there is implicit competition for students, the laws of supply and demand dominate decisions on resource allocation, with the unit of measurement being simple quantity-only (grades and pupils) metrics. The system therefore creates winners and losers for 'suppliers' (schools) and 'consumers' (children). Such an approach generates annual (in the case of national and international league tables) and headline (in the case of Ofsted gradings) distractions for our education Cerberus' heads, taking the focus away from what is best for our children.

What has such a system led to?

It can be argued that this approach helps elites become world-class elites and deliver academic excellence in selected subjects for focused pupils. If only a rising average matters, then our country can look strong in global league tables. If the point of the system is to maximise progression to university, then it can work. But surely those aren't the measures that deliver in the best interests of all the country's children?

Even before the COVID-19 pandemic, UK data showed increased numbers of school leavers feeling anxious or depressed and disconnected from their communities. Lower numbers reported high life satisfaction or being satisfied with their health.[27] The latest international benchmark data show that British pupils rank 69th out of 72 countries for satisfaction with life.[28] School curricula and environments aren't necessarily to blame, but have they helped?

Consider the assessment system, the design of which means nearly one-third of pupils finish their subject-based GCSEs having not met the national standard or 'pass rate'. There are complex reasons behind this, but some might argue that forcing pupils to 'fail' without offering viable and valuable alternatives to demonstrate their knowledge and skills is unethical.

How about the workforce? International comparisons show that teachers in England at both primary and secondary level work significantly more than the average hours than other OECD countries, but they spend a similar amount of time teaching.[29] Teachers work under undue and unnecessary pressure and are physically and mentally exhausted.[30] The result is that recruitment and retention is difficult – 33 per cent leave the profession within five years of starting,[31] with workload the most important factor cited.[32]

Money is an issue. The difference in 'per pupil' funding between state and private schools has doubled over the last 10 years (£3,100 in 2009–10 to over £6,500 in 2021), while public expenditure on education as a percentage of GDP has fallen from its peak in 2010–11.[33] OECD analysis put UK public spending on education at 3.9 per cent in 2018, 19th out of 37 countries,[34] and below the OECD average.[35]

There is another way

At the beginning of this chapter, I shared a young man's reflection on how his academic grades were the sole, tangible, measured thing he took away from his years in the education system, despite attending a great school. Our young people are leaving school without a fair record of their success, achievements and personal developments beyond their exam results. But for some young people, the exam itself is a barrier to achievement. Exams have their place in the system – they are proven to be less open to bias than something like teacher assessment – but not everyone is able to perform to their ability.

Sophie Maxwell may have an answer. Sophie is quite simply one of the most impressive people I know, and I admit I'm a little bit in awe of her vision and ability to make change. A note of warning, though: her essay contains a first-hand account of neglect and physical, sexual and emotional abuse.

The difference between an exam and a game? It's all in the mind

Sophie Maxwell, founder and CEO of The Really NEET Project and of Escape Assessments

> Sophie, dissociation was an escape from a reality so intolerable that your mind shut down and disconnected from what was happening to you.

I sat with the neurologist, not sure what to do with the information he was telling me, as I received a diagnosis of functional neurological disorder. At 17 I was experiencing violent shakes and tremors, loss of speech and complete paralysis – enough to scare the life out of any teenager. But I had no one to talk to, being homeless at the time. Ten years of sexual abuse and domestic violence as a child led to me being pulled out of an education system that labelled me 'unteachable', fleeing violence by constantly moving around the country to finally being homeless and alone by age 16.

This was the intolerable reality, and my brain was shutting down.

But I found that being a child susceptible to dissociation came with an upside: it made me susceptible to an imagination that would thrive in adulthood.

The story of Theseus and the Minotaur has stayed with me throughout my journey. Theseus was trapped in a labyrinth with no knowledge of how to escape, with a bloodthirsty Minotaur hot on his heels. All hope was lost until Ariadne left golden threads to lead him to safety. 'Ariadne's threads' is now a recognised philosophy that can be applied to life. It's the ability to problem solve out of situations where all can appear lost. Essentially there are 'golden threads' all around us; we just need to know how to look for them.

I have applied these principles from an early and significant age. They have transformed my life path and enabled me to be successful, despite my childhood experiences.

Threading together experience and hope

At 17 years old I was living in a homeless hostel surrounded by young people like me who felt excluded not only from education, but also from life and society itself. One awful day set me on an incredible transformation of mind and self. My friend took his last ever hit of heroin and never woke up. Trying to revive him and having to recount to his parents his last moment in a coroner's court significantly changed the way I viewed life and human vulnerability.

Instantly I recognised that something needed to change, and that no person other than myself could do it. I walked into my local college and asked to be enrolled. Despite my lack of qualifications, I was taken on by an incredible person. Paul, a sports tutor at the college, spent countless hours supporting me to make it through the very system that had let me down. Tragically, Paul had terminal cancer, but still spent the last two years of his life supporting others to succeed. To witness first-hand someone like Paul became the foundation for how I wanted to live my life, and gave me an unwavering persistence to problem solve my way out of the dark places I found myself in. He helped me see the 'golden threads'.

After graduating from university, I founded The Really NEET Project, NEET standing for Not in Education, Employment or Training. Our mission is to make education accessible to young people who wouldn't make it through a mainstream setting. Our programmes focus on meeting a young person's basic needs. This is aimed at embedding stability in situations where a young person has experienced a lack of nurture and love, key components that contribute tremendously to a strong sense of identity, confidence and self-esteem, secure attachment and a positive outlook. Over the course of ten years, Really NEET has worked with over 1,000 of the UK's most vulnerable and marginalised young people, giving us an insight into the education system, and why so many young people are slipping through the net.

Through this work I noticed one common theme. Most of the young people at Really NEET struggle with traditional exams. I dug deeper, and my findings would begin a seven-year campaign to change the system.

The issues for those struggling with exams include:

- low self-esteem, anxiety and a fear of failure;
- other more pressing priorities and external factors occurring at the time of the exam;
- communication, interaction difficulties and challenges around concentration due to ADHD (attention-deficit hyperactivity disorder) or external factors;
- not seeing the relevance in taking exams in relation to the current journey they are on.

I reflected on the distress I could see the exams were causing our students, pushing their mental health to, and in some cases, over, the very brink, just at the very mention of sitting an exam.

At the end of exam week in 2015, as a reward, we took them on a night out to an 'escape room game' experience. During the evening, I watched in amazement as our learners cracked codes and solved puzzles to escape a room within a 60-minute time-pressured environment. Not only did our students tackle basic numeracy in the form of multiplication, division and code breaking, showing their working on the board provided, they positively loved the experience, and were relaxed and engaged in the activity, demonstrating skills that would have intimidated them in a traditional maths exam.

I saw, with crystal clarity, that the fundamental difference between exam and game for our young people was simply being immersed in an experience that felt safe, exciting and relevant. It made me question why we insist all pupils take traditional paper-based exams when the world has advanced so significantly.

We know that special considerations are already in place via Exam Access Arrangements, such as extra time, scribes, separate exam rooms, and so on, but these simply look at ways to support young people within the current system instead of providing an alternative assessment to suit the different ways in which young people can best demonstrate their skills and knowledge. An innovative approach to assessment has the potential to change the UK assessment system, making it accessible to all.

Following the thread to escape rooms

At Really NEET, we believe we can harness the design of escape rooms to immerse learners in a creative and engaging assessment that challenges the status quo and better meets the needs of students with specific barriers, providing more equality within the exams sector.

I met the CEO of a large examinations awarding body, who, disappointingly, was sceptical about making any changes to the exams system at all. I, however, believe we should stop worrying about how students get there, and find more ways of assessment that work for them. If no one believes change is possible in life, then nothing ever changes. So I continued. Successfully.

The educational qualifications awarding body NCFE has just funded us to pilot the first ever story-based assessments centred round the principles used within escape rooms. We are following the 'golden threads' and they are getting thicker by the day; it's time to let imagination loose in the exams sector! We will continue to follow the threads, collate evidence, and harness the bravery of the education establishment to rethink and reimagine what assessments and examinations are. I am confident many others will join us, changing the education system to build equality and accessibility for all young people.

Sophie's attitude of overcoming resistance, actively looking for different ways to do things and then making them happen, is one that needs to be emulated across the education sector.

Different ways to deliver education

Broadening skills and subjects taught

England's National Curriculum's stated aim is to be 'an introduction to the essential knowledge they [pupils] need to be educated citizens'.[36] However, it frequently comes under fire for being too narrow in its scope and aims. For example, by age 14, students may opt out of learning history, geography, music, art, languages and design technology. Some, including the government's own adviser, feel that what is taught within its scope is too prescriptive,[37] with endless spelling and facts to be memorised rather than teachers having the freedom to respond to cultural contexts, individual abilities and pupil needs. Of course we want young people to be knowledgeable, but what about their wider development?

The International Baccalaureate (IB) is a not-for-profit foundation that offers programmes at all stages of education, and is internationally acknowledged for its academic rigour, broad curriculum and the personal development of its pupils. Its aims are to: 'develop inquiring, knowledgeable and caring young people who help to create a better and more peaceful world through intercultural understanding and respect ... to encourage students across the world to become active, compassionate and lifelong learners who understand that other people, with their differences, can also be right'.[38]

The differences between these aims and those of the English National Curriculum are stark. Running throughout all of the IB programmes is knowledge − not just the encyclopaedic accumulation of facts, but also an ability to critically analyse. Students' voice is central: they can influence the content of their learning and are expected to lead on projects to realise and then demonstrate that they can have influence on the world around them. Older pupils undertake volunteer work, and graduates leave with a diploma held in high regard by universities.

This IB approach, encompassing not only academic but also vocational aspects, is popular with influential voices, including former Prime Ministers Tony Blair and John Major, as well as ten former education secretaries calling for the wider curricula to be 'more IB-like'.[39]

Mainstreaming the IB would allow for flexibility in the curriculum for individuals, offering a wider array of subject options. It also would allow for flexible assessment (such as Sophie's idea) to recognise a range of skills and achievements. And importantly, it would put back onto the education system the need to provide broad possibilities and experiences for children. Trials for a British Baccalaureate are already taking place – it's time to get behind them.

Narrowing the inequality gap

In England it is the independent, fee-charging schools (that educate only about 7 per cent of all pupils) that have most taken up IB curricula (nearly 60 per cent of IB courses).[40] Independent schools are a political hot potato. On the one hand, they undoubtedly engrain inequality and inequity into the education system and beyond. For example, by summer 2022, 45 out of the 55 British Prime Ministers had attended fee-paying schools (20 of whom attended Eton College).[41] A recent study found that people with 'elite' jobs were five times more likely to have attended private school than not.[42] On the other hand, their supporters argue that independent schools raise overall standards and national attainment, and reduce pressure on the state capacity.

So what role might independent schools have in a future where the goal is that all children can thrive and thereby the inequality of opportunity will narrow? Is the solution to ban private schools? Or is it to open them up to wider groups of families? Is it to deny their (controversial) charitable status and the tax breaks that come with this? Should we be creative in spreading their assets to provide a much wider public benefit and tax their alumni at a higher rate? The solution may or may not be binary, but leaving things as they are is not compatible with a democracy that strives for a better future for all.

Alan Milburn is no stranger to the way democracy works. He was a Cabinet Minister for over five years and has chaired the Social Mobility Commission. Taking up this challenge, he has written this essay on why it is vital that quality education is available to children from the widest variety of backgrounds and socio-economic circumstances.

An end to educational inequality

Rt Hon Alan Milburn, former Minister of Health, ex-Chair of the Social Mobility Commission and Chair of the Social Mobility Foundation

The world is in the midst of a perma-crisis, placing an unprecedented strain on liberal democracies. In Britain there is another profound crisis: a social one. Over recent decades Britain has become an ever more divided nation – not just by income or class, or gender or race, but also between geographies and generations. The growing gulf between the haves and the have-nots is multi-dimensional in its nature. It is a crisis that is corroding the sense of our cohesion as a nation.

Young people on the frontline of inequity

Young people are at the sharp end of this great divide. The 20th-century expectation that each generation would be better off than the preceding one is no longer being met. Home ownership, the aspiration of successive generations of ordinary people, is in sharp decline, particularly among the young. Compared to other developed nations, Britain has higher levels of child poverty[43] and lower levels of social mobility.[44] Over many years Britain has become a wealthier society, but has struggled to become a fairer one.

A divided Britain

Whole tracts of Britain feel left behind, because they are. Whole communities and sections of society feel they are not getting a fair chance to succeed, because they are not. There is a growing gulf between our country's great cities and the new social mobility cold spots, which are concentrated in remote rural or coastal places and in former industrial areas. These towns and counties are being left behind economically and hollowed out socially. They are places where the public mood oscillates between sullen sourness and downright anger.

Our politics are polarising too. Unless mainstream politics can find solutions to this problem, the answer will come from the extremes. A narrow nationalism is eating into the gains made by a more globalist politics. Mainstream political parties seem discombobulated by the new politics that has emerged in recent years of identity, immigration and inequality. These three are changing the shape of politics across the developed world – and not necessarily for the better.

Change is coming...

So far, then, so bad. But here is where I believe there are good grounds for optimism: there is a mood for change in the nation. Shocks on the scale of the pandemic produce change. Think of how the Second World War ushered in an era of collectivisation. Of course people want a return to normality, but they also want a better world to emerge from the pandemic than the one that went into it. Change is the currency of the times.

It is sorely overdue. COVID-19 has not only exposed the fragility of our care system; it has exposed the fragility of our society. In this context it is welcome that 'levelling up' is on the domestic policy agenda. And important though levelling up between places is, it is not the only equity issue that must be addressed if the discontents of modern Britain are to be addressed. Inequality hurts people, not just places. There needs to be far greater alignment between the spatial and social agendas if levelling up is to succeed.

'Education: the key to a fairer society'

After leading the government's Social Mobility and Child Poverty Commission and chairing the Social Mobility Foundation I know that time spent in education – including the vital early years – is the most important determinant of future social status, and success in schools is the most important factor determining mobility. Over decades standards have risen in our schools, but there is a long tail of underachievement that is failing to realise the innate potential of huge numbers of youngsters. Around one in three children on free school meals (FSM) gets good exam results aged 16 compared to two in three of other children.[45] This is not innate. Low-ability children from wealthy families overtake high-ability children from poor families during primary school. Despite some recent successes in narrowing the gap in educational attainment between poorer children and their better-off classmates, the deep-seated social gradient in how well children do in school has not been flattened. From the early years through schools and on to universities, there is an entrenched and unbroken correlation between social class and educational success. The income gap is larger than either the ethnicity gap or the gender gap in schools.

It is time to put the ending of that profound unfairness at the heart of our country's education policy. The government should set clear objectives for breaking the link between educational attainment and social background, and it should commit to a redistribution of education resources to those areas that need them most. Since global evidence points to the quality of teaching being the key factor in helping close attainment gaps, the government should find new ways of giving the best teachers better incentives to teach in the worst-performing schools.

But it will not be a job for the state alone. In the end the biggest influences on children's life chances are parents. Two in five children from the poorest homes are read to every day compared to nearly four in five of those from the richest families,[46] with consequences that are felt throughout their later lives. More support is needed to bridge that parenting gap because it is so crucial to closing the life chances gap.

Reasons for optimism

For those who think this cannot be done, it is worth remembering that just a few short decades ago, London state schools were routinely described as the worst in the country. Now they are the best. The education attainment of disadvantaged children in particular has dramatically improved, thanks to initiatives like London Challenge. Similarly, there is not a university in the country today that does not have a programme to widen participation and improve fair access. Of course, the pace of change can be frustratingly slow. But progress is being achieved. There are more working-class youngsters in higher education than ever before, and the gap between those parts of the country that send most to university and those that send the least has narrowed. This is because social mobility has moved from being marginal to being mainstream business for universities.

None of these things are impossible to do. But it will require a far bigger national effort to break the transmission of disadvantage from one generation to the next. The prize on offer could not be greater – a nation at ease with itself. A society where aspiration and ability, not birth or background, dictate progress in life. A Britain with a level playing field of opportunity. Most importantly of all, a generation of children who get a fair chance to realise their full potential.

It is clear there are challenges to solve over the breadth of subject matter and depth of fair access to the best quality education. It is equally clear there is tension, complexity and stress in the English system, and that the multi-headed Cerberus still stands guard over it. We have begun to explore intriguing opportunities and solutions, but where can we look to be inspired to act and make the best decisions?

Finland's holistic approach

In mid-2022, British politics was even stranger than usual, as minister after minister resigned from Boris Johnson's Cabinet, and then he, closely followed by his short-lived successor, also resigned. During the course of one week, those working in the education sector had three different secretaries of state. In fact, between the 2010 General Election and 2022 there have been ten. That's ten people who needed time to get on top of their brief, to then make their marks with initiatives and pet projects. But it doesn't have to be that way.

Finland is often held up as an example of excellence in education internationally. It certainly has a different model to England: no high-stakes standardised testing until the final year of school, a rigorous entry level for those entering teaching (all teachers have to have a Master's degree), no competition or ranking of schools (cooperation is the norm), accountability measures that are low for teachers (they're already high quality, and the point is individual teacher improvement), and teachers who stay with cohorts so students might have their the same teacher for up to six years. ... The list goes on. Of course, simply copying and pasting a national education system with its cultural and contextual differences won't work, so what interests me is *how* Finland established such a different system.

I think the key is in the way decisions *about* education are made. Since the 1990s, respective Finnish governments have worked to a Development Plan for Education and Research.

This covers all aspects of education and looks at education as a whole. Targets and financial strategy typically cover a five-year span (bridging incoming and outgoing governments) to provide stability across changes of government. The Ministry of Education and Culture is responsible for creating these plans, but they do so in collaboration with schools, teachers and the third sector. Each plan is based on consensus,[47] so all players move in the same direction. Finally, the culturally established goal that all families should have access to a good school means that parents, on the whole, do not need to worry about the quality of their children's education. The UK could learn a lot from such long-term visions and plans for schooling. What a refreshing difference that could make for our schools, and ultimately, for our children.

Conclusions

Running through this chapter is the question of goals. What are the aims of society, and therefore of education? At present education goals are largely aligned to economic growth, but louder and louder voices are calling for broader thinking about educational success. While work is an important aspect of citizenship, a citizen is also someone who cares for neighbours and strangers they'll never meet, who engages in democracy, contributes to the greater whole and who is entitled to call on collective institutions to help build a decent life. Education is the way we share society's values. It is about creating citizens. Yet, as we have seen, under the current model there are huge flaws in achieving this. Neither market-oriented outcomes nor conformity of the process of, or content within, knowledge sharing is fit for purpose.

The critical question in education, before we tinker, or radically reset our system, is to work out what it is for. As Valerie noted in her essay, this means focusing on meaningful relationships – understanding each other and the world around us. Even more concisely, the student I mentioned at the start of this chapter understood great education as finding 'a diverse understanding of the world'. The clarion call quote that started this chapter nails it: education must be structured so that it lights fires that ignite young people's curiosity and relationships.

Four more essays, containing additional proposals for government, are hosted at www.raisingthenation.co.uk:

- Jo Rhodes is a dance artist, creative consultant and founder of Challenge 59 and the Co:Lab Collective. She makes a powerful argument for why creative expression is a critical skill to thrive as an educated citizen.

- Will Orr-Ewing is an educationist and founder of Keystone Tutors. He challenges private schools to justify their public benefit by implementing some thought-provoking ideas.

- Tim Baker has been a primary school headteacher for almost 20 years. He uses that experience to write of the power of teaching through real life, and of the benefits of 'learning studios'.

- Joe Hallgarten is a teacher and CEO at the Centre for Education and Youth, a think-and-action tank. Jo Franklin is an ex-headteacher and CEO at The LETTA Trust, a multi-academy trust in London. Together they highlight the need for space in school curricula for 'non-National Curriculum learning'.

7

Health

If a child dies, the government is always serious about it. So, if the child doesn't die, they should be serious about the child anyway.

Ayo (age 12)[1]

In our garden stands an eight-foot bear we call Pablo. Luckily for us, Pablo is made of fibreglass! He has a dove painted around his shoulders and two chillies tattooed on one leg. The dove is based on a doodle Pablo Picasso made on a napkin in Butler's Cafe in Sheffield in 1950 when he was visiting the World Peace Council Congress. Butler's Cafe later became Butlers Balti House, which still serves delicious curries to this day, hence the chillies on Pablo's leg. Pablo is with us because I bid for him in an auction for a charity very close to my heart: The Children's Hospital Charity, which supports the NHS' Sheffield Children's Hospital, one of just three specialist children's hospitals in the UK. Pablo is majestic, but the hospital is even more so. It is unique in the broad range of services it delivers: looking after the mental and physical health of children and young people. And that is why I have introduced you to Pablo. To me, the scary bear with his peaceful dove represents the two sides of health: the physical side, which is obvious and so often dominant, and the mental side, which is like a fragile and often unseen protective cloak. Sheffield Children's Hospital works to protect and repair both sides for its patients. In this chapter I'll explore the extent to which we support and promote the two sides of health for all our children.

This question came into stark relief during the COVID-19 pandemic. As the Nuffield Trust reported in 2022, children were least likely to suffer physical illness from the virus but suffered most from the policy response. Children had the highest growth in need for mental health services and the highest disadvantage in terms of their development and social isolation. In addition, the number of children waiting for a referral relating to a food disorder increased fourfold between 2019 and 2022.[2] This was replicated globally. In the USA, the CEO of the Boston Children's Hospital flagged similar concerns, saying: 'Prior to the COVID-19 pandemic, we thought that the number of children we were seeing per day with (behavioural and mental health) issues was already extremely high – that number was in the 20s. During the pandemic, and currently, those numbers are in the 50s to 70s.'[3]

COVID-19 has exacerbated two of the major long-term health challenges facing children today: healthy weight and mental health, or lack of both. I have chosen to narrow the focus of this chapter, which could otherwise be potentially unending, on these two ongoing and deteriorating issues. Both have a clear correlation to poverty,[4,5] so the solutions need to be more than just patching up individuals: they need to be both systemic and radical.

Unhealthy weight

Two 11-year-old friends, let's call them Oli and Harry, sit next to each other at the Emirates Stadium every match day and are inseparable for a couple of hours as they share their love for Arsenal Football Club and their future aspirations. Although they both live in London, the single biggest predictor of whether their dreams might come true is their postcode. Let's say Harry lives in the Borough of Richmond and Oli in the Borough of Brent. All other things being equal, this single fact means that Oli is likely to die over eight years before Harry, and have a significantly increased chance of living with obesity.[6,7]

Now let's now imagine two five-year-old friends who don't live in different boroughs but on the same street; we'll call them Chloe and Pippa. Their life chances diverge fundamentally, as one of Chloe's parents lives with obesity. This means that Chloe is 300 per cent more likely to develop the same condition than Pippa.[8]

Even within the same family life chances can hugely diverge. If, for example, within Pippa's house she watches TV adverts for high fat, salt or sugar foods once a day but her brother doesn't, she will be twice as likely than her brother to buy such foods regularly throughout their lives,[9] increasing the chances that Pippa, and those like her, will live their lives with an unhealthy weight.

Being overweight or obese in childhood damages health now and in the future. Childhood obesity can lead to:

- early onset of conditions traditionally associated with old age, such as type 2 diabetes, poor oral health and cardiovascular disease;[10]
- poor psychological and emotional health, lower educational attainment and poor sleep;[11]
- a high likelihood of experiencing bullying;[12]
- a high likelihood of becoming obese for life, and a greater risk of morbidity, disability and premature death;[13]
- a higher likelihood of experiencing tooth decay.[14]

The accelerating prevalence of childhood obesity is a big deal for society and for our ability to build a thriving future. Data from the National Child Measurement Programme (NCMP) 2020–21 shows the highest annual rises in obesity since the NCMP began in 2006.[15] However, obesity is just the most extreme manifestation of unhealthy weight: more than a quarter of four-year-olds and 40 per cent of 11-year-olds are unhealthily overweight, but not yet obese. These average figures mask the reality that the prevalence of unhealthy weight among children living in the most deprived areas is almost double that in the least deprived areas.[16]

The consequences of unhealthy weight among children stretch to the future health of our society, public services and economy. They bring a range of economic and social costs, including large expenses to the NHS and a reduction in skills and productivity. In 2014–15 the NHS spent £6.1 billion on overweight and obesity-related ill health, a sum greater than that spent on the police, fire service and judicial system combined. More broadly, the overall annual cost of obesity to wider society is estimated at £27 billion.[17]

A personal mission

When I was CEO of Ella's Kitchen, we undertook several significant projects to tackle the diet-related crisis. One day, back in 2011, I read two newspaper articles. The first said that of the girls born that year, one-third would live to see their 100th birthday.[18] The other said that by 2050, 50 per cent of adults in the UK would be obese.[19] The children of 2011 are the mid-life adults of 2050. It made me question what sort of society those children would inherit if one-third of them would live to be 100, but half would die much younger due to obesity? At Ella's Kitchen we undertook research to give evidence to politicians to act. In 2014 we worked with Leicester City Council to implement some of our campaign's proposals, and called on political parties to commit to a coordinated 'Food Manifesto for the Under-Fives' as part of their 2015 UK election manifestos.[20] Later, I led an evidence-based, public advocacy campaign to convince Public Health England to revise weaning advice to prioritise early, varied and persistent use of vegetables to reduce chances of childhood obesity and poor health.

After I stepped away from Ella's Kitchen, Sadiq Khan, Mayor of London, appointed me as Chair of London's new Child Obesity Taskforce. His challenge, in a city where nearly 40 per cent of children are not a healthy weight, was to find actions that would change this. We brought together a diverse taskforce and started with a simple, but audacious, aim: to unleash a transformation in London so that every child would have every chance to grow up eating healthily, drinking plenty of water and being physically active.

We set out three core principles – ones at the heart of virtually every issue explored in this book – to:

- place children at the centre of everything. Well-meaning actions would work only if based on an understanding of the realities of the lives of London's children. To fix the system, we'd have to know how children experienced it from the inside. We developed profiles of London's children,[21] and continued to engage them, especially those living in poverty, in co-designing solutions;

- take a 'whole-systems' approach and disperse leadership across communities and sectors, so that everyone would feel responsible for shared ambitions;
- be bigger and bolder in amplifying positive initiatives already happening, albeit often at a small scale. We also wanted to trial new actions.

The result was an action plan, *Every Child a Healthy Weight*,[22] containing 20 varied and interconnected actions.★

Reflecting on the work of the Taskforce, I take two learnings. Both are relevant to creating a future where children flourish.

The first is that unhealthy weight and obesity in childhood are invariably symptoms of an underlying real problem: poverty. Poverty means living in cramped, poor-quality homes, with unstable tenancies in locations where healthcare support is patchy, where parks and walkways can be unsafe, and where takeaways are plentiful and cheap. It is poverty that forces parents to work long hours or to take multiple jobs, which, in turn, undermines family time and the capacity to shop for and cook fresh food. The day-to-day, cognitive attention of any family in such circumstances would be focused on survival.

My second learning is of the power of lived experience in understanding where solutions may lie. The true experts are not really the policy makers, politicians, NHS or public health staff, food scientists or academics: they are the children and families of the communities living in poverty. Those communities know what needs to change. And it is they to whom policy makers need to pay most attention.

I'll come back to health inequalities driving public and individual health later. In the meantime, my taskforce colleague Corinna Hawkes has written this essay for us on a food system utopia.

★ The plan is shared via a QR code at the end of this chapter.

Food for thought: how a child-orientated food system is possible

Corinna Hawkes, Professor of Food Systems and Director of the Division of Food Systems and Food Safety at the FAO

A child running to the ice cream van. Another jumping for joy in a sweet shop. Another devouring a piece of cake, bright-eyed. These things are a pleasure to behold. So if we're to invite kids to design a world where they eat healthily, would we just get groans about too much broccoli? Maybe.

But not if we, as a society, had done our jobs properly. If we had done so, children would love, value and aspire to eat healthy food most of the time, and enjoy sweets, cake and ice cream as treats. Children would want to eat wholegrains, fruits and vegetables, nuts, pulses, milk and dairy, fish and (for non-vegetarians) modest amounts of meat – food that science shows clearly benefits their bodies and minds.[23]

Nurturing strong and healthy children is as much a social responsibility as teaching kids English and maths. But, unlike English and maths, policy makers and indeed society tend not to see it like that.

Just imagine if it were. Let's sketch out what it would entail.

Children would have easy access to healthy, nourishing food. First, their nurseries and schools would provide spaces where they would learn to love and value good food. This is far from the case now: evidence from around the world shows that all too often food in schools is unhealthy and/ or unappealing for kids.[24,25] Healthy food on journeys to and from school is also hard to find.[26]

Second, children would also have easy access to healthy food at home. That, in turn, would require parents to have the capacity to provide it. Yet too many children live in resource-constrained households where parents lack the financial resources to prioritise healthy food.[27] They likewise lack the necessary material resources to store, cook and eat healthy meals – such as decent kitchens, ovens and dining tables.[28]

Emotional resources matter as well: evidence shows that higher work–life stress among parents – so common in these times – leads to less healthy family food environments.[29] This relates to the importance of having time: parents who face time pressure are less likely to engage in healthy food-related activities.[30]

We know that parents facing these multiple overlapping pressures *want* to provide healthy foods for their children, but there are just too many constraints to make it happen.

Children, however, could and should be free of these pressures. In our imagined future, everywhere they go children would be stimulated to eat healthy, nourishing meals, drinks and snacks. The nudges and signals they see and hear would steer them towards foods that support their health and development. This is sadly not the case. Take food packaging: packaging for unhealthy foods is used to attract children and parents' attention, shaping product associations and motivating them to choose energy-dense food products with high levels of sugar, fat and salt.[31] It's the same for other forms of marketing and promotion: a plethora of evidence shows that globally, children are over-exposed to ads for unhealthy foods and beverages on TV and a wide array of digital media.[32]

Children should be well informed about healthy eating and have high levels of food literacy, enabling them to 'understand food in a way that they develop a positive relationship with it, including food skills and practices across the lifespan in order to navigate, engage and participate within a complex food system'.[33] Yet evidence suggests that food education is not typically designed in a way that can most effectively help children eat well.[34] Nor are children sufficiently taught the skills they need to buy, cook and prepare healthy food, or navigate unhealthy food environments.

Children would find value and meaning in eating well. Yet, given all the above factors that conspire against it, they tend not to. A study in Newcastle found that children preferred to take packed lunches to school because they enjoyed trading the unhealthy food items they contained with their friends.[35] In our vision for the future, children would have the social support they need to eat well. Their peer influencers would reinforce and lift each other up towards healthier options, making them 'cool' and aspirational.[36]

What needs to happen

A child-oriented food system is possible – provided adults, specifically adults in government, do their job properly.[37] Every ministry and agency across government has the power to enact policy to ensure kids eat well by:

- providing sufficient capacity to schools to offer healthy food for all kids, along with a comprehensive curriculum for food literacy;
- supporting the medical community to spend time talking with children about diets and health, especially those facing mental health problems;
- imposing heavy fines on companies violating basic norms of healthy food marketing for children;
- ensuring adequate social safety nets for all families to afford healthy food;

- equipping housing with proper spaces and resources to prepare food;
- championing local food initiatives where food is celebrated and enjoyed in social, community settings;
- establishing initiatives to connect farmers of healthy food to children, turning them into trusted figures children aspire to eat from.

The solution is for all government departments to act in tandem, to all commit, to all act. It is up to the Prime Minister to set the tone and hold them accountable for doing so. Failing to do so is failing our children and the multiple benefits across the economy and society that these policies could stimulate for and beyond the diets of children.

Child-first, whole-systems and brave policy prioritisation could bring Corinna's vision within reach.

But obesity is only one side of the malnutrition coin. The other, hunger, shames a society among the richest in human history, yet one in which in 2020 had 4.3 million British children growing up in poverty.[38] Growing up in poverty not only means increased risks of obesity through eating cheap and readily available – but also highly processed, calorie-dense and nutrition-light – foods, but also an acute risk of lacking sufficient food at all. For example, The Trussell Trust saw a 15 per cent increase in food parcels provided for children between 2020 and 2022.[39]

In 2021, the Child Poverty Action Group (CPAG) reported that children in low-income families were going hungry and missing out on healthy food and social activities that their peers take for granted.[40,41] For these children, lack of food causes physical pain, feelings of guilt and shame and a sense of social exclusion; their parents often skip meals so their children can eat. CPAG also highlighted that most children growing up in poverty have at least one parent in paid employment. It reported that children in lone-parent families are at greater risk of food poverty than others, reflecting broader poverty trends, and that since most lone parents are mothers, the health implications of parental sacrifice are gendered. As 11-year-old Shaniya's mum explained: 'last week I didn't even eat for four days … I have to lie to my kids and tell them I've eaten so that they're okay, because as long as my kids are eating then I'm okay'.[42]

CPAG's report concludes that food charity is not the answer. While aid such as food banks can help meet the immediate needs of some families, it does not address the causes of poverty, and can lead to further shame, stigma and social exclusion. The report calls for healthy free school meals to be available to all children at school and provided as part of the normal school day, to mitigate some of the effects of poverty on children's health and education. It also states that solutions to food poverty must address its root causes: low and irregular wages, inadequate benefits and the high costs of essentials that leave parents struggling to make ends meet.[43]

Poor mental health

To thrive in a VUCA world children need persistence, resilience, determination and mental agility. They require a tenacity that can only be achieved if the structures of society – family, institutions, community and public services – support them to navigate the future and believe it is theirs to harness, shape and thrive within. However, such structures have failed to adapt and support our children, and the consequence is an explosion in the toxic stress discussed in Chapter 3 and a crisis in children's mental health.

In the last century mental health was barely acknowledged as 'a thing'. For virtually the whole century, and indeed for every century previously, if it was acknowledged at all, it was framed in a completely different way to how it is discussed today, even at times blamed on the supernatural![44] Support and treatment for 'mental illness' included brutal, uncaring asylums,[45] overprescribing addictive tranquillisers,[46] and damaging, 'just man up'-style advice.[47]

Young people in particular are driving a different approach and opening up conversations about mental health.[48] In doing so, they have moved society forward, reduced its stigma and positioned it firmly on the public radar.

Of course, given underreporting, we don't know the exact number of children battling issues such as anxiety and depression, but government data from 2020 suggests one in six children aged five to 16 is likely to have had a mental health disorder,[49] an increase of almost 60 per cent from three years earlier.[50] Half of all mental health problems start by the age of 14.[51]

Many young people would prefer to access mental health support without going through their GP;[52] stigma remains, but also the challenges young people carry are often beyond what GPs are trained to do.

Most support is through the NHS' Child and Adolescent Mental Health Services (CAMHS). I know much about the service as I'm beyond proud that my daughter works within it. CAMHS provides a wide range of services: some require referral, others do not; some are provided by in-house specialists, others by health professionals in general services (such as school nurses); and some are light-touch designed to protect good mental health, while others treat severe disorders for in-patients. Funding is from various national and local sources, but crucially, the services are organised locally, engaging with the community.[53]

The concept and intention of CAMHS is world-leading, but its Achilles' heel is in funding, scalability and, I'd argue, its structure. Between April and June 2021 190,271 children were referred to CAMHS, an increase of 135 per cent from a year earlier.[54] Demand has skyrocketed, with more:

- emotional disorders, particularly anxiety and depression;
- experiences of adversity, such as living in poverty, parental separation or financial and cost of living crises;
- young people identifying as LGBTQ, a group that is disproportionately affected by mental health issues;
- children having experience of the care system; 'looked-after' children are four times more likely to experience mental health issues than their peers;
- children entering the youth justice system, with one-third estimated to have a mental health issue.

At the same time that demand is exploding, funding is stagnating. Local Clinical Commissioning Group areas spend less than 1 per cent of their overall budget on children's mental health. Funding for school nurses and public mental health services has seen a £700 million reduction between 2015 and 2021 – a cut of almost 25 per cent per person needing treatment.[55] Finally, there continues to be limited investment in mental health support for the under-fives – 42 per cent of local CAMHS do not provide any services for children under two years old.[56]

The reality, and tragedy, of having a potentially world-class children's service underfunded and unprepared to truly tackle the root causes of mental health fragility is that the system will break.

Nick Wilkie has written this essay offering a three-stage solution to our endemic children's mental health problem.

Through the looking glass: how reframing policy can transform childhood

Nick Wilkie, Chair of the Parent–Infant Foundation, UK Director of Save the Children and policy adviser to the Cabinet Office and HM Treasury

Mental health: 'it's not all about me'

The term 'mental health' describes a 'state of well-being'.[57] Material, social and cultural factors, and early life experiences, significantly influence children's mental health.[58]

Yet, in stark contrast, public understanding of mental health is often couched in individualistic terms. So when people experience problems in mental health, the starting point is almost always to consider it as a chemical imbalance in the brain, or deficits in personal motivation or character, or both.[59]

As a result of this misconception, our mental health policies and services are typically operated with the same narrow framing at their core: fixing deficits in individuals, or empowering individuals to better deal with adversity – rather than addressing wider challenges in their families, communities and society.

In recent years, a key focus of children's mental health policy in England has been the increased provision of therapeutic interventions in schools. While this is helpful for many children, it is a policy focused on addressing the symptoms of mental health problems rather than their causes. England has made a start in attending to causes by introducing some social prescribing where GPs and other health services refer people to non-clinical services.[60]

The Parent–Infant Foundation supports specialised parent–infant relationship teams working with families when a baby's development is at risk because their parents find it hard to provide the sensitive, responsive care that all babies need to flourish. Our research describes these teams as rare jewels because, like precious stones, they are small, valuable and scarce.[61] Part of the reason for their rarity is that this work can be perceived as not within the domain of mental health services: because it is not based on diagnosis, but on the *relationship* between a baby and their primary carer. Yet there is strong evidence that these teams, led by mental health professionals and focused on supporting parent–infant relationships, directly improve babies' mental health.

Of course, diagnosis and treatment have a crucial role to play. But to truly transform the childhoods of our most vulnerable, we need policies and services that address relationships and environments, not simply *treating* the individuals who are grappling with the damage of poor relationships and unsupportive circumstances.

One practical step towards this could be to task the minister for care and mental health with a cross-government remit to develop a strategy that both builds on therapeutic support and also encompasses tackling the poverty, intergenerational trauma and other adversities that feed poor mental health in the first place. In such a world, services such as specialised parent–infant relationship teams would be an inherent component of mental health services. Older children would also benefit from services tackling the wider risks to their mental health, working with the key adults in their lives to create deep, lasting change.

Children before institutions

Throughout my time as a community worker, chief executive, volunteer and chair, I have been struck by the self-defeating propensity at all levels to tackle symptoms in isolation from one another – as opposed to truly focusing on the whole child and addressing the range of interlocking and reinforcing dynamics holding each back.

It is understandable how we got here. Everything needs organising, and institutions offer up clear and discrete ways of arranging things. But the idea that life can be tidied into straight lines and neat boxes is a fiction. If policy focused on children and their outcomes, rather than institutions and isolated levers, the 'national mission' would have a far greater chance of success.

Working across the whole system around the child is undoubtedly hard, but it is possible. Organisations such as West London Zone are pointing the way to collective impact.[62] And in-roads were made by the Department for Children, Schools and Families, which housed policy teams working on cross-government issues relating to children, such as child poverty and youth justice.

Focusing on the whole child, including their relationships and the context in which they live, is a transformative change in how policy making and services are approached and organised. It involves looking at the evidence about what really makes a difference to a child's outcomes, and then pulling all the policy levers and practical services that drive change, wherever they may sit.

Four 'Rs', not three

For as long as anyone can recall, the essential framing of early education has been anchored in the three 'Rs': reading, 'riting and 'rithmetic. There should be four – the fourth being self-regulation.

Self-regulation describes the ability to notice, monitor and recognise feelings, and then control how one reacts to a situation. Compared to academic ability at age ten, self-regulation has a greater effect on adult mental well-being, and a similar impact on health and income.[63]

There is a remarkable degree of consensus that the making of a good life lies not only in our formal skills and knowledge, but also equally in our wider abilities, ambition and attitudes. And not only do they matter; they matter more than ever. The shift to a service economy, more open routes through education and into employment, together with the emphasis of choice in public and consumer services, all combine to make individual agency and capabilities more important than ever.[64,65]

Crucially, too, we know that individuals' capabilities aren't given or fixed. They can be developed. And science shows that at the heart of such skills sits 'self-regulation'.[66]

It's not hard to see why self-regulation shapes life experiences and opportunities. A child who has self-regulation at the start of school can sit and focus on their learning. Out of the classroom, self-regulation is at play, too, helping children navigate social interactions. And so on, through life. Self-regulation is a cornerstone for flourishing. Yet, while mentions of social and emotional skills, including self-regulation, have been scattered across policy documents for many years, they are invariably never prioritised. Instead, they should be a focus of policy, an outcome measured and reported alongside traditional academic measures.

Conclusion

I suggest three straightforward ways in which reframing our national approach to children's policy could lead to better public spending, significantly improved childhoods and enduringly greater life chances. I argue for new and better lenses:

- moving away from a narrow, individualistic view of mental health – seeing it as the result of an interplay of individual characteristics, relationships and environments;
- focusing on children rather than on presenting symptoms, and thus isolated interventions and individual institutions;

- prioritising self-regulation as an indicator of whether public services are providing good enough support to children and young people.

None of these ideas are new. Nor are they controversial. Embracing their adoption wholesale could, however, fundamentally change how policy is made, delivered and experienced.

Yet, while these are not easy shifts, it is time to shake up briefs and policy-making infrastructure (alongside service design), and reframe policy and programme goals by slaying some long-established shibboleths. Success depends, ultimately, on whether we keep on ploughing narrow furrows, driven by good intentions, but adhering to profound misconceptions, or whether we look up and look out, looking again at what the evidence is really showing us.

Nick touches on the idea of a cross–government minister to deliver child–centred change. Corinna alluded to something similar. It's an idea that chimes with the key call from this book: the establishment of a National Children's Service, as set out later, in Chapter 14.

Ellen O'Donoghue is CEO of the suicide support charity for young men, James' Place. She sees the impact of growing toxic stress in young people and the consequences on their mental health in her daily work. She has written this essay around the importance of early intervention policies.

Mental health, well-being and suicide prevention
Ellen O'Donoghue, CEO at James' Place

Children and young people's mental health needs are not supported early enough, and often only when they have reached crisis point.

Given that half of all adult psychiatric problems are diagnosable by age 14,[67] and 75 per cent by age 24,[68] the lack of adequate and early support is particularly concerning. We need to take concrete action to reverse that.

In my day job, I work as CEO of James' Place, a charity that treats men in suicidal crisis. We listened and consulted with men to create a clinical intervention and therapeutic programme, built on the evidence base delivered by professional therapists designed to help them get through their crisis and be able to go on to live their lives.

In previous roles, I have worked on public health campaigns, as a member of the Mayor of London's Child Obesity Taskforce and as a school governor. This has distilled a key question: what could early intervention and effective mental health support look like for children?

Give young people a voice

Not only is it essential that children get the support they need early on, but they should also be given the opportunity to co-create the space and tools to improve their own well-being and mental health.

After all, there are many pressures on children, such as bullying and the pressure to fit in, and fear about the world around them, especially given that climate change is an issue that they will have to deal with as adults. Naomi Watkins-Ligudzinska of the NW Counselling Hub CIC, which offers means-tested therapy to adults and young people, said: 'Young people don't feel heard or listened to. We need to take what they are saying seriously, listen properly to what they have to say and stand up for what they believe in. They need to know that we will do the best we can.'

The charity Young Minds has produced an excellent strategy for young people's mental health, which identifies that their 'needs are not supported early enough, and often only when they have reached crisis point'.[69] Young Minds advocates for action in three areas, so that young people:

- are helped to look after their own mental health;
- have adults around them who are equipped to recognise emerging needs and provide support;
- have their powerful voices placed at the heart of any change needed.

Start with quality of life

If we want to give children better mental health, we must look to improve their overall quality of life. Good mental health does not exist in a vacuum. The social determinants of health include housing, education and an absence of racism and discrimination. Children and young people's mental health is affected by psychosocial influences: bullying, sexual violence, loneliness.

Some children and young people are particularly vulnerable and may need further targeted support. For example, the Care Quality Commission reported, 'a third of people in the youth justice system are estimated to have a mental health problem',[70] and the government's own Green Paper identified, 'young people involved in gangs face particularly high rates of mental illness … as many as one-in-three female and one-in-ten male gang members are considered at risk of suicide or self-harm'.[71]

Listen and understand

We need to ensure that all children are equipped with the emotional resources to manage and protect their own feelings, and that adults understand enough that at every touchpoint children are met with compassion and understanding.

How are we going to do this? First, by listening. I asked children what adults could do to support young people's mental health. One said they wanted it to be more common:

> for kids to have a school counsellor they can talk to. And more clubs, and more action stations, which is a little box where if there's something that's really troubling you, you can write it on a slip of paper and put it in a box and a teacher or counsellor at school will read it and help.

Kelly Thorpe manages the HOPELINEUK service at the suicide prevention charity Papyrus. When we spoke, she highlighted that there is more to be done in schools and beyond to create safe spaces where children can go to talk openly: 'Young people are carrying a lot of their own stuff, and their friends' too. It would be wonderful if we could lighten that load. Young people want a non-judgemental space where they are taken seriously and their voices are heard.'

Intervene early and appropriately

Charities can move at speed to innovate and work with people who are not getting the support they need from statutory services. James' Place is a good example of innovation in the charity sector, and was set up to meet a specific and recognised gap. It provides something that isn't duplicating what's already happening in the NHS, but works alongside it.

This is the kind of innovation that we need to support children and young people, and to facilitate that, we need consistent and reliable statutory services. For example, the charity Place2Be does excellent work providing a range of mental health support and services to children based in schools that buy in its services. Dr Niki Cooper, Clinical Director of Place2Be, said to me:

> There are rising levels of need for mental health support for children and young people. According to NHS data, prevalence has increased, and

currently one in six children and young people experience diagnosable mental health problems. We want to see a focus on prevention and early intervention, so that we can stop young people from reaching crisis point and needing to be referred for specialist treatment.

Yet, as not all schools are able to fund services like this, not all children access the benefit. Underinvestment in mental health and suicide prevention means that the statutory sector offering is not predictable: care varies in different areas, and children, parents and professionals themselves often don't know what to expect when they seek help. This is a missed opportunity when early intervention can make a huge long-term difference.

Prioritise children and young people's mental health

Four key actions government can take to prioritise children and young people's mental health are:

- embed early intervention and support in all primary schools;
- ensure school counsellors and mental health practitioners are available in every school to children who need them, when they need them;
- focus on providing urgent support when it's needed, with a commitment to a maximum waiting time for referrals to statutory services, and associated funding;
- give consistent funding to charities that are providing essential services and whose support should be standard for all children and young people.

This is precisely what the child I spoke to wanted to see. They finished by saying that they would like 'every building [to have] an action station. School, home, anywhere. Because you can get a worry anywhere.'

Health inequalities: determined by what's going on around us

Ellen and Nick rightly homed in on how critical social determinants are to individual mental (and physical) health, and it is to these factors that I now turn in imagining actions to deliver a future where all can thrive. Social determinants are the non-medical factors that influence health outcomes. They are the conditions in which people are born, grow, work, live and age, and the wider set of forces and systems shaping the conditions of daily life. These forces and systems include economic policies and systems, development agendas, social norms, the quality of homes and jobs, social policies and political systems. In the UK, they are highly unevenly distributed and lead to avoidable, unfair and systematic differences in health between different groups of people.[72]

Social determinants are the upstream causes of much poor health. They mean that children growing up in more deprived areas often suffer disadvantages throughout their lives, from educational opportunities through to employment prospects, which, in turn, affect their physical and mental well-being. Educational attainment is, in turn, strongly linked with health behaviours and outcomes, for example more educated individuals are less likely to suffer from long-term diseases and report themselves in poor health or suffer from mental disorders such as depression or anxiety.[73]

As an example, let's take one socially determined outcome, 'school-readiness', on which children are assessed having completed Reception Year, at around five years of age. To achieve a 'good level of development' a child should have reached the expected level in early learning goals around communication and language, physical development and personal, social and emotional development.[74] Measures of this include paying attention, listening to stories, using the toilet, dressing themselves and starting to read, write and do simple sums. In 2016 nearly half of five-year-olds who were eligible for free school meals (FSM) were not ready for school, compared with just under a third of their peers from wealthier families.[75]

Recognising the correlation between poverty, the social determinants of health, health inequalities and health outcomes has been noted or nodded to in government policy frameworks for decades. Sometimes the response is simple: fluoride in water, universal inoculations and means-tested FSM. Sometimes it is clunky as government tries to fit holistic, (necessarily) multi-system solutions within the siloed department of state bureaucracies, where, for example, childcare provision, budgeting and policy delivery often falls between 'multiple stools'.

One of the most comprehensive attempts to place public health solutions in the context of social determinants and health inequalities was a 2010 independent study, *Fair Society, Healthy Lives (The Marmot Review)*,[76] led by Sir Michael Marmot, a world-leading academic and epidemiologist. The key message was of creating conditions for people to control their own lives. This requires action across the social determinants of health, many of which are beyond the reach of the NHS alone.

The Marmot Review stressed that disadvantage starts *before* birth and accumulates throughout life. This is reflected by the fact that of its six policy objectives, he gave the highest priority to the first: 'Giving every child the best start in life.' The second objective was also *Raising the Nation*-esque in nature: 'Enabling all children, young people and adults to maximise their capabilities and have control over their lives.'[77]

I recently spoke with Michael about the Review, and he still is adamant that the empirical evidence overwhelmingly shows that early years matter for future life changes, and what is going on around children shapes good early years.

The UK government welcomed *The Marmot Review*, pledging to put the reduction of health inequalities at the centre of its public health aims and base its strategy on its recommendations.[78] But, with the austerity of upcoming public spending cuts and a fundamental reorganisation of the NHS, political priorities changed. In 2020 Michael Marmot authored a follow-up report, *Health Equity in England: The Marmot Review 10 Years On*,which opened with the damning words, 'Since 2010 life expectancy in England has stalled; this has not happened since at least 1900 … [this] is a sign that society has stopped improving', and noted that, 'there has been no national health inequalities strategy since 2010 … an essential first step in leading the necessary national endeavour to reduce health inequalities'.[79]

Michael's work provides the keys to unlock health inequalities' doors, yet they largely remain locked. The siloed nature of government departments makes it difficult, seemingly too difficult, to commit to, and implement, a single, workable, coordinated strategic framework. One politician who has used his statutory powers and personal manifesto to try is Sadiq Khan, Mayor of London. Sadiq has written this essay on his approach to the multi-tentacled challenge of London's health inequalities.

Politicians have a moral obligation to invest in children's futures

Rt Hon Sadiq Khan, Mayor of London and former Government Minister

Healthier and happier children should be a primary, headline goal for every government.

As policy makers, all politicians have a moral obligation to ensure their citizens have the opportunity to reach their potential. We know that our children's health and well-being is linked to every feature of our city: from the homes they live in, to the way they travel to school and the quality of their education once they are there. All these factors, and many more, play an integral role in determining their health outcomes. We must also recognise that this is a matter of social justice and the extent to which health and economic inequalities are inextricably linked.

There are some who want to blame poor health on personal choice, but this is purely an excuse for inaction. Individuals cannot redesign roads to make it safer to cycle, or fund the building of new sports facilities, or dramatically clean up toxic air in their community.

Research shows that social determinants can be more important than healthcare in influencing health. Income, for example, has a huge impact on health, which is one of the reasons I am committed to ensuring every Londoner receives a fair day's wage for a fair day's work. The number of London Living Wage employers has quadrupled since I became Mayor, and this commitment has been supported by 14 NHS trusts in London, although our ambition is to strive for compliance across all 30. This policy demonstrates that the challenge of improving the health and happiness of our children is not the responsibility of one single organisation.

And as no one agency has the power to solve them alone, mayors across the country are taking a lead in tackling health inequalities. As London's Mayor, I have a duty to deliver these changes and ensure our city becomes an environment in which Londoners can live healthier lives.

But everyone has a vital role to play, and I am fortunate to work alongside local authorities, our NHS and regional partners to ensure that the health and well-being of our children is at the forefront of everything we do at City Hall. Our aim is to create a healthier, fairer city, where nobody's health suffers because of who they are or where they live.

Taking bold policy steps

Although there is no silver bullet to tackling the drivers of poor mental health, poverty or obesity in our children, ambitious policy making can deliver meaningful change.

In February 2019, in the face of opposition, I banned junk food advertising on the entire Transport for London network. This means that no adverts for less healthy food and drink are allowed on the world's largest transport system, which serves millions of Londoners daily. The move was considered controversial by some at the time, but evidence has shown that the restrictions work. Indeed, the policy's impact has been far greater than we could have imagined. Researchers at the University of Sheffield found that the policy has prevented almost 100,000 obesity cases, and is expected to save our NHS in London £200 million over the lifetime of the current population.[80] And a London School of Hygiene and Tropical Medicine study revealed that the ban has contributed to a 1,000 calorie decrease in unhealthy purchases in Londoners' household weekly shops.[81] The ad ban shows how improving the health of London's children means ensuring that families find the healthier choice the easiest choice. It is an example of international best practice, delivering multiple benefits for our city. The policy is now supported by Londoners and has been taken forward by several local authorities. I believe the national government should now follow our lead and ban junk food advertising.

In London we know all too well the horrifying consequences of poor air quality, particularly on our children. The case of Ella Adoo Kissi Debrah, a nine-year-old who died in 2013 of asthma contributed to by excessive air pollution, has been a clarion call for action. We have made huge strides in cleaning London's toxic air through the Ultra Low Emission Zone (ULEZ). The ULEZ was first introduced in central London in April 2019 and then expanded to cover the whole of inner London in October 2021. It has been supported by £171 million in scrappage funding to help those on low incomes, with disabilities, charities and small businesses prepare for the scheme, as well as work to clean up our bus and taxi fleets.

The ULEZ has transformed the air millions of Londoners breathe. There are 74,000 fewer polluting vehicles in the zone on an average day and harmful nitrogen dioxide concentrations are estimated to have nearly halved in central London and are a fifth lower in inner London. Independent experts have praised the ULEZ for the impact it has had, and other cities have followed in rolling out similar schemes. The ULEZ will be expanded London-wide in August 2023, meaning cleaner air for every Londoner.

In February 2023 I announced an unprecedented new scheme to ensure every London primary schoolchild receives free school meals for a year during the cost-of-living crisis. This £130 million investment will ensure an additional 270,000 children receive healthy free school meals across the academic year, beginning in September 2023. It should mean that none of these children's health will suffer because they miss the chance to have a hot nutritious meal.

I also know the joy that simple things can bring, like a dog walk in your local park, and so we continue to make the places and spaces our children live and play in healthier.

Through our London Plan, we have introduced restrictions that mean no hot food takeaways will be allowed within 400 metres of a school. Through our school Superzones initiative we are working with local authorities, communities and families to give young people a voice, so they can influence the changes they want in their neighbourhoods and co-produce the solutions required to create healthy urban environments around schools.

I am supporting more changes to the built environment by creating healthy streets, including School and Play Streets, so young people can independently and safely move around and play. We have also invested millions of pounds in community sports schemes aimed at children and young people.

My administration has shifted the dial to enable more walking and cycling, delivering a fivefold increase in protected cycling lanes, reducing speed limits on London's largest roads and introducing local traffic reduction schemes.

It is crucial that we continue to ensure all our communities have a stake in the future of our city. Real progress has been made where we have been able to mobilise and galvanise Londoners around the issues that matter to them most. We can make a difference to children's lives, but we have much more to do to ensure every young Londoner has the chance to lead a healthy and fulfilling childhood.

Sadiq's essay addresses some of the social determinants of health from a practical perspective, showing that both local and national governments are vital to achieve a future where children's health is protected.

Conclusions

This chapter has focused primarily on the two endemic public health issues of unhealthy weight and mental health, as they both have spiralling and wide consequences. It also sought to show how they are tied to the social determinants of health. Michael Marmot couldn't have been clearer, or more right, in his 2010 review, or in his choice of words to open his report in 2020, 'if health has stopped improving, then society has stopped improving'.[82]

It is no accident that the thread of a multi-touchpoint, whole-systems solution called for by Corinna chimes with Michael's report and other evidence shared in the chapter. Nor is it that Nick and Ellen each called for co-design of solutions to protect mental health, as young people's insights into what will work are invaluable. Each shared visions of how a new world is possible, and how, with political will, it could be probable. Perhaps in assessing that possibility we ought to focus our minds back to the words of Ayo, who opened the chapter: 'If a child dies, the government is always serious about it. So, if the child doesn't die, they should be serious about the child anyway.'

One of the multiple new challenges and opportunities that this generation of children faces is the ubiquity of technology in their lives. It can be used to underpin many of the solutions to challenges they face, perhaps especially around health: the opportunities of using artificial intelligence, data science, robotic support and personal profiling are immense, but an always-on 'digital' world can be dangerous too. It is to this subject that we'll next travel to explore how 'digital' can help in *raising the nation*.

Three additional essays, containing more proposals for government, are hosted at www.raisingthenation.co.uk:

- Sharon Hodgson MP chairs the All-Party Parliamentary Group on School Food. She has written on the subject she has tirelessly campaigned upon for many years: action to end holiday hunger.

- Patrick Barwise is Emeritus Professor of Management and Marketing at London Business School. He has written with a call for universal free school meals.

- Robin Hewings is Director of Programmes at the Campaign to End Loneliness. He has written on how loneliness is one consequence of a lack of variety of meaningful relationships, and a significant contributor to poor mental health in young people.

In addition, the website hosts the *Every Child a Healthy Weight* plan.

8

Digital

We have allowed a situation to develop in which it is legal for a multibillion dollar industry to own, wholly and in perpetuity, the intimate and personal details of children.

Baroness Kidron[1]

I started this chapter as the inquest into the death of Molly Russell was headline news in the UK. Molly took her own life in 2017, aged 14, after seeing thousands of graphic images of self-harm and suicide on Pinterest and Instagram. Molly went into her Instagram account around 120 times a day, had a secret Twitter account, and through her YouTube account regularly 'liked' a high number of disturbing video posts concerning anxiety, depression, self-harm and suicide.[2] Her family had no idea of this world she had entered. The companies that own the social media platforms had, at their fingertips, the data to warn of the patterns of Molly's likes and views. The inquest found their algorithms were, and still are, designed to push, amplify and widen access to images, videos and messages likely to resonate with someone like Molly. Such content was, and is, totally unsuitable for children. Molly's father powerfully reflected that: 'It's time to protect our innocent young people, instead of allowing platforms to prioritise their profits by monetising their misery.'[3]

The main social media platforms allow 13-year-olds to set up their own accounts.[4] Yet they have no processes to distinguish whether it is 13-year-old children or adults accessing content, although platforms such as Pinterest warn in their terms of service that users may be exposed to material that is 'inappropriate for children'.[5]

Molly had sought help, but not from her family, or from the platforms that granted her access to material 'inappropriate for children'. She sent posts for help to social media influencers and her idols, who, with millions of followers and thousands of daily posts, would never realistically see pleas from a lonely and desperate schoolgirl. As Molly's father put it, 'she was calling out into an empty void'.[6]

Molly's is a thoroughly tragic case, but it is by no means unique. Suicide rates among teenagers almost doubled in the eight years to 2018.[7] This trend has fuelled alarm about the influence of social media on young people. The number of young people taking their own lives speaks to the priorities of our society. The extent to which our future is child-centred depends on how society balances social media companies maximising profits against privacy rights and the protections for our children. This balance is something governments often seem incapable of even seeking to strike, perhaps, because:

- social media does not recognise national borders;
- institutions (global, national and sectoral) are unprepared to tackle them;
- government processes are too slow to react;
- those in positions of power lack the expertise to act;
- the challenge is evolving with accelerating speed.

Let's take a breath, and a step back. At its best, the digital★ environment offers important opportunities for children, such as self-expression, acquiring knowledge and socialising with peers. It exposes them to new ideas and more diverse sources of information. It can expand possibilities, reduce inequalities and contribute to realisation of their rights. 'Digital' has utterly transformed education and learning, the formation of friendships, leisure time and the nature of engagement across wider society.

★ I use the word 'digital' to encompass digital electronic systems including websites, cloud servers, search engines, social media platforms, mobile apps, audio and video services, and other web-based resources. In this sense it includes online services, television, podcasts and radio.

It has helped create the most informed, connected, confident, aware and creative generation that has ever lived. One in three internet users globally is a child.[8] In the UK almost nine in ten children aged 10 to 15 years report that they go online every day.[9] The UN has declared access to an internet connection vital to the enjoyment of human rights, stating that universal access should be a priority for all states.[10] While the digital environment and its services will evolve, it is here to stay.

Yet, the digital age also brings a range of risks. Digital technologies have increased the scale of child sexual abuse and exploitation, whether through child sex offenders having increased access to children, or children sharing personal information (for example, intimate photos of others without their consent).[11] In addition, cyberbullying means bullies can hurt and humiliate with the click of a button, all day, every day. Words and images posted online are also difficult to delete, increasing the risk of re-victimisation.[12]

There are disturbing statistics about the number of children involved in risky online behaviours. In 2020, although the majority of children only exchanged messages with people online that they knew in person, around one in six 10- to 15-year-olds had spoken with someone they had never met.[13] Further, one in 50 said that they had spoken to or messaged someone they thought was their age, but later found out was much older. Five per cent of 10- to 15-year-olds (212,000 children) met in person with someone they had only spoken to online, and one in ten 13- to 15-year-olds reported receiving a sexual message, with one in 100 sending a sexual message themselves. These risks are often more acute for children who live with disadvantages as they are more likely to be vulnerable online.[14]

In addition to online content and contact risks, many parents are concerned about the time their children spend using digital technology and its effect on their physical activity and mental health. Evidence suggests that while moderate use of digital technology can be beneficial to children's mental well-being, excessive use can be detrimental.[15]

So what can be done? Where to start?

The challenge is to maximise access possibilities while minimising the risks and harm of inappropriate content or contacts. Let's start with what governments can do to widen access through infrastructure and investment, and to tackle unequal access that flows from social, economic or geographic circumstances.

The UK is actually world-leading in many aspects of the digital world. Internet availability for children is universal, schemes exist to address barriers to access, and legislation is pioneering regarding safety. Indeed, the British government has committed the country to be the safest place in the world to be online.[16] But 'world-leading' isn't the measure of success, not when those with ill intent are moving and evolving so quickly. What is needed is utter dedication to maximising opportunities for children to thrive and minimising all risks that they will be harmed. And here there are still many choices to be made.

Maximising opportunities for children from digital services

Since 2018, 100 per cent of all British households with children have had internet access at home.[17] But children still face a digital divide in utilising that internet. For example, families who do not have a laptop, desktop or tablet at home must access digital services via a smartphone. The stark implications of such constrained access were evident during the COVID-19 crisis. The government did respond with a £100 million package to send 200,000 devices and 50,000 4G routers to some vulnerable pupils, care leavers and disadvantaged students nearing their exams. However, only 37 per cent of those eligible were actually allocated a device.[18] Those who weren't were at risk of social and educational disadvantage. Even for families that had a computer, the reality of lockdown was that access to a device was not the same as having *enough* access: poor bandwidth, costs or having to share all hinder actual use.

One solution is to make broadband a public utility: free at the point of access, potentially in public and private spaces, like health services and fluoridated water. This was previously floated as a policy by the Labour Party,[19] and is working successfully in other countries. Switzerland, Poland and Latvia, for example, offer free and safe Wi-Fi in most public places. Helsinki offers free Wi-Fi across the city that is faster than the subscription connections in citizens' homes.[20]

Other solutions to maximise opportunities to increase digital inclusion for all children are offered by Amy Jordan and Ellen Helsper in an essay they have co-written for us.

A child-centred approach to digital inclusion

Amy Jordan, Professor and Chair in the Department of Journalism and Media Studies, Rutgers University and *Ellen Helsper*, Professor of Digital Inequalities in the Department of Media and Communications, London School of Economics and Political Science

We could begin with numbers that highlight digital divides: between countries in the Global North versus the Global South, between families who are economically secure versus insecure, and between children who are White versus Black. But our research has found that the digital divide is not only about access to the internet or ownership of devices; it is also about the social, economic, political and physical structures that determine whether and how participation in digital spaces can be meaningful for children. These are shaped by government policies and funding mechanisms that leave rural communities invisible to internet providers, overlook the digital needs of teachers, and leave young people out of the conversation.

Lessons learned from digital history

Decades of interventions have shown that programmes need to be carefully considered, well targeted and future-proofed to be sustainable and effective in reducing the digital divide. In this we can learn from failures.

One of the first US government programmes to address digital inclusion focused on access. In 1996 the E-Rate programme was set up to help schools and libraries obtain affordable broadband. At that time, the internet was dial-up and funding came from surcharges on telephone bills. The programme's discounts for support depended on levels of poverty and whether the school or library was located in an urban or rural area. By 2013, the economic model and programme were both obsolete. Only one-third of schools had high-speed connections and few students had access to Wi-Fi in the classroom. Legislation had to be fundamentally updated, after which billions more dollars were poured into a revised programme. Today, nearly 99 per cent of schools in the USA have high-speed internet.[21] In its early days, the E-rate programme shone a spotlight on the needs of children who were being left out of what policy makers called the 'information superhighway'. But it wasn't future-proofed for when technologies and economic models became obsolete. Moreover, its cultural assumption that children's need to connect to the internet stopped at the grounds of schools and libraries proved to be flawed.

Other interventions have sought to provide children with devices to connect with the internet. For example, the non-profit initiative One Laptop Per Child, established in 2005, distributed basic computers to low-income communities. But the devices were often sources of frustration for teachers who were expected to incorporate them into their curricula without training, and for children who often couldn't connect to the internet. The computers came with software, but it was basic and uninteresting.[22] Adults were unequipped to guide children's use of the laptops, and communities were often unable to fix devices when they malfunctioned. Evaluations of the programme's efficacy showed negligible effect,[23] and the programme shut down in 2014.[24]

What can we learn from well intentioned, but fundamentally flawed, programmes like these to achieve full digital inclusion? We could begin with a need to shift focus from functional, instrumental skills centred on (passive) consumption of content and lowest common denominator access towards a more critical, engaged approach. In other words, we could adopt an (active) child-centred approach using more holistic thinking about digital skills.

Starting with the child

A child-centred approach recognises that the environments within which children live and grow matter. This builds in support for adults in children's lives, so they can guide and participate alongside their charges. Such support can come from community organisations, for example the Good Things Foundation in the UK. Key to success is embedding learning and content creation in shared activities and experiences in locations where children live their everyday lives. Research and recent interventions show that much learning about technology takes place informally and collectively through learning-by-doing and observing others rather than formal training. This is why children's everyday social and digital environments and experiences are so important in shaping digital behaviours and views of the digital world.

A 'digital inclusion agency'

Policy making around the internet has tended to focus on the negative: how to keep children safe from bullies, predators and content that might be harmful. Or it has only focused on disadvantaged children. These are important goals, but what would a more holistic viewpoint look like?

It would involve the use of digital spaces to connect children with people who are important in their lives – families, teachers, peers – and in spaces they live in. It also means moving from the typical approaches – which urge vulnerable or disadvantaged young people to 'catch up' – to a collective responsibility for creating a more inclusive online environment.

Governments should provide universal and affordable internet access as a fundamental obligation to its children, much like public education or public health. It is essential to create a central place that is focused on enhancing young people's digital inclusion. A 'digital inclusion' agency could go a long way towards ensuring that disparate efforts are accessible, effective, coherent and coordinated. Such an agency would:

- foster dialogue with young people and the adults in their lives;
- connect with organisations in local communities;
- privilege equity and ethics in its decision making;
- be well resourced;
- have staff who are creative and experienced, advocating for digitally marginalised youth.

We must invite diverse children and young people's voices into the conversation and shift priorities away from protectionism into engagement. Only then will digital inclusion result in young people feeling connected to fellow citizens, peers and family, having opportunities to be creative and funny, and having agency to shape conversations about people, places and events that impact them.

A focus, like Amy and Ellen's, on equitable access to digital services and bridging digital divides, is fundamental to helping all children thrive. Mike Adams is passionate about disability inclusion and has lived with significant physical disability all his life. He is founder and CEO of Purple, an organisation that is changing the disability conversation. He has written this essay calling on government to recognise the variety of abilities of child users of digital services.

Voice activated

Mike Adams OBE, campaigner for disability rights and founder and CEO of Purple

To change the conversation requires a voice. For so many disabled children, this right is denied.

I'm the father of a 10-month-old baby who is just realising he has a voice. First words. He's got me thinking about other 10-month-olds, born without the ability or opportunity to express. Communication isolation from day one, locked out of a society they only recently entered. Instead. Deemed the responsibility of government and the welfare state. Positioned as an issue of charity. Choice, control and independence hampered before life has really begun.

For the next generation of young disabled children, society is at a crossroads. But the direction is very clear. The signpost says 'inclusion'! In 2022 'accessibility' needs to be redefined and 'enabling technology' embraced. For years technology has provided support to those with physical mobility. Wheelchairs. Manual and electric. Scooters. So why don't we harness it the same way when it comes to communication? Why isn't technology better utilised to give people a voice?

In our modern world speaking is only one way to be heard. The transformation in digital technology and social media has radically changed the way we communicate. Yet it has not been mainstreamed to support those with vocally or communicatively challenging conditions.

Disabilities such as autism affect at least 1 per cent of the population and up to 30 per cent of autistic people are non-speaking.[25] This is similar to other conditions such as cerebral palsy and Rett syndrome. One in 200 people would benefit from access to augmentative and alternative communication (AAC),[26] a form of communication other than spoken or oral language used to express thoughts, needs, wants and ideas.

The technology to drive AAC exists. But current NHS England specialist hubs are only funded to meet the needs of about 10 per cent of people who require AAC.[27] The other 90 per cent are denied. A key pillar of independence slammed shut. Potential contribution to wider society stopped in its tracks. While in other countries, such as the USA and Germany, the provision of AAC happens at scale.

So the technology exists and demand is growing. Non-speaking children need to be empowered. Today. Not in ten years, and certainly not never.

The importance of voice shines a light on wider issues faced by disabled people. In the UK there are 14.6 million disabled people who have rights under current disability legislation, including 1 million disabled children.[28] To put that into context, disabled people are the largest minority group in the world.[29] Two other eye-watering and humbling statistics: 83 per cent of disabled people acquire their disability in their lifetime and 80 per cent of disabilities are hidden.[30] Both impact children.

The COVID-19 pandemic crossed a Rubicon. One in six COVID-19-related deaths in England were disabled people.[31] Disabled people were disproportionately isolated as information, services and the power to purchase moved online. The level of online inaccessibility was laid bare. But this was a problem long before COVID-19. Only 3 per cent of the most visited websites meet minimum accessibility standards. The loss to business in the UK alone of not providing accessible websites stands at £17.1 billion, and is rising.[32] This digital exclusion has also had a significant impact on disabled children, as the ability to switch to online education services proved enormously difficult. A growing dependence on digital could exacerbate the opportunity gap for our disabled children.

There is an irony. A disconnect. For while mainstream online services are broadly inaccessible to many of those with disability, the actual technology to support people within the AAC community is advanced. The art of what is possible is enabling. The ability to interact with the family WhatsApp. Latest Twitter debate. Weekly Teams meetings. Conversation. Engagement. At one end of the spectrum think Stephen Hawking. His contribution to our current and future world. More Stephens can be enabled.

Meet Joe. He is now 20 years old. He has a condition known as athetoid dystonic cerebral palsy, meaning, in part, that he cannot vocalise words. But Joe is a 'total communicator', using a mix of different methods. As a young child he signed and used picture symbols, but after starting with AAC his life was truly transformed. AAC gave him a voice in his childhood. The ability to fit in. Be a kid. He now expresses himself, makes more choices and steers a conversation. Joe now participates fully at college and in extra-curricular activities. His reading and spelling comprehension is way beyond what was thought possible. He makes friends, flirts and makes jokes.

Enabling his voice has been a game changer. Joe can make himself understood if his parents and/or carers are not there. Everyone understands him quickly.

Without ACC, Joe would have been essentially locked in his own world throughout his childhood, with limited opportunity to voice what he wanted to. He wouldn't have been able to show his understanding of the world, or what a bright and sparky child he was.

The value of having a voice is compelling. The technology exists to ensure all disabled people can have a voice regardless of whether they are non-speaking individuals. Hearing different voices enriches the conversation. Especially for disabled children. It gives them a voice. A bigger variety of experiences. It protects their well-being.

Funding cannot be the new barrier to playing a full part in society. If there was a medical operation available to give a child the opportunity to speak, there would be no questions, no deliberation. It would happen. Technology should be seen as the alternative treatment and offered as a right.

Let's make sure every child can have their voice activated, now, and throughout their lives.

Amy, Ellen and Mike have laid down a challenge to those of us thinking about what an inclusive child–centred future means. Convincing policy makers will be easier by showing what is already proving effective. That effectiveness can be seen in one country that prides itself for abolishing its digital divide. With good cause, Estonia is seen as being the 'gold standard' for digital services.

E-Stonia

Following decades of investment in infrastructure, content development, education and support, Estonian digital public services are fully integrated, universal and reliable. Since independence in 1991, Estonia has harnessed technology to help citizens live supported, independent and fulfilling lives. It ranks first in the world for public digital services.[33] Estonia's innovative approach includes:

- a proactive childcare digital system that guarantees that as soon as a child is born their details are registered and their family automatically receives all benefits to which they are entitled, throughout the child's life;[34]

- the ProgeTiger programme to improve technological literacy and digital competence of students (from kindergarten) and their teachers;
- a large-scale digitalisation of educational materials and wide use of smart technologies such as e-learning materials and digital databases, textbooks, class diaries and assessments;[35]
- a commitment to collaborate with other Baltic and Nordic countries;
- opening up its e-learning content, resources, insights and research for any school or education system to use, for free, under the Education Nation programme.[36]

When COVID-19 hit, education in Estonia actually thrived, with a virtually seamless transition to cloud-based homeschooling and distance learning. The whole country had access to fast, secure, safe and often free broadband or Wi-Fi; investment had never been squeezed; and children, teachers and parents were 'digitally literate'; the teaching materials and services were already online.

Is it any wonder that Estonian children are thriving? Seventy-eight per cent of 15-year-olds have a high satisfaction with their lives, against 64 per cent in the UK.[37]

Not all moves to a future where digital technology plays a positive role in children's thriving need be complex, expensive or have long implementation timelines. Henry Warren and Oli Barrett have found a simple, transformative idea that they, as co-founders of the TOTS campaign, are trying to encourage governments and digital platforms to adopt. They have shared their idea in this essay for us.

Turn on the subtitles!

Henry Warren and Oli Barrett MBE, entrepreneurs and co-founders of the TOTS campaign

People assume that politics and policy making is a zero-sum game with inherent trade-offs and sacrifices, and that we will have to make some tough choices. This isn't one of those times.

Sometimes an idea comes along and it's so blindingly obvious and powerful that we all step back and ask, 'Why hasn't this been done before?'

Our work originated in 2020 when we happened upon a news article that claimed that turning on subtitles on children's TV could double their literacy acquisition – we had to know if this was as brilliant as it appeared. Lots of discussions with academics and even more ongoing conversations with broadcasters led to the inception of our charitable endeavour Turn On The Subtitles (TOTS). We are on a mission to improve literacy for children everywhere, by simply 'turning on the subtitles'.

What is the problem that TOTS is trying to solve?
Most children come to school ready to learn and leave with a solid reading foundation. However, 25 per cent of British children leave primary school having not met their expected reading level, which jumps to 45 per cent for those from low-income families.[38]

What happens if you leave education with low literacy levels? As an adult, you are three times more likely to die young, three times more likely to be incarcerated, and three times more likely to be hospitalised.[39]

Literacy clearly matters. There are some great initiatives, but the vast majority don't go wide enough. We need to look for solutions that will impact *all* children. While we still don't have a way of solving this issue on a scale or budget so that countries (or their citizens) can afford to reach all the children that require help, there is a way to improve literacy for every child in the country (well, actually, almost every child in the world). It won't cost the public or the government a penny. In fact, it won't cost anyone very much money at all.

The mechanism is subtitles. Subtitles running on children's TV programmes* can massively improve children's literacy. It doubles the chance of each of them becoming a good reader.[40] Therefore, what TOTS proposes is that children's TV content has subtitles shown by default.

The 'by default' part is key, and is why policy is needed, rather than simply asking parents to select the 'Subtitle' button on their remote control. To reach families that need this the most, changing the default setting is the most effective method. Think of it as similar to the intervention in the 1960s, where a small amount of fluoride was added to all drinking water in the UK

---

* We define children's TV content as programmes made primarily to be watched by children aged 6–10 as it is this age group that receives the maximum impact through subtitles.

to help reduce tooth decay. A simple intervention that helped everyone in equal measure.

The evidence base for subtitles is vast. It turns out many academics have known about the power of subtitles for years.[41]

How does it work?

Subtitles cause automatic reading behaviour among children and adults. Viewers who have some reading ability – even partial letter-to-sound correspondence – can't just ignore subtitles, and will exhibit automatic reading responses, tracking subtitling on screen automatically.

The key to reading fluency, however, is practice, practice, practice. An important learning from neurocognitive science is that 'neurons that fire together, wire together'. To raise a good reader, those neurons need to fire sufficiently and over a long enough period of time to happen automatically.[42]

So how do subtitles get children to keep up that unwitting practice?

The key is high-interest content. MIT's John Gabrieli, a leading cognitive neuroscientist, explains that emotion and motivation 'propel learning very powerfully'.[43] Subtitling content that is interesting to children fires a steady stream of consistent letter–sound associations in the brain, and therefore reinforces language and what letters sound like.

In the case of popular songs, nursery rhymes and repeatedly watched cartoons, there is the additional advantage of predictable text. The visual and auditory pathways involved in reading are strengthened gradually and subconsciously, and all as a by-product of watching content that the child has an inherent motivation to watch.

Put subtitles on a programme that a child wants to watch and they are going to read it again and again!

Does subtitle exposure lead to improved reading skills?

In a nutshell, yes! Results from a study where subtitles were used continuously in the home led to children scoring significantly higher on word identification and comprehension than children who had not been exposed to subtitles.[44,45]

Making changes to policy

In the past, using subtitles was difficult. No doubt some of us can remember hitting '888' on the remote control and having to do so *every time* the TV was switched on. But now, children's profiles can be created that identify which programmes should have subtitles. Now we need a policy to help make things happen.

We want all media catering to under-12-year-olds to have subtitles on by default.* We are working with broadcasters to change their default settings. However, if this does not occur in a timely manner, we are seeking to change broadcast legislation and regulators' powers in this space.

Policy change is possible. India is already leading the way. It has implemented a national policy across terrestrial TV to aid literacy, and requires 50 per cent of content to have subtitles shown by default by 2025.

Having subtitles on children's TV to improve literacy is a universally popular idea in government and beyond. It's simple and quick to implement, and won't cost the taxpayer a thing, yet could have a profound impact on life chances for our children. As gifts to the next generation go, this is right up there as one of the simplest and smartest things we can do.

Harnessing the power of digital technology to create the brightest future can be simple!

Minimising the risks to children from digital services

I often hear people of my parents' generation talk about sending their kids outside to play and having no idea where they were until they came home when it was dark or they were hungry. In Chapter 5 I discussed the way that this culture has fundamentally changed, meaning children today do less exploring, less evaluating of risk, and even less choosing of their friends.

But in the online world things are very different. Parents generally have no idea how long their children are online, where they spend time, with whom or what they are doing there. Some parents feel unequipped when it comes to digital spaces, and perhaps hope that government regulation and laws will keep their children safe online, the way the Highway Code, driving licences, the police and laws do on the roads.

But the reality is that the online world is infinite, complex, under-regulated and contains unique risks for children. So what are these risks and how can the government minimise them?

---

* This is for all children's content that isn't broadcast live. With live shows, subtitles have to be generated automatically by machines, and this causes a few issues with quality.

Digital risks and challenges

The best outline of the different types of risk children face online that I have seen comes from the OECD. Its 'typology' sets out the types of risk, how many cut across different aspects of children's well-being and how the risks manifest themselves. Take a look:

Risk categories	Content	Conduct	Contact	Consumer
Cross-cutting risks	Privacy risks (interpersonal, institutional and commercial)			
	Advanced technology risks (eg, AI, predictive analysis, biometrics)			
	Health and well-being risks			
Manifestations	Hateful content	Hateful behaviour	Hateful encounters	Marketing
	Harmful content	Harmful behaviour	Harmful encounters	Commercial profiling
	Illegal content	Illegal behaviour	Illegal encounters	Financial
	Disinformation	User-generated problematic behaviour	Other problematic encounters	Security

Source: Based on the OECD's *Revised Typology of Risks*[46]

Let's consider a fictional example of what these might mean for a young teenager. Thirteen-year-old Noah is searching for videos online when pop-up advertisements with pornographic or violent content appear (content risk). He opens his social media messaging account and sees one of his peers 'sexting' in a group chat (conduct risk). On his social media profile, he receives messages telling Noah his skin colour makes him less attractive (contact risk). While scrolling he comes across content that advertises gambling to him, offering free bets on signing up (consumer risk). It paints a scary picture. Evaluating and mitigating those risks will be by individual children, parents or citizens. Ideally it should also be collectively, via governments and the responsibilities demanded of digital corporations.

The UK is leading efforts to mitigate risks of the digital world to children. The UK Parliament has set global standards with which digital corporations must comply. Leading this drive has been Baroness Beeban Kidron, a crossbench Peer in the House of Lords, film producer and founder of the 5Rights Foundation. 5Rights works to ensure children secure their five rights when using online services: the right to remove, to know, to be safe and supported, to be informed and conscious when using, and to digital literacy. 5Rights' work and Beeban's steadfast resolve have resulted in landmark legislation that has raised the bar for the rest of the world.

The Age Appropriate Design Code

The *Age Appropriate Design Code* (aka *The Children's Code*) was written into British law at the same time as General Data Protection Regulation (GDPR) was implemented. The Code mandates website and app owners take the 'best interests' of children using their sites into account, otherwise face fines of up to 4 per cent of annual global turnover.[47] The definition of 'best interests' or 'age appropriate' was cleverly given little detail in the legislation, other than simply requiring the independent UK Information Commissioner to define what each means. This gives flexibility to evolve or adapt definitions. Coupled with an increase in the powers of the Information Commissioner's Office, the result has been transformative.[48] Unless they can prove their service is not likely to be used at all by children, companies face a choice: make their entire offering compatible with the Code, or find a way to identify younger users and treat them with care. The Code also prohibits the use of 'nudge' techniques aimed at encouraging children to give up more of their privacy than they would otherwise choose to. It calls on companies to minimise data they collect about children, and requires privacy options that default to the maximum security.[49]

This legislation has already had an impact, including:

- TikTok turning off notifications for children past bedtime;[50]
- Instagram disabling targeted adverts for under-18s entirely;[51]
- YouTube turning off autoplay for teen users;[52]

- Google allowing anyone under 18, or their parents, to request the removal of images from search results, while it has also acted to disable entirely its location history service for children;[53]
- a plethora of changes at Facebook bringing tighter default sharing settings and protection from 'potentially suspicious accounts' (namely adults blocked on the site by large numbers of young people).[54]

The Code is landmark legislation, but it is not enough. For example, while it deals with age-appropriate content, it does not deliver assurance regarding who is viewing that content. An age-assurance process would offer important due diligence, but wouldn't mitigate children's privacy and safety risks. The core challenge to age-assurance solutions, however, as the 5Rights Foundation noted in its seminal report *But How Do They Know It Is a Child?*,[55] is that they all are currently undermined by the lack of common definitions, agreed standards and regulatory oversight. Each social media service effectively comes up with their own definition of an adult, almost always at a different age to society's norms, national legislations and the United Nations Convention on the Rights of the Child (UNCRC). Most social media accounts can be set up if the user confirms they are 13 years of age or older.[56] Self-confirmation, at the time of writing, is the only mechanism to check if the user is an 'adult'.

The 5Rights Foundation also notes that statutory codes for age assurance will drive the development of new products and services, and create a richer and more diverse digital ecosystem in which children are an acknowledged user group. A regulatory age-assurance framework offering certainty to businesses and trusted by parents and children will drive innovations and redesigns that better support children's participation in the digital world, maximising opportunities and minimising risks.[57] Indeed, Beeban told me that, if successful, not only would children thrive online, but it would also help businesses differentiate their offering between teens and adults, thus creating market sectors, advertising opportunities and products for different age groups. The likelihood of success, she added, depends on the incorporation of children's voices, views and experiences when developing legislation, definitions and age-relevant content and products.

Children co-designing content, user experience, safeguards and legislation will help ensure children's online experience is safe and beneficial. Michael Preston, Zaza Kabayadondo and Stacy Galiatsos know this. Together they have written this essay.

Designing for thriving – by, with and for children

Michael Preston, Executive Director at the Joan Ganz Cooney Center and commissioner in the UK's Digital Futures Commission, *Zaza Kabayadondo*, designer and researcher in EdTech and *Stacy Galiatsos*, consultant in digital learning systems

Many of the world's nearly 2 billion children do not have access to the internet, but for those who do, childhood has become defined by the digital experience. Today's youth move seamlessly among face-to-face conversations, texting, watching videos, gaming and so on, often synchronously and in coordination with each other.

Smart government policies have a significant role in setting standards, applying pressure and creating incentives for actors to develop a digital world where children are not just safe, but can thrive.

At the Joan Ganz Cooney Center at Sesame Workshop, our team of researchers and practitioners are leading efforts to augment good policy with good collaborative practice. Through various initiatives we partner with corporate and non-profit product teams in *designing by, with and for children*.

New playgrounds

Industry favours those who can bring digital products to market quickly, but rapid cycles of innovation come with a heavy price: often innovators only have time to design for a 'general audience' and fail to consider children. Yet children are often the earliest adopters. Today's creators *must* assume that their digital product or service will be used by children in some way.

Online video platforms are a prime example, offering opportunities as valuable tools for learning and for amplifying and elevating youth voice. However, they collect large amounts of personal data and can also increase children's exposure to developmentally inappropriate and even illegal content. Their algorithms encourage children to watch one video after another, known as 'going down the rabbit hole', and create bubbles of information (or misinformation) that can mislead children.

From safe to thriving

We know from 50-plus years of *Sesame Street* that it *is* possible to centre children's learning, development and equitable experience in product development *and* be successful in the market. In the 1960s, our organisation's co-founder Joan Ganz Cooney proved that families and children should not settle for what was once described as 'a vast wasteland' on television, and advocated for television's potential as a learning medium.

We help developers define, integrate and measure 'what good looks like' in designing for kids. We've outlined three levels at which products should be judged:

1. At the *safe* level, designers must minimise risks to privacy and safety and also ensure that children's best interests[58] are honoured. In the UK, standards are legislatively mandated by the *Age Appropriate Design Code*.[59]
2. At the *inclusive* level, designers should create environments for wide accessibility, consider developmental appropriateness and design for inclusion by serving populations too often not prioritised (such as youth with learning differences or from different backgrounds and communities).
3. At the *thriving* level, designers should look to empower children to find meaning in digital encounters by enabling play, collaboration and creativity and promoting well-being as an outcome.

The traditional approach of playtesting with children tends to focus on identifying problems and getting user feedback. Our Center supports product developers to co-design with children by engaging them as design partners at the *beginning* of product development cycles, thus emphasising the opportunities to move from 'safe' to 'thriving'. Co-design with children from diverse backgrounds as equal partners is a 'win–win': product teams benefit from new ideas and the unique perspectives of their target audience, while participating children develop skills as their ideas impact real-life products.

Policies that incentivise and support children's digital thriving

Many of the companies we work with undertake co-design because they have missions to foster kids' learning and healthy development. Others respond to customer, employee and leadership demands for exploring new approaches to building better products beyond safety and privacy features.

Government policy can encourage more companies to build digital products that prioritise children's thriving.

The UK government[60] and international organisations[61] have built a foundation for this work, setting out important corporate context, guidance and accountability for digital products to attain the 'safe' level. The UNCRC Comment No 25 on children's rights in the digital environment[62] goes further, detailing all the rights that must be supported for children to have an opportunity to reach their full potential online – not only safety, but also access to information, freedom of assembly and the right to play.

Beyond safety and privacy, what can government do to propel digital media companies to go further and design for children's thriving? Here are three ideas:

- *Promote a common understanding of children's digital well-being.* Promoting an accessible and research-based definition of digital well-being can help companies set goals and change practice accordingly.
- *Accelerate research that informs industry practice.* Develop a digital well-being repository so research and evidence-based examples are accessible to development teams. Fund better understanding of connections between children's digital media use and thriving, including longitudinal studies.
- *Incentivise industry change.* Incentives should recognise industry's challenges and elevate good practice as they shift from 'safe' to 'thriving'. One method is to publicly recognise companies that lead in this space. Support certifications that help companies designing for inclusion and well-being to stand out as the gold standard. Another is to enable and reward sharing of best practices so they become more of a public good than a trade secret. This could also include grants for product development or manufacturing changes or tax credits for companies that illustrate product changes informed by the principles of children's thriving.

We believe that children's safety is only the starting point. Children's right to thrive is paramount and must remain constant throughout the emergence of new media and technological innovation. We are on the cusp of a new wave of ideas to create a digital world that prioritises the well-being of children and puts their thriving at the centre of design. The companies that emerge as the most innovative will be those that see children's best interests as a marker of excellence.

The Online Safety Bill

The other game-changing and globally relevant piece of British legislation (albeit not yet passed into law, and therefore not yet an Act, at the time of writing in mid-2023), is the Online Safety Bill.[63] It has proven a difficult commitment because it raises the question of what society prioritises: the safety of its children, or the right to express 'harmful but legal' statements (that children can see). The Bill has been much delayed in its progress as government grapples with this challenge. As I write, there is a danger that the Bill will fall because of the nuance of this prioritisation, which would catastrophically fail children.

The Bill is focused on 'user-to-user services',[64] and would create a duty of care for online platforms, requiring them to act against harmful content, whether illegal or legal. Platforms failing this duty would face fines up to £18 million or 10 per cent of their annual turnover. It would also empower Ofcom to block access to particular websites. If passed, the duty of care would apply to services where there are reasonable grounds to believe that there is a material risk of significant harm; and that such services have a significant number of UK users, or target UK users, or are capable of being used in the UK. This would challenge platforms that do not currently age-verify users to prevent children from being exposed to unrestricted legal, but harmful, content adults may access.

The success of the Bill is vital to helping children thrive in the digital world. It goes some way in addressing the age-assurance hole in online child safety protection (although the need to overcome the lack of common definitions, agreed standards and regulatory oversight could remain), and in mandating age checks for pornography websites. If passed into law, how the British government enforces it and how the digital platform companies respond is critical.

As I write this paragraph, the words of the coroner at the conclusion to the inquest into Molly Russell's death ring in my head. He said: 'It would not be safe to leave suicide as a conclusion. She died from an act of self-harm while suffering from depression and the negative effects of online content', adding that the images of self-harm and suicide she viewed online 'shouldn't have been available for a child to see'.[65] There cannot be a bigger imperative to pass the Bill.

Conclusions

There can be few things more indispensable to a 21st-century childhood than digital connectivity. Digital will continue to evolve at a dizzying speed, and so we will continue to grapple with the opportunities and risks it presents. Solutions have been found, for example Estonia has set precedents in harnessing opportunities and the UK has enacted world-leading legislation, especially if it does pass the Online Safety Bill. We know, however, with the pace of evolution, solutions invariably fall short of our future aspirations in *raising the nation*.

This chapter has presented lots of ideas on how to bridge that gap. Henry and Oli shared a simple one: subtitles by default. Beeban's expertise, passion and persistence helped push Parliament to legislate. Amy and Ellen focused on equitable access and distribution, while Michael, Zaza and Stacy looked at content and services. What unites them and others, however, is that children must be an active part of solutions. Co-design has been a concept that has flowed through most of the ideas presented here. It is critical to a child-centred digital future, and therefore simply the future.

This chapter started with Molly Russell. Her death is an example of how society fails its children. But society can look at itself, learn, adapt and act. As we digest that thought, the next chapter considers other children society has failed, and how that could change if the determination is there.

One additional essay, containing another proposal for government, is hosted at www.raisingthenation.co.uk:

- Nicholas Carlisle is a child psychotherapist who, for 20 years, has campaigned to improve children's digital well-being. He founded No Bully and Power of Zero, and has written on how governments can support children's well-being in a digitised world.

9

Children society fails most

Surely the greatest burning injustice ... is the poverty of the innocent ... of children too young to know they are not to blame.

Gordon Brown[1]

I'm a hopeless gardener. Whether it's a flower bed or veg patch: nothing thrives. This summer I was given a beautiful potted plant, which sits across from my desk as I write. It struggled to thrive from day one. I under- and over-watered it, moved it to and from sunny and shady spots, all to no avail. It wasn't until my wife suggested the soil might need some attention that it started to perk up. It's now positively blooming!

I share this to reflect that when a plant wilts we consider all conditions within its ecosystem that help it thrive. But do we do the same when a child struggles?

This chapter is all about the children our society fails, the groups of children with common experiences that, because of collective choices, we have, implicitly or explicitly, chosen to under-support.

I start with an essay that is the story of one person's lived experience shared in a raw, insightful and defiant way. When the author first spoke to me about it, I felt ashamed of our society. That author is Jemeillia, who was 16 years old at the time of writing and, a word of warning, her essay contains a first-hand account of neglect and physical, sexual and emotional abuse.

Government parents

Jemeillia, young person in the care system

I'm a nobody in the eyes of society, only someone to be judged and misunderstood due to my title as a 'care leaver', someone who has left the care system. I am a 16-year-old who has gone through 13 years of abuse: physically, emotionally and sexually. A 16-year-old who was neglected yet was a carer for her bi-polar mum, despite what she did to me.

I entered a system with protocols, safeguarding and risk assessments that determined and restricted my freedom. They promised love and support, but where was it? Government parents* are emotionally neglectful ones, with only a shallow understanding based on their official training and 'experience'. The system created to serve children has become over-professionalised, and it actually ruins any opportunity for children in care to heal from their trauma and grow within society. This is clear in the numbers: one-third of care leavers become homeless in the first two years after they leave care.[2] Despite children in care making up less than 1 per cent of the population, care leavers make up a quarter of the prison population.[3] Further, 45 per cent of looked-after children (and 72 per cent of those in residential care) have a mental health disorder – compared to one in ten in the general population – and looked-after children and care leavers are between four and five times more likely to attempt suicide in adulthood.[4]

Social services have been involved in my life since 2008. Before I was taken into the care system, two social workers saw the emotional abuse, but did nothing beyond sit on the sofa and watch. At home, before or after school, my back would meet a belt. Endless tears soaked my pillows every night. His hands would meet my skin. It was never a kind touch. It was never one of love. It was of lust and anger. I was my parents' ragdoll. The cries for help were quickly dismissed. My tears quickly wiped away.

By 11 years old I had no hope left. Life as I knew it was nothing but pain. I began drowning in depression and anxiety. At 13, I came into the care system, freshly diagnosed with complex post-traumatic stress disorder (PTSD). The only time I was allowed outside my placement was to go to therapy. I was

---

* By 'government parents' I'm referring to the corporate parents/social workers who hold parental responsibility over children in care and care leavers. However, they are far from parents, and, ironically, I see them as just professionals who are there to check in once a month, risk assessing decisions and behaviour issues young people display.

constantly moved from placement to placement, so there was no stability. I had been removed from my mum, my dog and from my home because of her parenting and her poor mental health, only to enter environments that mimicked it in a different way. I went from one hell to another, being hurt and neglected in a different way, albeit this time in a professionally accepted way. The only thing you learn from the system is how not to get attached to anyone, social workers or carers, because they will be gone, or you will be gone in a couple months.

By the time I turned 14, I was deemed 'unsuitable' for family life and was put into care homes. Social workers define young people by risk assessments and what's written on paper. They define young people by their mental health issues. They were so fixated on keeping me safe, I couldn't even have a shower by myself without supervision. In care I was retraumatised and triggered by other young people self-harming in front of me. Some stole my stuff, while others taught me how to cut myself from a mug or a grater. After a while, I was desensitised to blood in the bathroom, the headbanging and the screams.

Running away felt safer for me, just as it does for almost 150 children in care who run away every day.[5] What does this say about the system? The fact that one in ten young people in care last year felt the need to escape a place meant to be their *home*? I'm here to voice the words that the system silenced. We were given a sentence for our parents' mistakes. A sentence of neglect, pain, trauma and heartache. A sentence that leads to drug addiction, unhealthy relationships and with no trust left to give or receive.

In being given the opportunity to show the world the truth, I hope to ignite passion in others. I've found my voice. I've found a purpose. I've found hope again. I learned things I shouldn't have, but I'm in a better place now. I live by myself. Surviving, not thriving, but I have freedom, which is all I ever wanted.

If you are a social worker, a government official or anyone working with children and young people, does it go against protocols to comfort us? Hug us? It seems that way to me. Instead, you just move us constantly, leave us to a new social worker, and make it hard for us to build trust. All I ask is that you listen to young people's voices and help them to achieve their goals.

If you are a child in care or a care leaver, believe me when I say 'this will end'. You will once again be in control of your life. Don't allow this artificial system to dampen your personality, your fierceness. What the system views as risk is what the real world sees as opportunity. Every single one of us dreams of something, and it's so important not to let that dream die. Love yourself, even if no one else has.

When I was younger, I thought the system was there to save me. But it only broke me more. All I want now is that future generations growing up within this system are genuinely safe, cared for and loved, and treated like children and not convicts.

So who am I? I'm a somebody. Someone special. Someone whose abilities and potential have constantly been undermined due to my age and circumstances. The government and government parents may think that I am a nobody right now, but they are wrong. I am not just the voice of one; I'm the voice of every child in care, the thousands who've faced this injustice. The reason I didn't end up killing myself is because I realised I would be allowing the injustice to win, I realised that the children left behind would continue to suffer. I realised that this can't continue.

Knowledge is power, and now you, anyone reading this, know the pain children in care carry. Now you have the power. What will you do to use it and make a difference?

It is certainly an uncomfortable read. Children treated like convicts, not children, and for crimes they did not commit. Jemeillia's story illustrates systems designed for efficiency over the well-being of vulnerable children, for 'computer says no' risk assessment over human love. It's vital we don't shy away from very real consequences when, as a society, we fail to get things right for children. In this, the airline industry is a good place to start: its culture of open communication and communal learning has been essential for reducing accidents. The industry prioritises looking at all relevant factors where things have gone wrong, and asks 'why?'

We know some reasons why children end up vulnerable. They include adverse childhood experiences (ACEs)[6] that increase risk of poorer health and ability to reach one's potential in life. They also include risk factors beyond the capacity of a child or family to protect against, such as living in an area with high levels of crime or unstable housing,[7] growing up in poverty, or simply having a particular ethnic heritage.[8]

Taking the impact of wider contexts seriously demands we ask: are we proud of the services we provide for children who draw the short straw at the start of their life? To answer, we'll look closely at the circumstances of certain groups of vulnerable children: those in care, those living with special educational needs and disabilities (SEND), those who are displaced from their homeland, and those in poverty.

A careless social care system

When I first read Jemeillia's essay, I naively hoped her experiences were exceptional. Tragically not. In 2022, the independent MacAlister Review of children's social care reported: 'What we have currently is a system increasingly skewed to crisis intervention, with outcomes for children that continue to be unacceptably poor and costs that continue to rise … a radical reset is now unavoidable.'[9]

The care system exists to safeguard and protect children vulnerable to domestic neglect and abuse, support families to care for their children and, where necessary, provide an alternative safe, stable and loving home. It therefore exists for those children in the absolute greatest need. Local authorities have the legal duty to provide this acute support, and unfortunately, demand is growing.

So what do children and families experience when they come into contact with the children's social care system?

First, they encounter a workforce under strain – two-thirds of whom report deteriorating personal mental health due to working conditions.[10] Social workers have to ration scarce resources. It is a workforce with a burdensome bureaucracy, spending 80 per cent of their time on paperwork and just 20 per cent in direct contact with children and families.[11]

Graham Handscomb, with lived experience as a child in care, has written this essay on what government should do to better support social workers' vital work.

Between a rock and a hard place
Graham Handscomb, Professor of Education and ex-local authority Director of Education

> High caseloads and limited resources to support me in my job, as well as support services available for families, leave me stretched physically

in terms of time and availability, but also emotionally. It leaves more room for mistakes when working with vulnerable children and families. (Social worker, Liverpool)[12]

Children are magnificent and special. This is not just because today's children are tomorrow's society, but also because the integral qualities children have are so valuable for our world. So, the care and welfare of children is perhaps our most important responsibility, and yet, we are falling short, particularly for children who are most vulnerable and for those in the care system.

Sadly, the awful stories that hit the headlines of the abuse of children, often within their own homes, are familiar. In the post-mortems, social workers are typically in the firing line. But where there is fault, it is often in the system as much as the shortcomings of individuals. Social workers are often caught between a rock and a hard place – forging trusting relationships with at-risk families while at the same time ensuring robust safeguarding and protection – all against diminishing resources and huge caseloads.

A personal journey and reflection

First, let me set some context. I grew up within the care system, beginning in a children's home during my early years, and then fostered by my grandmother. I became a teacher, followed by a career in school improvement services, and then Professor of Education.

A few years ago, on something of a whim, I contacted my childhood local authority to ask about records of my early youth. What then happened was extraordinary! First by email and then by post, I received a raft of information, including every social workers' report on me, submitted almost every month throughout my first 18 years. My whole childhood mapped out via third parties' paperwork.

Among this was a report of when a social worker took my brother and me to visit my mother, who was in a mental hospital, where she was incarcerated, on and off, for much of her life. This led me to penning a poetic reimagining of this visit, using extracts from the verbatim written record of the social worker. Responses to the poem have been interesting, but the most intriguing was of a friend who heavily sympathised with the social worker. I see her point, and have since reconsidered the challenges facing those who work in social care.

Stressed, overworked and overwhelmed

The resounding message from social workers' unions, the Association of Directors of Children's Services and even the government itself is of a crisis in children's social work. Responding to a survey from their trades union Unison, social workers described rising levels of anxiety from being unable to meet the needs of children with whom they work: 'Caseloads have increased and resources are decreasing' (social worker, Basildon); 'We struggle to deliver vital services to young children and their families because of the cuts' (social worker, Worsley).[13]

During the pandemic chronic conditions became even worse. The government's longitudinal study of social workers[14] that found a growing majority 'are feeling overworked and stressed, while job satisfaction – though still high – is falling'.[15] Many were looking to change their career and more local authorities now recruit non-permanent staff.

Major factors contributing to this crisis are burgeoning caseloads, inadequate management and poor support. Indeed, where councils are judged 'inadequate', measures put in place often prove counterproductive. For instance, in Bradford the approach to improve services entailed a 'culture of "doing to" rather than "working with"'. Staff felt disempowered and that many of the bureaucratic changes 'did not make sense' and limited their ability to 'exercise their professional judgement'.[16,17] The government commissioner reporting these concerns concluded that a focus on process rather than practice undermined the professional autonomy of experienced practitioners and 'their ability to make decisions based on the needs and circumstances of individual children'.[18] This situation is also often compounded by a succession of temporary senior leadership teams being installed following a poor inspection report.

All this leads to multi-causal stress and instability for social workers. Their well-being has diminished considerably, with a growing number saying that their mental health has 'got worse', and some even saying that it has 'collapsed'.[19]

A call for radical change

A radical government could:

- increase funding, targeted to enable staff to work professionally and effectively;
- reduce caseloads, via recruitment and streamlining reporting to focus on what is essential for children's well-being;
- invest in mental health and well-being support for social workers;
- address shortcomings robustly, but not through a blame regime;
- establish stable management mobilising resources, enabling professionals to do their job well.

Unsung heroes

Social workers are crucial in helping support, care for and protect children at risk. Responding to numerous concerns raised by the evidence cited in this essay a government spokesperson said: 'Social workers are often our unsung heroes, doing their best in very difficult jobs, and their welfare and well-being is of huge importance.'[20] It's time this well-meaning rhetoric was accompanied by sustained action if these vital workers are to give of their best for our most vulnerable children.

Graham makes a powerful case for the *unsung heroes*. We know that they and the care system more broadly must sometimes decide that a child's best interests are served by being taken away from their family and placed into foster care or a care home. But are those places actually fit for purpose?

Care homes

As a society we have got muddled, creating a system where private profit competes with child well-being in goal setting. While children's care homes in England were once run by local authorities and charities, they are now dominated by for-profit private businesses that demand extraordinary returns above market rate. For example, the Competition and Markets Authority (CMA) found that the 15 biggest private providers of children's homes made average annual operating profits of 22 per cent between 2016 and 2022. Contrast this with Amazon, which made 6 per cent, or Tesco, at 7 per cent.[21] Annually £250 million of profit is taken out of the system by their owners, rather than being reinvested in quality provision for children in their care. It is worth noting that the Welsh and Scottish governments are taking steps to end profit making in children's care, while in England the Conservative Children's Minister Will Quince told the Commons he has no issue with profit in general – only profiteering.[22] It is a similar issue to that of nursery provision addressed in Chapter 3, on which June O'Sullivan focused her essay.

Some argue that, with appropriate regulation and competition, the market should ensure value for money for the state and provide an optimal service for children. But current outcomes do not seem to justify such a scenario. The CMA has concluded that the profits of the big providers are above those expected in a well-functioning market.[23] A 2022 BBC investigation into one large private provider of care homes led the regulator Ofsted to re-inspect five they had previously rated 'good' or 'outstanding', closing three immediately and re-rating the others as 'inadequate', after finding 'serious and widespread failures'.[24]

The (English) Children's Act 1989 sets out how society sees the role of the state in looking after children who need care. It places responsibility with local authorities to safeguard and promote the welfare of children, and costs taxpayers £10 billion per year.[25] Rather than drawing on and supporting family and community, the system too often tries to replace human bonds and relationships with professionals and services.[26] Demand for the care system is shaped by other professions (health, education and the wider economy), but the system is unable to shape the forces that drive demand for its activities. Ostensibly with good intentions, the care system tries to compartmentalise and solve complex problems that do not fit neatly into boxes.

Joined-up services

The children's social system was not designed to be this way. Back in 1968 concern over such siloed boxes led to the Seebohm Report, which recommended establishing a single local government social services department encompassing health, education, income, housing and social welfare, together with new responsibilities including community well-being, as well as directing additional resources to areas with higher need.[27] Yet structural, economic and cultural barriers prevented progress, and instead, social care separated into adult and children's work and the recognition that children and their needs cannot be separated from the families and the communities in which they live was lost. I think it is time to revisit the ideas and principles of the Seebohm Report.

As mentioned earlier, the MacAlister Review[28] found a system increasingly skewed to crisis intervention rather than the long-term outcomes for children. It made radical recommendations towards a service that provides intensive help to families in crisis, acts decisively in response to abuse, unlocks the potential of wider family networks to raise children, puts lifelong loving relationships at the heart of the care system, and lays the foundations for a good life for those who have been in care. It is a powerful document that the government is currently evaluating.

The ethos of both the MacAlister and Seebohm reports, although separated by over 50 years, chime with the principles I envisage at the heart of a National Children's Service.

Special educational needs and disabilities

In 1994 a global conference was held in Salamanca, Spain, adopting a framework that called on all schools to 'accommodate all children, regardless of their physical, social, intellectual, emotional, linguistic or other conditions'.[29] The resulting UNESCO *Salamanca Statement* is perhaps the most significant document on SEND,* not just because of the momentum it sparked and its push towards inclusive education, but because it also explained why an inclusive education matters:

> Regular schools with this inclusive orientation are the most effective means of combating discriminatory attitudes, creating welcoming communities, building an inclusive society and achieving education for all; moreover, they provide an effective education to the majority of children and improve the efficiency and ultimately the cost effectiveness of the entire education system.[30]

In other words, it is not just beneficial for children with additional needs; it is beneficial for all children, for communities and for society at large, and is likely to be less economically costly.[31]

---

* A child or young person has special educational needs and disabilities if they have a learning difficulty and/or a disability that means they need special health and education support. This covers four broad areas: communication and interaction, cognition and learning, social, emotional and mental health difficulties and sensory and/or physical needs.

There are 1.4 million children in England who have SEND (16 per cent of pupils).[32] Most have their needs met by schools without additional funding. Families and schools can, however, apply to have a formal assessment by the local authority for additional resources. If the application is successful, they get an Education, Health and Care Plan (EHCP), a legally binding document describing a child's SEND and necessary support.

So why is it that three decades after the *Salamanca Statement*, SEND provision in England is in crisis? Why did the cross-party Education Select Committee in 2019 report that there is 'overwhelming evidence' that a generation of young people are being let down despite 'good intentions'?[33] Let's take a closer look.

The English SEND ecosystem currently has:

- increasing numbers of children with EHCPs; in 2022 there were 475,000, nearly double those in 2015;[34]
- a 40 per cent increase in pupils with an EHCP attend special (not mainstream) schools or independent schools (local authorities have to fund these more expensive places);[35]
- an adversarial process, where too many parents have to take their case to tribunal to get funding, even though 95 per cent of such cases are found in favour of parents;[36]
- joint working between health and education ministries is poor, so consequently intervention is often missed and a postcode lottery of provision results;[37]
- a school system that is not always inclusive. There may be little impetus for schools to 'do the right thing' in supporting children with SEND, particularly when the EHCP does not bring adequate financial support to cover provision.

Funding is often blamed for the system not working for many children – the National Education Union estimates there is a £2 billion shortfall.[38] But regardless of funding, a huge cultural shift is needed at all levels to transform from 'unlawful practices, bureaucratic nightmares, buck passing and a lack of accountability'[39] to deliver the aims of the *Salamanca Statement*.

This can be done. For example, Italy has had a ground-breaking policy since the 1970s, Integrazione Scolastica[40] ('integrated or inclusive schools'). It has no specialist schools or dedicated settings, instead aiming to be truly inclusive. Additional support is provided within the mainstream setting including via support teachers in all schools who work with children with additional needs, doing so in collaboration with teachers and other professionals to ensure sound provision.[41] Class sizes are limited to 25 students, with a limit of two students who have additional needs per class.

In England, the 2022 Green Paper★ *Right Support, Right Place, Right Time* sought to make changes to turn 'a vicious cycle into a virtuous one',[42] by establishing a national system for SEND support provision. This proposal has been received with cautious optimism by those working in the sector, given its ambition for change, but also with ongoing frustration over a continued lack of focus on a culture of inclusive mainstream education.[43] Even if the Green Paper becomes law, until the principles of the *Salamanca Statement* are embraced and implemented in systems and culture, children with SEND will remain part of those whom society fails most.

Child refugees

Perhaps the most vulnerable people on earth are those who are stateless. And the most vulnerable people who are stateless are children. At the end of 2021 there were 27 million refugees,[44] 12 million of whom were stateless,[45] and over half of whom were children.[46] They are children who have been forced to leave their country, and at times, their own family, to escape war, persecution or natural disasters. In a VUCA world the number of refugee and stateless children is likely to continue to rise.

Why does this matter in seeking to build a country whose future is brighter because its children thrive?

It matters in cold numbers

In the year to December 2022, excluding Ukrainians, there were 75,000 applications for asylum in the UK, of which one in

---

★ Green Papers are consultation documents produced by the government. They give the opportunity for feedback and expert insight on policy or legislative proposals.

five related to a child and over 5,000 related to unaccompanied children.[47] In addition, over 100,000 refugees arrived from Ukraine,[48] one in three of whom was a child.[49] That is a lot of children, some of whom were totally alone, most of whom did not speak English well, did not know British culture, and all of whom needed support in navigating systems to ensure they received their rights and entitlements. My family has the privilege of hosting one such family, but we can see, on a daily basis, the barriers they face in securing the services they are entitled to for their four-year-old son – despite the unanimously warm, kind and genuine intentions from those within the welfare system.

It matters on a 'human' level

Although the vast majority of refugees will remain in refugee camps and/or in countries neighbouring their own, providing sufficient support to people forced to leave their homes (perhaps especially children) is a moral responsibility of all global citizens.

I have experienced first-hand the abject vulnerability of refugees when I visited the Kakuma refugee camp in Kenya. The terror of one young mother in particular, etched on her face, has stayed with me. She had just crossed into Kenya from South Sudan with her baby and toddler. She was petrified of having her children taken from her, of them all being sent back, of her abusive husband finding them, and of the South Sudanese militia finding her, or, more accurately, her children. Meeting her and hearing her story has had a profound and enduring impact on me.

It matters on an economic level

There is a dividend in both welcoming refugees claiming asylum (for example, in the UK) and in supporting their welfare in countries to where they first flee (and where the vast majority stay).[50] The fact that refugee populations are young and include many children means dividends to the countries where they find new homes pay back for longer too.

Sherrie Westin is President of Sesame Workshop, the creator of the iconic television show *Sesame Street*. She has led many programmes to support young child refugees to have better outcomes, and has written this essay on why it is in a government's interest to fund such work.

A big opportunity in a narrow window: early childhood investments in humanitarian crises

Sherrie Westin, President of Sesame Workshop

Meet Somaya. A vibrant six-year-old girl, she climbs trees, loves to learn and knows she can become anything she wants.

Somaya can dream big for her future because she has opportunities to learn, play and build the skills she needs to reach her full potential – opportunities that she didn't always have. Somaya and her family are among almost one million Rohingya refugees who fled violence in Myanmar and who now live in sprawling camps in Bangladesh. When they first arrived at the camp, Somaya's parents were concerned about lack of access to education and safe spaces for their daughter to play during the most crucial years of her life.

Decades of research demonstrate the importance of a child's early years in shaping the developing brain, and how exposure to adversity can inhibit brain development, with long-term repercussions.[51,52] This is an especially high risk for millions of children, like Somaya, who have been forced to flee their homes, and the growing number of young children caught up in crises around the world. But we also know that quality early childhood development support – including education, health, nutrition, safety and positive relationships with caring adults – can help children overcome adversity and build a brighter future.[53]

A few months after Somaya's family arrived in the refugee camp, an opportunity opened for her to begin attending a BRAC Humanitarian Play Lab, where she could learn, play and grow in a safe and nurturing environment. The more she learns, her parents notice, the happier and more confident about her future she becomes.

As President of Sesame Workshop, the non-profit educational organisation behind *Sesame Street*, I have had the privilege of meeting families like Somaya's. Whether it's a Syrian father in a refugee camp in Jordan or an Afghan mother who has fled her country, they all say they want a brighter future for their children.

For more than 50 years, Sesame Workshop has harnessed the power of media through its beloved Muppet characters to help children grow smarter, stronger and kinder. We have addressed some of the biggest challenges facing the youngest children and their families – always through the lens of a child: from helping families cope with homelessness in the USA, to modelling gender equity in India and teaching life-saving hygiene habits in Ghana. Sesame Workshop works in more than 150 countries, and continues to look for ways to support the world's most vulnerable children.

In the Middle East, we're reaching millions of children affected by the Syrian refugee crisis through direct services in partnership with the International Rescue Committee, and our Arabic-language television show *Ahlan Simsim* (*Welcome Sesame*). Designed in collaboration with local advisers and consultation with families, *Ahlan Simsim* features characters children can relate to. One is a shy Muppet named Jad, who had to leave his home and recently moved to the Ahlan Simsim neighbourhood. He becomes best friends with Basma, a gregarious Muppet, who welcomes Jad to the neighbourhood with open arms. Together, they go on adventures, learn through play and practice, identifying and managing 'big feelings' – helping children build the social-emotional skills and resilience they need to overcome adversity and reach their full potential.

Rohingya girl playing with Basma
© Sesame Workshop. Photographer: Ryan Donnell

Our partnership with BRAC reaches children like Somaya in the Rohingya refugee camps and host communities in Bangladesh through direct services in homes, child-friendly spaces and health centres. Working with caregivers and community-based facilitators, we promote playful learning and nurturing care via videos, storybooks, posters and more. We know children learn best when they can see themselves and their own experiences reflected in our content. That's why we introduced Rohingya Muppets – six-year-old twins Noor and Aziz, who live in the refugee camps in Cox's Bazar. Rooted in the rich Rohingya culture and informed by extensive research and input from Rohingya families, Noor and Aziz enable Rohingya children to see themselves in our content. For most Rohingya children, Noor and Aziz are the very first characters in media who look and sound like them.

Our partnerships in Bangladesh and the Middle East are among the largest early childhood interventions in the history of humanitarian response, and we are rapidly expanding our work to reach families affected by crises around the world. This work will expand the existing evidence base on early childhood development in crisis contexts. We will share what we learn to empower others to adapt, scale and build on these lessons to support children and families affected by crises.

This transformation is overdue. Despite clear evidence that early childhood development programming has both immediate and long-term benefits, it is dramatically underfunded, so children who experience crises at the most consequential time in their lives – and who stand to gain the most from quality interventions – are the least served in humanitarian response.

Policy change is needed in three areas.

First, we need to ensure that the needs of young children affected by crisis are visible and understood, so investments can match the urgency. Globally, only 2 per cent of humanitarian assistance is dedicated to education, with only a tiny sliver allocated for early learning and nurturing care. We need humanitarian actors, donors and governments to lead efforts to ensure that early childhood development programming in crisis contexts is given the attention it deserves.

Second, we must engage all potential early childhood development financiers (state, but also private sector and international actors) to support a multi-sectoral approach that promises multi-sectoral impacts in return. If you care about nutrition, gender equity or shrinking disparities between rich and poor families, you should care about early childhood development too. It's crucial that policy makers and funders alike understand these connections.

Finally, it's time to normalise the importance of funding not only programme delivery, but also research, monitoring, evaluation and advocacy. Research helps implementers understand how to tailor programmes to suit specific contexts and assess impact. Monitoring and evaluation provide opportunities for course correction at important junctures. Funnelling this insight into advocacy means that initial investments can catalyse even more – reaching new stakeholders and investors committed to a child-centred future.

Investing in early childhood development is not only the right thing to do to protect the prospects of the youngest generation; it's also the smart thing to do for economic and social development. The UN has recognised early childhood development as a key driver of the Sustainable Development Goals – a powerful way to promote lifelong learning and well-being, reduce poverty and inequality, advance gender equity and build more peaceful and prosperous societies. If we are to achieve the future we want, we know that investing in children, especially the most vulnerable, is where it all begins.

Sherrie's case is difficult to argue against. It also allows us to reflect on why society should be urging government and global institutions to act for those who might never step foot in our own country. However, for those who do, the likelihood is that they will join the biggest group of children our country fails, those without enough to live on. Children living in poverty.

Poverty

In the UK we have chosen (through political priorities and choices endorsed by democratic mandates) to fail our children by increasing their chances of growing up in poverty on both an absolute and relative level.[54] In Chapter 2, I noted that the proportion of British children growing up in relative poverty has doubled since I was a baby. Meanwhile, inflation-adjusted GDP per person has more than doubled.[55] If that growth was evenly distributed, everyone in the UK would be more than twice as wealthy, in real terms, as each person was when I was born. To be really blunt, poverty in the UK is a matter of distribution, and therefore of political decisions. Or bluntly and uncomfortably – of democratic choice.

Anne Longfield has spent decades working to address child poverty. For six years she was the Children's Commissioner for England, the person at the heart of government, delivering for children and championing their voices and needs, especially the children we most fail. She continues as Chair of the independent

Commission on Young Lives that seeks to redesign the system of support for young people at risk, and has written this essay for us on child poverty.

Imagine if all kids counted

Anne Longfield CBE, campaigner, Chair of the Commission on Young Lives and former Children's Commissioner for England

Growing up in poverty is hard. It's not only the bare cupboards and the constant strain on your parents' faces as they try to make sure you get enough to eat, sometimes going without meals themselves; it's all the extras that poverty can bring with it: bad housing, poor health, not being able to go places and do things other children are doing and the long grind of low expectations that life isn't likely to get any better. Apart from the practical realities of not having enough money, poverty can eat away at self-belief and confidence. It limits opportunities, and ultimately limits life chances and ambitions.

I've worked with vulnerable children and families all my working life. Some of the stories I have heard over recent years from them wouldn't be out of place in a 19th-century Dickens novel. Children can have extraordinary resilience, and despite their circumstances are able to achieve remarkable things. But growing up poor is a tough mountain to climb, and for many children, particularly some of those who experience entrenched poverty over years (and generations), it can be an overwhelming burden.

A total of 4.2 million children live in poverty in the UK.[56] They are the group of the population most likely to have felt the impact of the COVID-19 pandemic, and their families are facing a deepening cost-of-living crisis. In several towns and cities in England, more than half of children live in poverty. Even prior to the pandemic, the number of children in poverty had already increased, and that number is likely to grow even further in the immediate future.

Poverty diminishes life chances

The UK is a prosperous nation, but the number of children living in poverty casts a long shadow; it stymies opportunity and wastes talent. Over recent years the educational achievement gap between children eligible for free school meals (FSM) (a widely used measure of low parental income) and their peers has widened, limiting not only the life chances of individuals, but also the prosperity of the whole nation. The consequences of poverty in childhood can affect adulthood, and then pass down from generation to generation. Failing to turn around the blight of child poverty is storing up social and economic problems for the future.

If we are serious about the need to 'level up' those parts of our country and society that are currently falling behind, decisive and bold measures need to be put in place to reduce child poverty, and quickly.

Previous governments have cut child poverty. The current government did too, briefly, when it raised Universal Credit during the pandemic. So it can be done, but it requires determination and political will. However, the difference to the lives of millions of children – and our collective futures – would be transformational.

What would it take? How could we transform these children's futures to give every child the opportunities they deserve?

Being bolder to help all children succeed
It seems obvious, but the starting point is a simple one: poor families need higher and more sustainable incomes. To achieve this requires more help to find secure employment that pays decent wages alongside low-cost childcare – 70 per cent of children living in low-income households have working families, but still face poverty.[57] Affordable and reliable childcare is an essential building block for families, alongside support for parents to build skills or even develop small businesses. Increasing social security support to low-income families (whether in work or otherwise) is an important way to get money directly to families. The two-child benefits policy (that prevents benefit payments to a third and subsequent children) has been a disaster for some families. Scrapping it would have an immediate impact on some of the poorest households.

It is also important to break the link between poverty and opportunity. Here we need to be much bolder, determined and more creative.

Imagine if children in the poorest neighbourhoods had the richest early years experiences with state-of-the-art centres, staffed by our most promising and skilled early years workers, working closely alongside health professionals to identify if children need additional support and provide it.

Imagine if we offered the least advantaged children the best opportunities to learn in schools: the most skilled teachers, the highest achieving schools and the best support to help them succeed in school and in life.

Imagine if all our schools were open from dawn until late, weekends and holidays – a bright beacon in the community – places full of good activities going on to develop hobbies and interests. All supported by adults children trust and are inspired by.

Imagine if our poorest communities were brimming with community activities, with libraries full of books, reading and storytelling, sports and arts activities, youth groups as well as programmes for caregivers to gain new experiences and skills as well as access to advice and support.

Imagine that all housing was decent and family-friendly, with enough room for children and their parents and safe outdoor places to live and play.

Imagine if poor families had access to affordable childcare to enable parents to develop their skills, take up training and extend their working hours.

Imagine if we made children growing up in poverty a political priority and chose to provide the best opportunities and support we could help them overcome the challenges they face, with the biggest springboard possible into adult life.

How shameful we do not.

Time to make all children a political priority

This is what our country could do if we chose to. Child poverty is not going away on its own, so we must decide to act and eliminate it. Talent is everywhere, but opportunity is not. It's time for us to raise our ambition and aspirations for those growing up in poverty so all children have the best possible start in life to help them succeed.

This is a challenge all political parties must take on. A strategy to eliminate child poverty must be a central priority at the next general election. If we want our country to succeed, we must help all our children succeed. Politicians need to choose to make all children count.

In 2022 the Commission on Young Lives, that Anne chairs, published *Hidden in Plain Sight*,[58] a significant report, which recommended a national plan of action to support vulnerable teenagers, including those living in poverty, to succeed and to protect them from adversity, exploitation and harm. It proposed radical ideas around the introduction of hubs, in and close to schools, bringing local services together and providing bespoke services for families and children who need them. It argued for the creation of 1,000 Sure Start Plus Hubs by 2027 to coordinate and deliver health and education support for vulnerable teenagers; it is another very *Raising the Nation*-esque call for integrated, cross-department, cross-sector support to ensure the most in need teenagers can thrive.

It's now time to go to the root cause of child poverty and consider ideas to reset the economic system and improve support via the welfare system.

Resetting our economic system

In the last century there were three competing global economic systems: capitalism, fascism and communism. In this VUCA 21st century, just one remains. To improve more lives, there is no alternative to making capitalism work and evolve. Right now, it is failing to do either. If we want a society whose future is bright, because its children are thriving, we need to start by resetting capitalism so it:

- recognises the interdependence between a finite, fragile environment; caring, flourishing communities and healthy, sustainable enterprises is needed to create wealth to improve a population's lives;
- operates in a way that is free and fair so all can participate in employment, investment and consumption;
- is accountable to all its stakeholders, not primarily its shareholders, and including children.

Outside this book I have argued for such a resetting to include:

- a change in the metrics of economic success, whether those of firms or the macroeconomy, away from short-term incentives that excessively influence decision making;
- a widening of capital ownership so that all – *including* children – have a vested interest in the economic system succeeding;
- a return to a people-centred calculation of value, so that it matters, and shapes economic decision making if, for example, child poverty is increasing, literacy levels are falling and children are breathing unclean air.

There are policies that could make a difference, including:

- raising the National Minimum Wage and National Living Wage to a real living wage (underpinned by sufficient guaranteed hours), thereby ensuring that parents do not have to work multiple jobs to make ends meet, at the expense of their children's well-being. This would also mean that taxpayers (including the low paid) no longer effectively subsidise rich corporations that 'underpay' their employees to the extent that they need to seek state benefits to augment their low wages;

- requiring companies to account for any 'negative externalities' they create. Currently others (taxpayers) pay, funding the required public services that tend to the damage done, for example, water companies that discharge raw sewage into open water, or confectionery companies that focus their marketing on children who consequently live with unhealthy weight and decaying teeth;

- granting all children 'Baby Investment Bonds' at birth that mature on their 18th birthday, similar to the Child Trust Funds issued by the Blair government in 2002,[59] but with more meaningful sums. Public funds could top these up each birthday for children from low-income families. These bonds, tax-free, long-term savings or investment accounts, would help widen capital ownership while narrowing the gap in opportunities to thrive at 18 years old.

Such actions would super-charge momentum towards helping children, yet none are being seriously addressed by 21st-century capitalism or by governments.

Welfare reform

The concept of the 'welfare state' is one of the most shining examples of civilised behaviour: collective support enshrined in both law and culture that recognises that 'we', not just 'I', matter. Things like the NHS, free school education, public parks and social housing ensure our children have a chance to survive. If, however, ensuring every child could thrive and not just survive, became our goal, where would we prioritise resources, and what should our government's north star be?

Eliminating child poverty would be an awesome place to start. This has been a north star for at least one previous British administration. The Blair government of 1997 set out a path to end child poverty through a 20-year mission. Its commitment was driven by the centre of government and came with a series of actions across a range of policy areas and departments (some of which have been discussed elsewhere in this book). It introduced tax credits and increased spending, resulting in an additional £18 billion of benefits for families with children. The then Prime Minister Tony Blair claims that this lifted 1 million children out of poverty.[60] That government lost some focus, the complexities of implementation diluted impact, the 2007–08 global economic crisis hit, and then a change of government came, reversing many of the decisions, policies and programmes under its austerity drive. The point is that it is possible to set a different future as a nation's north star, and that the welfare state has proven to be a critical and successful lever to deliver transformation.

To reinvigorate a commitment to eliminate child poverty, we could start by reorganising the welfare state and government departments to allow families and children better access to the rights and support to which they are entitled. There is an opportunity to make it easy for families to receive help and support *across* governmental departments so that the departments don't operate in silos, distinct and unreflective of the ways families live their lives.

The UK's welfare benefit for those of working age is Universal Credit. It was introduced in 2013, designed to replace six existing benefit entitlements and make the system fairer, more efficient to administer and to incentivise work. Significant changes were made in 2017, when the Conservative government chose to prioritise £3 billion of welfare budget cuts in its policy of austerity. The simplified system and the 2017 cuts have created winners and losers. The biggest losers are single parents and families with three children, who have lost an average of £2,380 and £2,540 a year respectively.[61] These are some of the children society fails most. As former Prime Minister Gordon Brown put it, the shameful impact of these cuts is in 'children having to go to school ill-clad and hungry. It is the poverty of the innocent – of children too young to know they are not to blame'.[62]

There remain opportunities to support children to thrive and best contribute to society throughout their lives, including:

- ensuring in-work claimants with children don't have to pay for childcare upfront, or wait for Universal Credit payments in arrears, as they currently do.★ The Work and Pensions Select Committee (WSPC) maintains this is a 'barrier to work'. Many such families are in perilous financial positions and unless the payment timings are reversed, 'too many will face a stark choice: turn down a job offer or get themselves into debt in order to pay for childcare'.[63] I have seen this challenge first-hand with the choices faced by our Ukrainian guests;

- shortening the period between applying for Universal Credit and receiving initial payment. The goal is to turn applications around in six weeks. The WPSC says reducing the delay would make the policy more likely to succeed.[64] The six-week goal is also often missed, with about one in five applicants waiting nearly five months.[65] The result of the payment policy and its inefficiency is that children are suffering from increasing instances of eviction, hunger and toxic stress, with parents resorting to loan sharks to make ends meet;

- affording every person in the Universal Credit system the same rights and dignity. This just does not happen. Since 2017 the third child (and all subsequent children) in a family receives no child tax credit benefit at all. This is worth £2,900 per child per year.[66] In its first three years, 243,000 families were affected by the two-child limit – that's over one million children.[67] Nearly all families so affected have reported cutting back on essentials such as food, medication, heating and clothing.[68] Finally, despite being a crass way to manage costs and assert controlling influence over personal parental behaviour; the cruellest (and possibly illegal) aspect is it discriminates against the third and subsequent children in any family entitled to Universal Credit. The credit is paid to support the well-being and welfare of the individual child, and the state therefore has chosen not to financially support some children purely on the basis of the accident of their birth order. It is an outrageous

---

★ In the March 2023 Budget, the UK government committed to ensure parents on Universal Credit could access funds needed for childcare up front from Summer 2023; see https://educationhub.blog.gov.uk/2023/03/16/budget-2023-everything-you-need-to-know-about-childcare-support

consequence to a morally dubious aspect to government policy, with its associated tinge of social engineering.

Conclusions

This chapter has covered stark examples of how society is failing its most vulnerable. It holds a mirror up to ourselves and reflects who we are. Children suffering, facing obstacles and challenges that other children, and many adults, never even think about. From living in a system that stops someone from hugging you, to having no rights because you belong to no state, from not knowing where the next meal is coming from, to being denied support that your brothers and sisters enjoy – it's all an accident of birth, and, to borrow Jemeillia's phrase, to those children it must seem like a punishment for a crime they did not commit. But the chapter also offers ideas and examples of how a better child-centred future can be built.

This chapter also brings into focus children's fundamental rights and society's responsibilities. It exposes shortfalls in securing both, and that challenge leads us to our next chapter looking at democracy and in particular, how children can participate in it to ensure their best interests are recognised with the same gravity and importance as those of anyone else.

Five additional essays, containing more proposals for government, are hosted at www.raisingthenation.co.uk:

- John Phillips MBE, Ciara Lawrence and Katie Hollier have each worked for, and volunteered at, Mencap for over 20 years. Both John and Ciara have a learning disability and all three find strength in volunteering. Together they share policy ideas to encourage inclusion for all types of children.

- Katharine Sacks-Jones is Chief Executive of Become, the national charity supporting children in care and young care leavers. She writes on a campaign she is leading for government to #EndtheCareCliff of young care leavers being left isolated and ill prepared for life on their own.

- Sir Stephen O'Brien CBE co-founded, was the initial CEO and is now Vice-President of Business in the Community. He highlights how business could benefit from employing care leavers.

- Mark Russell is CEO of the Children's Society, a charity that supports young people that society has failed. He believes joined-up youth services can act as a pre-emptive measure to lower the chances of young people ending up in the system.

- John Dickie is Director at the Child Poverty Action Group (CPAG) in Scotland. He has worked with children and families in poverty for decades. He has written with ideas regarding child poverty, born from actions taken by the Scottish government.

In addition, the website hosts the poem Graham Handscomb wrote and referred to in his essay.

10

Democracy

*We children are doing this to wake the adults up. We children
are doing this for you to put your differences aside and start
acting as you would in a crisis. We children are doing this
because we want our hopes and dreams back. I hope my
microphone was on. I hope you could all hear me.*

Greta Thunberg (age 15)[1]

In June 2016 the UK held its referendum on whether to remain
a member of the European Union; 17.4 million Britons, just
under 52 per cent of those voting, voted to leave.[2] It was the most
seminal demonstration of democracy this country has seen. But
13 million Britons were not permitted to vote in that democratic
exercise – children[3] – despite the fact that they will live longest
under the decision's consequences.

Brexit was a binary and emotionally charged example of
democracy in action. Our parliamentary representatives drew
an arbitrary age line in the rules for a decision of immeasurable
consequence. Legally a child is a child until their 18th birthday, and
the call was that children could not vote. Except in the Scottish
Independence Referendum of 2014 some could, when 16- and
17-year-olds were allowed to vote. Indeed, they had a higher
turnout rate (75 per cent) compared to the next age bracket, 18- to
24-year-olds (54 per cent).[4] And when I was born, it was different
again, as only people over the age of 21 could vote. Of those child
citizens legally denied a vote in the Brexit referendum, thousands
were paying tax on their earnings (taxed, but not represented). Of
them 2,300 served in the armed services[5] (legally child soldiers).
A further 171 got married[6] (child brides or grooms, legally so).

It doesn't quite seem right to me.

Nor does it seem right considering many children's political engagement. A Greta Thunberg quote opens this chapter, but there are endless examples of less famous children, like Ciara De Menezes who, at ten years old, pointed out the flawed logic in who can vote:

> Older people should have the right to vote, but I don't think they should have the right to vote on all subjects. I've seen lots of stories on the news about issues that affect the whole of my life, but won't really affect older voters. I'm thinking of climate change ... and it's going to affect children more because we're going to live longer.[7]

Why is it that children's thoughts are deemed less relevant than those of other citizens? Seventeen-year-old Cameron Kasky, a survivor of an unimaginable mass school shooting in Parkland, USA and co-founder of March for Our Lives, called it out perfectly: 'just because we are little, does not mean we are inadequate when it comes to being part of the conversation'.[8] And if society were to say, 'well, they shouldn't be less relevant', why are our institutions and democracy designed in a way that lowers their agency and undermines their power to be heard, let alone influence public policy?

David Runciman has staked his credibility and reputation in making the case that six-years-olds should have the right to vote.[9] He is currently working with primary schools on a project exploring children's franchise, and has written this essay for us.

Democracy for children

David Runciman, Professor of Politics, University of Cambridge and host of the Talking Politics podcast

There are two very different ways of understanding democracy. It's important not to confuse them. The classic version is highly demanding – pioneered in ancient Athens – and it requires full-blooded commitment. Here, democracy means taking part. People are expected to participate in community life, to look out for each other, share common goals and generally think that public service matters more than anything. The other version, representative democracy, is much more minimal. It involves voting for other people – that strange breed we call politicians – to take decisions for us, meaning we get only an occasional say. This is the democracy we have today.

When I go into schools to see how young people learn about democracy – especially primary school children – I'm struck by how often the more demanding version is pushed. I have sat through lessons in citizenship that emphasise the importance of democracy as active, where what matters is getting involved in the life of the community. We encourage children to become informed about what's going on around them, to raise issues that concern them and contribute where they can in helping others. Plant a tree! Write a letter! Start a campaign!

What could be wrong with this? It sounds like just what we should be teaching children, so that they can be better citizens. But to my mind, it's a mistake. In fact, it is deeply unfair. The truth is that we introduce expectations of children that we don't make of adults. In the adult world, democracy is the minimal version. You don't have to be a good citizen to take part. You don't even have to take part at all if you don't want to. Adults get to vote regardless of how much they know or how public-spirited they are.

There is growing evidence that young people are becoming disillusioned with democratic politics, which can appear to them as a game they stand little chance of winning.[10] Part of the frustration is that older voters dominate by sheer weight of numbers. But it is also true that the democracy young people encounter when they leave school has little in common with the one they've been taught about and encouraged to practice. It's demoralising to discover that far from being an active, engaged, demanding kind of politics, democracy mainly consists of politicians making promises to voters to secure election.

And that's the other puzzle. It's not just that we ask things of children that we don't expect of adults. We also deny children things we grant adults: we don't let children vote. Yet voting is not the demanding, difficult version of democracy. It's the easy version. It takes little commitment and little knowledge, just an ability to express a preference. Children can do that – they express preferences all the time.

The familiar arguments against letting children vote are that they lack capacity and experience. I think this confuses the two kinds of democracy and shows that many adults don't understand the difference. If we genuinely lived in a participatory democracy, I would be against expecting children to join in fully. For instance, I don't believe that children should serve on juries. Nor do

I think that young children have the capacity to be Members of Parliament. But voting would simply mean children get to voice their preferences and adult politicians would have to take them seriously.

Of course, voting is a serious business and elections are at the heart of representative democracy. Winning the franchise for various excluded groups – from women to minority ethnic groups and religious minorities – has been a vital part of political progress over the last century or more. But, in each case, doubts were expressed about the capabilities of the then excluded to take part. Women, for instance, were said to lack relevant knowledge and experience. These doubts were nonsense.

Another argument sometimes expressed against enfranchising children is that because electoral politics is such a grubby business, the very young should be protected from it. Who wants politicians coming into schools touting for votes? I think this argument gets it the wrong way round. It is precisely because electoral politics is increasingly fraught and the techniques involved ever more pernicious, that we should do what we can to protect *everyone* from the worst. We are all at risk from misinformation and manipulation. The great thing about schools is that they are places where protecting people from falsehood is taken seriously. In some ways, we would benefit from thinking of all voters as being like school children, in need of a safer information environment. I don't believe that if politicians came into schools the children would end up behaving worse. I think the politicians would end up behaving better.

I have spent the past year working in a primary school with children aged between six and ten, exploring what their political preferences actually are. After all, they are rarely asked. Because children don't get to vote they don't get polled, so we have little idea of what they think about political questions. What I have discovered is that while some children are surprisingly well-informed about what's going on in the world – from the war in Ukraine to the cost-of-living crisis – some of them know very little. But that's true of adults, too. Any electorate will contain a wide mixture of levels of knowledge and ignorance – of engagement and indifference. Children are no different. That some six-year-olds can explain climate change and some don't have a clue means they are just like adults.

What I also discovered is a real enthusiasm for expressing their political opinions, from the sensible to the crazy, from ones that sound like they come from their parents to ones that sound like only they could have thought of themselves. How many of us adults can say for sure where our political preferences come from? It might be family, it might be education, it might be prejudice, it might be the most recent thing we have read. What matters is that we get to express them.

It is wrong to ask more of young people than we do of adults, while at the same time denying them the means to express and act on their preferences. School children should be allowed to vote. It would be good for children to have the capacity to make their views known and to be taken seriously. It would be good for politicians, who would have to broaden their horizons. It would also be good for that thing we call democracy. It wouldn't make it live up to the ancient ideals of full participation – that ship sailed long ago – but it would make it live up to the ideals of representative democracy: we call it 'universal suffrage'. So let's make it universal.

David's call for a truly universal franchise of 'easy' democracy may spark scepticism, but let's reflect on the words of Greta and Ciara, which speak to an issue where children and young people seem more engaged than older generations. That is, of course, the environmental crisis, and in particular, the devastating implications of climate change.

The environmental crisis and children's activism

UNICEF has declared that 'the climate crisis is a child's rights crisis'[11] as it no longer only impacts children when they reach adulthood. Today, nearly 1 billion children globally live in places deemed 'extremely high risk' due to exposure to multiple environmental and climate shocks, impacts exacerbated by inadequate essential services.[12] Many children are demanding their voices be heard, even bringing litigation cases against companies and governments.[13]

In the UK young people are calling out for change too. Sisters Ella and Caitlin McEwan, for example, then aged nine and seven, were upset about the impact of plastic in the oceans. They began a petition for fast food giants to reduce the amount of plastic in the free toys given away with children's meals.[14] With the petition gaining momentum, they visited the headquarters of McDonald's, taking with them 1,600 plastic toys, the amount they calculated were being given out every five minutes with a Happy Meal. They were not given access, but Burger King immediately acted to be more sustainable (with no impact on sales), and McDonald's eventually followed suit.[15]

For many years, I have been an activist with ShareAction, a campaigning organisation to democratise business, that has ensured that children (as proxy shareholders) have been able to ask direct and poignant questions at the Annual General Meetings (AGMs) of public companies. For example 11-year-old Lucas Pinto challenged Tesco's board in 2014 over why they didn't pay their employees the living wage.[16] It was interesting to watch their chairman try to answer without being patronising.

Nell Miles spent her teenage years being an activist for environmental issues. Now completing a biology degree at the University of Oxford, she works closely with campaigners Zero Hour. Her essay's title says it all.

We don't have time to wait until my generation is in charge – pass the Climate and Ecology Bill now!

Nell Miles, undergraduate student and environmental activist

Greta Thunberg began her school strike for what was supposed to be a three-week period before the 2018 Swedish elections.[17] Those three weeks turned into over a year out of education for a 17-year-old girl who should have been enjoying secondary school.

I adored secondary school and left after five years with 100 per cent attendance. I told everyone this was because I wanted the promised certificate, but truthfully, I just couldn't bear the thought of missing lessons. My favourite GCSE subjects were biology, geography and English, and I left, ready to get stuck into A Levels, keen to learn more about the natural world I had fallen in love with. But within a few months I informed my college principal that I'd be leading a group of students to leave lessons on Friday 15th March 2019, in protest at the lack of climate action taken by the UK government. That Friday, over a million young people across 125 countries joined the Fridays For Future movement calling for climate action,[18] and action has continued since then, with 18 million strikers estimated to have protested.[19] That's 18 million children like me, sacrificing their time in education because they feel so strongly that those in power need to do better.

Over two-thirds of 18- to 24-year-olds were more worried about climate change in 2020 than they were the previous year.[20] There's not a friend I talk to who isn't concerned about the climate and biodiversity crises, and I increasingly encounter the nihilistic outlook that 'the planet's screwed, so what matters anyway?' Like Greta and thousands of other young climate activists around the world, my friends and I have had to suddenly grow up and fight what sometimes feels like a losing battle, and doing so has taken its toll.

Fighting a feeling of hopelessness as I started university, I was determined to meet others involved in climate and biodiversity action, hoping to find solace in a community fighting for change. That's where I was introduced to the Climate and Ecology (CE) Bill. A piece of potential legislation, led by backbenchers in Westminster, mandating a science-led, joined-up approach to the climate and biodiversity crises,[21] and placing them centrally in national priorities. The CE Bill gave me hope in the possibility of keeping 1.5°C alive and reversing biodiversity loss through serious, science-based solutions backed by hundreds of businesses, charities and politicians and with strong public support. In short, the transformative action we so desperately need.

If passed, the CE Bill would help tackle the persistent, pervasive worries of younger people, giving us faith that the UK government values our future and wants to see us thrive. If passed, its annual targets would reassure us that we're on the right path and, if not, allow us to change course appropriately. I'm fed up with being told our 'generation will change things' when we need to turn the ship around now. We don't have time to wait until my generation is in charge. We need the CE Bill passed into an Act and acted on now, as a critical first step on that 'right path'. We then need to see further legislation, regulation and behaviour change to build on that act of reassurance.

I don't just want to see the CE Bill become law to simply begin to ease the worries of today's children. I want it for our futures, for us to live our adult lives in a prosperous, sustainable economy and healthier society. I grew up in Yorkshire, in an area left with high poverty rates[22] after the demise of the mining industry. The CE Bill would require that any strategy should have an overall positive impact on local communities with high deprivation rates – as well as on young people. It means communities like mine wouldn't be left behind but would directly benefit from a just transition. My family and friends could retrain in green jobs, those younger than me wouldn't have to move away for their career, and instead, they'd be empowered to help build a greener future where they live.

It's well known that nature has a well-being value[23] – and with it visibly and measurably on the path of recovery by 2030, as the CE Bill requires, I could find joy in seeing species reappear in my local parks, take time to appreciate nature and feel content surrounded by a network of ecosystems recovering around me.

And these ecosystems aren't just important for their aesthetic value. The natural world provides ecosystem services vital to human prosperity that are valued at over US$33 trillion per year.[24] These include pollination, waste treatment and food production, and provide the foundations for our societies and economies to prosper. Ecosystem services also include climate regulation[25] – and the CE Bill promotes nature-based solutions to tackle both biodiversity and climate crises, holistically addressing the issues that worry me so much.

While I let myself dream of what legislation like the CE Bill could bring, I try not to think of the counterfactual. Without drastic global action, which the UK should lead, humanity is headed for dark times. By 2070, large swathes of land across Africa, Asia and South America are predicted to become virtually uninhabitable under a business-as-usual scenario,[26] predicted to displace 3.5 billion people. How many children will lose their homes then? How much disruption will my children face as school sizes triple under the mass migration of climate refugees seeking shelter from pains we have, in part, caused?

And ours may not be a prosperous country for climate refugee children seeking shelter. Nature may have continued to decline, with flora and fauna dwindling until what we took for granted becomes rare or extinct. I don't want these remaining years of my youth to be the last when I see swifts arrive in April or watch bluebells bloom in spring. But without action, there's no certainty that these things will continue; we stand to lose what we hold dear.

The nature around me has made me who I am. I ask you to protect it and help it thrive by imploring our politicians to pass legislation such as the CE Bill and more. By doing so, the government could gain a world-leading reputation for green credentials and deliver its responsibility to children and young people of today. It has a chance to do the right thing. I truly believe this is a first, but precedent-setting, step.

I speak on behalf of thousands of young people across the UK when I say we need our political leaders to tackle the climate–nature crises now, enacting the CE Bill before it's too late, and thereafter building on such a meaningful first legislative step.

I was born when the Earth's carbon dioxide concentration was 365 parts per million – it's 420 now.[27] Don't let any more children grow up with this as a measure of change. Let them instead watch nature – and a greener, more sustainable society – grow with them. Let them grow up safe in the knowledge that the law of the land will protect their future and help them thrive.

Nell's essay in many ways overlaps with Valerie Hannon's essay in Chapter 6, which recognised that the well-being of children is reliant on the well-being of their relationships with themselves, others and the planet. Without a well planet the concept of a child-centred future becomes meaningless. The necessity for a sustainable planet dwarfs all other issues.

It is humbling and embarrassing that children and young people need to find ways to teach adults how to campaign, create an argument and act. It's shameful that they have found ways to do David's 'hard' democracy, despite being denied the 'easy' version.

Preparing children to participate in democracy

We've established that children can participate in liberal democracies as activists. However, the vast majority of children have opinions and preferences on how society should function, but are not activists. Consequently, unlike similar adults, their voice is never counted in the 'easy' democracy ledger, since they can't cast a vote. How can we at least prepare them to make their vote count when the time comes?

The answer may surprise you: ensure children play. We have seen in Chapter 4 that play is critical to child development. It turns out it is also critical to human, societal and cultural development too. Nancy Richards Farese understands why. Nancy is a social documentary photographer and former Fellow at the Harvard Kennedy School. For her latest book, *Potential Space: A Serious Look at Child's Play*,[28] she saw children at play all over the world and, partially from that experience, has written this essay for us.

Just outside the frame: how play and democracy are inextricably linked

Nancy Richards Farese, photographer

Few visuals are as unsettling as watching people forced from home with meagre belongings and faces lined, uncertain where to live safely. Even now, we watch a record number fleeing conflict and vanishing resources, crossing political borders to become refugees.[29] They ask for assimilation, access to economies and a fair shot at finding a new home. The host country is inevitably besieged, and this act of desperate migration often results in violent political and social upheaval. Yet sometimes societies adjust and begin to see benefit from inclusion. This shift sometimes happens peacefully and efficiently, sometimes awkwardly and chaotically. Why is it that democracies are particularly successful at the assimilation of refugees?

One theory is related to play.

Childhood play can be an essential training ground for social adaptation and self-governance: the foundation skills of a liberal democracy. As children play, they learn quite naturally the emotional regulation, collaboration and cooperation necessary to achieve the higher goal, which is always to play for as long as possible. Consider a game of backyard tag: rules are established at the outset, players are determined, boundaries set and the selection of leaders established. New arrivals are invited in and violators of the rules are tossed out. 'Peaceful transfer of power' is the norm. Assuming no adult intervenes, these kids are learning to govern themselves and manage a fluctuating world around them. Their goal is to maximise play; society's goal is for them to develop the skills to make democracy last for as long as possible.

A game of tag, the banter of jokes or the decision of who climbs to the highest tree branch are risks and skills that seem insignificant – 'child's play'. But this play is quite serious. In the US Constitution, Thomas Jefferson identifies 'the pursuit of happiness' as a fundamental right of citizens of a democracy; child's play is an essential tool for the achievement of that right.

How we look at play

As a photographer, I have created a visual survey of children at play around the world. I work with international aid organisations to watch how children turn to games, toys and imagination to adapt and heal from some of the most extraordinary trauma. For example, I enter an emergency refugee camp to document loss, yet on the edge of every frame, or just behind my lens, I see kids playing 'cirque' with old bicycle tires, flying down a hill of mud that has become a slide, or fashioning sticks and fabric into baby dolls. These games, whether in the deserts of Burkina Faso or the hills of Guatemala, are our games too. I'm always amazed that we know play when we see it, anywhere in the world. We recognise what it means to be lost in play.

Photographing kids at play allows for open-ended storytelling where my goal is for you to remember what it was to be a kid, and then ask what these kids know that adults have perhaps forgotten. Play is a fundamental tool of well-being and creativity. It is also how we learn to adapt to a chaotic and uncertain world. When we take play seriously, we understand that it

Acrobatics on the beach, Haiti, February 2010,
one month after the earthquake
© Nancy Richards Farese, 2010/2019

Playing with shadows, Spain, August 2019
© Nancy Richards Farese, 2010/2019

is a muscle of resilience and a joy that powerfully shapes who we are as individuals, and as a society.

When Alexis de Tocqueville came to America in the 1830s, he noted that Americans had created a brand-new mechanism for self-governance and problem-solving that negated the need for a higher authority such as a monarch. Recently, it seems our self-governance muscle is flagging. 'We have become less artful at democracy', suggest Jonathan Haidt and Greg Lukianoff in a *New York Times* opinion piece entitled 'How to play our way to a better democracy.'[30] Is this decline of democracy related to the decline of free play?* They suggest that hypervigilant parenting and over-scheduled kids may have broader implications for our society. Individually, kids are struggling with soaring rates of anxiety, depression and narcissism as they move uncertainly into an adult world. As a society, we just don't seem to be able to cooperate and manage dissent.

Economist Steven Horwitz saw this phenomena within the political framework of cooperation, or its opposite, coercion. Democracy is based on cooperation, with rules and norms built to accommodate fluctuation and deliver stability and economic success.[31] Coercion is based on authoritarianism and control. Rules are dictated and autonomy disallowed. A controlling parent who repeatedly negates a child's ability to navigate solutions to social problems in childhood could have longer-term implications for society. 'If we parent or legislate in ways that make it harder for children to develop these skills, we are taking away a key piece of what makes it possible for free people to generate peaceful and productive liberal orders', warned Horwitz.

What can be done?

'In a perfect world we would say to our kids "you can't do your homework until you've gone out to play"', says Brendan Boyle, toy inventor and partner at IDEO, a California-based firm dedicated to harnessing creativity for business design. Families can be intentional about how to bring more play into their lives by taking a critical look at scheduling and their own comfort levels in allowing kids freer rein in the community. This involves the neighbours too – kids, after all, need friends to play with. Broad and clear boundaries can be established for kids to play in homes, schools and neighbourhoods. If kids participate in setting these rules, they learn to hold the responsibility for their own safety. Local governments could offer support with access to resources to guide such conversations, perhaps from libraries, town halls and online.

Lenore Skenazy, founder of Free-Range Kids, works to challenge the creep of parental overprotection and 'helicopering' with the tagline 'All the worry

---

* By 'free play' I mean the unsupervised, ideally outdoor play that we allow for our children, where they learn to resolve conflicts on their own and manage uncertainty.

in the world doesn't prevent death, it prevents life.' Free-Range Kids offers a 'Parents Bill of Rights',[32] further promoting the idea that public interest and individual well-being is best served when kids walk and cycle to daily activities and play outside unsupervised. The Bill has been voted into legislation in a handful of US states, supporting the right of parents to not be found criminal or negligent when they let kids 'roam' freely.

In 1989 the UNCRC established an international mandate to protect 'the right of all children everywhere to leisure and play'.[33] We should hold governments accountable for promoting the 'right to play' as an unalienable personal right and essential public value; 190 countries have ratified the agreement, legally bound to acknowledge the right in their domestic policies. The best way to enforce compliance would be to adopt the UNCRC into statute and give children a legal recourse should their government fail to provide safe access to, and provision for, their right to leisure and play.

If we insist that governments promote play as a kind of social glue and fundamental necessity for a healthy democracy, then we can align and incentivise behaviour from the rule makers into local societies, schools, neighbourhoods and homes. Play is that serious.

Nancy's reflections on play as the building block for democratic participation are at once original and yet completely obvious. The foundations of democratic behaviours practised in play are then picked up and continued in formal education.

Schools are microcosms of society, and so have a critical role when it comes to promoting democratic behaviours. For many young children this might be first experienced in the form of a school council to which they elect counsellors to represent their class and attend meetings with the headteacher. Both my children relished being elected food counsellors, but were ultimately disappointed that their influence was not what they had hoped it would be, which was perhaps a great experience for understanding democratic participation and strategies to use 'power' effectively. There is good news in that increasing numbers of schools are deepening the roles and responsibilities of school councils, developing new structures and seeing value in listening to and amplifying children's voices. A good example is the New School in London, which, although not a 'mainstream' school, operates under the core ethos that its students should be involved in school decision making as equals, and focuses on ensuring that children are aware of their own agency. One way it does this is through 'the circle', a daily meeting where children raise concerns, challenge decisions and can expect to be heard. The school describes 'the circle' as: 'a mechanism by which young people can tackle challenges with staff and to develop inclusive and emotionally intelligent relationships. Everyone participating has an equal vote and right to speak regardless of their age or job title.'[34]

A further step is democratic schools, which embed and embrace a fuller democracy across all decision making and actions. For example, in Chapter 11 Charlotte Church writes of her experience setting up an active democratic school in the 'hard' democracy vein.

Outside school there are spaces for children to organise and have their views heard under democratic mandates. Many countries have different forms of youth parliaments or councils. One example is the UK Youth Parliament (UKYP), with 354 11- to 18-year-old representatives elected to the position of MYP, rather than MP. But, merely imitating Westminster models of election, with its flaws in terms of representation,[35,36] means voices of marginalised young people are not heard.[37] Ireland's Youth Assembly demonstrates a different approach. It seeks to combine demographic knowledge around characteristics (as examples: experience of the care system, racial group, LGBTQ+, disability, young carers, eligibility for free school meals, religious belief and gender) with a random selection of (anonymised) applicants to ensure that the Assembly membership is fully representative. This was recently repeated to form a special interest Children and Young People's Assembly on Biodiversity Loss to explore action to protect and restore Ireland's biodiversity.[38]

Children's rights upheld and respected

Claudette Colvin was 15 years old in 1955 when she boarded a busy bus in Montgomery, Alabama. A short way into the journey, the bus driver told her to give up her seat for a passenger standing nearby. Claudette was a young Black student; the passenger was White. Claudette refused. Nine months before Rosa Parks made a similar refusal, Claudette was dragged from the bus by two police officers and charged with violating segregation laws as she repeatedly shouted, 'It's my constitutional right.' It is worth spending time reading about why hers was not the name most famously associated with the bus boycotts, but her age was certainly one factor. I am profoundly moved by Claudette's story,[39] and those words she repeated, '*It's my constitutional right.*'

So far in this chapter we've thought about how we can encourage and support children to participate in democracy. What we haven't yet tackled are the democratic legal responsibilities we should have to children. What legislation is needed to optimise their '*constitutional rights*', and how can they be implemented to deliver a country whose future is better because its children thrive?

One cornerstone could be to lower the voting age. David powerfully articulated why this should be so in his essay. But any such move would raise the key question: 'to what age?' Unless the answer is 'everyone', it will likely be as arbitrary as the current age, while raising further questions about other age-related rights and responsibilities. When we look at historical, successful civil rights legislation that extended voting franchises, we see that they are universally borne from movements and demands from those groups themselves. In all honesty, I don't hear such demands to lower the voting age in this country right now.

It is true, however, that without equal votes and without hearing the voices of all citizens, our democracy is discriminatory and unfair. As a result, children are currently being failed. I think a national debate and citizens' assembly is the best next step towards working out where the franchise should extend. Any such debate and assemblies must be multi-generational and children's voices respected.

In the meantime, I suggest five pieces of legislation that would utterly transform children's rights and voice in our democracy, and reframe the responsibilities of political representatives without changing the age at which citizens can vote.

1. Automatic voter registration

The first is ensuring the right to vote. At present, in the UK, citizens can vote, once they are 18 years old, *if* they proactively register, and with new legislation, only then if they produce an approved photo ID document at the polling station.[40] Young people are less likely to already possess documentation, such as passports, and the authorised documents appear to be age discriminatory in themselves (for example, a senior citizen bus pass is authorised, a young person's railcard is not; an Oyster card 60+ is okay, an Oyster card 18+ is not[41]).[42] National Insurance (NI) numbers are issued automatically to those approaching their 16th birthday, so there should be no reason why voter registration is not automatically triggered from NI number issuance alongside approved, free Voter Cards, with advice to help 16- to 18-year-olds make the most of their right when their opportunity to vote comes. Our representation and therefore democracy would benefit accordingly.

2. Protected rights

The Equality Act 2010★ is the core piece of UK legislation that shields people from discrimination because of protected characteristics.† It is designed to protect each of us against direct and indirect discrimination, harassment and victimisation. It requires public bodies and businesses to consider how their decisions and policies affect different people, including age.[43] The Act gives adults (over-18s) alone full legal protection from age discrimination (with the exception of those children in employment),[44] although children are protected from discrimination based on other characteristics. So there is an opportunity to extend the Act to secure specific additional protected rights for children. In this respect I see their protections as similar to those for other minority groups. On occasion children's rights come into conflict with adults' rights, and sometimes a child cannot fully utilise the benefits of public spaces, services or assets. The law should be used to redress such disadvantage. For example, babies could feed

---

★ The Act applies in England, Scotland and Wales in full, and partially in Northern Ireland.

† The nine protected characteristics are: age, disability, gender reassignment, marriage and civil partnership, pregnancy and maternity, race, religion or belief, sex, and sexual orientation.

in spaces where the rest of us can eat; young children could be protected from corporal punishment as older people are from violence;[45] those designing public transport services would need to make 'reasonable adjustments' for travellers with young children;[46] and teenagers could not be discriminated against in public places through the deployment of the Mosquito device that I shared in Chapter 5.

3. The Wellbeing of Future Generations Bill

You will remember from Chapter 2 that Wales became the first nation in the world to create a future generations commissioner post, underpinned by ground-breaking legislation. Now is the time to build on that precedent and legislate for a UK commissioner, through Parliament passing a Wellbeing of Future Generations Bill. Such a bill has been introduced,[47] led by the *Big Issue* founder and cross-bench peer Lord John Bird, and is slowly gaining momentum. However, no major political party has yet adopted it as a core part of delivering their vision, and without that, its route to success is difficult. The Bill would require the UK government to:

1. Work to prevent problems, including the climate crisis, poverty and pandemics from happening, and not just deal in emergencies.
2. Give current and future generations a voice in decision making and protect them from global threats.
3. Deliver a new, sustainable vision for the nation that prioritises our environmental, social, economic and cultural well-being.

4. Extending the powers of the children's commissioners

Each of the UK's four nations has a children's commissioner who must promote the 'rights, views and interests of children in policies or decisions affecting their lives'.[48] While the powers are different in each devolved nation,* the commissioner's role

---

* For example, the commissioner for Northern Ireland has a Legal and Investigative Team that can support children and families for individual cases in court, whereas the other commissioners cannot.

is to listen to children and their experiences and commission research and reports. All four commissioners have a duty to contribute to a report for the UN Committee on the Rights of the Child every five years, assessing how the UK's governments are progressing towards the commitment to the UNCRC.[49] There is scope to extend their statutory powers beyond advisory, advocacy and convening, to bring legal rights and redress for children, especially if granted in synchronicity with my final, and most consequential, change in statute to deliver a future where all children can thrive, by...

5. Adopting the UNCRC into UK statute

Although the Equality Act 2010 is a central piece of human rights legislation that offers legal protections and cultural guidance, and while – as we have seen – age is a protected characteristic within the Act, for children it is only relevant in respect to employment. So where can children look to ensure their rights are respected and upheld beyond this realm?

The answer lies in the UNCRC.[50] You will recognise that it is referred to on numerous pages throughout this book. It comprehensively outlines the rights of under 18-year-olds. You may also remember that it is the human rights document with the most governments' signatories (only one member of the UN has not ratified the agreement: the USA). It lists 54 specific rights that all children have.[51] These include all those secured by adults, plus extra rights they need to learn, grow, play, develop and reach their full potential. Each signatory government has agreed to acknowledge these rights by considering them (not protecting them) when passing and enforcing national legislation.

There are two opportunities to improve implementation to help in *raising the nation*.

The first concerns responsibility for interpretation, monitoring and the boundaries of the UNCRC work. Signatories must submit reports to the Committee on the Rights of the Child★ every five years, on which the Committee passes

★ Which comprises 18 independent experts and operates from within the Office of the United Nations High Commissioner for Human Rights.

'*concluding observations*'.[52] Much can be learned from how the Committee responds to discrimination (addressed in Article 2 of the UNCRC) in its *concluding observations* that tend to be overwhelmingly directed at tackling discrimination against traditionally disadvantaged groups of children: such as girls, minority ethnic groups and racial minorities and children with disabilities. In other words, the Committee rarely frames discrimination as being against children on the basis of childhood itself. There appears to exist an assumption across most societies that this is unproblematic, and perhaps that, 'by reason of age alone, children should be afforded less and lesser legal rights than adults'.[53] If we aspire to a child–centred future and enforce the UNCRC, the Committee on the Rights of the Child needs to be bolder and more consistent in its recognition of discrimination primarily on the basis of childhood. Governments could take the lead to encourage this.

The second opportunity would be transformational: to legislate the UNCRC UK–wide, giving children rights enforceable by law, dovetailing with the Equality Act 2010 (and filling its holes with respect to children). Such a move would build a society where our children have special rights and protections that are not advisory, or principles, but *legally enforceable*.

Nancy touched on such action in her essay. Lawyer Yasmin Waljee, supported by her colleague Haylea Campbell, has written an essay for us wholly focused on this very concept. It makes an impressive case.

The best way to guarantee children their rights is ...

Yasmin Waljee OBE, Pro Bono Lawyer and Partner at Hogan Lovells with *Haylea Campbell*, Associate at Hogan Lovells

We often under-estimate how much children can take on board the complexities of the world: but they can be hugely insightful. On one walk to school, my then primary school-aged son volunteered that child rights ought to include, at a minimum, the right to adequate food, water, a house, clean air and the internet.

As it happens, *none* of those rights are fully guaranteed by domestic law. How absurd is that?

We increasingly find that neither our national law and courts nor our political system can be relied on to protect the rights of children. But incorporating the UNCRC into UK-wide statute might just change that.

Background

Almost 100 years ago, the League of Nations adopted the Geneva Declaration of the Rights of the Child – the first international human rights document to address the rights of children specifically. As well as listing obligations on citizens of all nations to care for children, and ensure their safety, it clearly states that humankind needs children to contribute to and improve our societies, and so it is in all our interests to make sure they have the best environment in which to grow.

It took until the 1980s for the United Nations Convention on the Rights of the Child (UNCRC) to be fully drafted, with the United Nations adopting the document in 1989. It consists of 54 articles that set out children's rights and how governments should work together to make them available to all children. It is a legally binding international agreement, encompassing the civil, political, economic, social and cultural rights of every child, regardless of their race, religion or abilities. The UNCRC is now the most widely ratified human rights treaty in history – a hopeful sign that the majority of the world's countries recognise the importance of strengthening and protecting our youth.

While the UK ratified the UNCRC in 1991, and therefore must take it into consideration, there have been no laws passed that incorporate it into domestic legislation. The effect of incorporation would be to ensure that children's rights are binding in court, and that legislation could not be passed in contravention of the UNCRC. The arguments for incorporation are not just 'child's play' – they are the transformational step from which we can't row back.

Incorporation of the UNCRC is vital where politics fails children

It has long been thought that the rights of children are effectively guaranteed by ensuring those of adults, but the interests of adults and children may diverge. For example, when adults' pensions are increased by investment decisions that undermine the environmental integrity of the planet, children's rights are harmed to serve those of adults. Incorporation of the UNCRC would give weight to the needs of children and help to rebalance this inequality.

One key recent example is the way in which the Nationality and Borders Act impacts how child victims of trafficking and modern slavery are treated and assessed, with their best interests not always taken into consideration.[54] Peers in the House of Lords called on MPs to ensure that age assessments based on international legal principles, protections from prosecution and an exemption from penalties for missing deadlines on disclosing trauma and abuse be included in the final legislation. While the final Act confirms that children will not be penalised for missing deadlines, the other important safeguarding provisions have not been incorporated, with children now more at risk.

Successive governments have said that it is not necessary to incorporate the UNCRC because it is unlikely to be breached by legislation. However, this Act and two recent Supreme Court decisions[55] demonstrate that young people can no longer rely on Parliament or the courts to protect their interests.

The Supreme Court examples are worth sharing as the Justices ruled that it is not open to them (as the Supreme Court) to determine whether or not the UK is acting in compliance with its human rights obligations when the issue pertains to a treaty that has not been incorporated into domestic legislation. The first ruling asked if child tax credit rules are discriminatory to families with more than two children: the court said that UNCRC provisions requiring the best interests of the child to be a primary consideration need not be taken into account. In the second, the appeal of a 15-year-old who was remanded in solitary confinement was dismissed. While the UN Committee on the Rights of the Child stated that solitary confinement of those under 18 should be prohibited in all cases, the court ultimately ruled that it was not bound by the UNCRC.

The judges in the child tax credit appeal specifically referred to politically motivated legal challenges by charities, such as the Child Poverty Action Group (CPAG), stating that they 'present a risk of undue interference by the courts in the sphere of political choices'.[56] However, these organisations are a rare avenue for children to influence political power.

Scotland[57]

We don't have to look very far to see the effects of making UNCRC part of domestic law, with the Scottish Parliament passing the United Nations Convention on the Rights of the Child (Incorporation) (Scotland) Bill in 2021.[58]

The intent behind this Scottish Bill speaks of an 'everyday accountability' that would both require all of Scotland's public authorities to take 'proactive steps' to ensure that children's rights are protected and also give children the ability to enforce their rights in courts. Importantly, children have been at the heart of moving this legislation forward, with the Scottish government receiving responses from organisations that represent the views of young people and children.[59] One of the findings of the consultation was that children are not fully aware of their rights, which exacerbates the rights protection gap.

During the pandemic, the Children (Equal Protection from Assault) (Scotland) Act came into force, making it the first country in the UK to ensure that, like adults, children have unequivocal protection from assault. It is widely known as the 'smacking ban' and specifically draws on Articles 19* and 37† of the UNCRC. It means that Scotland has now implemented the UN's specific recommendations to the UK to prohibit corporal punishment.[60] I note here that while some people still believe that smacking is an effective way of disciplining children with no real harmful effects, multiple studies have shown[61] that physically punishing children has an adverse effect on their mental health and development.

My call to action

As with any group in society, rights will only move forward if there are structures in place that allow for public authorities to be challenged and held to account. With British children increasingly unable to secure protection through the courts or through political representation, their rights can only be truly realised and enforced by incorporation of the UNCRC into domestic law. While Scotland will continue to pass legislation at Holyrood, the real difference to the lives of all British children, and especially those who are most vulnerable to harm, will be found when Westminster follows its lead. We have a responsibility to ensure that the rights of children across the UK are protected, and the UNCRC is the best legislative tool to guarantee that they are, by being codified in the law.

I'll return to Yasmin's essay in the last chapter of this book. In the meantime, it is interesting to note that when the four children's commissioners reported to the Committee in 2020,[62] they noted, like Yasmin, that many young people were unaware of their rights and called for more work to raise understanding. Some schools

---

* Article 19 requires a state to take all appropriate measures to protect a child from violence carried out by a caregiver.

† Article 37 requires protection from torture or other cruel, inhuman or degrading treatment.

have decided to do this work themselves. Over 1.6 million British children now go to Rights Respecting Schools – a status awarded by UNICEF when a school has embedded a rights approach based on the UNCRC.[63]

This is great, but why should this be left to chance and reliant on the decisions of school leadership teams? Why is this not a fundamental part of the curriculum for all children? It can be!

Conclusions

The right for children to vote needs national, inclusive discussion if elected public servants are to serve *all* people and represent their collective interests. It is the obvious way to ensure all voices count.

There are other, potentially more effective, ways to ensure democracy and rights thrive. Nancy shared her photographer's perspective to show how children need to be children and play, and how that helps secure a sustainable, inclusive democracy. Yasmin raised rights-based arguments to deliver a child-centred future. And Nell set the context of rights and democracy in terms of a thriving planet.

These disparate ideas go to the very heart of the challenge this book seeks to address: building a future where every child can become the person they have the potential to be. Participating in our democracy across their entire lives is critical to achieve this. The challenge is captured by human behaviour expert Alfie Kohn: 'Children, after all, are not just adults-in-the-making. They are people whose current needs and rights and experiences must be taken seriously.'[64]

One additional essay, containing proposals for government, is hosted at www.raisingthenation.co.uk:

- Jude Kelly CBE is a theatre director and arts producer who, as a feminist and campaigner for girls' and women's rights, founded the WOW Foundation. She shows how the education system can better support gender equality, and thereby a more equitable and truer democracy.

11

Voice

So here I stand, one girl among many.
I speak not for myself, but for all girls and boys.
I raise up my voice — not so that I can shout, but so that
those without a voice can be heard.

Malala Yousafzai (age 16)[1]

Three golden threads have weaved their way through the chapters of this book. They have left a trail showing us that children are best provided for when:

- they and their families have agency, a voice, to shape their lives;
- their childhood is full of varied positive experiences;
- their well-being is prioritised.

It's time to look more closely at the threads of voice, variety and well-being in these remaining chapters by reviewing what they reveal across the broad landscape of childhood. We start with voice.

Voice: ensuring more children and families have more control over their lives, with more agency and involvement in what is best for them, including the support some may need to effectively use their voice.

Having a voice is about more than children and families having the power to articulate what they need; it is equally about making certain that the ears of our institutions and civic society are tuned in and are listening. After all, children need to be seen *and* heard.

This must start at birth, when, unable to speak for themselves, a child's parents must have a voice that is attended to. Parents need a stable environment, in their home and locally, where they can best meet their children's needs. They invariably know what support they need to achieve this, and broader society should listen and respond as Heckman's evidence is strong: effective interventions at the very start of life pay dividends not only for individuals but for the nation as a whole.

When they are able, we must involve children in the decision-making processes about issues that impact them. We've seen ways in which children's ideas and voices are successfully embraced, such as in the design of local spaces, but more can and must be done. After all, their world is one in which many adults (including parents and lawmakers) have little understanding of the ecosystem. We saw this in digital spaces where the velocity of change is incomparable to the speed with which institutions respond, and the consequences of not listening can be fatal.

If all children are to count, we need to start by listening to the voices of those children the rest of us have let down. Listening to young people like Jemeillia, who, as a 16-year-old, could articulate the impact of a policy designed in Whitehall that risked unconsidered consequences through exclusively prioritising safeguarding at the expense of well-being. A small example of why those with power must listen and learn from those with lived experience.

Children's agency can only be effective if they have both knowledge and a platform. School should provide both, helping children grow into fulfilled citizens. Sir Anthony Seldon doesn't believe it does. He is an accomplished historian and educator, with over 30 years' experience as a headteacher, and so he has clear insight into our education system's failings, and has written for us on ideas of how they could be put right.

Children need agency to reveal the colourful rainbow of their intelligence

Sir Anthony Seldon, headteacher, ex-university vice-chancellor, author, political commentator, historian and educator

In education, our young are mired in a puerile-powered past and constrained by a toxic present.

Here in the UK, we are living in the 21st century in one of the most technologically developed countries on Earth. But we have a Victorian education system that infantilises and patronises our young, holds them back and restricts their achievement for life while claiming to do exactly the opposite.

Children are capable of doing far more than we entrust them with today. Trust is the key word: they thrive on it and rise to the challenge.

No one wants to hurry up childhood: it is the most precious time of life and one that can never be repeated. But we should be looking to give our young the opportunities to take appropriate responsibility and to step progressively up the ladder of maturity.

Is it surprising that employers tell us that the attributes that school leavers have acquired in formal education are not the ones they want in the world of work? Or that so many young people are unhappy, and rising numbers are suffering from mental distress? How outrageous is it that our school system tells one-third of our students – who come disproportionately from disadvantaged backgrounds – that they have failed to make the grade, a label of failure that they carry throughout life?

Governments the world over have reduced human intelligence and dignity to a narrow range of logical and linguistic skills. Why? Because they can be tested, examined and compared. Limited content is drummed into young people, while the glorious gamut of human intelligence in all its fullness is shunned.

What a joy it is when one sees young people full of life, with a passion to build a better world and with values of kindness, consideration and respect embodied in their very actions. Too often, though, they have emerged like this not because of the education system, but despite it.

A school system that denies young people agency is bad enough. If this denial is layered into the lives of young people already experiencing poor and inadequate home backgrounds, it becomes toxic. I've seen the impact of such instability in childhood directly: not just on my wards at Wellington and Brighton Colleges, but also in my own family. My father's parents were killed by the influenza plague in 1918, shortly after they arrived from Ukraine, and he was passed around from home to home before finding loving foster parents when he was nearly three. But then his stepfather died, his life was plunged back into uncertainty, which affected him all his life.

As a country we are doing nothing like enough to ensure that every child is part of a loving family and safe home. Those families experiencing difficulties need more help and support if the cycles of deprivation and incomplete parenting are not to be repeated down the generations.

The rainbow of a child's intelligence

Human intelligence is multi-faceted. Let's, for the sake of argument, say that there are seven human intelligences – the logical, the linguistic, the creative, the physical, the personal, the social and the moral. All these aptitudes remain dormant unless they are developed at home or school. We can compare the seven intelligences to the colours of the rainbow. No one would think that a proper job of schooling has been done if we concentrated on just two colours. Only when the intelligences are all taught together in balance is the whole child educated. And only when the seven interact does an eighth colour manifest – white light – which we might associate with holistic or, dare I say, spiritual intelligence or wisdom.

Is it surprising that when these wider intelligences are not being assessed and measured at school, that they are marginalised? Indeed, devoting time to their development might be folly because it will take away from time that could be spent on maths or grammar.

Traditionalists ask why should young people have *any* freedom in schools? Why not insist that they don't talk in corridors or in class, and sit passively absorbing what they're told, uncritically and regurgitating it in exams? Surely that's the very zenith of what good schools should be doing? If children are trusted to take their own decisions, it can cause mistakes and hazards, which is messy. It can also damage league table positions, and risk the opprobrium of Ofsted, which sniffs out records on bad behaviour. But the risk is that the young person will not be able to thrive when they move beyond that rigid structure.

Agency: disperser of clouds, revealer of rainbows

Giving young people agency is indeed a risky business. We can be sure that the more freedom the young are given, the more mistakes they will make. We can also be certain that the more mistakes they make, the more likely they are to learn right from wrong, good from bad, than they would learn from mere instruction.

In my 20 years as a headteacher, I noticed how even those students dismissed as 'bad cases' could carry out a task extraordinarily well and effectively when they were trusted with it. The young can be given quite significant responsibilities in their final year at primary school, but then go down to the bottom of the rung when they join senior school, and they have to wait for an absurdly long time before they are given responsibility again.

Some examples include volunteering: we need an explosion of it at the heart of every school. Take assemblies away from dull heads like me and have older students delivering the key messages. Have students doing the speaking on open days, speech days and all other major events. Let them select their year representatives and school leaders, and comment regularly on the performance of their teachers. Allow the students to choose the values they want to see in their schools. Give them some say in the curriculum, and over rules and punishments. Few things can teach young people better about the way society works than involving them in devising the social guidelines by which they should all live together and deciding what to do when infringements occur.

Agency is, of course, about much more than this. It is down to the very way subjects are taught. If young people are regularly told the answer, rather than having the chance to work it out, then the material will always belong to someone else. The moment students are told the answers, they cease to think, and much of the depth of learning is lost. The best teachers, in my experience, never actually teach in the sense of instructing the young: rather, they guide them to finding the answers for themselves.

This future is vital and entirely possible. All we need to do is to learn to trust and respect our young people. We start by blowing away the grey clouds and damp rain of our current Victorian education system to reveal the colourful rainbow of their intelligences in an entirely new, 21st-century one. And to start this we must give them more agency in their education.

Another, still experimental, way of ensuring children have a voice in shaping their lives, and one that builds on Anthony's vision, is through 'democratic schooling', an educational system that advocates for student-run schools and decision-making processes. It values the belief that all students should have the right to self-determination and the ability to make decisions about their educational environment. It operates by helping children develop social and democratic skills (such as negotiation, compromise, collaboration and listening) and then by acting on what they have to say. As a child, Charlotte Church was a globally recognised singer, and so experienced a highly unusual childhood. Ironically, the girl known to have the 'voice of an angel' had her voice taken away from decisions about her own childhood as her life became highly managed. Partially based on this lived experience, she is now such an advocate for the power of democratic schools that she established her own, and has written this essay for us on why – and how – they give children agency over their own childhoods.

Democratic schooling – a voice for our children
Charlotte Church, singer, songwriter and founder of The Awen Project

Trusting young people is something a lot of us struggle to do. This is not without good cause. Brain puberty makes the neural connections that formed in childhood literally tear away. These dendrite nerve cells are then floating around, looking to find new connections. This is why most teenagers, from an adult's perspective, often behave like absolute tools. So we don't trust them, especially not with responsibility for themselves or with choices of their own, because we adults are scared that they will ruin their lives.

There is a tendency to view children as potential adults who need to be crammed with information so they can move up to our level. We are blinkered to their immediate needs and desires and rights, and we lose sleep over their futures: their potential. That word 'potential' is so tenderly dehumanising. It's a promise of a shiny bauble in the future accompanied by a silent slander: 'you are not enough'. But age hierarchy dictates that young children be dragged upward, not fulfilled in their present state. The conversation is never allowed to become 'what does the 11-year-old need to best be the 11-year-old?' Older students are becoming physically and emotionally ready for responsibility, especially that of choice, but they are kept from making decisions about their own lives because it is assumed they will make bad ones.

The journey to Awen
When my own children approached school age, I was torn. I could send them to private school, but I didn't feel comfortable with that. We had

found a kindergarten that kept kids on until age seven – which was more in line with what I'd been learning about child development – but the holistic, organic, knit-your-way-to-knowledge wasn't right for us either. So instead, I homeschooled my kids for four years.

Then my daughter started saying that she really wanted to see what school was like. Banging on about children's rights and autonomy, I had to respect her wishes, and we enrolled her in a local primary school. For her, it wasn't about the change of education. She wanted to be in a large social group and experience THE DRAMA. So and so has a crush on so and so, who has a crush on … you get the picture!

But secondary school was different. Looking at friends' teenagers who were struggling and losing themselves in a system that feeds children to the exam monster, I could not, in good conscience, stand by and not do anything. Instead, I could set up a school, not in competition with the state system, in collaboration, but free from the demands of the state. Not some middle-class cutesy private school, but one that does not ask for fees, yet provides an education that is fit for the future. So I set about my research, visiting many schools doing things their own way to develop my vision.

Democratic schools

During these visits I came across democratic schools like Sands School in Devon. Here, all operational decisions are made by the school council, from the budget and the hiring and firing of staff, to the writing of school rules, including the appropriate justice for any students who break them. Every pupil and staff member has an equal vote on all matters and via peer review matters are dealt with in a way that supports the community. A student caught bullying at Sands, for example, has to face a jury of their peers, who then decide on a fitting and fair punishment. Even the process of having judgement put on you by your friends seems enough of a roasting before the penalty itself. It certainly works as a deterrent, far more than detention in any case. The responsibility for the school and community is in the hands of the children, who learn how to conscientiously contribute to the society at large.

Now Sands is very small, it is fee paying, although with means testing. It cannot avoid appearing to be a cosy enclave of loveliness. Crack it open, though, and you find that the process of their democracy is anything but cosy. The kids are shown trust and allowed to take risks. Of course, they fail. But they fail better each time, all the while participating in a living democratic system that is a hell of a lot fairer than most.

The Awen Tribe

Democratic schools like Sands inspired me to found The Awen Tribe, a self-directed, consent-based learning community for young people to focus on their own education. Awen students learn to love learning freely, but are, by social necessity, required to be responsible members of the community and participate in a community founded on robust debate and mutual respect.

Our tribe is governed by 'The Gathering', a democratic meeting held every week, where any member of the tribe can voice concerns, put forward ideas and address behavioural issues that may arise. Each member has an equal vote, and through practising deep democracy exercises and upholding the importance of individual consent, 'The Gathering' promotes social learning, tolerance and the development of communication and collaboration skills.

During an Awen education, students amass a portfolio that can be used as a record of their achievements. We do not follow any exam curriculum for traditional subjects; however, if students decide that they would like to study for a qualification, they will be supported as part of self-directed learning. Our pedagogy focuses first on well-being, understanding that if a young person is not okay, they will struggle to learn anything at all.

Why give our children a voice within their education?

Our young people need to feel trusted. And so often they don't.

The philosophy being pushed, that children need to learn rigour and compliance, without listening to what they need, is frankly insulting and dehumanising to young people. Of the carrot and the stick, the stick can work in creating uniformity, in the short term. But the psychological effects are not things that we would tolerate as adults, and yet some say they are the best way to educate our kids. I say more carrots.

I'm not naive in thinking that an Awen education is for every child and their family, but what I do want recognised is that for some children it is better to have the option of attending schools like ours. There are significant numbers of young people who feel that mainstream education is not where they belong. The label they are given is 'school refusers',* which in itself summons up images of an obstinate stroppy teenager, rather than a child who finds themselves lost in the mainstream.

---

* A 'school refuser' is a child who has not been excluded for behaviour or one who is truanting, but for emotional reasons, and, with the knowledge of their parent/carer, is not attending school.

But if young people felt that their school was a society they were a part of, that they could change, rather than a sort of probation they need to wait out until they are old enough to be allowed rights, we might see more young voters. We might see more young people engaged in social enterprise, with a sense of civic duty, with a passion for societal change.

It's something government should chew over.

Kerry Kennedy is one of the most effective advocates and campaigners for children's voices being heard. She is my friend and colleague, and has developed a different, but complimentary, approach to Charlotte's, in helping children know that their voice counts. Hers is through human rights education, taught as an essential skill to understand human relationships and be able to express compassion, fairness and justice. Kerry has written this essay making the case for embedding human rights education at the heart of school curricula to empower children and young people to speak truth to power.

Uplifting the voices closest to the solution

Kerry Kennedy, human rights lawyer and President of Robert F. Kennedy Human Rights

It is a difficult time to be a child. We face existential challenges that threaten the very existence of our species: global warming, a pandemic killing almost 7 million people,[2] and the threat of nuclear annihilation. The world order is at risk – China is on the rise economically, militarily and politically; Russia's horrific invasion of Ukraine terrorises its neighbours and the world – democracies are in decline, not only from outside forces, but also from the very real populist enemy within. Hatred based on race, gender and sexual orientation target the innocent, and has an outsized impact on those who are already homeless, hungry, poor, on the move, subjected to violence and criminalised not just for what they do, but for who they are. Meanwhile, a billion children[3] worldwide face the life-threatening challenges of meeting basic requirements for food, clothes, medical supplies, shelter and safety, while others are sold as chattel, enslaved in garment factories, prostitution houses and agriculture fields, or forced to pick cocoa for more privileged children to gobble on at Halloween.

What to do?

Solutions must be an interwoven fabric of legislation, administrative steps, litigation and community action. Governments have a major role to play, as do families and our schools.

All this change will require the qualities of youth, 'Not a time of life', as Robert Kennedy put it, 'but a state of mind, a temper of the will, a quality of the imagination, a predominance of courage over timidity, of the appetite for adventure over the love of ease'.[4]

Our Speak Truth to Power education curriculum

We know that those closest to the problems are closest to the solution. So we must listen to children and respond with concrete action. In order for those children to be heard, they need tools, too. That's why Robert F. Kennedy Human Rights established the Speak Truth to Power (Speak Truth) education curriculum.

At Speak Truth, we train the next generation of human rights defenders. We teach students, kindergarten through law school, to know their rights and understand how to assert them. We teach them community-organising skills so they can be effective change makers within their communities, and we teach social-emotional skills, so they are able to manage emotions, develop healthy identities, feel empathy for others and make responsible decisions.

All our lesson plans begin with the story of a human rights defender. They are people like Elie Wiesel, who survived the Holocaust as a child. He said, 'My dream for the future is that your children won't have my past.'[5] And Archbishop Desmond Tutu, the great South African anti-apartheid activist, who said 'We don't have a God who says, "ahhh, got you", we have a God who lifts us up, dusts us off, and tells us to try it again.'[6] These are the bookends of human rights – on the one hand, trying to stop the atrocities, and on the other hand, having faith in the power of the human spirit, even under the worst of circumstances.

Students learn from people like the founder of the US-based Children's Defense Fund, Marian Wright Edelman, whose lesson plan recounts a conversation she had while working as a lawyer for Dr Martin Luther King. He told her: 'Fly. If you can't fly then run; if you can't run then walk; if you can't walk then crawl; and if you can't crawl, just keep on moving, keep on moving.'[7]

Students learn about His Holiness the Dalai Lama from Tibet, Malala Yousafzai from Pakistan and Jamie Nabozny, a high school student who considered suicide in the wake of brutal bullying because of his sexual orientation, until he hired a visionary lawyer, sued the school district and set a precedent to protect all children.

As students learn the stories of defenders, they note the heroes all have one quality in common: courage. Courage consists of bravery – a willingness to overcome fear, *combined* with compassion – a willingness to act on behalf of others. Moral courage is the rarest form of valour in the adult world; it is the willingness to risk being rejected by one's community for what one believes is right.

These stories resonate with students because it is they who are called on to muster moral courage every day. In chat rooms, in hallways, scribbled on bathroom walls, sung by favourite artists in popular music, words of hatred are daily fare: 'fatso', 'retard', 'homo' and more. Every time they hear a sexist joke or a racial slur, they must ask themselves, 'Will I be a perpetrator, a victim, a bystander or a human rights defender?' And each time they make the decision on which role they will play, they are exercising a 'muscle', making that 'muscle' stronger. And that 'muscle' is defining who they are. This can happen 10 or 15 times a day, every day, throughout middle and high school.

By the time they enter the adult world, they are no longer making a conscious decision. They are relying on muscle memory to decide how to act. So, as they engage with the stories of the defenders, they are exercising the 'defender muscle' and emerge as advocates who know their rights, how to assert them, how to listen with empathy and how to act and create change.

Learning about their rights fosters students' sense of self-worth, as well as the importance of being advocates for the betterment of all. By working together with leaders and partners to devise local-, state- and national-level curricula, we develop the next generation of leaders.

Embed human rights education at the heart of school learning

The current challenge is that school systems too often address human rights as an add-on or one-off programme rather than as a mechanism that underpins the core principles of education.

There is another way. That's why we advocate for a whole-school approach. This involves each of the constituents (teachers, students, administrators and parents) that make up a school agreeing to take a human rights-based approach.

So students are observing each group treating the others not in a hierarchy, but with mutual value and respect. This informs how the grounds crew are treated by teachers, how teachers are treated by administrators, and so on.

By centring human rights education at the core of our curriculum, we then extend the impact of traditional social-emotional learning, transforming personal empowerment into democratic engagement and social change.

That's why political leaders who care about community, democracy and the dignity of all must embed human rights education and a rights-based approach in every school.

Abubacar Sultan, a teacher from Mozambique, worked with child soldiers who had been forced to witness and commit murder, torture and rape – often members of their own families – during his country's brutal civil war. I asked why he risked his life doing this.

He explained,

> It is something strong which is within yourself. You feel you are a human being and there are other human beings there suffering. You are better off. So, you need to sacrifice. It's hard to explain. It's perhaps a kind of a gift that you have inside yourself, a gift to be able to give.[8]

Anyone who works with children has that gift inside themselves. For that, we can all be truly grateful.

There is now a UK-specific Speak Truth programme, taught in some schools in England. One such school has evidence that violence (in and around the school) declined by 50 per cent after introducing a daily 30-minute Speak Truth lesson.[9]

Conclusions

When children have their voices heard, society shows them that their words matter while also demonstrating inclusion and trust. The outcome is a better understanding of children's needs and how to support them, while those empowered to change things learn a different and vitally relevant perspective. We have seen too many children and their families who can't currently control their daily lives and who are forced, voiceless, to fit into a system that they can't shape. For too many, nobody asks them about what they think is best for them, and on the rare occasions that they do, little is done with such insight and knowledge. Finding ways to give this an agency – listening to such voices and using them to co-design solutions – would bring better outcomes, not only for the children and their families, but also for all of society and its future.

This short chapter should have helped us re-find, recognise and re-grasp the thread of 'voice' that has weaved through previous chapters, and remind us of how connected the different ideas, evidence and policy proposals are when considered from the viewpoint of agency and the power, impact and necessity of being heard.

Two more essays, containing additional proposals for government, are hosted at www.raisingthenation.co.uk:

- Gerard Silverlock was a headteacher and, with Prashant Raizada, is now involved in a schools' entrepreneurship project: the Lumi network. They set out how the education system must adapt to teach and develop 'future' skills necessary for a thriving economy and society, and to do this, how children must be seen *and* heard.

- Michael Tyler is a poet and writer from Chicago. He makes clear how literacy and access to books are both critical to children discovering their full potential and purpose, and how both can be enhanced to give children the confidence and imagination to articulate and own their agency.

12

Variety

[N]ot every child has an equal talent or an equal ability or equal motivation, but they should have the equal right to develop their talent and their ability and their motivation, to make something of themselves.

John F. Kennedy[1]

Variety: ensuring all children get to experience a wide array of learning, ideas, activities, environments and people (especially people 'not like them'), so they can find their passions and tolerances and develop open mindsets.

We have seen evidence of the importance of variety from the early years onwards. We caught a glimpse of it from intergenerational learning and relationship building, when care homes have been integrated with nurseries, bringing benefits to the very young and the very old. We saw the child-inspired mindset in the incredible projects Erion Veliaj has undertaken in Tirana in Albania. Every physical and mental piece of that city's public furniture is now designed by and for children with the simple goal of creating a city built for those aged eight and 80.

We learned how broadening the variety of how, where and with whom children play adds to accelerating the learning that helps them thrive, and how 'helicopter' and 'snow plough' parenting actually reduce children's experiences. As we saw in Bo Stjerne Thomsen's essay, the Danes have begun to harness a variety of ways to teach and incorporate play into the classroom and through teacher training.

A wider, more varied curriculum, taught through varied teaching techniques, is crucial to thrive in a VUCA world. As is the need to have a variety of assessment methods to ensure all children can fulfil their potential, and Sophie Maxwell's essay gave much food for thought on this in Chapter 6.

Widening the variety of experiences is critical to finding a route for vulnerable children to thrive. That way they will own the power to break the vicious cycles they are often trapped within. Our essayists wrote of the related dangers within separate state systems (such as care, justice, education, health or employment), and inferred how easy it can be, once caught in one system, to find oneself reeled into the negative aspects of others. Indeed, it is clear that solutions to help such children thrive lie in connecting the positive opportunities that link the systems and designing ways to navigate a beneficial path across each.

Ndidi Okezie has spent her career supporting vulnerable young people with youth work and life skills development. She has written this essay on how access to the variety of support services can be more easily accessible to young people, and consequently improve their opportunities to succeed.

Youth work: an idea to interlock the jigsaw pieces

Ndidi Okezie OBE, CEO of UK Youth

Before taking on my current role, my 20-year career was varied, but the unifying thread was a dedication to serving young people within the education sector. I have been a classroom teacher, a school leader, an executive director of an education charity and a vice-president of digital strategy for a global commercial education publisher.

Like many in the education sector, my experience had led me to believe that schools play *the most* critical role in developing young people, providing them with a quality education full of a variety of learning opportunities that would enable them to fulfil their potential.

In 2020, I became CEO of UK Youth, a leading national charity with an open network of over 8,000 youth organisations working right across the UK. In this role, I have been struck by the depth of expertise of the youth workers who so effectively navigate mental health, community and social challenges despite constant funding and capacity pressures. The experience has caused a humbling realisation: in those previous 20 years I'd not really known to engage the resource of professional skills from the youth sector to deliver the impact I'd worked so hard to achieve.

Youth work is a jigsaw puzzle

As professionals working to support young people, we are extremely fragmented and inclined to operate within silo-reinforcing frameworks. Although we each bring something of unique value to a young person's life, despite our best intentions, none of us is able to meet all the needs of the young people alone.

One of the key reasons that most professionals working with young people are on their knees with unmanageable workloads and growing pressures is that we commit so much valuable time trying to 'make up' for the gaps we see young people are facing, many of which exist beyond our own sphere of provision.

As professionals we have a duty of care and a burning desire to make things better for young people. Yet too many of us continue to feel overwhelmed and under-resourced, constantly facing insurmountable pressures.

Being young is a complicated path to navigate. These complications are further compounded when also coping with difficult family circumstances, living in socially or economically deprived environments, or having special educational needs.

There is an understandable tendency for professionals – across youth, education, social work and so on – to believe that we have the relationships, experience and training to take the leading role in equipping young people with what they need. That we are best placed to support the young person through the life path they need to navigate. The inference is that it is us alone who know what's best for them. On reflection, this is what I had thought about teachers.

But I am increasingly of the belief that this pattern of thinking is a key part of the problem. In our eagerness and compassion we can too easily over-estimate our individual importance in the lives of any one young person.

There are many pieces to the jigsaw

Think of all the variety of influences a young person encounters in any given week across their physical and virtual worlds – teachers, youth workers, sports coaches, parents/carers, siblings and peers in and out of school – let alone the numerous online celebrities and influencers across music, sports, film and social media.

The truth is that each one of us is just a piece of the complicated jigsaw of the life that young people are trying to build – often without the exposure or confidence to know what their puzzle could eventually look like. This is not to say that one individual cannot have a profound influence on a young person's life at key moments. But there are, more than likely, going to need to be many influences. A jigsaw with hundreds of small pieces is a lot harder to finish, especially if those pieces don't fit together very well. We don't want to overcomplicate things or force collaboration for the sake of it, but there is no such thing as a 'jigsaw' with a single piece, and likewise, one sector cannot be all a young person needs to thrive.

By having the clarity and humility to recognise that each of us working in the education, youth, social and health sectors are but one piece in the lives of the young people we support, we can stop exhausting ourselves trying to do it all. We can become a proactive piece, seeking to work across a more integrated and joined-up ecosystem. We cannot afford to continue to invest in broken, siloed systems that are exhausting the professionals and failing the young people they should be serving.

Here is my call for how we can reimagine our approach and become more effectively joined-up.

Interlocking the jigsaw pieces

We are all familiar with smartphones and the apps that operate on them. They each work within an intentionally built operating system that allows us to seamlessly use different apps to check emails, send messages, watch videos, play games, plan a journey and so on – whatever we want to do, 'there's an app for that'. Behind the scenes the apps work together on our behalf. They share information related to our behaviours, locations and preferences. When we want to do something – such as book a holiday, translate an article or monitor our expenditure – we can be confident that there is a specialist app that will draw on insights we've made available to it, and use information to increase the quality of our experience and the effectiveness of our activity. Most of that knowledge transfer happens without the need for our intervention. Because someone has thought ahead about the operating system, it all just works.

Just imagine if young people – most of whom have never known a world *without* smartphones – could seamlessly navigate through the variety of experiences and services they need to support their development and well-being in such an integrated fashion. Imagine a digitally powered ecosystem that could create a transformational model of insight-led delivery. The work of schools, youth, social organisations and network services would be interconnected, drawing on insights from each other's activity, and flexibly adapting services for the ever-changing needs of young people.

How empowering would it feel to navigate through an interconnected ecosystem where each of us youth professionals is free to focus on our specialist areas, but we are also able to be more than the sum of our parts for all young people. As government seeks to integrate its services through digital-enabling technology (thereby becoming more efficient and 'user-friendly'), it should be even bolder, working with key sectors to transform the development experiences and well-being of our young people. With all the advances technology has brought in the last few decades, we must be more committed to making it easier for young people to effectively navigate and access all that they need. We can achieve this by helping key sectors interlock their individual puzzle pieces, thereby unlocking far more effective expertise across the jigsaw kaleidoscope that is our youth development system.

Like Ndidi, Jon Yates leads a youth-focused charity. He is also the author of *Fractured*,[2] which tells the story of how our nation is divided and how to fix it. Those fixes are creative ways to bring us into contact and friendship with those in our country who might seem different to us. This perspective flows through this essay – Jon asks, what if our children met and connected with people from all walks of life? What might it do for their health, happiness and opportunity?

'No child is an island' (with apologies to John Donne)
Jon Yates, Executive Director of the Youth Endowment Fund and author

Be careful if you visit my house. My children surround visitors with toys to display and tales to tell. When the storm breaks, my dazed visitors normally say one of three things: 'Well, they seem healthy', 'At least they're happy' or 'What on earth do you think they'll do when they're older?'

Health, happiness and a good job. Isn't that what most of us want for our children? So how are we doing at providing them?

There are reasons to worry. A third of our children now leave primary school overweight, raising the risk of high blood pressure and other health problems. Survey after survey suggests that our children are less happy than children in Europe.[3] And as for getting a good job, it still depends on your parents' wealth. It takes five generations for a low-income family to have a child who will get a well-paid job.[4]

When it comes to health, happiness and opportunity, it's not just what you know, it's who you know that counts, as three stories reveal.

Stewart Wolf and the mystery of Roseto

In the late 1950s, Dr Stewart Wolf made a visit to the village of Roseto, Pennsylvania, where he was introduced to a medical mystery. The villagers had very unhealthy lifestyles. They smoked, drank and ate pizza covered in sausages. They hardly exercised. And yet, hardly anyone had a heart attack.

This was extraordinary. Heart attacks in the 1950s were the main cause of death for middle-aged men. Wolf was cynical. He reviewed medical records and conducted blood tests before believing it. But sure enough, the youngsters had no signs of heart disease and the elderly had half the rate of other Americans.

There was another odd thing about Roseto. Everyone knew each other. Rosetans stopped in the street and chatted. Neighbours cooked for each other. Homes had three generations living under one roof. The local church bustled with people, as did the 22 different social clubs. The town had just 2,000 people, but they were incredibly well connected.

Dr Wolf had a theory. Could this wide set of friendships be what was keeping Rosetans in good health? Time would prove him right. Today, Rosetans' lifestyles have not changed: cigars are still smoked and exercise is rarely taken. But one thing has changed: community life has largely gone. And the remarkable health of the people of Roseto? It is also in the past: today, Rosetans die of heart attacks at the same rate as everybody else.[5]

The professors and the stress test

Two professors, Elizabeth Page-Gould and Rodolfo Mendoza-Denton, conducted an experiment about friendship. They paired up strangers and asked them simply to talk to each other. Before and after the strangers met, they did a swab test[6] for one hormone – cortisol.

Cortisol matters. It regulates blood pressure and supports our immune system; it gives us energy. We need it when we exercise. We shouldn't need it when sitting and talking.

And yet, at the end of the strangers' meetings, there was the cortisol. This didn't make sense. These volunteers weren't doing any exercise. There was something even odder. Cortisol only showed up when the volunteers thought the person they were meeting for the first time was 'not like them'.

There is one other thing that causes cortisol: stress. What the experiment had shown was that spending time with people who seem 'unlike us' causes us stress. This sounds like bad news for our children. They are growing up in societies full of difference – whether by race, age, income, politics or religion – so does this mean they are destined to be anxious?

But there is good news. The professors got the strangers to meet each other twice more. At the end of the third meeting, they took swab tests. The high cortisol level had gone. It had taken just three conversations for them to feel at home and at ease with strangers who initially seemed different. How do we protect our children from anxiety in a world full of difference? We get them mixing and meeting people – and realising that we have more in common than we thought.

The fair city

Harvard-based economist Raj Chetty was on a mission: he wanted to know if poor children could still get ahead. And so he started analysing the salary of every American born between 1980 and 1982 and the salary of their parents. He identified the children born into poverty who were now doing well and marked where they had grown up. Bingo. He had a map of the places where poorer children could still get ahead.[7]

I want to tell you about one of those places. Maybe you picture it as a diverse, creative location with a reputation for innovation? Lots of manufacturing on the outskirts, to provide jobs for all? One of the highest spenders on education, presumably? Probably with a population that is left-leaning, secular, even hipster?

Far from it. It sits in a state that is strongly Republican, mostly White, and with no big manufacturing base. It is not secular; it is deeply religious. It is the capital of a state that funds its schools less than any other in the country. Our social mobility utopia is Salt Lake City.

The answer, again, is relationships. Salt Lake City's schools continue to educate richer and poorer children side by side. Outside school, almost half of Salt Lake children attend the Mormon Temple – where they meet people who are rich and those who are poor. Poorer children have access to the same friendships, the same networks, the same expectations. It's not what you know, it's who you know that counts.

So what do we do?

Here's the problem. Our children are growing up in a country that has become divided. Half of graduates have almost exclusively graduate friends. A quarter of us have no friends who voted the other way on Brexit. Half of us have no friends from a different ethnic group. The largest divide remains class – the average barrister would have to invite 100 friends to a party to be confident of inviting a single person who was unemployed.

Our three stories show why this matters. Division makes our children less happy, less healthy and less well off.

It doesn't have to be this way. We could give our children the connections they need.

We could start with school admissions. Half of our poorest children are educated together in a fifth of our schools. The government recently gave every school the power to reserve places for families who can't afford to live in the catchment area.[8] If you're a school governor, you could make this happen.

And how about the curriculum? Most children spend over 100 months learning maths, English, history and science. The government could protect just one month for children to take on a project together in their local community. One month to learn how to work and have fun with people from all backgrounds.

Finally, there are so many local charities that would love to work with our schools, getting children involved in the community. Why doesn't it happen? Partly because these charities don't know who at the school to contact. This is easy to fix. Each school should have a single point of contact for local charities to contact.

I am proposing three small changes that will make our children happier, healthier and better off. It takes a village to raise a child. It's time we brought the village back together.

Finally, we have Janice Allen, a headteacher in Rochdale, who sees the role of her school within her community as one beyond just providing a good education. In this essay she argues that schools are places in 'the village' that are ideally placed to provide a variety of support and intervention for children and families beyond quality education.

Schools: the hubs of community

Janice Allen, headteacher

Many of us have become accustomed to reading about child poverty, poor mental health and high levels of anxiety in young people, of the Child and Adolescent Mental Health Service (CAMHS) waiting lists, and of communities scarred by years of austerity. All of these realities are interlinked: solving one requires a broad view and an understanding of the others. I have put this theory into practice with the idea that schools can act as *the* community hubs, the place that provides the link between connected challenges, by hosting and working alongside charities and statutory services, to provide streamlined services to support affected children and their families. Our pilots show how the 'power of place and convenience' can lead to behaviour change among professionals, and support families and wider communities better, to not only survive, but to thrive.

I've been a headteacher since 2015. I work in an environment that is not 'neat' – my school has over 1,000 pupils from dozens of heritage backgrounds. The complexity of problems they face means there is no single logistical or procedural solution to any. They are all interlinked. The problems our community faces are not abstract concepts: we live and breathe them, every day. Yet there is extraordinary hope in children, and I have found by developing community partnerships that we can best help our young. By focusing on place-based, local change – with schools as hubs for social and health services and through bonding with local community partners and families – we have found a way to navigate some of the barriers in our engrained systems. At Falinge Park High School we began the process by building a community wing to the school.

Our vision

Two pieces of knowledge started our thinking journey.

First, discovering 'only 30 per cent of the explanation for variations in school achievement appears to be attributable to factors in the school'.[9] This led us to explore the question: 'What can schools do to influence the 70 per cent of variation that is a consequence of factors in the public realm, outside the school environment?'[10]

Second, discovering social relationships determine learning and that pupils' primary audience and influence is their peers: 'When there is a clash between the peer culture and the teacher's management procedures, the peer culture wins every time.'[11]

We committed to think about how we could influence the public realm and the peer world in order to ensure better equity in achievement opportunities for all students. We realised that community investment was as important as academic attainment to build necessary social capital. So we set about building connections with third sector (charity) and statutory (public) organisations to enhance the variety and quality of networks and support our pupils and families could experience. We quickly found that the best partners, and the greatest impact, were generated when the partnerships were hyper-local. We therefore didn't seek to bring in large national organisations, but instead built on connections with our local authority and community-based organisations. Here are two examples:

1. Reducing youth violence

Working with Early Break, a local substance misuse charity, and Rochdale Youth Service, we built a strong three-way partnership that enabled us to bid for funding to tackle youth violence in the area. The partnership involved Early Break and youth workers coming into school to work alongside staff, individuals and groups of pupils, especially in those crucial 'after-school' hours of 3–6pm, when all would go out together into the local community. Early Break provided 'Teen Yoga' for pupils with high levels of anxiety during the school day, and youth workers provided support for groups of pupils at risk of exclusion and involved in antisocial behaviour outside school. The magic ingredient was that activities happened both in school *and* in the community.

2. Wraparound care for families

We supported our pupils to help with volunteering at local charities to extend their social awareness. By engaging them in social action, we created and evolved partnerships with local place-based charities that then came into school to support school-families in crisis or in need of help. Parents built on the relationships to develop a Parent Pantry, and we brought Greater Manchester food banks into the partnership circle together with our local community centre to offer targeted sessions for parents who needed help with Universal Credit, housing, asylum status or managing home finances. The convening of such needed and trusted partners has proved how central schools are beyond providing education to the lives of local families.

What next?
This is just a snapshot of our work to positively influence the circumstances pupils encounter beyond the school gate. There is more that we can do to make a real difference. Schools could:

- place health practitioners in schools to limit the need for parents to take children to appointments at inconvenient times and places. Parents currently tell us that attending appointments at hospitals, which may be two bus journeys away, make it difficult in terms of work, and taking children out of school for these appointments can often take a full morning. If health practitioners operated from school premises after the school day, these issues could be minimised and result in greater attendance at both appointments and lessons;
- develop place-based partnerships with social services. Local partnerships could operate from a 'hub' school and local issues could be identified so support can be targeted by place. This could create better information sharing and cross-school working between different types of schools via the hub school;
- provide space for local charities to operate so that social prescribing can take place and be easily accessible.

Rethinking schools as community hubs and investing in community education coordinators to create and deliver local partnerships can make change happen that will improve families' lives, which is therefore likely to improve educational attainment. This does not necessarily require funding but rather redeployment of staffing resources, which could, in turn, lead to more intelligent and responsive data sharing.

Yet our piloting experience highlighted that bureaucracy can be a huge barrier to implementation. Schools are often seen by policy makers as recipients of programmes rather than active participants and partners with expertise held within the school. By schools working with communities and agencies, we could cut down on bureaucracy and inaction and act before problems occur.

Mobilising the potential of schools as community hubs for support and services beyond learning is not new thinking. But our pilots and experience have shown that by acting, even with a small but committed team of community leads working in partnership with different agencies, we can begin to address problems faced within local communities, and ensure that while we continue to strive for educational excellence, children no longer need go without food, live in unsafe areas or not have a bed to sleep in. A variety of services can support them in one place. School.

Conclusions

Being exposed to a variety of people, activities and experiences helps children understand that the world is made up of different cultures, perspectives and social experiences. Variety allows them to develop skills and interests. It is key in helping children become thriving individuals who not only have more understanding and capabilities, but also more opportunities to find their passions.

This short chapter should have helped us re-find, recognise and re-grasp the thread of 'variety' that has weaved through previous chapters. It's also a reminder of how connected the different ideas, evidence and policy proposals are when considered from the viewpoint of variety. It is worth reflecting on the power, impact and necessity of experiencing a childhood that offers a wide variety of positive experiences from which to find passions and a purpose, as well as the best opportunity to discover oneself.

One additional essay, containing another proposal for government, is hosted at www.raisingthenation.co.uk:

- Mahamed Hashi is founder of Brixton Soup Kitchen and New Beginnings Youth Provision, and has much experience of youth work. He focuses on the variety of opportunities work and work schemes can offer young people in search of their purpose in life.

13

Well-being

We hold these truths to be self-evident, that all men are created equal, that they are endowed by their Creator with certain unalienable Rights, that among these are Life, Liberty and the pursuit of Happiness.

Thomas Jefferson[1]

Well-being: ensuring children are thoroughly supported in developing strong mental health and meaningful relationships: with themselves, their friends, society at large and in their connection to the planet.

I like the definition of 'well-being' as being the experience of health, happiness and prosperity. It includes having good mental health, high life satisfaction, a sense of meaning of purpose and the ability to manage stress.[2] Without a strong foundation of being well, nothing else is possible for children. This aspiration is not a fluid, difficult-to-measure, 'modern' concept pushed by progressive liberals. As you can see from the quote that begins this chapter, this core aspiration is baked into the formation of the United States of America. In many respects, it's why the country exists. It forms part of the legal responsibility of the US government, and for over 250 years has underpinned, as a foundation, the world's oldest written constitution. It is that serious.

Too often in this book we've seen examples of how efficiency, cost management or certain social philosophies interfere with the deployment of optimal support for children. Unsurprisingly we have found confused results, rarely in the interests of the recipient child's well-being.

I have argued that an education drenched with economic agendas cannot also be one that delivers broader well-being for all students. It should be no surprise that the market concept of 'winners and losers' at the heart of a competitive system is felt by children every day. Where each of us lives, its safety and appearance, how easy it is to get around, the opportunities we can access nearby and the messages we see around us – these are all factors that matter to our ability to become the person we have the potential to be. In this we have seen, as ever, inequality of opportunity and social deprivation undermine well-being chances.

Our collective actions must be at the service of well-being, not at the expense of it. The obvious conclusion, the reality, is that if we want well-being for all, we can't tackle it through siloed approaches.

Well-being is critical in every part of each childhood, from holistic culture and metrics to specific environments and choices, including in decisions taken by the state. Ruth Luzmore has much experience as a school designated safeguarding lead,★ witnessing numerous families' experiences with the social care system, and how the system is, or isn't, equipped to cope with best protecting a child's, and also a family's, well-being in challenging circumstances. She has also been a teacher and headteacher at an inner-city primary school, and has written this essay for us.

How best to support each 'child in need'

Ruth Luzmore, former headteacher

For those working in schools, concerns about the well-being of a child rarely start with the type of crisis you see in TV dramas. In most cases, little bits of seemingly insignificant information come together over time, like putting together a jigsaw, before there is a trigger event that prompts you to refer

---

★ A 'designated safeguarding lead' is the person who is appointed to take lead responsibility for child protection issues in school. They work with all school staff to make sure there is a culture of safeguarding, keeping and monitoring all records and providing advice. They also manage referrals to social care or the police.

a family for support. It could perhaps be the mental health of a parent, a breakdown in a relationship at home, a concern about a child's physical appearance or their housing situation. In most cases, referrals are made for early help* with the permission of the child's legal guardians.

As a professional, I'm always relieved when that referral goes in: it means support is on its way. For less complex cases, this may mean an assessment takes place with a 'team around the family or child' meeting. Here a small group of relevant professionals and the family discuss the issues and a plan of action is agreed. This might be as simple as signposting a parent to a structured parenting programme, or a support worker helping to negotiate with housing or debt. Home visits might occur, or the school may make adjustments in provision of their support. The intervention is time-restricted so that once the piece of work is done, the family is signed off the system. For most, this is all that is needed – timely intervention for a particular problem.

More complex cases may lead to a Section 17 assessment, known as a 'child in need'. This occurs where the local authority is required to step in and support in a much more formal way because there is concern that the child is at risk of harm, or is unlikely to be able to achieve or maintain reasonable health or development without intervention. Here professionals from multiple agencies (such as social workers and professionals with health, housing and education specialist expertise) get involved to put together a 'child in need' plan. After the initial early help interventions, another round of assessments takes place.

While the intentions of those around the table are good, and information sharing ensures a coherent planning of interventions, I have no doubt that it can be an overwhelming experience for the parent whose family life is suddenly under scrutiny, not only from strangers, but also those they know professionally. I've been in meetings where one parent has sat with ten professionals, each sharing reports and expressing opinions on their life. I've often wondered whether I'd be as dignified as the families I've worked with in such circumstances – but in those initial meetings, they always are. They desperately want to make things better for their family.

Yet the faces of those in the meetings seem to change regularly – families are referred to different services and have to explain their very personal and sometimes quite traumatic circumstances over and over again. I've seen families build effective relationships with one social worker only for that social

---

*   'Early help' intervention is support given to a family when a problem first emerges rather than waiting for a situation to escalate.

worker to be moved to another team or leave the profession and another put in their place. It becomes a negative pattern that leads to cynicism, not only for the family, but also, I have to admit, from people like me who, while maintaining a professional front, find it frustrating. Let me be clear, I don't think this is the fault of social workers or their teams, but rather a symptom of the system they are working in which is under pressure.

Over time I've seen the trust parents put in the process designed to support them ebbing away, particularly when professionals can be quick to say it's not within their service's remit to support with certain problems, when the reality is that there is no one else to step up. It is even worse when the family's circumstances don't meet the threshold for support or intervention. That one really stings – a family is essentially told that instead of intervening now to prevent a situation getting worse, they'll need to wait until they are in crisis to get help. It's not surprising that tensions can become very high. At this stage, engaging with a 'child in need' plan is voluntary for the family, and sometimes they disengage from the process completely by removing their consent.*

The Children's Act 1989 imposes on local authorities a duty to 'safeguard and promote the welfare' of children. It is a duty designed to 'promote the upbringing of children by their families', and one that is designed to be supportive, flexible and, more importantly, preventative. But the evolution of an underfunded and constrained system means that genuine early help is so closely guarded that those families who voluntarily stand up and say 'I need help' are being triaged as not needing it enough. While everyone wants to do what is in the best interests of the child, you just know that they are being further damaged by the system, which is not prepared to put in the resources to allow for long-term relationships that can hold steady a family through their difficult times. My experiences of the system are not unique. The 2022 independent MacAlister Review into social care[3] is a difficult but important read as it holds a mirror up to such imperfections. It has hit the nail on the head with its recommendations for change, being to:

1. Bring together the work undertaken at early help and 'child in need' level rather than place it under separate teams. Make sure these teams include a multi-disciplinary workforce, for example having social workers in a

---

* Where there is evidence that a child is suffering or is likely to suffer significant harm, a Section 47 is completed, and if it meets the threshold, a statutory child protection plan is put together, and there is a legal requirement for families to engage.

team with family support workers, youth workers, probation officers and more. This will minimise the number of referrals, assessments and bureaucracy needed, meaning families get the support they need in a much more timely sense. This is happening in some local authorities, but requires a significant push and cultural change to make it widespread.

2.   Put in place greater transparency and consistency about what it means to be eligible for support. Sadly the thresholds for support differ depending on the local authority, and probably the resources they have available. The mere act of asking for help is a good indication that a family should be provided with signposts and an indication of what they can expect.

In my experience, schools are ideal places that these 'family help' teams could be located. They are the one place in the community that those with children have to engage. Conversations at pick-up time at the school gate are extremely powerful in getting information out. By having a presence in schools, the stigma of asking for help could be further broken down. Clearly this will only work, though, if the help then offered is itself de-stigmatised and impactful. We owe it to children to make it so.

While Ruth focuses on the challenges within a system supporting a public service in order to prioritise children in need's well-being, Kirsty McNeill has developed ideas on a very different aspect of child well-being – the design of public spaces and the consequent impact on all children's well-being. Kirsty has written this essay highlighting how children are often ignored by society, by design. She proposes steps that would enhance their well-being, bringing their experience of the public environment and collective life to a level that adults already enjoy.

Inclusive by default

Kirsty McNeill, Executive Director for Policy, Advocacy and Campaigns at Save the Children UK

People who have children or who work with them know this feeling well: the sense that there will *always* be someone else who is the first thing we think about when we wake up and the last thing we think about before we go to sleep. Those of us responsible for children think about them *all the time*.

Somehow, however, the systems and structures that govern our lives seem not to have been designed with children in mind at all. What might our country look like if we flipped that – if everyone providing a service or designing a system had to be inclusive by default?

Let's take just one day as an example of what I'm talking about. My family and I leave our flat and are immediately surrounded by dangerous levels of pollution. Remember that UNICEF UK found that one in three children are breathing harmful levels of dirty air *every day*.[4] We're going to the station to get an intercity train. We go via the shop for snacks for the journey. Junk food and energy drinks are everywhere, some obviously marketed at children – a reminder of why the UK's childhood obesity rates are worse than anywhere else in Western Europe.[5] We get on the train where there are quiet carriages to allow workers to be productive, but no family-friendly carriages with smaller seats, where playing games or watching cartoons would be welcome. The toilet doesn't have baby changing facilities. There is nowhere to breastfeed.

How many parents could tell the story of a day like this? At Save the Children we work with parents on low incomes, those living at the sharp end of decisions made by people who simply don't understand their lives or those of their little ones. Families now, faced with spiralling bills, who say they are 'constantly stressed and worrying. The government really don't have a clue what it's like for people who are struggling to survive.'[6]

I believe life for these families – for all families – could be transformed if legislation mandated that products and services must be inclusive by default. There will, of course, be some things (like cigarettes) that should never be available for children and some environments (like nightclubs) that can never be made safe for them. Likewise, laws that prohibit child labour and child marriage should be, if anything, strengthened. Beyond such exemptions, surely we should not allow the legal exclusion of children from environments and experiences from which they could benefit or simply enjoy.

Some people might object that a legal default to inclusion represents an unwarranted intrusion into the mechanics of the market or the public sector. That doesn't bear much scrutiny: there are plenty of instances where we have mandated providers to do (and not do) things because we think fairness should trump their freedom to do as they please. The Equality Act 2010 exists to do exactly this, ensuring, for example, that buses accommodate wheelchairs and councils provide information in accessible formats. That we still have a long way to go in securing full equality and inclusion for groups who have been traditionally discriminated against or left out is an argument for raising the legal floor, not for failing to set one.

Others might claim that children already enjoy legal protections, such as a right to schooling and to be free from cruelty and neglect, but beyond that society has no obligations. In this line of thinking, it is for parents alone to provide and fight for their kids. But let's consider for a minute how big a potential lobbying group parents are, yet how weak their political impact remains.

There are more than 14 million adults who are parents or caregivers to children under 18.[7] There are also more than a million people working in schools, a large workforce of children's social workers, paediatricians, midwives, play workers and youth workers and hundreds of thousands of people volunteering with children. You'd think that would be an unstoppable force, but you'd be wrong.

We can tell how little children's interests are fought for by the fact that it is estimated that another 500,000 children will be in absolute poverty in 2024.[8] By the fact, as James Kirkup of the Social Market Foundation noted in the summer of 2020, that we were able, 'as a country ... to reopen pubs, shops, hair salons and holiday cottages' during COVID-19 but not to 'find a way to educate our children'.[9] And by the fact that Robert Hughes and colleagues in the *British Medical Journal* (*BMJ*) reported that the terms of reference for the UK's COVID-19 public inquiry 'do not include the words child, childhood, babies, toddlers, school, childcare, college, or for that matter, play, interaction or socialisation'.[10]

For whatever reasons – perhaps circumstantial (parents are, famously, perennially exhausted), perhaps structural (there are no trades unions or trade bodies for parents) and perhaps based on demography (parents of new-borns may not see themselves as having the same identity and interests as those looking after teens) – the latent power of families has yet to be realised.

Another hesitation raised by some is that it would be very onerous to implement and would require a total rethink from every government department, every council, every business. That is indeed true – and is somewhat the point.

Let's retrace my day's journey from this perspective. Imagine if my council had to consider, in every transport and planning decision, what the implications would be for the level of pollution and the health of children's lungs? Imagine if my train provider had an obligation to explain to me why they *wouldn't* provide carriages that were safe, comfortable and fun for kids who would be in them for hours on end? Imagine if baby changing and breastfeeding facilities were available *as standard*?

Imagine, too, a world in which the families Save the Children works with have the security of a welfare safety net strong enough to catch them when it's needed and an employment market providing jobs with family-friendly pay and conditions as the norm. Imagine a world in which it's cheaper to fill the shopping basket with nutrients for hungry minds than processed food that makes our children ill.

This future is more achievable than we think. Getting to it will take three things:

- The first operates at the level of a paradigm shift – this book and the wider push for a child-centred future is part of that. Every reader we can persuade to make children central to their thinking gets us closer to that new reality.
- The second is building what I've previously called 'a broad and diverse families' movement dedicated to putting children's futures at the heart of our national recovery'.
- The third is finding and backing policy entrepreneurs inside the system who can devise pilots, write laws and drive implementation. Who will be the first council, the first corporate, the first MP to take up the cause?

If we can meet all three conditions simultaneously, we can make our country inclusive by default, and in the process, deliver not simply a society where children can thrive, but where we all can. For centuries children's well-being has been out of mind. It's time to make it top.

Finally, David Gregson, a successful businessman, investor and philanthropist, has spent much time and energy considering broad and holistic well-being for children and young people – what it is, how it might be best measured and what can be done with the findings to improve it. He has written an essay specifically covering the incredible project he has created for children and young people to be involved in defining, measuring and supporting their well-being.

'I'm learning about myself'

David Gregson, founder of #BeeWell, co-founder of Phoenix Equity Partners, Executive Committee Member of the Institute for Fiscal Studies and Director of the Barclays Women's Super League

Every few years the Organisation for Economic Co-operation and Development (OECD) publishes its influential and comprehensive Programme for International Student Assessment (PISA) on the global status of student learning outcomes. The publication of its latest report, at the end of 2018, was a sobering moment.

While the UK rose in the academic attainment rankings from 23rd to 13th, our young people were shown to have the fourth lowest levels of life satisfaction across the 79 countries surveyed.[11] Further analysis completed by my family's Foundation[12] showed that young people in five other European countries enjoyed considerably higher life satisfaction levels than British kids, while achieving similar attainment levels in the core subjects of maths, reading and science.[13]

I'm British but have lived in the Netherlands for over 15 years. How could it be that Dutch young people could enjoy a much more positive view of their lives compared to those in the UK? Reasons I've reflected on include that for the Dutch, the gap between rich and poor is narrower; the country's public infrastructure is well invested; and the country is smaller, with a clear system of devolved authority to local areas.

However, two other significant differences stand out.

First, the Dutch culturally believe that 'a satisfied child is a learning child'.[14] Policy reflects this belief, evidenced through the delivery of a nationwide well-being survey of young people by Youth Monitor. This survey has been delivered for some 40 years through almost every school in the country, and seeks to understand children's lives, so that everyone involved in their upbringing can act on the findings.[15]

Second, Dutch children have real agency in helping shape the system that is assisting them to create their own futures. This starts from the very top, with, for example, the Prime Minister encouraging young people during the pandemic to share their views on education with the government.[16]

By contrast, policy makers (as opposed to practitioners) within the English education system often feel divided by opposing perspectives that are hard to bridge. On the one hand, there are those who believe in a knowledge-based education, with success measured largely in terms of exam results. On the other hand, others focus on well-being and the importance of child agency.

This divide in perceptions is not actually shared by British parents. In 2021, my family Foundation co-funded a survey of British parents with the Youth Sport Trust.[17] It showed that the well-being of their child was the single most important criterion by which parents judge their choice of secondary school. However, parents also gave great weight to attainment. They want both.

British employers are also concerned about the English education system. In 2022, the Times Education Commission surveyed directors of large companies and found strong support for a shift of emphasis in school.[18] Over half would like to see a greater emphasis on personal skills, and 70 per cent thought that the system focused too much on grades.

Against all this background, in 2019, I approached Dame Nancy Rothwell, Vice-Chancellor of the University of Manchester, with a proposal: a well-being questionnaire delivered to as many young people of secondary school age as possible across Greater Manchester. The results would help us design new frameworks and actions that would improve the well-being of young people and be a template for other regions to follow. This would not be at the expense of learning and attainment. Far from it; it would actually complement it.

Professionals and senior executives from across the city region were keen to build on their existing work in this area, and from these embryonic beginnings the #BeeWell programme was born. It has three core elements:

- listening to the voices of young people through a standardised and validated questionnaire reflecting the issues that young people themselves have identified;
- inspiring a coalition of local and national partners to act on the results of what the young people have said;
- celebrating the well-being of young people across the relevant city regions.

It's extraordinary to realise how far our thinking has come, thanks to various catalysts on the way. First, as the tide went out during the pandemic, the rocks of inequality and mental health issues became all too visible right across British society. Second, there is a growing awareness of the benefits of prevention (well-being) as opposed to cure (mental health intervention). Finally, the government's focus on the power of data in inspiring the Levelling Up agenda has shone a light on programmes such as #BeeWell, which are considered exemplars of this type of thinking.

#BeeWell has, in fact, seemed to catch a moment in time: some three-quarters of mainstream secondary schools across Greater Manchester, to date, have taken part, and as a result we have already heard the voices of over 50 per cent of all young people in the relevant age groups across Greater Manchester in the first two years of delivery. This isn't a survey – it's a census.

Meaningful analysis of this rich data source can now guide how to improve the well-being of young people in the coming years, both in schools and in neighbourhoods. The #BeeWell framework of well-being drivers covers six areas: health and routines, hobbies and entertainment, school, environment and society, relationships, and young people's views of their futures.

As I write this, we are barely at the end of the beginning. We are partnering with the Greater Manchester Combined Authority (GMCA), its ten local authorities and multiple other partners to embed the programme across Greater Manchester. In addition, we are now working with partners across the Hampshire and Isle of Wight Integrated Care System region to tailor and then deliver, with excellence, the #BeeWell programme in this second area from Autumn 2023.

We envision many developments in the coming years, building the case for policy change by 2030. I have drawn out four in particular below:

- The steady adoption of consistent, regular measurement of young people's well-being in regions across England. How can we improve something when there are as many as 200 different surveys of well-being operating in English schools today?
- The publication, by neighbourhood, of well-being data, without reference back to participating schools, to inspire action across civil society, as is already happening in Greater Manchester.
- An increasing perspective across civil society, led by the views of young people themselves, that equal priority should be given to attainment and well-being.
- Ultimately, policy makers wishing to adopt a more balanced regulatory framework for schools.

And so finally back to the Dutch. In 2021, I visited a secondary school in the Netherlands and asked a 13-year-old girl what she was learning. I expected her to talk about algebra, the books she was reading or the chemical reactions she was studying. Far from it. She told me that she was learning about the most important thing – herself. There would still be plenty of time to learn about other things.

It was an answer that feels important for British young people to be able to give in the years to come, if they are to thrive in a modern world. The early beginnings of #BeeWell suggests that there is an appetite across society for us to move that way.

We are determined to create an environment where the voices of young people are heard, where reliable and consistently measured data can drive a broader approach, so that our young people become fulfilled and productive citizens within their own country and within a changing world. They, and we, deserve nothing less.

Conclusions

Well-being helps children recognise their strengths and weaknesses and develop an understanding of their emotions, and how to manage them when forming meaningful relationships. It also helps children develop a sense of purpose and connection to their communities and the environment. If their well-being has been taken care of, children can learn to develop the skills and positive attitudes needed to reach their full potential. It just takes a society and a government to prioritise their well-being as its measure of national success to begin to build a better future.

This short chapter should have helped us re-find, recognise and re-grasp the thread of 'well-being' that has weaved through previous chapters, and remind us of how connected the different ideas, evidence and policy proposals are when considered from the viewpoint of ensuring children are supported and have opportunity for thriving relationships – so they can have every opportunity to pursue happiness in childhood and throughout their lives.

Two additional essays, containing more proposals for government, are hosted at www.raisingthenation.co.uk:

- Laurence Guinness is CEO of The Childhood Trust, London's leading child poverty charity. He picks on a particular aspect of being a child in poverty, asking: what happens to their well-being during school holidays?

- Iqbal Wahhab OBE is a successful entrepreneur, philanthropist and restaurateur, and founder of The Cinnamon Club and Roast restaurants. He has supported many projects tackling injustice in the criminal justice system and how business can help government solve youth inequalities of opportunity and justice. He has written about an idea to create an 'Investors in Children' award and Kitemark for businesses.

14

A National Children's Service

Article 3: The best interests of the child must be a top priority in all decisions and actions that affect children.

Article 6: Every child has the right to life. Governments must do all they can to ensure that children survive and develop to their full potential.

Extract from the United Nations Convention
on the Rights of the Child[1]

This morning, a misty, winter's morning, I sat at my desk and looked out of the window, pondering how to start this concluding chapter. Deep in thought, I noticed a snail's trail winding its way across the pane and a little spider's web, full of dew, in the window's corner. These two little creatures' work offers a metaphor for the challenge in writing an inherently linear book on a subject like this. People don't lead linear and compartmentalised lives. Everything is connected. Yet government structures, systems and solutions don't reflect the way we live our lives.

The snail spent last night crossing the window, meandering a bit, but essentially spending its time going from A to B. Such a path has essentially been the way this book has enabled me to share my vision for raising a nation of thriving children. Taking you on a journey, hopefully meandering on the scenic route and pointing out sights to see along the way: ideas small charities have delivered on a local scale, programmes other nations have implemented, research insights academics have produced and lived experiences essayists have shared. With one chapter following the next, we've crossed the terrain and are at the next juncture, ready to act.

But it wasn't just the snail that was busy overnight. The spider, instead of going from A to B, spent the night weaving its web, exploring its corner of the world by connecting all the strands of its yarn together. Its interconnected web brought all the bits together. Its strength is dependent on its collective strands working together. It is designed to capture anything that comes by. So it is with the arguments and stories shared in this book: their potential impact depends on the strength of the connections between them. A future in which children thriving will only be achieved if policies, services and support are integrated. Like the spider's web.

The spider is our hero. Its design gives us the structure of a National Children's Service that can support all children to grow into the people they have the potential to be.

Before progressing, we need to remind ourselves that the structure of government in the UK devolves certain responsibilities to its nations: the Scottish and Welsh Parliaments and the Northern Ireland Assembly, while the UK Parliament has responsibility for equivalent matters in England. Devolved powers vary across the nations, but generally include education, housing, environment, social care and health. I have therefore used the term 'National Children's Service' as shorthand for a collective of 'Nations' Children's Services' to reflect the fact that four separate services would likely evolve from the proposals in this chapter. A similar distinction is true for the National Health Service, which is, more accurately, four National Health Services.

Building a spider's web

Spinning silk

Spiders' silk, called gossamer, is about six times stronger by weight than high-grade steel. It is stronger than any known natural or synthetic fibre, more durable and elastic than the strongest man-made fibre and extremely pliable. These properties mirror those needed for bindings that will harness a system worthy of our children's potential. And its chemical design – the interaction of ingredients that create the gossamer and give it its properties – is akin to the way evidence, research, reports, pilots, programmes, knowledge, lived experiences and ideas must combine to create the supporting structure where all children have a chance to flourish.

Our web's spokes

The preceding chapters are a journey through the challenges children face. We've seen how society has tried to respond and adapt to changing circumstances and equip new generations to thrive, using both cultural and legal structures. Culture is a living mechanism; it adapts in real time and evolves. It binds movements, evolves by trial and error, through an invisible hand, as some fads and trends fall away and others become cultural norms. In many ways culture is the 'bottom-up' agent of change. This book has focused on culture indirectly, largely as an influencer of policy change, or as a response to such change, but of course young people have also always played significant roles in shaping human culture.

In contrast, legal structures are defined by institutions and statutes. These invariably are fixed in time and respond through rules. They are clunky and don't easily evolve. They require concerted effort to shift. This book has focused more directly on changing legal structures.

Just as my spider tethered its web to my window frame, so, too, cultural and legal structures shape the circumstances affecting different aspects of children's lives.

Spiders first construct spokes that frame the whole web. In our case, the spokes were constructed by the themes in Chapters 3 to 10, being:

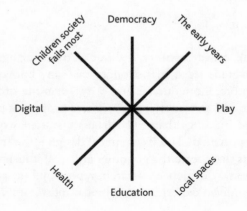

These spokes begin to pull together all aspects of children's lives, but they don't prevent what (in Chapter 7) Nick Wilkie captured so succinctly, 'the self-defeating propensity at all levels to tackle presenting symptoms in isolation from one another'. To conquer that challenge our spider needs to *connect* the spokes by weaving a series of concentric rings. The first outer ring it weaves brings shape and foundation to the whole web. The building of a coherent child-focused momentum has to be constructed on such a stable foundation.

Ring 1: Legislation

Adopting the UNCRC into UK legislation would be a life-changing move, giving children the right to a stronger voice, more variety of childhood life and protecting and enhancing their well-being. The legal position of children would be utterly transformed, and so this is the key legislative change called for in this book. But, as we saw in Chapter 10, other legislative changes are needed, including: automatic voter registration as a child reaches adulthood; adoption of the Wellbeing of Future Generations Act; extension of the reserved rights for children in the Equality Act 2010; and, as Nell Miles' essay calls for, passing the Climate and Ecology Bill.

Ring 2: The economy

Once transformational legal rights are established, the next ring must be delivering sufficient and consistent funding. True investment in children's lives can't be exposed to short-term economic and political headwinds. Transformed life chances bring benefits in both human and economic terms, for individuals and for communities. Resources must be assured in times of prosperous growth and in recession, in times of public infrastructure investment and of public spending cuts.

In Chapter 3 we saw the impact of the Heckman Equation. The empirical evidence is strong, and its logic is sound. Its core message is that for every £1 invested in early years child development, society reaps a £7 return over the lifetime of that child. It even generates an estimated return on investment of 13 per cent each year. This country is blessed with over 700,000 new children each year; they are a sustainable, high-return investment.

Away from the economics of it, investment in children brings the intangible joy, security, dignity, compassion and the simple beauty of a fulfilled childhood. So how can we make the investment case persuasive enough to overcome short-termism, competing agendas and the dead hand of indifference to ensure more children thrive so our country's future is brighter?

First, the economics work if framed more as a home mortgage, rather than an everyday, salary-constrained household budget. I propose that the big cross-sector programmes, which deliver the long-term returns Heckman described, be funded from the national capital account rather than the current account, and from borrowing rather than taxation. The net outcome, socially and economically, would be a strong rate of return for the whole country *and* for each child and family. We have explored programmes that have not had enough investment (such as Sure Start, quality affordable childcare and CAMHS) as well as more generic opportunities to reframe and reinvest in things such as early years settings, education and the children's social care system.

There are numerous ways in which capital for investment could be borrowed without undermining 'sound money' principles:

- 'Children's Gilts' could be one mechanism: government bonds, issued specifically to raise capital to invest in long-term children's development programmes. A precedent exists in the Green Bonds that the British government has issued since 2021. Children's Gilts, given Heckman-expected rates of return, could offer attractive and safe interest rates and yields for investors. Such Gilts should attract Bank of England investment and commercial market interest. In 2021, the first year of the Green Gilt offer, the government raised £16 billion for investment specifically in green projects, with the order book being 12 times oversubscribed.[2] The bonds mature after 32 years. It seems likely that a 50-year Children's Gilt could also raise significant sums on an annual, sustained basis.
- Social Impact Bonds (SIBs) are also an interesting and highly feasible route to build investment capital. SIBs help solve entrenched social problems that, due to their intersecting

nature, have been consistently hard to address via conventional approaches to public service commissioning. SIBs are outcome-based contracts that use private funding to cover the capital required for a provider to set up and deliver a service. The service is set out to achieve measurable outcomes established by the commissioning authority (that pays for outcomes). Investors are repaid only if these outcomes are achieved. For example, payments would be made if a young person enters a job or if a child mental health support programme reduces the number of children using CAMHS during their teenage years. SIBs differ from traditional fee-for-service contracts due to a focus on outcomes rather than inputs or activities.

The first UK SIB was implemented in Peterborough in 2010 with the goal of reducing reoffending rates. They have grown rapidly over the last decade, and are working across a range of sectors, including supporting children on the edge of the social care system, helping homeless people find sustainable housing and supporting children and young people into education, employment or training. Over 80 SIBs have been launched across the UK.[3] I advocate that they are scaled and become a key route to funding programmes needed to deliver a country that will prosper because its children have thrived.

- Government itself could utilise reserves, existing capital budgets and the investment potential on a (future) National Wealth Fund[4] to invest tax receipts in Heckman's theory and the practical programmes necessary to deliver them.

Government will need to invest on a massive scale. General current account, taxation and borrowing-funded budgets will also be needed. The ideas and suggestions in this chapter are presented simply as examples to stimulate debate and alignment towards the optimal funding routes. Nevertheless, they clearly show the case for funding and the potential sources to fulfil the opportunity.

Ring 3: The structure of government

Throughout this book's narrative, and amplified by many essays, I have built the case that the current design of government does not support citizens' needs in an optimal, efficient and complete way.

The bureaucracy of today is not fit to respond to this VUCA 21st-century world, and was not planned to enhance intersectional, interdepartmental or interdependent relationships. Government structures are not nimble enough to respond in a targeted and impactful way. They are mechanical in construction and therefore cannot easily evolve or adapt to changed circumstances or needs.

While this book is not about tearing apart the structures of government and rebuilding all from scratch, the evidence, stories, voices, arguments and ideas contained in these pages demand that the way government operates, budgets and interacts with children and their families evolves. Here I have a single transformative proposal.

The issues facing children – their lack of voice and agency in shaping their lives, the limited variety in their experiences and the support for their well-being – are unlike those of other citizens. Their vulnerability, democratic deficit, limitless potential and longevity each merit special and specific attention within government. Yet the siloed system of the Departments of State drives more competition for resources than collaboration. In addition, the ministerial and civil service cultures and structures tend to result in inward-looking strategies and policies, often (in the case of ministers) with short-term focuses for personal or political reasons.

The answer at the national level is to create a Department for Children,* led by a Cabinet-level minister, whose responsibilities would:

- deliver the legislative changes proposed in these pages;
- include representing the voices and well-being of children across government;
- include delivering cross-departmental programmes supported by current and capital budgets;
- extend to holding other departments to account for ensuring that children thrive;

---

* In reality this would be four separate, national Departments for Children, each responsible to their devolved first minister, or, in the case of England, the UK Prime Minister.

- mean reporting directly to the Treasury with protected budgets for long-term delivery.

This is radical and vital. Departments of State do morph as issues and focuses require. Former Prime Minister Gordon Brown restructured the Department for Education and Skills into the Department for Children, Schools and Families (2007–10). Recently issues such as exiting the European Union and climate change have warranted new ministries. Collaboration and aligning goals are possible, evidenced with the COVID-19 vaccine roll-out. Finally, there is precedent for Treasury-led programmes, for example Sure Start was first the responsibility of the Chancellor of the Exchequer. In Norway the Minister for Children and Families sits on the Council of State and in Denmark the Minister of Children and Education is a senior Cabinet member. It can, and must, be done.

At local authority level there is also scope for creating an empowered position that is a 'children's first' role. The position could be the specific responsibility of a council cabinet member or, more excitingly, a 'children's champion' – who could be an elected young person, elected just by young people, and someone empowered to champion children's interests in the services provided, and budgets allocated, locally, such as town planning, education, transport, care and health provision.

The restructure of government is the vital middle ring in creating our resilient and sustainable spider's web.

Ring 4: Democracy in action

The penultimate ring of our web involves how policy and decision making can be best made by Ministers for Children across the UK nations. Who do they collaborate and consult with? How are they accountable in managing budgets efficiently? And how might they achieve some consistency across the UK without compromising nationally devolved powers?

Answers may be found in the Nordic Council of Ministers, specifically, in how they set their children and young people's cross-sectoral strategy,[5] a six-year strategy designed to make the Nordic region the best place for children and young people.

Ministers work under the UNCRC and provide opportunities for children to exercise their rights, to participate in society and to enjoy a decent standard of living. The ministries involved include Nordic Cooperation, Labour, Gender Equality, Culture, Regional Development, Health and Social Affairs and Education. They are advised by the Nordic Committee for Children and Young People, which, notably, is full of young people. At six years, the strategy spans changes of national governments and reports on progress every two years.

Another example of collaborative, stable, strategy development and execution is the Finnish Education and Research Development Plan, which we were introduced to in Chapter 6. Its targets and financial strategy typically cover a five-year span (bridging incoming and outgoing governments). The Ministry of Education is responsible for creating these plans, but it does so in collaboration with schools, teachers and the third sector.[6]

We can learn from these Nordic examples. Our visionary, cross-sector strategy must be built on aligned interests between the UK nations' (Cabinet-level) Ministers for Children and the respective children's and future generations commissioners from each nation. All need guidance, advice and expertise from professional bodies, trades unions, metropolitan mayors, children's charity leaders and critically, families, young people and children themselves. The key thing to ensure is that the strategy is designed with the input and direction of those it is intended to help.

Ring 5: Services and programmes

The innermost ring of our web is the one that makes the web work. This ring is all about delivery to ensure a complete, fit-for-purpose structure. When the spider has spun its final ring, the one closest to the centre, it goes to the centre and tightens all the spokes, adjusting the tension in this ring. This critical ring makes the web taut, yet flexible, and ready to deliver on its purpose of providing protection and sustenance.

This book is packed with ideas for policy, services and programmes that show what is possible. They range from tiny nudges to existing programmes, such as making subtitles the default option for all children's programming, as proposed by

Henry Warren and Oli Barrett; to fundamental reorganising of the way we do things, such as the ideas by David Runciman (children should vote), Sophie Maxwell (reconstructing assessment and examination of children's academic learning) and Corinna Hawkes (reimagining our food system). There are things that can be done, should society, through its government, choose to reimagine successful childhoods. Not every example needs to be adopted, but everything should be considered.

We also have opportunities to learn from, adapt and adopt programmes and services from other parts of the world. Examples include the all-encompassing digital approach in Estonia, training teachers in play in Denmark, the Mayor of Tirana's holistic approach and early years childcare in Cuba. There are also the small, local ideas that government could harness and scale, such as Torbay Council's initiative to co-locate toddler and older people services, the Children's Wood in Glasgow protecting open-play spaces and Charlotte Church's Awen Project in democratic schooling. There are dozens of ideas in this book and many more on its companion website (see www.raisingthenation.co.uk). This final chapter draws out the commonality within them to show what could be possible under a child-centred strategy.

Significant steps could and should be taken by the respective Departments of State themselves. Others could be co-designed by local authorities and local communities. Others will need some debate and finessing by people with a range of expertise. Those that could be supported by a National Children's Service include:

- a 2020s version of the Sure Start programme, shared in Chapter 3;
- the Sure Start Plus programme for teenagers, as proposed by the *Hidden in Plain Sight* report noted in Chapter 9;
- a digitised 'complete childhood' Redbook including meta-analysis to optimise the impact of personal and population level interventions, as proposed in Chapter 3;
- universal provision of quality, affordable, regulated and Kitemarked childcare, both for pre-school children and after school for primary school-aged children; Nicole Green spoke specifically to this in her essay in Chapter 3;

- responsibility for commissioning a 'Seebohm Report 2.0' and for implementing the MacAlister Report recommendations for children in care, as set out in Chapter 9;
- responsibility for implementing the *Salamanca Statement* recommendations for children with special educational needs and disabilities (SEND), as set out in Chapter 9;
- transfer of responsibility for delivery of CAMHS from the Department of Health and Social Care so that it is better funded, coordinated and integrated with other children's services, and both prevents decline to poor mental health as much as treats and supports those already experiencing it, as set out in Chapter 7;
- responsibility for a child-first, child-friendly urban strategy, as delivered by Erion Veliaj in Tirana, and proposed by both Tim Gill and Rachel Toms in their essays, all in Chapter 5;
- revisiting opportunities to act on disadvantageous social determinants to health through cross-departmental policies that narrow childhood inequalities in line with the Marmot Review principles considered in Chapter 7;
- a National Play Network, reflecting contributions from Samira Musse, Alice Ferguson and Ingrid Skeels, and Sophia Giblin, in their essays in Chapters 4 and 5;
- the establishment of Baby Investment Bonds so children are vested in the economic system with capital on reaching adulthood, as set out in Chapter 9;
- the establishment of a mechanism for democracy to better capture the preferences and opinions of children, through various ideas shared in Chapter 10.

This list could go on and on. Suffice to say, services and programmes need to be prioritised and co-designed with children and their families.

What I am not proposing, however, is a definitive list of such programmes and services, but ideas to be considered. For, as Valerie Hannon observed in Chapter 6:

> it would be strange to prescribe here the shape of that in detail. We do, however, have a responsibility to begin the debate, to assist young people to participate

in it, and to create the enabling environment for its realisation. We need a new and different public discourse to help that happen.

She, like me and most other voices in this book, are convinced that 'young people themselves must be empowered to design and create the kind of future they want'. The lack of this has been the root of the failings of the approach to date, thereby excluding the huge power of lived experience for understanding where solutions may lie. The true experts are not really the policy makers, politicians, NHS or public health staff, educators, city planners, youth justice judges, academics or entrepreneurs. They must learn from children and families (especially those living in poverty). These are the people who know what needs to change. And it is they to whom policy makers must turn their ear most acutely.

Conclusions

An overall National Children's Service, comprising coordinated and aligned devolved nations' children's services, is the product of our five rings: legislation, economics, structure of government, democracy in action and services and programmes. Together they bind the spokes of the other chapters: the diverse yet connected aspects of childhood that siloed departments have failed to adequately address. The spokes and rings together form our spider's web structure to create and execute policy to deliver a brighter future.

Key to what eventually emerges is that the National Children's Service:

- helps all children thrive by giving them and their families meaningful voices to shape their lives;
- ensures all children have opportunities for the widest possible positive experiences in their childhood so that they can find their passions and purpose, develop their tolerances for differences and discover the person they have the potential to be;
- meaningfully measures and acts to protect all children's well-being, be that in their relationship with themselves, with their friends and families, with the broader community or with the planet itself.

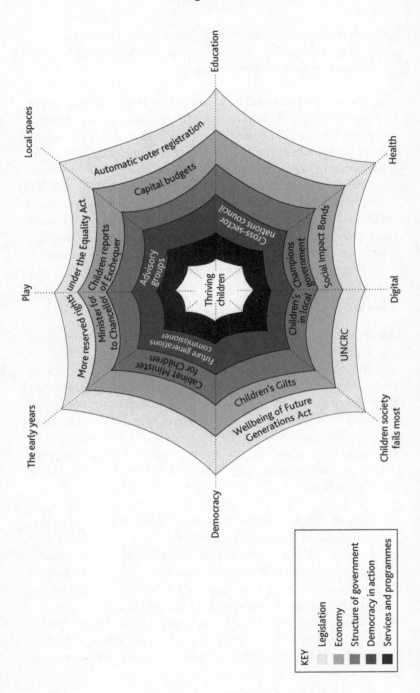

Education

Local spaces

Health

Play

Digital

The early years

Children society fails most

Democracy

Automatic voter registration

Capital budgets

Cross-sector nations council

More reserved rights under the Equality Act

Children reports to Chancellor of Exchequer

Minister for

Advisory groups

Children's Champions in local government

Social Impact Bonds

Thriving children

Future generations commissioner

UNCRC

Cabinet Minister for Children

Children's Gilts

Wellbeing of Future Generations Act

KEY

Legislation

Economy

Structure of government

Democracy in action

Services and programmes

We need a national debate to kick-start our way to truly delivering on a promise to raise the nation. Not a dinner party discussion, or a Twitter rant; not an intellectual evaluation, or a series of opinion pieces; but a serious, structured process that involves the voices of all those vested in our future.

Which is everyone, but particularly children, young people and those living in spaces and places where no one ever truly listens to them.

In starting that national debate, and in inviting everyone to participate with value and confidence, let us focus our minds back to Nelson Mandela's words that I shared in the Preface: 'There can be no keener revelation of a society's soul than the way in which it treats its children.'[7]

It is now up to us. Are we curious enough to look into our soul? And if we don't like what we see, are we brave enough to act? I am confident that we are and we will.

For our brightest possible future, let's begin.

Keep smiling!

Paul

@Paul_Lindley
#RaisingtheNation

Notes

Preface

[1] Mandela, N. (1995) 'Address by President Nelson Mandela at the launch of the Nelson Mandela Children's Fund, Pretoria', 8 May, www.mandela.gov.za/mandela_speeches/1995/950508_nmcf.htm

[2] Mandela, N. (1995) 'Address by President Nelson Mandela at the dedication of Qunu and Nkalane Schools', 3 June, www.mandela.gov.za/mandela_speeches/1995/950603_qunu.htm

Chapter 1

[1] Kennedy, R.F. (1963) 'Address at a meeting of the University of South Carolina Chapter American Association of University Professors', 25 April.

[2] ONS (Office for National Statistics) (2019) 'Families and households in the UK: 2019', 15 November, www.ons.gov.uk/peoplepopulationandcommunity/birthsdeathsandmarriages/families/bulletins/familiesandhouseholds/2019

[3] ONS (Office for National Statistics) (2019) 'Families and households in the UK: 2019', 15 November, www.ons.gov.uk/peoplepopulationandcommunity/birthsdeathsandmarriages/families/bulletins/familiesandhouseholds/2019

[4] DWP (Department for Work and Pensions) (2010) 'Government gives grandparents more credit', Press release, 15 October, www.gov.uk/government/news/government-gives-grandparents-more-credit

[5] JRF (Joseph Rowntree Foundation) (2022) *UK Poverty 2022: The Essential Guide to Understanding Poverty in the UK*, York: JRF, www.jrf.org.uk/report/uk-poverty-2022

[6] Sonuga-Burke, E., Danese, A. and Knowles, G. (2022) 'An isolated generation: The impact of COVID-19 on children and young people', King's College London, 9 February, www.kcl.ac.uk/an-isolated-generation-the-impact-of-covid-19-on-children-and-young-people

[7] Henricson, C. and Bainham, A. (2005) *The Child and Family Policy Divide: Tensions, Convergence and Rights*, York: Joseph Rowntree Foundation.

[8] Blair, T. (1996) Speech to the Labour Party Conference, Blackpool, 1 October, britishpoliticalspeech.org/speech-archive.htm?speech=202

[9] Indigo Anchor (2018) 'On the origins of VUCA and how it affects decision making', www.indigoanchor.com/blog/2019/10/31/on-the-origins-of-vuca-and-how-it-affects-decision-making

Notes

10 Statista (2021) 'Proportion of GCSE entries awarded a A/7 or higher in the United Kingdom between 1998 and 2022', www.statista.com/statistics/282537/gcse-highest-pass-rate-in-uk

11 ONS (Office for National Statistics) (2021) 'National life tables – Life expectancy in the UK: 2018 to 2020', 23 September, www.ons.gov.uk/peoplepopulationandcommunity/birthsdeathsandmarriages/lifeexpectancies/bulletins/nationallifetablesunitedkingdom/2018to2020

12 ONS (Office for National Statistics) (2022) 'Child and infant mortality in England and Wales: 2020', 17 February, www.ons.gov.uk/peoplepopulationandcommunity/birthsdeathsandmarriages/deaths/bulletins/childhoodinfantandperinatalmortalityinenglandandwales/2020

13 Silver, C. (2021) 'The top 25 economies in the world', Investopedia, 1 September, www.investopedia.com/insights/worlds-top-economies

14 ONS (Office for National Statistics) (2022) 'Gross Domestic Product: Chained volume measures: Seasonally adjusted £m', 10 February, www.ons.gov.uk/economy/grossdomesticproductgdp/timeseries/abmi/pn2

15 Connolly, P. (2018) 'Counting the cost: Antidepressant use in children' [radio programme], *File on 4*, 24 July, https://downloads.bbc.co.uk/rmhttp/fileon4/20_Counting_the_Cost.pdf

16 The Childhood Trust (2021) *Bedrooms of London: The Context to London's Housing Crisis and Its Impact on Children*, London: The Childhood Trust, www.childhoodtrust.org.uk/wp-content/uploads/2021/01/Bedrooms-Of-London-Report-1.pdf

17 UN (United Nations) (2022) 'COVID-19: How the Omicron variant affects Europe?', 20 January, https://unric.org/en/covid-19-how-the-omicron-variant-affects-europe

18 Quoted in Lindley, P. (2017) *Little Wins: The Huge Power of Thinking Like a Toddler*, London: Penguin, p 179.

19 Quoted in Levy, B.S. (2022) *From Horror to Hope: Recognizing and Preventing the Health Impacts of War*, Oxford: Oxford University Press, pp 240–52.

20 Lyons, L. (1947) 'Loose-leaf notebook', *The Washington Post*, 30 January, p 9.

21 Department for Levelling Up, Housing and Communities (2020) 'Guidance on devolution', 28 September, www.gov.uk/guidance/guidance-on-devolution

Chapter 2

1 Roosevelt, F.D. (1940) 'Address at University of Pennsylvania', 20 September, www.presidency.ucsb.edu/node/210464

2 Del Col, L. (1832 [2002]) *The Life of the Industrial Worker in Nineteenth-Century England*, Life, 1, https://dragifhistory.weebly.com/uploads/1/2/6/3/126335822/the_life_of_the_industrial_worker_in_nineteenth_century_england.pdf

3 Jal, E. (2010) *War Child: A Child Soldier's Story*, New York: St Martin's Griffin.

4 Volk, A.A. and Atkinson, J.A. (2013) 'Infant and child death in the human environment of evolutionary adaptation', *Evolution and Human Behavior*, 34(3): 182–92.

5   Volk, A.A. and Atkinson, J.A. (2013) 'Infant and child death in the human environment of evolutionary adaptation', *Evolution and Human Behavior*, 34(3): 182–92.

6   Ariès, P., Baldick, R. and Phillips, A. (1996) *Centuries of Childhood: A Social History of Family Life*, London: Pimlico.

7   Orme, N. (2003) *Medieval Children*, New Haven, CT: Yale University Press.

8   Reissland, N. (2019) '*Medieval children* by Nicholas Orme', *Common Knowledge*, 25(1): 413–14.

9   Sigelman, C. and Rider, E. (2009) *Life-Span: Human Development*, Boston, MA: Cengage Learning.

10 Locke, J. (1690 [2013]) *An Essay Concerning Human Understanding*, Lanham, MD: Start Publishing LLC.

11 Locke, J. (1690 [1824]) *Some Thoughts Concerning Education, Posthumous Works, Familiar Letters. The Works of John Locke in Nine Volumes* (Volume 8, 12th edn), London: Rivington, p 192. See https://stephenhicks.org.wp-content/uploads/2011/09/locke_john-poe.pdf

12 Fox, V. (1996) 'Poor children's rights in early modern England', *Journal of Psychohistory*, 23(3): 286–306.

13 Cohen, E. and Reeves, M. (2018) *The Youth of Early Modern Women*, Amsterdam: Amsterdam University Press.

14 Del Col, L. (1832 [2002]) *The Life of the Industrial Worker in Nineteenth-Century England*, Life, 1, https://dragiffhistory.weebly.com/uploads/1/2/6/3/126335822/the_life_of_the_industrial_worker_in_nineteenth_century_england.pdf

15 Daniels, B. (2003) 'Poverty and families in the Victorian era', Hidden Lives Revealed, www.hiddenlives.org.uk/articles/poverty.html

16 Galbi, D. (1997) 'Child labor and the division of labor in the early English cotton mills', *Journal of Population Economics*, 10(4): 357–75.

17 Malkovich, A. (2012) *Charles Dickens and the Victorian Child*, London: Routledge.

18 Boehmer, E. (2004) *Notes to 2004 Edition of Scouting for Boys*, Oxford: Oxford University Press.

19 *Tes Magazine* (2015) 'Timeline: A history of education', 1 November, www.tes.com/magazine/archive/timeline-history-education

20 Education and Skills Act 2008, www.legislation.gov.uk/ukpga/2008/25/part/1/chapter/1

21 GOV.UK (no date) 'Age of criminal responsibility', www.gov.uk/age-of-criminal-responsibility

22 Scotland's age of criminal responsibility is eight years old, but this is not full criminal responsibility, as children under 12 cannot be prosecuted.

23 DfE (Department for Education) (2010) *United Nations Convention on the Rights of the Child (UNCRC): How Legislation Underpins Implementation in England*, 15 March, www.gov.uk/government/publications/united-nations-convention-on-the-rights-of-the-child-uncrc-how-legislation-underpins-implementation-in-england

24 Zelizer, V. (1994) *Pricing the Priceless Child*, Princeton, NJ: Princeton University Press.

25 Sustrans (2019) 'The role of transport in supporting a healthy future for young people', Blog, 17 October, www.sustrans.org.uk/our-blog/research/all-therems/all/the-role-of-transport-in-supporting-a-healthy-future-for-young-people

26 Sustrans (2019) 'The role of transport in supporting a healthy future for young people', Blog, 17 October, www.sustrans.org.uk/our-blog/research/all-themes/all/the-role-of-transport-in-supporting-a-healthy-future-for-young-people

27 Future Generations Commissioner for Wales (2021) *A Future Fit for Wales: A Basic Income for All*, November, Crookham Village: Autonomy, www.futuregenerations.wales/wp-content/uploads/2021/11/2020_DEC29_UBI-v4.pdf

28 UN (United Nations) (2021) *Our Common Agenda: Report of the Secretary-General*, www.un.org/en/content/common-agenda-report/assets/pdf/Common_Agenda_Report_English.pdf

29 Forsyth, J. (2013) 'Eglantyne Jebb: A true children's champion', Save the Children blog, 25 August, www.savethechildren.org.uk/blogs/2013/eglantyne-jebb-%2525e2%252580%252593-a-true-children%2525e2%252580%252599s-champion

30 League of Nations (1924) *Geneva Declaration of the Rights of the Child*.

31 UNICEF (United Nations Children's Fund) (1989) *The United Nations Convention on the Rights of the Child*, www.unicef.org.uk/wp-content/uploads/2010/05/UNCRC_united_nations_convention_on_the_rights_of_the_child.pdf

32 Machel, G. (1996) *Impact of Armed Conflict on Children*, New York: United Nations Children's Fund and the United Nations Department of Public Information, https://digitallibrary.un.org/record/223213

33 Office of the Special Representative of the Secretary-General for Children and Armed Conflict (no date) 'The six grave violations', https://childrenandarmedconflict.un.org/six-grave-violations

34 UNICEF (United Nations Children's Fund) (2014) 'With 15 million children caught up in major conflicts, UNICEF declares 2014 a devastating year for children', Press release, 8 December, www.unicef.org/mena/press-releases/unicef-declares-2014-devastating-year-for-children

35 UNICEF (United Nations Children's Fund) (2022) *25 Years of Children and Armed Conflict*, www.unicef.org/reports/25-years-children-armed-conflict

36 Machel, G. (1996) *Impact of Armed Conflict on Children*, New York: United Nations Children's Fund and the United Nations Department of Public Information, https://digitallibrary.un.org/record/223213, para 317.

37 UN (United Nations) (2022) 'One month of war leaves more than half of Ukraine's children displaced', 24 March, https://news.un.org/en/story/2022/03/1114592

38 UNHRC (United Nations Human Rights Council) (2022) 'Ukraine refugee situation', https://data.unhcr.org/en/situations/ukraine#_ga=2.42943909.1086535942.1650548497-1018768493.1646415527

39 Home Office (2022) 'Ukraine Family Scheme, Ukraine Sponsorship Scheme (Homes for Ukraine) and Ukraine Extension Scheme visa data', www.gov.uk/government/publications/ukraine-family-scheme-application-data

40 Frank, A. (1952 [2004]) *The Diary of a Young Girl*, London: Longman.

41 Woodward, M. (2017) 'How to thrive in a VUCA world', *Psychology Today*, 31 July, www.psychologytoday.com/us/blog/spotting-opportunity/201707/how-thrive-in-vuca-world

42 Sinek, S. (2016) 'Millennials in the workplace', *Inside Quest* with Tom Bilyeu, https://youtu.be/hER0Qp6QJNU

43 De Veirman, M., Hudders, L. and Nelson, M.R. (2019) 'What is influencer marketing and how does it target children? A review and direction for future research', *Frontiers in Psychology*, 10: 2685.

44 Geyser, W. (2022) *The State of Influencer Marketing 2022: Benchmark Report*, Influencer Marketing Hub, https://influencermarketinghub.com/influencer-marketing-benchmark-report

45 Lewis, P., Barr, C., Clarke, S., Voce, A., Levett, C. and Gutiérez, P. (2019) 'Revealed: The rise and rise of populist rhetoric', *The Guardian*, 6 March, www.theguardian.com/world/ng-interactive/2019/mar/06/revealed-the-rise-and-rise-of-populist-rhetoric

46 ONS (Office for National Statistics) (2021) 'Children's online behaviour in England and Wales: Year ending March 2020: 2. Children's online activity', www.ons.gov.uk/peoplepopulationandcommunity/crimeandjustice/bulletins/childrensonlinebehaviourinenglandandwales/yearendingmarch2020#childrens-online-activity

47 Hopkins, L., Brookes, F. and Green, J. (2013) 'Books, bytes and brains: The implications of new knowledge for children's early literacy learning', *Australasian Journal of Early Childhood*, 38(1): 23–8.

48 Macrotrends (2022) 'UK birth rate 1950–2022', www.macrotrends.net/countries/GBR/united-kingdom/birth-rate

49 ONS (Office for National Statistics) (2020) 'Births in England and Wales: 2019', www.ons.gov.uk/peoplepopulationandcommunity/birthsdeathsandmarriages/livebirths/bulletins/birthsummarytablesenglandandwales/2019

50 ONS (Office for National Statistics) (2019) 'Families and households. Table 1. Update November 2019', www.ons.gov.uk/peoplepopulationandcommunity/birthsdeathsandmarriages/families/datasets/familiesandhouseholdsfamiliesandhouseholds/current

51 Self, A. and Zealey, L. (eds) (2007) *Social Trends No 37*, Office for National Statistics, http://news.bbc.co.uk/1/shared/bsp/hi/pdfs/11_04_07_social_trends.pdf

52 Macrotrends (2022) 'UK life expectancy 1950–2022', www.macrotrends.net/countries/GBR/united-kingdom/life-expectancy

53 ONS (Office for National Statistics) (2018) 'Living longer: How our population is changing and why it matters', www.ons.gov.uk/peoplepopulation

andcommunity/birthsdeathsandmarriages/ageing/articles/livinglongerhow
ourpopulationischangingandwhyitmatters/2018-08-13

54 ONS (Office for National Statistics) (2018) 'Living longer: How our population is changing and why it matters', www.ons.gov.uk/peoplepopulation andcommunity/birthsdeathsandmarriages/ageing/articles/livinglongerhow ourpopulationischangingandwhyitmatters/2018-08-13

55 ONS (Office for National Statistics) (2018) 'Living longer: How our population is changing and why it matters', www.ons.gov.uk/ peoplepopulationandcommunity/birthsdeathsandmarriages/ageing/articles/ livinglongerhowourpopulationischangingandwhyitmatters/2018-08-13

56 ONS (Office for National Statistics) (2018) 'Living longer: How our population is changing and why it matters', www.ons.gov.uk/peoplepopulation andcommunity/birthsdeathsandmarriages/ageing/articles/livinglongerhow ourpopulationischangingandwhyitmatters/2018-08-13

57 Runciman, D. (2021) 'Votes for children! Why we should lower the voting age to six', *The Guardian*, 16 November, www.theguardian.com/ politics/2021/nov/16/reconstruction-after-covid-votes-for-children-age-six-david-runciman

58 Social Mobility and Child Poverty Commission (2014) *Social Mobility in the UK: State of the Nation 2014 report*, www.gov.uk/government/publications/ state-of-the-nation-2014-report

59 Francis-Devine, B. (2022) 'Poverty in the UK: Statistics', UK Parliament House of Commons Research Briefing, 29 September, https:// commonslibrary.parliament.uk/research-briefings/sn07096

60 Francis-Devine, B. (2022) 'Poverty in the UK: Statistics', UK Parliament House of Commons Research Briefing, 29 September, p 28, https:// commonslibrary.parliament.uk/research-briefings/sn07096

61 Centre for Ageing Better (2022) *The State of Ageing 2022*, https://ageing-better.org.uk/state-of-ageing

62 Owen, D. (1995) *Ethnic Minorities in Great Britain: Patterns of Population Change, 1981–91*, Warwick: Centre for Research in Ethnic Relations, University of Warwick.

63 ONS (Office for National Statistics) (2022) 'Ethnic group, England and Wales: Census 2021', www.ons.gov.uk/peoplepopulationandcommunity/ culturalidentity/ethnicity/bulletins/ethnicgroupenglandandwales/ census2021

64 Phillips, K.W. (2017) 'How diversity makes us smarter', *Greater Good Magazine*, 18 September, https://greatergood.berkeley.edu/article/item/ how_diversity_makes_us_smarter

65 Weale, S. (2020) 'Almost half of English schools have no BAME teachers, study finds', *The Guardian*, 14 December, www.theguardian.com/ education/2020/dec/14/almost-half-of-english-schools-have-no-bame-teachers-study-finds

66 UNICEF (United Nations Children's Fund) (2020) 'UK youth justice system risks breaching children's rights, says UNICEF UK', Press release,

8 December, www.unicef.org.uk/press-releases/uk-youth-justice-system-risks-breaching-childrens-rights-says-unicef-uk

Chapter 3

1   https://checkyourfact.com/2019/04/30/fact-check-frederick-douglass-easier-build-strong-children-repair-broken-men
2   ONS (Office for National Statistics) (2021) 'Births in England and Wales: 2020', www.ons.gov.uk/peoplepopulationandcommunity/births deathsandmarriages/livebirths/bulletins/birthsummarytablesengland andwales/2020
3   Hall, E. (2021) *Born in Lockdown*, Mothership Writers.
4   Hall, E. (2021) *Born in Lockdown*, Mothership Writers, Chapter 20, p 61.
5   First Things First (2022) 'Brain development', www.firstthingsfirst.org/early-childhood-matters/brain-development
6   Oxford Brookes Babylab (2022) 'Social distancing and development', https://babylab.brookes.ac.uk/research/social-distancing-and-development
7   Gabriel, T. (1997) 'Was modernism born in toddler toolboxes?', *The New York Times*, 10 April, www.nytimes.com/1997/04/10/garden/was-modernism-born-in-toddler-toolboxes.html
8   Froebel Trust (2022) 'Froebelian principles', www.froebel.org.uk/about-us/froebelian-principles
9   Early Education, the British Association for Early Childhood Education (2022) 'Friedrich Froebel', 10 December, https://early-education.org.uk/friedrich-froebel
10 Center on the Developing Child (no date) 'Brain architecture', https://developingchild.harvard.edu/science/key-concepts/brain-architecture
11 Center on the Developing Child (no date) 'Brain architecture', https://developingchild.harvard.edu/science/key-concepts/brain-architecture
12 Center on the Developing Child (no date) 'Serve and return', https://developingchild.harvard.edu/science/key-concepts/serve-and-return
13 Center on the Developing Child (2021) 'Three principles to improve outcomes for children and families', https://developingchild.harvard.edu/resources/three-early-childhood-development-principles-improve-child-family-outcomes
14 Center on the Developing Child (no date) 'InBrief: The impact of early adversity on children's development' [video], https://developingchild.harvard.edu/resources/inbrief-the-impact-of-early-adversity-on-childrens-development-video
15 National Scientific Council on the Developing Child (2005/2014) *Excessive Stress Disrupts the Architecture of the Developing Brain*, Working Paper 3, Center on the Developing Child, Updated edition, https://developingchild.harvard.edu/wp-content/uploads/2005/05/Stress_Disrupts_Architecture_Developing_Brain-1.pdf
16 Center on the Developing Child (no date) 'Toxic stress', https://developingchild.harvard.edu/science/key-concepts/toxic-stress

17 Center on the Developing Child (no date) 'InBrief: The impact of early adversity on children's development' [video], https://developingchild. harvard.edu/resources/inbrief-the-impact-of-early-adversity-on-childrens-development-video

18 Children's Commissioner (2020) 'Best beginnings in the early years', 17 July, www.childrenscommissioner.gov.uk/report/best-beginnings-in-the-early-years

19 NHS England (2016) *Healthy Children: Transforming Child Health Information*, Novemb, www.england.nhs.uk/wp-content/uploads/2016/11/healthy-children-transforming-child-health-info.pdf

20 RCOG (Royal College of Obstetricians & Gynaecologists) (2017) *Maternal Mental Health – Women's Voices*, February, www.rcog.org.uk/media/3ijbpfvi/maternal-mental-health-womens-voices.pdf

21 CQC (Care Quality Commission) (2020) *2019 Survey of Women's Experiences of Maternity Care: Statistical Release*, January, www.cqc.org.uk/sites/default/files/20200128_mat19_statisticalrelease.pdf

22 Robson, S. (2022) 'Parent charity NCT deletes natural birth guidance that says "mothers will be more satisfied"', inews.co.uk, 31 March, https://inews.co.uk/news/parent-charity-nct-deletes-natural-birth-guidance-ockenden-report-national-childbirth-trust-1549547

23 WHO (World Health Organization) (no date) 'Breastfeeding', www.who.int/health-topics/breastfeeding#tab=tab_1

24 The Infant Formula and Follow-on Formula (England) Regulations 2007, www.legislation.gov.uk/uksi/2007/3521/contents/made

25 McFadden, A., Gavine, A., Renfrew, M.J., et al (2012) 'Support for healthy breastfeeding mothers with healthy term babies', *Cochrane Database of Systematic Reviews*, 2(2), doi:10.1002/14651858.cd001141.pub4.

26 Muller, C., Newburn, M., Wise, P., et al (2009) *NCT Breastfeeding Peer Support Project*, London: NCT.

27 Kendall-Tackett, K. (2007) 'A new paradigm for depression in new mothers: The central role of inflammation and how breastfeeding and anti-inflammatory treatments protect maternal mental health', *International Breastfeeding Journal*, 2: 6.

28 Uvnäs Moberg, K. and Prime, D.K. (2013) 'Oxytocin effects in mothers and infants during breastfeeding', *Infant*, 9(6): 201–6.

29 Linde, K., Lehnig, F., Nagl, M. and Kersting, A. (2020) 'The association between breastfeeding and attachment: A systematic review', *Midwifery*, 81: 102592.

30 Hallowell, S.G., Froh, E.B. and Spatz, D.l. (2016) 'Human milk and breastfeeding: An intervention to mitigate toxic stress', *Nursing Outlook*, Jan–Feb, 65(1): 58–67.

31 Rollins, N.C., Bhandari, N., Hajeebhoy, N., et al (2016) 'Why invest, and what it will take to improve breastfeeding practices?', *The Lancet*, 387(10017): 491–504.

32 Chzhen, Y., Gromada, A. and Rees, G. (2019) *Are the World's Richest Countries Family Friendly? Policy in the OECD and EU*, UNICEF, June, www.unicef-irc.org/family-friendly

33 OECD (Organisation for Economic Co-operation and Development) (2022) PF3.4: 'Childcare support', www.oecd.org/els/soc/PF3_4_Childcare_support.pdf

34 Pregnant Then Screwed (2022) '1 in 4 parents have had to cut down on heat, food & clothing to pay for childcare', Press release, 25 March, https://pregnantthenscrewed.com/one-in-four-parents-say-that-they-have-had-to-cut-down-on-heat-food-clothing-to-pay-for-childcare

35 Sylva, K., Melhuish, E., Sammons, P., et al (2004) *The Effective Provision of Pre-School Education (EPPE) Project, Technical Paper 12: The Final Report: Effective Pre-School Education*, https://discovery.ucl.ac.uk/id/eprint/10005308/1/EPPE12Sylva2004Effective.pdf

36 Coleman, L., Dali-Chaouch, M. and Harding, C. (2020) *Childcare Survey 2020*, London: Coram Family and Childcare, www.familyandchildcaretrust.org/sites/default/files/Resource%20Library/Coram%20Childcare%20Survey%202020_240220.pdf

37 Ofsted (2022) 'Main findings: Childcare providers and inspections as at 31 March 2022', www.gov.uk/government/statistics/childcare-providers-and-inspections-as-at-31-march-2022/main-findings-childcare-providers-and-inspections-as-at-31-march-2022

38 TUC (Trades Union Congress) (2022) 'Cost of childcare has risen by over £2,000 a year since 2010', 13 June, www.tuc.org.uk/news/cost-childcare-has-risen-over-ps2000-year-2010

39 Early Years Alliance (no date) 'Families set to foot the bill as new figures reveal half a billion shortfall in childcare funding', www.eyalliance.org.uk/families-set-foot-bill-new-figures-reveal-half-billion-shortfall-childcare-funding

40 Social Mobility Commission (2020) 'The stability of the early years workforce in England', 5 August, www.gov.uk/government/publications/the-stability-of-the-early-years-workforce-in-england

41 Topping, A. (2022) 'Childcare costs have spiralled for two-thirds of UK families, survey shows', *The Guardian*, 25 March, www.theguardian.com/money/2022/mar/25/childcare-costs-spiralled-uk-families-survey

42 OECD (Organisation for Economic Co-operation and Development) (2016) 'Starting Strong IV: Early Childhood Education and Care Data Country Note: Finland', www.oecd.org/education/school/ECECDCN-Finland.pdf

43 Salary Explorer (2022) 'How much money does a child care worker make in Sweden?', www.salaryexplorer.com/salary-survey.php?loc=209&loctype=1&job=699&jobtype=3

44 Gromada, A. and Richardson, D. (2021) *Where Do Rich Countries Stand on Childcare?*, UNICEF, www.unicef-irc.org/publications/pdf/where-do-rich-countries-stand-on-childcare.pdf

45 OECD (Organisation for Economic Co-operation and Development) (2019) 'Net childcare costs', https://data.oecd.org/benwage/net-childcare-costs.htm

46 Lawler, E., Kersley, H. and Steed, S. (2009) 'A bit rich: Calculating the real value to society of different professions', New Economics Foundation, 14 December, https://neweconomics.org/2009/12/a-bit-rich

47 Centre for Progressive Policy (2022) 'CPP's latest report finds caring responsibilities are disproportionately impacting women in the UK', Press release, 11 April, www.progressive-policy.net/publications/press-release-cpps-latest-report-finds-caring-responsibilities-are-disproportionately-impacting-women-in-the-uk

48 Usdaw (2017) *Parents and Carers: Looking After Grandchildren?* [leaflet], www.usdaw.org.uk/CMSPages/GetFile.aspx?guid=a3a73702-9a9d-4a04-aeec-5ecce2cc0181

49 Rose, A. (2019) *The Alison Rose Review of Female Entrepreneurship*, London: HM Treasury, https://assets.publishing.service.gov.uk/government/uploads/system/uploads/attachment_data/file/784324/RoseReview_Digital_FINAL.PDF

50 Berry, C. (2022) 'The government's stance on childcare reveals its character – and it's ugly as hell', *The Guardian*, 18 April, www.theguardian.com/commentisfree/2022/apr/18/childcare-costs-rishi-sunak-spring-statement

51 Lloyd, E. and Simon, A. (2022) 'Large for-profit nursery groups are becoming more common – with negative consequences for parents and the sector', The Conversation, 16 February, https://theconversation.com/large-for-profit-nursery-groups-are-becoming-more-common-with-negative-consequences-for-parents-and-the-sector-175759

52 Hobbs, A. and Bernard, R. (2021) 'Impact of COVID-19 on early childhood education & care', UK Parliament, 27 October, https://post.parliament.uk/impact-of-covid-19-on-early-childhood-education-care

53 Women's Budget Group (2016) *Investing in the Care Economy: A Gender Analysis of Employment Stimulus in Seven OECD Countries*, March, www.ituc-csi.org/IMG/pdf/care_economy_en.pdf

54 Hutchinson, J., Reader, M. and Akhal, A. (2020) *Education in England: Annual Report 2020*, London: Education Policy Institute.

55 Global Education Monitoring Report Team (2010) *Reaching the Marginalized: EFA Global Monitoring Report*, UNESCO, https://unesdoc.unesco.org/ark:/48223/pf0000186606

56 Lloyd, E. and Penn, H. (2012) *Childcare Markets: Can They Deliver an Equitable Service?*, Bristol: Policy Press.

57 OECD (Organisation for Economic Co-operation and Development) (2019) *Good Practice for Good Jobs in Early Childhood Education and Care: Eight Policy Measures from OECD Countries*, Paris: OECD, https://oe.cd/pub/ecec2019

58 Quoted in Berry, C. (2022) 'The government's stance on childcare reveals its character – and it's ugly as hell', *The Guardian*, 18 April, www.theguardian.com/commentisfree/2022/apr/18/childcare-costs-rishi-sunak-spring-statement

59 Melhuish, E., Belsky, J. and Barnes, J. (2010) 'Evaluation and value of Sure Start', *Archives of Disease in Childhood*, 95(3): 159–61.

60 HM Treasury (1998) *Modern Public Services for Britain: Investing in Reform, Comprehensive Spending Review: New Public Spending Plans 1999–2002*, https://assets.publishing.service.gov.uk/government/uploads/system/uploads/attachment_data/file/260743/4011.pdf

61 Melhuish, E., Belsky, J. and Barnes, J. (2010) 'Evaluation and value of Sure Start', *Archives of Disease in Childhood*, 95(3): 159–61.

62 Cabinet Office (2011) *Early Intervention: Smart Investment, Massive Savings* (Allen Report), www.gov.uk/government/publications/early-intervention-smart-investment-massive-savings

63 Cattan, S., Conti, G., Farquharson, C., Ginja, R. and Pecher, M. (2021) *The Health Effects of Universal Early Childhood Interventions: Evidence from Sure Start*, No W21/25, IFS Working Paper, London: Institute for Fiscal Studies, https://ifs.org.uk/sites/default/files/output_url_files/WP202125-The-health-effects-of-universal-early-childhood-interventions-evidence-from-Sure-Start.pdf

64 DfE (Department for Education) (2011) *National Evaluation of Sure Start Local Programmes: An Economic Perspective*, Research Report, https://assets.publishing.service.gov.uk/government/uploads/system/uploads/attachment_data/file/182194/DFE-RR073.pdf

65 Rigby, L. (2017) 'Sure Start worked. So why is Theresa May out to kill it?', *The Guardian*, 6 February, www.theguardian.com/commentisfree/2017/feb/06/sure-start-children-worked-why-theresa-may-out-to-kill-it

66 Eisenstadt, N. (2013) 'How the government discovered early help' [video], TEDx Talk, www.youtube.com/watch?v=3blQ46eEcc4

67 Butler, P. (2018) '1,000 Sure Start children's centres may have shut since 2010', *The Guardian*, 5 April, www.theguardian.com/society/2018/apr/05/1000-sure-start-childrens-centres-may-have-shut-since-2010

68 Action for Children (2019) *Closed Doors: Children's Centre Usage Between 2014/15 and 2017/18*, https://media.actionforchildren.org.uk/documents/Action_for_Children_-_Closed_Doors_Report_June_2019.pdf

69 DWP (Department for Work and Pensions) (2022) 'Households below average income, statistics on the number and percentage of people living in low-income households for financial years 1994/95 to 2020/21, Table 1.4b', www.gov.uk/government/statistics/households-below-average-income-for-financial-years-ending-1995-to-2020

70 Children's Commissioner (2020) 'Best beginnings in the early years', 17 July, www.childrenscommissioner.gov.uk/report/best-beginnings-in-the-early-years

71 Heckman (no date) 'The Heckman Equation', https://heckmanequation.org/the-heckman-equation

72 Heckman, J.J. (2011) 'The economics of inequality: The value of early childhood education', *American Educator*, 35(1): 31–47, p 47.

73 Heckman (no date) 'Perry Preschool: Intergenerational effects toolkit', https://heckmanequation.org/resource/perry-preschool-midlife-toolkit

74 Heckman (no date) 'Perry Preschool: Intergenerational effects toolkit', https://heckmanequation.org/resource/perry-preschool-midlife-toolkit

75 Heckman (no date) 'Fadeout toolkit', https://heckmanequation.org/resource/fadeout-toolkit

76 Hansard (2022) 'Early Years Educators, Volume 707: Debated on Tuesday 25 January 2022', https://hansard.parliament.uk/Commons/2022-01-25/debates/22012545000001/EarlyYearsEducators

77 Executive Office of the President of the United States (2015) *The Economics of Early Childhood Investments*, January, https://obamawhitehouse.archives.gov/sites/default/files/docs/early_childhood_report_update_final_non-embargo.pdf

78 Nightingale Hammerson (2018) *Building Relationships Between the Generations: The Case of the Co-Located Nursery*, p 6, https://applesandhoneynightingale.com/wp-content/uploads/2021/07/Building-relationships-between-the-generations.pdf

79 Nightingale Hammerson (2018) *Building Relationships Between the Generations: The Case of the Co-Located Nursery*, p 14, https://applesandhoneynightingale.com/wp-content/uploads/2021/07/Building-relationships-between-the-generations.pdf

80 George, L. (2018) *Starting Young: Lifelong lessons from Intergenerational Care and Learning*, Winston Churchill Memorial Trust, https://media.churchillfellowship.org/documents/George_L_Report_2017_Final.pdf

81 Jansen, T. (2016) 'The preschool inside a nursing home', *The Atlantic*, 20 January, www.theatlantic.com/education/archive/2016/01/the-preschool-inside-a-nursing-home/424827

82 Providence Mount St Vincent (no date) 'Intergenerational Learning Center', www.providence.org/locations/wa/mount-st-vincent/facility-profile/intergenerational-learning-center

83 Powell, C.A., Walker, S.P., Chang, S.M. and Grantham-McGregor, S.M. (1991) 'Nutritional supplementation, psychosocial stimulation, and growth of stunted children: The Jamaican study', *The American Journal of Clinical Nutrition*, 54(4): 642–8.

84 Gertler, P., Heckman, J.J., Pinto, R., et al (2021) *Effect of the Jamaica Early Childhood Stimulation Intervention on Labor Market Outcomes at Age 31*, No w29292, Cambridge, MA: National Bureau of Economic Research, http://dx.doi.org/10.2139/ssrn.3931815

85 UNICEF (United Nations Children's Fund) (2016) *Early Childhood Development in Cuba: Sharing the Experience of a Scaled-Up Integrated System that Promotes the Best Start in Life for Every Child*, www.unicef.org/cuba/media/591/file/early-childhood-development-cuba-2016.pdf

Chapter 4

1 Rogers, F. (no date) 'Thoughts for the week, Programs 1486-1490', Fred Rogers Institute Archive, www.fredrogersinstitute.org/files/archive/records/32/thoughts1486%2d1490%2epdf

2   Sharpe, L.L. (2019) 'Fun, Fur, and Future Fitness: The Evolution of Play in Mammals', in P.K. Smith and J.L. Roopnarine (eds) *The Cambridge Handbook of Play: Developmental and Disciplinary Perspectives*, Cambridge: Cambridge University Press, pp 49–66.

3   Rogers, F. (no date) 'Thoughts for the week, Programs 1486-1490', Fred Rogers Institute Archive, www.fredrogersinstitute.org/files/archive/records/32/thoughts1486%2d1490%2epdf

4   Stevenson, A. and Waite, M. (2011) 'Play', *Concise Oxford English Dictionary*, Oxford: Oxford University Press.

5   Piaget, J. (1962) *Play, Dreams, and Imitation in Childhood*, New York: Norton.

6   Pellegrini, A.D. (2013) 'Object use in childhood: Development and possible functions', *Behaviour*, 150(8): 813–43.

7   Vygotsky, L.S. (1967) 'Play and its role in the mental development of the child', *Soviet Psychology*, 12: 6–18.

8   Hart, J.L. and Tannock, M.T. (2019) 'Rough Play: Past, Present and Potential', in P.K. Smith and J.L. Roopnarine (eds) *The Cambridge Handbook of Play: Developmental and Disciplinary Perspectives*, Cambridge: Cambridge University Press, pp 200–21.

9   Quoted in Veronese, G., Pepe, A., Jaradah, A., Murannak, F. and Hamdouna, H. (2017) '"We must cooperate with one another against the enemy": Agency and activism in school-aged children as protective factors against ongoing war trauma and political violence in the Gaza Strip', *Child Abuse & Neglect*, 70: 364–76.

10 Lynneth Solis, S., Liu, C. and Popp, J. (2022) *Learning to Cope through Play: Playful Learning as an Approach to Support Children's Coping During Times of Heightened Stress and Adversity*, Billund: The LEGO Foundation, https://cms.learningthroughplay.com/media/jqifsynb/learning-to-cope-through-play.pdf

11 Blair, C. (2002) 'School readiness: Integrating cognition and emotion in a neurobiological conceptualization of children's functioning at school entry', *American Psychologist*, 57: 111–27.

12 McClelland, M.M., Cameron, C.E., Connor, C.M., Farris, C.L., Jewkes, A.M. and Morrison, F.J. (2007) 'Links between behavioral regulation and preschoolers' literacy, vocabulary, and math skills', *Developmental Psychology*, 43(4): 947–59.

13 Kochanska, G., Murray, K.T. and Harlan, E.T. (2000) 'Effortful control in early childhood: Continuity and change, antecedents, and implications for social development', *Developmental Psychology*, 36(2): 220–32.

14 Whitebread, D., Coltman, P., Jameson, H. and Lander, R. (2009) 'Play, cognition and self-regulation: What exactly are children learning when they learn through play?', *Educational and Child Psychology*, 26(2): 40–52.

15 Gopnik, A. (2016) *The Gardener and the Carpenter: What the New Science of Child Development Tells Us about the Relationship Between Parents and Children*, New York: Farrar, Straus & Giroux.

16 Murray, L., Rayson, H., Ferrari, P.-F., Wass, S.V. and Cooper, P.J. (2022) 'Dialogic book-sharing as a privileged intersubjective space', *Frontiers in Psychology*, 13: 786991.

[17] O'Farrelly, C., Booth, A., Tatlow-Golden, M. and Barker, B. (2020) 'Reconstructing readiness: Young children's priorities for their early school adjustment', *Early Childhood Research Quarterly*, 50(2): 3–16.

[18] All-Party Parliamentary Group for Childcare and Early Education (2021) 'Minutes', 22 November, Children's Commissioner, https://connectpa. co.uk/wp-content/uploads/2021/12/APPG-CEE-22-November-Minutes. pdf

[19] RCPCH (Royal College of Pediatrics and Child Health) (2020) *State of Child Health in the UK*, London: RCPCH, https://stateofchildhealth.rcpch. ac.uk

[20] Sadler, K., Vizard, T., Ford, T., Goodman, A., Goodman, R. and McManus, S. (2017) 'Mental health of children and young people in England 2017: Trends and characteristics', https://digital.nhs.uk/data-and-information/ publications/statistical/mental-health-of-children-and-young-people-in-england/2017/2017

[21] Creswell. C., Shum, A., Pearcey, S., Skripkauskaite, S., Patalay, P. and Waite, P. (2021) 'Young people's mental health during the COVID-19 pandemic', *The Lancet. Child & Adolescent Health*, 5(8): 535–7.

[22] Baines, E. and Blatchford, P. (2019) *School Break and Lunch Times and Young People's Social Lives: A Follow-Up National Study*, Final Report to the Nuffield Foundation, Ref EDU/42402, https://discovery.ucl.ac.uk/ id/eprint/10073916/1/Baines%2042402%20BreaktimeSurvey%20-%20 Main%20public%20report%20(May19)-final.pdf

[23] Bird, W. (2007) *Natural Thinking*, Royal Society for the Protection of Birds, www.rspb.org.uk/globalassets/downloads/documents/positions/health/ natural-thinking-report.pdf

[24] Ramchandani, P.G., Domoney, J., Sethna, V., Psychogiou, L., Vlachos, H. and Murray, L. (2013) 'Do early father–infant interactions predict the onset of externalising behaviours in young children? Findings from a longitudinal cohort study', *Journal of Child Psychology and Psychiatry*, 54(1): 56–64.

[25] Amodia-Bidakowska, A., Laverty, C. and Ramchandani, P.G. (2020) 'Father–child play: A systematic review of its frequency, characteristics and potential impact on children's development', *Developmental Review*, 57: 100924.

[26] Blalock, S.M., Lindo, N. and Ray, D.C. (2019) 'Individual and group child-centered play therapy: Impact on social-emotional competencies', *Journal of Counseling & Development*, 97(3): 238–49.

[27] PTUK (Play Therapy UK) (2011) *An Effective Way of Alleviating Children's Emotional, Behaviour and Mental Health Problems – The Latest Research*, Uckfield: PTUK, http://playtherapy.hk/wp-content/uploads/2022/12/ paperV2.pdf www.playtherapy.hk/paperV2.pdf

[28] Clear Sky (no date) Home page, www.clear-sky.org.uk

[29] The Children's Society (2021) *The Good Childhood Report 2021*, www. childrenssociety.org.uk/information/professionals/resources/good-childhood-report-2021

[30] Gray, P. (2011) 'The decline of play and the rise of psychopathology in children and adolescents', *American Journal of Play*, 3(4): 443–63.

31 Piaget, J., translated in C. Gattengo and F.M. Hodgson (1962) *Play, Dreams and Imitation in Childhood*, New York: Norton.

32 Rostad, W. and Whitaker, J. (2016) 'The association between reflective functioning and parent–child relationship quality', *Journal of Child and Family Studies*, 25: 2164–77.

33 Doyle, C. and Cicchetti, D. (2017) 'From the cradle to the grave: The effect of adverse caregiving environments on attachment and relationships throughout the lifespan', *Clinical Psychology: Science and Practice*, 24(2): 203–17, doi: 10.1111/cpsp.12192.

34 Hong, Y.R. and Park, J.S. (2012) 'Impact of attachment, temperament and parenting on human development', *Korean Journal of Pediatrics*, 55(12): 449–54.

35 Belsky, J. and Fearon, R.M.P. (2008) *Handbook of Attachment: Theory, Research, and Clinical Applications* (2nd edn), New York: Guilford Press.

36 Courtney, J. and Nowakowski-Sims, E. (2018) 'Technology and the threat to secure attachments', *Play Therapy*, September, https://cdn.ymaws.com/www.a4pt.org/resource/resmgr/magazine_articles/Article_2.pdf

37 Maskell-Graham, D. (2016) *Reflective Functioning and Play*, King's Lynn: Biddles Books.

38 Nuffield Foundation (2019) 'Reading with pre-school children boosts language skills by eight months', 9 January, www.nuffieldfoundation.org/news/reading-with-pre-school-children-boosts-language-skills-by-eight-months

39 Golinkoff, R.M., Hirsh-Pasek, K. and Singer, D.G. (2006) 'Why Play = Learning: A Challenge for Parents and Educators', in D.G. Singer, R.M. Golinkoff and K. Hirsch-Pasek (eds) *Play = Learning: How Play Motivates and Enhances Children's Cognitive and Social-Emotional Growth*, Oxford: Oxford University Press, pp 3–12.

40 Skene, K., O'Farrelly, C.M., Byrne, E.M., Kirby, N., Stevens, E.C. and Ranchandani, P.G. (2022) 'Can guidance during play enhance children's learning and development in educational contexts? A systematic review and meta-analysis', *Child Development*, 93(4): 1162–80.

41 Dodd, H.F., FitzGibbon, L., Watson, B.E. and Nesbit, R.J. (2021) 'Children's play and independent mobility in 2020: Results from the British Children's Play Survey', *International Journal of Environmental Research and Public Health*, 18(8): 4334.

42 Hofferth, S.L. (2009) 'Changes in American children's time – 1997 to 2003', *Electronic International Journal of Time Use Research*, 6(1): 26–47.

43 Baines, E. and Blatchford, P. (2019) *School Break and Lunch Times and Young People's Social Lives: A Follow-Up National Study*, Final Report to the Nuffield Foundation, Ref EDU/42402, https://discovery.ucl.ac.uk/id/eprint/10073916/1/Baines%2042402%20BreaktimeSurvey%20-%20Main%20public%20report%20(May19)-final.pdf

44 The World Bank (2021) *The State of the Global Education Crisis: A Path to Recovery*, www.worldbank.org/en/topic/education/publication/the-state-of-the-global-education-crisis-a-path-to-recovery

[45] International Commission on the Futures of Education (2021) *Reimagining Our Futures Together: A New Social Contract for Education*, https://unesdoc. unesco.org/ark:/48223/pf0000379707

[46] OECD (Organisation for Economic Co-operation and Development) (2017) *Social and Emotional Skills: Well-being, Connectedness and Success*, Paris: OECD, www.oecd.org/education/school/UPDATED%20Social%20and%20 Emotional%20Skills%20-%20Well-being,%20connectedness%20and%20 success.pdf%20(website).pdf

[47] Zosh, J.M., Hopkins, E.J., Jensen, H., et al (2017) *Learning through Play: A Review of the Evidence*, White Paper, Billund: The LEGO Foundation, https://cms.learningthroughplay.com/media/wmtlmbe0/learning-through-play_web.pdf

[48] Care, E., Anderson, K. and Kim, H. (2016) 'Visualizing the breadth of skills movement across education systems', Brookings, 19 September, http://skills.brookings.edu

[49] Cersoli, C.P., Nicklin, J.M. and Ford, M.T. (2014) 'Intrinsic motivation and extrinsic incentives jointly prejudice performance: A 40-year meta-analysis', *Psychological Bulletin*, July, 140(4): 980–1008.

[50] Phair, R. (2021) 'Should education leaders be listening to children?', OECD Education and Skills Today, 19 November, https://oecdedutoday.com/ should-education-leaders-be-listening-to-children

[51] Winthrop, R. and Ershadi, M. (2021) *Know your Parents: A Global Study of Family Beliefs, Motivations, and Sources of Information on Schooling*, Washington, DC: The Brookings Institution, www.brookings.edu/essay/know-your-parents

[52] Gottfried, A.W., Gottfried, A.E. and Wright Guerin, D. (2006) 'The Fullerton Longitudinal Study: A long-term investigation of intellectual and motivational giftedness', *Journal for the Education of the Gifted*, 29(4): 430–50.

[53] Gopnik, A., O'Grady, S., Lucas, C.G., Griffiths, T.L., Wente, A., Bridgers, S., Aboody, R., Fung, H. and Dahl, R.E. (2017) 'Changes in cognitive flexibility and hypothesis search across human life history from childhood to adolescence to adulthood', *PNAS (Proceedings of the National Academy of Sciences of the United States of America)*, 114(30): 7892–99, doi: 10.1073/pnas.1700811114

[54] Qvortrup, A., Lomholt, R., Christensen, V. Lundtofte, T.E. and Nielsen, A. (2023) 'Playful learning during the reopening of Danish schools after Covid 19 closures', *Scandinavian Journal of Educational Research*, 67(5): 725–40.

[55] Playful Learning (2019) *Playbook 1*, https://playful-learning.dk/wp-content/ uploads/2021/08/playbook-1-eng.pdf

[56] Skene, K., O'Farrelly, C.M., Byrne, E.M., Kirby, N., Stevens, E.C. and Ranchandani, P.G. (2022) 'Can guidance during play enhance children's learning and development in educational contexts? A systematic review and meta-analysis', *Child Development*, 93(4): 1162–80.

[57] Kingman, D. (2020) 'Green space inequality', Intergenerational Foundation, 20 May, www.if.org.uk/2020/05/20/green-space-inequality

58 ONS (Office for National Statistics) (2020) 'One in eight British households has no garden', 14 May, www.ons.gov.uk/economy/environmentalaccounts/articles/oneineightbritishhouseholdshasnogarden/2020-05-14

59 London skews the figures with its large and high-density population and relatively high number of parks. Lower-income families also have much less access to private gardens.

60 The average population per park in the UK is 2,000 households; for Clapham Common in London, for example, it's 46,000 households. See ONS (Office for National Statistics) (2020) 'One in eight British households has no garden', 14 May, www.ons.gov.uk/economy/environmentalaccounts/articles/oneineightbritishhouseholdshasnogarden/2020-05-14

61 Dodd, H.F., FitzGibbon, L., Watson, B.E. and Nesbit, R.J. (2021) 'Children's play and independent mobility in 2020: Results from the British Children's Play Survey', *International Journal of Environmental Research and Public Health*, 18(8): 4334.

62 Scott, J. (2014) 'Conker fights: Is it the end for the playground game?', BBC News Online, 10 October, www.bbc.co.uk/news/uk-england-29519601

63 Blunden, M. (2018) 'London borough of Wandsworth plans fines of up to £500 for climbing trees, flying kites or playing cricket in parks', *Evening Standard*, 16 February, www.standard.co.uk/news/london/london-borough-of-wandsworth-to-issue-fines-of-up-to-ps500-for-climbing-trees-flying-kites-or-playing-cricket-in-parks-a3768126.html

64 *National Post* (2015) 'Maryland parents who allowed their "free range" children to walk home on their own cited for neglect', 4 March, https://nationalpost.com/news/world/maryland-parents-who-allowed-their-free-range-children-to-walk-home-on-their-own-cited-for-neglect

65 Kline, S. (1995) *Out of the Garden: Toys and Children's Culture in the Age of TV Marketing*, London: Verso.

66 CLPE (Centre for Literacy in Primary Education) (2018) *Reflecting Realities*, London: CLPE, https://clpe.org.uk/research/clpes-reflecting-realities-survey-ethnic-representation-within-uk-childrens-literature-0

67 CLPE (Centre for Literacy in Primary Education) (2018) *Reflecting Realities*, London: CLPE, https://clpe.org.uk/research/clpes-reflecting-realities-survey-ethnic-representation-within-uk-childrens-literature-0

68 Sturdivant, T. (2021) 'What I learned when I recreated the famous "doll test" that looked at how Black kids see race', The Conversation, 22 February, https://theconversation.com/what-i-learned-when-i-recreated-the-famous-doll-test-that-looked-at-how-black-kids-see-race-153780

69 Sturdivant, T.D. and Alanis, I. (2021) '"I'm gonna cook my baby in a pot": Young black girls' racial preferences and play behavior', *Early Childhood Education Journal*, 49: 473–82.

70 Elvy, N. (2019) 'Outdoors: Is it a privilege?', Curious School of the Wild, www.curiousschoolofthewild.com

71 Weisgram, E.S. and Dinella, L.M. (2018) *Gender Typing of Children's Toys: How Early Play Experiences Impact Development*, Washington, DC: American Psychological Association.

[72] Cutts, E. (2019) *The Dear Wild Place: Green Spaces, Community and Campaigning*, Paisley: CCWB Press.

[73] Brooks, L. (2017) 'Glasgow Children's Wood saved from development', *The Guardian*, 2 January, www.theguardian.com/uk-news/2017/jan/02/glasgow-childrens-wood-saved-from-development

[74] Child Friendly Cardiff (no date) 'Play Lanes', www.childfriendlycardiff.co.uk/projects/play-lanes

[75] Department for Children, Schools and Families (2008) *The Play Strategy*, https://lx.iriss.org.uk/sites/default/files/resources/The%20Play%20Strategy.pdf

Chapter 5

[1] Quoted in Kuris, G. (2019) 'Reconstructing a city in the interests of its children: Tirana, Albania, 2015–19', Innovations for Successful Societies: Learning & Adapting Urban 95, Princeton, NJ: Princeton University, https://successfulsocieties.princeton.edu/sites/successfulsocieties/files/Albania_Tirana_Urban95.pdf

[2] Garrett, B.L. (2015) 'The privatisation of cities' public spaces is escalating. It is time to take a stand', *The Guardian*, 4 August, www.theguardian.com/cities/2015/aug/04/pops-privately-owned-public-space-cities-direct-action

[3] Quoted in Bray, A. (2018) 'Ex-magistrate defends using anti-child alarm on neighbour's six kids', DevonLive, 23 July, www.devonlive.com/news/celebs-tv/morning-anti-child-alarm-used-1815807

[4] Watling, G. (2021) 'Anti-loitering devices: Safety', *Hansard*, Volume 697, 16 June, UK Parliament, https://hansard.parliament.uk/commons/2021-06-16/debates/81F70BB5-C4E4-46A2-98F2-D53618641550/Anti-LoiteringDevicesSafety

[5] United Nations Committee on the Rights of the Child (2016) 'Concluding observations on the fifth periodic report of the United Kingdom of Great Britain and Northern Ireland', www.unicef.org.uk/babyfriendly/wp-content/uploads/sites/2/2016/08/UK-CRC-Concluding-observations-2016-2.pdf

[6] Council of Europe Parliamentary Assembly (2010) 'Prohibiting the marketing and use of the "Mosquito" youth dispersal device', Recommendation 1930, https://assembly.coe.int/nw/xml/XRef/Xref-XML2HTML-en.asp?fileid=17891&lang=e

[7] Watling, G. (2021) 'Anti-loitering devices: Safety', *Hansard*, Volume 697, 16 June, UK Parliament, https://hansard.parliament.uk/commons/2021-06-16/debates/81F70BB5-C4E4-46A2-98F2-D53618641550/Anti-LoiteringDevicesSafety

[8] United Nations Committee on the Rights of the Child (2016) 'Concluding observations on the fifth periodic report of the United Kingdom of Great Britain and Northern Ireland', www.unicef.org.uk/babyfriendly/wp-content/uploads/sites/2/2016/08/UK-CRC-Concluding-observations-2016-2.pdf, p 5.

9   Booth, R. (2019) 'Youth club closures put young people at risk of violence, warn MPs', *The Guardian*, 7 May, www.theguardian.com/society/2019/may/07/youth-club-closures-young-people-risk-violence-mps

10 DCMS (Department for Digital, Culture, Media & Sport) (2022) 'Government outlines ambitious plans to level up activities for young people', Press release, 1 February, www.gov.uk/government/news/government-outlines-ambitious-plans-to-level-up-activities-for-young-people

11 Association of Play Industries (2017) *Nowhere to Play: A Report by the Association of Play Industries on the State of England's Playgrounds*, Alrewas: Association of Play Industries, www.api-play.org/wp-content/uploads/sites/4/2018/02/NowheretoPlayFinal2.pdf

12 UNICEF (United Nations Children's Fund) (2012) *The State of the World's Children 2012: Children in an Urban World*, www.unicef.org/reports/state-worlds-children-2012

13 Ginsburg, K. (2007) 'The importance of play in promoting healthy child development and maintaining strong parent–child bonds', *Paediatrics*, 119(1): 182–91.

14 Gill, T. (2021) *Urban Playground: How Child-Friendly Planning and Design Can Save Cities*, London: RIBA Publishing.

15 Gromada, A. and Rees, G. (2020) *Worlds of Influence: Understanding What Shapes Child Well-being in Rich Countries*, Innocenti Report Card 14, Florence: UNICEF Office of Research – Innocenti, www.unicef-irc.org/publications/1140-worlds-of-influence-understanding-what-shapes-child-well-being-in-rich-countries.html

16 Shaw, B., Bicket, M., Fagan-Watson, B., Mocca, E., Elliott, B. and Hillman, M. (2015) *Children's Independent Mobility: An International Comparison and Recommendations for Action*, London: Policy Studies Institute.

17 Hörschelmann, K. and van Blerk, L. (2012) *Children, Youth and the City*, Abingdon: Routledge.

18 Blinkert, B. and Hank, A. (2005) *Aktionsräume von Kindern in der Stadt: Eine Untersuchung im Auftrag der Stadt Freiburg [Children's Play Spaces in the City: A Study Commissioned by the City of Freiburg]*, Herbolzheim: Centaurus Verlag.

19 Williams, S., Wright, H., Hargrave, J. and zu Dohna, F. (2017) *Cities Alive: Designing for Urban Childhoods*, London: Arup, www.arup.com/perspectives/publications/research/section/cities-alive-designing-for-urban-childhoods

20 Barcelona.cat (2021) 'Schools with street-calmed environments to number 155 in 2022', www.barcelona.cat/infobarcelona/en/tema/childhood/work-gets-under-way-at-the-75-schools-to-be-protected-from-traffic-in-2021-2_1114457.html

21 Transport for New Homes (2020) *Garden Villages and Garden Towns: Visions and Reality*, Foundation for Integrated Transport.

22 Quinio, V. and Rodrigues, G. (2021) *Net Zero: Decarbonising the City*, London: Centre for Cities.

23 Rittel, H. and Webber, M. (1973) 'Dilemmas in a general theory of planning', *Policy Sciences*, 4(2): 155–69.

24 Boardman, C. (2018) Speech to All-Party Parliamentary Group on Cycling, https://allpartycycling.org/2018/02/09/chris-boardman-speech-january-2018

25 Brown, P. (2004) 'Welcome to Tirana, Europe's pollution capital', *The Guardian*, 27 March, www.theguardian.com/environment/2004/mar/27/internationalnews.pollution1

26 Kuris, G. (2019) 'Reconstructing a city in the interests of its children: Tirana, Albania, 2015–19', Innovations for Successful Societies: Learning & Adapting Urban 95, Princeton, NJ: Princeton University, https://successfulsocieties.princeton.edu/sites/successfulsocieties/files/Albania_Tirana_Urban95.pdf, p 3.

27 Kuris, G. (2019) 'Reconstructing a city in the interests of its children: Tirana, Albania, 2015–19', Innovations for Successful Societies: Learning & Adapting Urban 95, Princeton, NJ: Princeton University, https://successfulsocieties.princeton.edu/sites/successfulsocieties/files/Albania_Tirana_Urban95.pdf, p 26.

28 Veliaj, E. (2017) 'Urban superheroes, a city transformed by kids', TEDxVitoriaGasteiz, www.youtube.com/watch?v=N7IahTl6JdM

29 Holich, V. (2021) 'Innovative Mayor: "You are not stuck in a traffic jam. You are a traffic jam"', Lviv Now, 25 October, https://tvoemisto.tv/en/news/we_capture_air_not_forest_the_mayor_of_tirana_about_the_city_development_124316.html

30 Veliaj, E. (2021) 'Tirana. Restoring the joy of parks in our communities', www.youtube.com/watch?v=9fKuodkno0I

31 Cleland, V., Timperio, A., Salmon, J., Hume, C., Baur, L.A. and Crawford, D. (2010) 'Predictors of time spent outdoors among children: 5-year longitudinal findings', *Journal of Epidemiology & Community Health*, 64(5): 400–6.

32 Play England (2010) 'ICM survey for Playday', http://playday.gn.apc.org/campaigns-3/previous-campaigns/2010-our-place/2010-opinion-poll

33 Shaw, B., Fagan-Watson, B., Fraudendienst, B., Redecker, A., Jones, T. and Hillman, M. (2013) *Children's Independent Mobility: A Comparative Study in England and Germany (1971–2010)*, London: Policy Studies Institute.

34 NHS Digital (2019) 'Statistics on obesity, physical activity and diet, England, 2019', 8 May, https://digital.nhs.uk/data-and-information/publications/statistical/statistics-on-obesity-physical-activity-and-diet/statistics-on-obesity-physical-activity-and-diet-england-2019

35 Gregory, A. (2021) 'Childhood obesity in England soars during pandemic', *The Guardian*, 16 November, www.theguardian.com/society/2021/nov/16/childhood-obesity-in-england-soared-during-pandemic

36 Local Government Association (2022) 'Children and young people's emotional wellbeing and mental health – Facts and figures', www.local.gov.uk/about/campaigns/bright-futures/bright-futures-camhs/child-and-adolescent-mental-health-and

37 Playday (2013) '2013 opinion poll summary', www.playday.org.uk/2013-opinion-poll

38 Read, J. (2022) *Child MPH: Delivering Safe Walking and Cycling Infrastructure for Children and Young People in Scotland*, Climate Action Ltd, https://2030.co.uk/Child%20mph.pdf

39 Rolfe, S., Garnham, L., Godwin, J., Anderson, I., Seaman, P. and Donaldson, C. (2020) 'Housing as a social determinant of health and wellbeing: Developing an empirically-informed realist theoretical framework', *BMC Public Health*, 20(1): 1–19.

40 Shelter (2005) *Full House? How Overcrowded Housing Affects Families*, https://assets.ctfassets.net/6sxvmndnpn0s/6dU8FFbZ6RnSk6DbnDOMHb/61e30884aff47a789891b2dce54fcbc7/Full_house_overcrowding_effects.pdf

41 Wilson, W. and Barton, C. (2021) *Overcrowded Housing (England)*, House of Commons Library, https://researchbriefings.files.parliament.uk/documents/SN01013/SN01013.pdf

42 National Housing Federation (2021) *People in Housing Need*, London: National Housing Federation, December, www.housing.org.uk/globalassets/files/people-in-housing-need/people-in-housing-need-2021_summary.pdf

43 Ministry of Housing, Communities & Local Government (2020) *English Housing Survey, Headline Report, 2019–20*, https://assets.publishing.service.gov.uk/government/uploads/system/uploads/attachment_data/file/945013/2019-20_EHS_Headline_Report.pdf

44 Wilson, W. and Barton, C. (2021) *Overcrowded Housing (England)*, House of Commons Library, https://researchbriefings.files.parliament.uk/documents/SN01013/SN01013.pdf

45 National Housing Federation (2021) *People in Housing Need*, London: National Housing Federation, December, www.housing.org.uk/globalassets/files/people-in-housing-need/people-in-housing-need-2021_summary.pdf

46 Wilson, W. and Barton, C. (2021) *Overcrowded Housing (England)*, House of Commons Library, https://researchbriefings.files.parliament.uk/documents/SN01013/SN01013.pdf

47 Venn, A.J., Cooper, M., Antoniak, M., Laughlin, C., Britton, J. and Lewis, S.A. (2003) 'Effects of volatile organic compounds, damp, and other environmental exposures in the home or wheezing illness in children', *Thorax*, 5(11): 955–60.

48 McCann, P. and Horsburgh, L. (2022) 'Awaab Ishak: Mould in Rochdale flat caused boy's death, coroner rules', BBC News, 15 November, www.bbc.co.uk/news/uk-england-manchester-63635721

49 Brittan, N., Davies, J.M.C. and Colley, J.R.T. (1987) 'Early respiratory experience and subsequent cough and peak expiratory flow rate in 36-year-old men and women', *British Medical Journal*, 294(6583): 1317–20.

50 Ghodsian, M. and Fogelman, K. (1988) *A Longitudinal Study of Housing Circumstances in Childhood and Early Adulthood*, Working Paper 29, London: NCDS (National Child Development Study) User Support Group.

51 Shelter (2006) *Chance of a Lifetime: The Impact of Bad Housing on Children's Lives*, https://assets.ctfassets.net/6sxvmndnpn0s/4LTXp3mya7IigRmNG8x9KK/6922b5a4c6ea756ea94da71ebdc001a5/Chance_of_a_Lifetime.pdf

52 Essen, J., Fogelman, K. and Head, J. (1978) 'Children's housing and their health and physical development', *Child: Care, Health and Development*, 4(19): 357–69.

53 Shelter (2018) *The Housing Crisis Generation: How Many Children Are Homeless in Britain, December*, https://assets.ctfassets.net/6sxvmndnpn0s/AGxzjr0tOiJqOgLXhRdg4/e123570ee8a8c34bd7053acf203d40e9/The_housing_crisis_generation_-_Homeless_children_in_Britain.pdf

54 Lavelle, D. (2022) '"I'm willing to take on absolutely everyone!" Kwajo Tweneboa on fighting for Britain's poorest tenants', *The Guardian*, 19 January, www.theguardian.com/society/2022/jan/19/im-willing-to-take-on-absolutely-everyone-kwajo-tweneboa-on-fighting-for-britains-poorest-tenants

55 Vostanis, P., Grattan, E. and Cumella, S. (1998) 'Mental health problems of homeless children and families: A longitudinal study', *British Medical Journal*, 316(199): 899–902.

56 Ministry of Housing, Communities & Local Government (2020) 'Complete ban on evictions and additional protection for renters', Press release, 18 March, www.gov.uk/government/news/complete-ban-on-evictions-and-additional-protection-for-renters

57 Shelter (2021) '200,000 children under threat of eviction this winter', 23 December, https://england.shelter.org.uk/media/press_release/200000_children_under_threat_of_eviction_this_winter_

58 DfE (Department for Education) (2022) 'Working together to safeguard children', www.gov.uk/government/publications/working-together-to-safeguard-children--2

59 See https://beyondcommandandcontrol.com/john-seddon-and-the-vanguard-method

60 Wellbeing Economy Alliance (2021) *Failure Demand: Counting the True Costs of an Unjust and Unsustainable Economic System*, https://weall.org/wp-content/uploads/FailureDemand_FinalReport_September2021.pdf

61 Chatterjee, K., Ricci, M., Cope, A., et al (2019) *The Role of Transport in Supporting a Healthy Future for Young People*, Report to The Health Foundation, www.sustrans.org.uk/media/5057/the-role-of-transport-in-supporting-a-healthy-future-for-young-people.pdf

62 Chatterjee, K., Ricci, M., Cope, A., et al (2019) *The Role of Transport in Supporting a Healthy Future for Young People*, Report to The Health Foundation, www.sustrans.org.uk/media/5057/the-role-of-transport-in-supporting-a-healthy-future-for-young-people.pdf

63 Department for Transport (2022) 'Demand responsive transport: Local authority toolkit', 13 April, www.gov.uk/government/publications/demand-responsive-transport-local-authority-toolkit/demand-responsive-transport-local-authority-toolkit

64 Our Pass (no date) '100,000 Our Pass cards issued since launch', https://ourpass.co.uk/10000-our-pass-cards-issued-since-launch

65 UK Parliament (2020) 'Free travel for children and young people in London', Early Day Motions, 20 July, https://edm.parliament.uk/early-day-motion/57279/free-travel-for-children-and-young-people-in-london

66 McCarthy, M. (2010) '1970 vs 2010: 40 years when we got older, richer and fatter', *The Independent*, 3 July, www.independent.co.uk/news/uk/this-britain/1970-vs-2010-40-years-when-we-got-older-richer-and-fatter-2017240.html

67 ONS (Office for National Statistics) (2019) 'Percentage of households with cars by income group, tenure and household composition: Table A47', www.ons.gov.uk/peoplepopulationandcommunity/personalandhousehold finances/expenditure/datasets/percentageofhouseholdswithcarsbyincome grouptenureandhouseholdcompositionuktablea47

68 Laville, S., Taylor, M., Bengtsson, H. and Zapponi, C. (2017) 'Thousands of British children exposed to illegal levels of air pollution', *The Guardian*, 4 April, www.theguardian.com/environment/2017/apr/04/thousands-of-british-children-exposed-to-illegal-levels-of-air-pollution

69 Carrington, D. (2021) 'Quarter of UK pupils attend schools where air pollution is over WHO limit', *The Guardian*, 17 June, www.theguardian.com/environment/2021/jun/17/quarter-of-uk-pupils-attend-schools-where-air-pollution-is-over-who-limit

70 Courts and Tribunals Judiciary (2021) 'Preventions of future deaths: Ella Kissi-Debrah', www.judiciary.uk/prevention-of-future-death-reports/ella-kissi-debrah

71 Marmot, M., Allen, J. and Goldblatt, P. (2010) *Fair Society, Healthy Lives: The Marmot Review: Strategic Review of Health Inequalities in England post-2010*, London: Department for International Development, www.gov.uk/research-for-development-outputs/fair-society-healthy-lives-the-marmot-review-strategic-review-of-health-inequalities-in-england-post-2010

72 Public Health England (2016) *Working Together to Promote Active Travel: A Briefing for Local Authorities*, https://assets.publishing.service.gov.uk/government/uploads/system/uploads/attachment_data/file/523460/Working_Together_to_Promote_Active_Travel_A_briefing_for_local_authorities.pdf

73 DePriest, K., Butz, A., Land, C., et al (2017) *Access to Greenspace and Asthma Symptoms in Urban Children with Persistent Asthma*, ERS (European Respiratory Society) Congress.

74 British Lung Foundation (2016) *The Battle for Breath – The Impact of Lung Disease in the UK*, London, www.asthmaandlung.org.uk/battle-breath-report

75 UNICEF (United Nations Children's Fund) (2019) 'Child health experts warn air pollution is damaging children's health', Press release, 5 February, www.unicef.org.uk/press-releases/child-health-experts-warn-air-pollution-is-damaging-childrens-health

76 Defra (Department for Environment, Food & Rural Affairs) (2019) *Clean Air Strategy 2019*, https://assets.publishing.service.gov.uk/government/uploads/system/uploads/attachment_data/file/770715/clean-air-strategy-2019.pdf

77 Public Health England (2018) *Estimation of Costs to the NHS and Social Care Due to the Health Impacts of Air Pollution*, https://assets.publishing.service. gov.uk/government/uploads/system/uploads/attachment_data/file/836720/ Estimation_of_costs_to_the_NHS_and_social_care_due_to_the_health_ impacts_of_air_pollution.pdf

78 Quoted in UNICEF (2019) 'Child health experts warn air pollution is damaging children's health', Press release, 5 February, www.unicef.org. uk/press-releases/child-health-experts-warn-air-pollution-is-damaging-childrens-health

79 Edwards, H. and Wellesley, L. (2019) *Healthy Air for Every Child: A Call for National Action*, UNICEF, www.unicef.org.uk/publications/healthy-air-for-every-child

80 Sustainable Development Commission (2011) *Fairness in a Car-dependent Society*, Cardiff: Sustainable Development Commission, https://road.cc/ sites/default/files/fairness_car_dependant.pdf

81 Roads Task Force (2013) 'Technical Note 20: What are the main health impacts of roads in London?', https://content.tfl.gov.uk/technical-note-20-what-are-the-main-health-impacts.pdf

82 TfL (Transport for London) (no date) *Walking & Cycling: The Economic Benefits*, https://content.tfl.gov.uk/walking-cycling-economic-benefits-summary-pack.pdf (updated regularly).

83 Rajé, F. and Saffrey, A. (2016) *The Value of Cycling: Rapid Evidence Review of the Economic Benefits of Cycling*, London, Bristol and Birmingham: Department for Transport, Phil Jones Associates and University of Birmingham, https://assets.publishing.service.gov.uk/government/uploads/ system/uploads/attachment_data/file/509587/value-of-cycling.pdf

84 Sustrans (2022) *Helping People Through the Cost of Living Crisis and Growing Our Economy: The Role of Walking, Wheeling and Cycling*, Walking and Cycling Index, www.sustrans.org.uk/media/11397/cost-of-living-report.pdf

85 DfT (Department for Transport) (2021) *Transport and Environment Statistics: 2021 Annual Report*, https://assets.publishing.service.gov.uk/government/ uploads/system/uploads/attachment_data/file/984685/transport-and-environment-statistics-2021.pdf

86 Holmes, R. (2019) 'We now see 5,000 ads a day … and it's getting worse', LinkedIn, 19 February, www.linkedin.com/pulse/have-we-reached-peak-ad-social-media-ryan-holmes

87 Vogels, E. (2019) 'Millennials stand out for their technology use, but older generations also embrace digital life', Pew Research Center, 9 September, www.pewresearch.org/fact-tank/2019/09/09/us-generations-technology-use

88 London's Child Obesity Taskforce (2019) *Every Child a Healthy Weight – Ten Ambitions for London*, London: Greater London Authority.

89 Yau, A., Berger, N., Law, C., et al (2022) 'Changes in household food and drink purchases following restrictions on the advertisement of high fat, salt, and sugar products across the Transport for London network: A

controlled interrupted time series analysis', *PLoS Medicine*, 19(2), https://doi.org/10.1371/journal.pmed.1003915

Chapter 6

1   See www.irishtimes.com/news/education/education-is-not-the-filling-of-a-pail-but-the-lighting-of-a-fire-it-s-an-inspiring-quote-but-did-wb-yeats-say-it-1.1560192

2   Fitzhenry, R.I. (ed) (1987) *Barnes & Noble Book of Quotations: Revised and Enlarged*, New York: Barnes & Noble Books, Division of Harper & Row, p 112.

3   DfE (Department for Education) (2019) 'Widening participation in Higher Education, England, 2017/18 age cohort', 17 December, https://assets.publishing.service.gov.uk/government/uploads/system/uploads/attachment_data/file/852633/WP2019-MainText.pdf

4   Busby, E. (2019) 'Gap between rich and poor students at university reaches widest point for a decade', *The Independent*, 17 December, www.independent.co.uk/news/education/education-news/university-poor-students-access-gap-disadvantage-government-pressure-a9250641.html

5   Mind (2022) 'Improving mental health support for young people', www.mind.org.uk/news-campaigns/campaigns/children-and-young-peoples-mental-health/improving-mental-health-support-for-young-people/#problem

6   States of Mind (no date) 'Breaking the silence', www.statesofmind.org/breaking-the-silence

7   Millar, F. (2022) 'Inspecting the inspectors: Students assess Ofsted regime's toll on wellbeing', *The Guardian*, 29 June, www.theguardian.com/education/2022/jun/29/inspecting-the-inspectors-students-assess-ofsted-regimes-toll-on-wellbeing

8   States of Mind (2022) '"The Framework" Documentary' [video], https://vimeo.com/725602882

9   Hannon, V. and Peterson, A.K. (2021) *Thrive: The Purpose of Schools in a Changing World*, Cambridge: Cambridge University Press.

10 Smith, S. (2020) *How to Future: Leading and Sense-Making in an Age of Hyperchange*, London: Kogan Page.

11 BBC News (2009) 'Depression looms as global crisis', 2 September, http://news.bbc.co.uk/1/hi/8230549.stm

12 Davies, A. and Bhatia, T. (2015) 'Can the NHS help tackle the UK's obesity epidemic?', Nuffield Trust Blog, 20 March, www.nuffieldtrust.org.uk/news-item/can-the-nhs-help-tackle-the-uk-s-obesity-epidemic?gclid=Cj0KCQiApL2QBhC8ARIsAGMm-KGiEmv3HANinVh-BThP65NG3amq03YIcI1COjEUxUptkgEyGPZjZ8oaAll5EALw_wcB

13 Flood, M. (2020) 'Pornography has deeply troubling effects on young people, but there are ways we can minimise the harm', The Conversation, 5 January, https://theconversation.com/pornography-has-deeply-troubling-effects-on-young-people-but-there-are-ways-we-can-minimise-the-harm-127319

[14] Anderson, J. (2019) 'Only 9% of 15-year-olds can tell the difference between fact and opinion', Quartz, 3 December, https://qz.com/1759474/only-9-percent-of-15-year-olds-can-distinguish-between-fact-and-opinion

[15] Winthrop, R., Ershadi, M., Alongi, J. and Harrington, G. (2021) *What We Have Learned from Parents: A Review of CUE's Parent Survey Findings by Jurisdiction*, September, Washington, DC: CUE (Center for Universal Education) at Brookings, www.brookings.edu/wp-content/uploads/2022/01/Parent_Survey_Findings_FINAL.pdf

[16] Raworth, K. (2017) *Doughnut Economics: 7 Ways to Think Like a 21st Century Economist*, New York: Random House.

[17] Lucas, B. (2021) *Rethinking Assessment in Education: The Case for Change*, CSE Leading Education Series Paper 2, Melbourne, VIC: CSE (Centre for Strategic Education).

[18] Waldington, R. (2016) 'What makes a good life? Lessons from the longest study on happiness', TED talk, www.youtube.com/watch?v=8KkKuTCFvzI&t=395s

[19] Hannon, V. with Temperley, J. (2022) *FutureSchool: How Schools Around the World Are Applying Learning Design Principles for a New Era*, Abingdon: Routledge.

[20] Brown, C. and Luzmore, R. (2021) *Educating Tomorrow: Learning for the Post-Pandemic World*, Bingley: Emerald Group Publishing.

[21] Kennedy, R.F. (1968) 'Remarks at the University of Kansas, March 18, 1968', www.jfklibrary.org/learn/about-jfk/the-kennedy-family/robert-f-kennedy/robert-f-kennedy-speeches/remarks-at-the-university-of-kansas-march-18-1968

[22] DfE (Department for Education) (2019) 'Graduate labour market statistics: 2018', 25 April, www.gov.uk/government/statistics/graduate-labour-market-statistics-2018

[23] ONS (Office for National Statistics) (2022) 'Why free school meal recipients earn less than their peers', 4 August, www.ons.gov.uk/peoplepopulationand community/educationandchildcare/articles/whyfreeschoolmealrecipients earnlessthantheirpeers/2022-08-04

[24] Farquharson, C., McNally, S. and Tahir, I. (2022) *Education Inequalities*, IFS Deaton Review of Inequalities, London: Institute for Fiscal Studies, https://ifs.org.uk/inequality/chapter/education-inequalities

[25] Farquharson, C., McNally, S. and Tahir, I. (2022) *Education Inequalities*, IFS Deaton Review of Inequalities, London: Institute for Fiscal Studies, https://ifs.org.uk/inequality/chapter/education-inequalities

[26] Henshaw, P. (2019) 'MPs urge DfE to make academy trusts more transparent and accountable to parents', SecEd, 30 January, www.sec-ed.co.uk/news/mps-urge-dfe-to-make-academy-trusts-more-transparent-and-accountable-to-parents

[27] ONS (Office for National Statistics) (2020) 'Young people's well-being in the UK: 2020', 2 October, www.ons.gov.uk/peoplepopulationandcommunity/wellbeing/bulletins/youngpeopleswellbeingintheuk/2020

28   OECD (Organisation for Economic Co-operation and Development) (2019) *PISA 2018 Assessment and Analytical Framework*, Paris: OECD Publishing, www.oecd-ilibrary.org/sites/b25efab8-en/index.html?itemId=/content/publication/b25efab8-en

29   DfE (Department for Education) (2019) *The Teaching and Learning International Survey (TALIS) 2018*, Research report, https://assets.publishing.service.gov.uk/government/uploads/system/uploads/attachment_data/file/919064/TALIS_2018_research.pdf

30   Green, F. (2021) 'Teachers under pressure: Working harder, but with less control over how they do their jobs', IOE Blog, 20 January, https://blogs.ucl.ac.uk/ioe/2021/01/20/teachers-under-pressure-working-harder-but-with-less-control-over-how-they-do-their-jobs

31   Long, R. and Danechi, S. (2021) *Teacher Recruitment and Retention in England*, House of Commons Library, 8 December, https://researchbriefings.files.parliament.uk/documents/CBP-7222/CBP-7222.pdf

32   DfE (Department for Education) (2018) *Factors Affecting Teacher Retention: Qualitative Investigation*, Research report, https://assets.publishing.service.gov.uk/government/uploads/system/uploads/attachment_data/file/686947/Factors_affecting_teacher_retention_-_qualitative_investigation.pdf

33   Sibieta, L. (2021) 'The growing gap between state school and private school spending', Institute for Fiscal Studies, 8 October, https://ifs.org.uk/articles/growing-gap-between-state-school-and-private-school-spending

34   Bolton, P. (2021) 'Education spending in the UK', House of Commons Library, 15 November, https://commonslibrary.parliament.uk/research-briefings/sn01078

35   Williams, M. (2017) 'International school spending – how does the UK compare?', NFER Blogs, 23 October, www.nfer.ac.uk/news-events/nfer-blogs/international-school-spending-how-does-the-uk-compare

36   DfE (Department for Education) (2014) 'National Curriculum in England: Framework for Key Stages 1 to 4', www.gov.uk/government/publications/national-curriculum-in-england-framework-for-key-stages-1-to-4

37   Vasager, J. (2022) 'Michael Gove's curriculum attacked by expert who advised him', *The Guardian*, 12 June, www.theguardian.com/education/2012/jun/12/michael-gove-curriculum-attacked-adviser

38   International Baccalaureate (no date) 'Our mission', www.ibo.org/about-the-ib/mission

39   Kiek, T. (2022) 'Plan to replace A Levels with a British Baccalaureate welcomed by ex-UK prime ministers', *The National News*, 15 June, www.thenationalnews.com/world/uk-news/2022/06/15/plan-to-replace-a-levels-with-a-british-baccalaureate-welcomed-by-ex-uk-prime-ministers

40   The Sutton Trust and Social Mobility Commission (2019) *Elitist Britain 2019: The Educational Backgrounds of Britain's Leading People*, London: The Sutton Trust, www.suttontrust.com/wp-content/uploads/2019/12/Elitist-Britain-2019.pdf

[41] Walker, A. (2019) 'Two-thirds of Boris Johnson's cabinet went to private schools', *The Guardian*, 25 July, www.theguardian.com/education/2019/jul/25/two-thirds-of-boris-johnsons-cabinet-went-to-private-schools

[42] The Sutton Trust and Social Mobility Commission (2019) *Elitist Britain 2019: The Educational Backgrounds of Britain's Leading People*, London: The Sutton Trust, www.suttontrust.com/wp-content/uploads/2019/12/Elitist-Britain-2019.pdf

[43] Statista (2022) 'Proportion of children living in poverty in the OECD countries in 2022', www.statista.com/statistics/264424/child-poverty-in-oecd-countries

[44] World Economic Forum (2020) *Global Social Mobility Index 2020: Why Economies Benefit from Fixing Inequality*, Cologny: World Economic Forum, www.weforum.org/reports/global-social-mobility-index-2020-why-economies-benefit-from-fixing-inequality

[45] Mansell, W. (2010) 'Poor children a year behind in language skills', *The Guardian*, 15 February, www.theguardian.com/education/2010/feb/15/poor-children-behind-sutton-trust

[46] Mansell, W. (2010) 'Poor children a year behind in language skills', *The Guardian*, 15 February, www.theguardian.com/education/2010/feb/15/poor-children-behind-sutton-trust

[47] Aho, E., Pitkanen, K. and Sahlberg, P. (2006) *Policy Development and Reform Principles of Basic and Secondary Education in Finland since 1968*, Education Working Paper Series Number 2, Washington, DC: The World Bank, https://pasisahlberg.com/wp-content/uploads/2013/01/Education-in-Finland-2006.pdf

Chapter 7

[1] Ayo, age 12, quoted in O'Connell, R., Knight, A. and Brannen, J. (2019) *Living Hand to Mouth*, London: Child Poverty Action Group, p 4.

[2] Morris, J. and Fisher, E. (2022) 'Growing problems, in depth: The impact of Covid-19 on health care for children and young people in England', Nuffield Trust Briefing, 18 February, www.nuffieldtrust.org.uk/resource/growing-problems-in-detail-covid-19-s-impact-on-health-care-for-children-and-young-people-in-england

[3] Quoted in Greenfield, M. (2022) 'Children's health during the COVID-19 pandemic: What have we learned?', McKinsey & Company, interview, 10 January, www.mckinsey.com/industries/healthcare-systems-and-services/our-insights/childrens-health-during-the-covid-19-pandemic-what-have-we-learned

[4] Batterham, R. (2020) 'Health inequalities and obesity', Royal College of Physicians, 28 October, www.rcplondon.ac.uk/news/health-inequalities-and-obesity

[5] Mind (2021) 'Facts and figures about poverty and mental health', www.mind.org.uk/about-us/our-strategy/working-harder-for-people-facing-poverty/facts-and-figures-about-poverty-and-mental-health

6   'Obesity' is a clinical term defined by the World Health Organization (WHO) as having a body mass index (BMI) of over 30. 'Overweight' is defined as a BMI of over 25. See WHO (World Health Organization) (no date) 'Obesity', www.who.int/health-topics/obesity/#tab=tab_1

7   The Health Foundation (2022) 'Map of healthy life expectancy at birth', 6 January, www.health.org.uk/evidence-hub/health-inequalities/map-of-healthy-life-expectancy-at-birth

8   NHS Digital (2018) 'Health survey reveals association between parent and child obesity', 4 December, https://digital.nhs.uk/news/2018/health-survey-reveals-association-between-parent-and-child-obesity

9   Cancer Research UK (2018) 'Obesity risk doubles for teens bombarded with junk food adverts', Press release, 15 March, https://news.cancerresearchuk.org/2018/03/15/obesity-risk-doubles-for-teens-bombarded-with-junk-food-adverts

10 Biro, F. and Wien, M. (2010) 'Childhood obesity and adult morbidities', *The American Journal of Clinical Nutrition*, 91(5): 1499S–505S.

11 London Child Obesity Taskforce (2018) *Unhealthy Weight in London's Children: What We Know*, www.london.gov.uk/sites/default/files/unhealthy_weight_in_londons_children.pdf

12 Morrison, K.M., Shin, S., Tarnopolsky, M. and Taylor, V.H. (2015) 'Association of depression and health related quality of life with body composition in children and youth with obesity', *Journal of Affective Disorders*, 172: 18–23.

13 Reilly, J. and Kelly, J. (2011) 'Long-term impact of overweight and obesity in childhood and adolescence on morbidity and premature mortality in adulthood: Systematic review', *International Journal of Obesity*, 35: 891–8.

14 Public Health England (2020) *The Relationship Between Dental Caries and Body Mass Index: Child Level Analysis*, https://assets.publishing.service.gov.uk/government/uploads/system/uploads/attachment_data/file/844121/BMI_dental_caries.pdf

15 NHS Digital (2021) *National Child Measurement Programme, England, 2020/21 School Year*, https://digital.nhs.uk/data-and-information/publications/statistical/national-child-measurement-programme/2020-21-school-year

16 Public Health England (2013) 'Obesity more likely in children from deprived areas', 16 May, www.gov.uk/government/news/obesity-more-likely-in-children-from-deprived-areas

17 Public Health England (2017) 'Health matters: Obesity and the food environment', 31 March, www.gov.uk/government/publications/health-matters-obesity-and-the-food-environment

18 Chapman, J. (2011) 'Girls of 2011 EIGHT times more likely to reach 100 than their grandmothers', *The Daily Mail*, 4 August, www.dailymail.co.uk/health/article-2022195/Girls-2011-EIGHT-times-likely-reach-100-grandmothers.html?ito=feeds-newsxml

19 Smith, R. (2007) 'Half of adults "will be obese by 2050"', *The Telegraph*, 17 October, www.telegraph.co.uk/news/uknews/1566436/Half-of-adults-will-be-obese-by-2050.html

[20] Morton, K. (2013) 'Health experts call on political parties to address diet-related disease in children', *Nursery World*, 7 February, www.nurseryworld.co.uk/news/article/health-experts-call-on-political-parties-to-address-diet-related-disease-in-children

[21] London's Child Obesity Taskforce (2019) *What Makes it Harder for London's Children to be Healthier?*, www.london.gov.uk/sites/default/files/what_makes_it_harder_for_londons_children_be_healthier.pdf

[22] Greater London Authority (2019) *Every Child a Healthy Weight*, www.london.gov.uk/city-hall-blog/every-child-healthy-weight-how-do-you-set-ten-ambitions-london

[23] BDA (British Dietetic Association) (no date) 'Healthy eating for children', Food Fact Sheet, www.bda.uk.com/resource/healthy-eating-for-children.html

[24] D'Souza, E., Vandevijvere, S. and Swinburn, B. (2022) 'The healthiness of New Zealand school food environments: A national survey', *Australian and New Zealand Journal of Public Health*, 46(3): 325–31.

[25] Pinheiro, A.C., Quintiliano-Scarpelli, D., Flores, J.A., et al (2022) 'Food availability in different food environments surrounding schools in a vulnerable urban area of Santiago, Chile: Exploring socioeconomic determinants', *Foods*, 11(7): 901.

[26] Kelly, C., Callaghan, M. and Gabhainn, S.N. (2021) '"It's hard to make good choices and it costs more": Adolescents' perception of the external school food environment', *Nutrients*, 13(4): 1043.

[27] Penne, T. and Goedemé, T. (2021) 'Can low-income households afford a healthy diet? Insufficient income as a driver of food insecurity in Europe', *Food Policy*, 99: 101978.

[28] van Kesteren, R. and Evans, A. (2020) 'Cooking without thinking: How understanding cooking as a practice can shed new light on inequalities in healthy eating', *Appetite*, 147: 104503.

[29] Bauer, K.W., Hearst, M.O., Escoto, K., Berge, J.M. and Neumark-Sztainer, D. (2012) 'Parental employment and work–family stress: Associations with family food environments', *Social Science & Medicine*, 75(3): 496–504.

[30] Fiese, B.H. (2018) 'Time allocation and dietary habits in the United States: Time for re-evaluation?', *Physiology & Behavior*, 193: 205–8.

[31] Ares, G., Velázquez, A.L., Vidal, L., Curutchet, M.R. and Varela, P. (2022) 'The role of food packaging on children's diet: Insights for the design of comprehensive regulations to encourage healthier eating habits in childhood and beyond', *Food Quality and Preference*, 95: 104366.

[32] Kelly, B., Vandevijvere, S., Ng, S.H., et al (2019) 'Global benchmarking of children's exposure to television advertising of unhealthy foods and beverages across 22 countries', *Obesity Reviews*, 20: 116–28.

[33] Cullen, T., Hatch, J., Martin, W., Wharf Higgins, J. and Sheppard, R. (2015) 'Food literacy: Definition and framework for action', *Canadian Journal of Dietetic Practice and Research*, 76(3): 140–5, p 143.

[34] Smith, K., Wells, R. and Hawkes, C. (2022) 'How primary school curriculums in 11 countries around the world deliver food education and

address food literacy: A policy analysis', *International Journal of Environmental Research and Public Health*, 19(4): 2019.

35 Briggs, L. and Lake, A.A. (2011) 'Exploring school and home food environments: Perceptions of 8–10-year-olds and their parents in Newcastle upon Tyne, UK', *Public Health Nutrition*, 14(12): 2227–35.

36 Ragelienė, T. and Grønhøj, A. (2020) 'The influence of peers and siblings on children's and adolescents' healthy eating behavior. A systematic literature review', *Appetite*, 148: 104592.

37 Hawkes, C., Fox, E., Downs, S.M., Fanzo, J. and Neve, K. (2020) 'Child-centered food systems: Reorienting food systems towards healthy diets for children', *Global Food Security*, 27: 100414.

38 DWP (Department for Work and Pensions) (2021) 'Households below average income: For financial years ending 1995 to 2020', www.gov.uk/government/statistics/households-below-average-income-for-financial-years-ending-1995-to-2020

39 The Trussell Trust (2022) 'Food banks provide more than 2.1 million food parcels to people across the UK in past year, according to new figures released by the Trussell Trust', 27 April, www.trusselltrust.org/2022/04/27/food-banks-provide-more-than-2-1-million-food-parcels-to-people-across-the-uk-in-past-year-according-to-new-figures-released-by-the-trussell-trust

40 O'Connell, R., Knight, A. and Brannen, J. (2019) *Living Hand to Mouth: Children and Food in Low Income Families*, London: Child Poverty Action Group.

41 O'Connell, R. and Brannen, J. (2021) *Families and Food in Hard Times: European Comparative Research*, London: UCL Press.

42 Quoted in O'Connell, R., Knight, A. and Brannen, J. (2019) *Living Hand to Mouth: Children and Food in Low Income Families*, London: Child Poverty Action Group, p 24.

43 O'Connell, R., Knight, A. and Brannen, J. (2019) *Living Hand to Mouth: Children and Food in Low Income Families*, London: Child Poverty Action Group.

44 Jutras, M. (2017) 'Historical perspectives on the theories, diagnosis, and treatment of mental illness', *British Columbia Medical Journal*, 59(2): 86–8.

45 Scull, A. (2017) 'The Asylum, Hospital, and Clinic', in G. Eghigian (ed) *The Routledge History of Madness and Mental Health*, Abingdon: Routledge, pp 101–14.

46 Metzl, J.M. (2003) '"Mother's little helper": The crisis of psychoanalysis and the Miltown Resolution', *Gender & History*, 15(2): 228–55.

47 Jobbins, J. (2017) 'Man up – The Victorian origins of toxic masculinity', *The Historian*, 12 May, https://projects.history.qmul.ac.uk/thehistorian/2017/05/12/man-up-the-victorian-origins-of-toxic-masculinity

48 World Economic Forum (2020) '7 ways young people are making a difference in mental health', 9 October, www.weforum.org/agenda/2020/10/7-ways-young-people-making-a-difference-mental-health

49 A 'mental illness' or 'mental health disorder' is an illness that affects that way people think, feel, behave or interact with others. There are many types of mental illnesses or health disorders with different signs and symptoms. See NHS Hampshire CAMHS (no date) 'Mental health/illness and resilience', https://hampshirecamhs.nhs.uk/issue/mental-health-and-mental-illness-yp

50 NHS Digital (2020) *Mental Health of Children and Young People in England, 2020: Wave 1 Follow Up to the 2017 Survey*, https://digital.nhs.uk/data-and-information/publications/statistical/mental-health-of-children-and-young-people-in-england/2020-wave-1-follow-up

51 Kessler, R.C., Berglund, P., Demler, O., et al (2005) 'Lifetime prevalence and age-of-onset distributions of DSM-IV disorders in the National Comorbidity Survey Replication', *Archives of General Psychiatry*, 62(6): 593–602.

52 The Children's Society (no date) 'Children's mental health statistics', www.childrenssociety.org.uk/what-we-do/our-work/well-being/mental-health-statistics

53 DCSF (Department for Children, Schools and Families) (no date) 'CAMHS: Four-tier strategic framework', https://webarchive.nationalarchives.gov.uk/ukgwa/20100202120904/http://www.dcsf.gov.uk/everychildmatters/healthandwellbeing/mentalhealthissues/camhs/fourtierstrategicframework/fourtierstrategicframework

54 LGA (Local Government Association) (2022) 'Children and young people's emotional wellbeing and mental health – Facts and figures', www.local.gov.uk/about/campaigns/bright-futures/bright-futures-camhs/child-and-adolescent-mental-health-and

55 LGA (Local Government Association) (2022) 'Children and young people's emotional wellbeing and mental health – Facts and figures', www.local.gov.uk/about/campaigns/bright-futures/bright-futures-camhs/child-and-adolescent-mental-health-and

56 LGA (Local Government Association) (2022) 'Children and young people's emotional wellbeing and mental health – Facts and figures', www.local.gov.uk/about/campaigns/bright-futures/bright-futures-camhs/child-and-adolescent-mental-health-and

57 WHO (World Health Organization) (2018) 'Mental health: Strengthening our response', https://cdn.ymaws.com/www.safestates.org/resource/resmgr/connections_lab/glossary_citation/mental_health_strengthening_.pdf

58 Curtis, S. (2020) 'The "wider" influences on mental health in childhood and adolescence', Medium, The British Academy, 3 March, https://medium.com/reframing-childhood-past-and-present/the-wider-influences-on-mental-health-in-childhood-and-adolescence-3bf32f166df6

59 Kendall-Taylor, N. (2009) *Conflicting Models of Mind in Mind: Mapping the Gaps Between the Expert and the Public Understandings of Child Mental Health as Part of Strategic Frame Analysis™*, A FrameWorks Research Report, Washington, DC: FrameWorks Institute, www.frameworksinstitute.org/wp-content/uploads/2020/03/childmentalhealthculturalmodels.pdf

60 OHID (Office for Health Improvement & Disparities) (2022) 'Social prescribing: Applying All Our Health', 27 January, www.gov.uk/government/publications/social-prescribing-applying-all-our-health/social-prescribing-applying-all-our-health

61 Hogg, S. (2019) *Rare Jewels: Specialised Parent–Infant Relationship Teams in the UK*, London: Parent–Infant Foundation.

62 West London Zone (no date) 'About us', www.westlondonzone.org

63 Feinstein, L. (2015) *Social and Emotional Learning: Skills for Life and Work*, London: Early Intervention Foundation.

64 Taylor, M., Marsh, G., Nicol, D. and Broadbent, P. (2017) *Good Work: The Taylor Review of Modern Working Practices*, London: Department for Business, Energy & Industrial Strategy.

65 Butler, D. and Margo, J. (2007) *Freedom's Orphans: Raising Youth in a Changing World*, Politics for a New Generation, Basingstoke: Palgrave Macmillan.

66 Feinstein, L. (2015) *Social and Emotional Learning: Skills for Life and Work*, London: Early Intervention Foundation.

67 CQC (Care Quality Commission) (2017) *Review of Children and Young People's Mental Health Services: Phase One Report*, www.cqc.org.uk/sites/default/files/20171103_cypmhphase1_report.pdf

68 Public Health England (2016) *The Mental Health of Children and Young People in England*, www.gov.uk/government/publications/improving-the-mental-health-of-children-and-young-people

69 Young Minds (no date) *You Matter: Our Strategy for 2020–2023*, www.youngminds.org.uk/media/ublkdysd/youngminds-strategy-2020-2023.pdf

70 CQC (Care Quality Commission) (2017) *Review of Children and Young People's Mental Health Services: Phase One Report*, www.cqc.org.uk/sites/default/files/20171103_cypmhphase1_report.pdf, p 7.

71 DHSC (Department of Health and Social Care) and DfE (Department for Education) (2017) *Transforming Children and Young People's Mental Health Provision: A Green Paper*, www.gov.uk/government/consultations/transforming-children-and-young-peoples-mental-health-provision-a-green-paper

72 Williams, E. (2022) 'What are health inequalities?', The King's Fund, 17 June, www.kingsfund.org.uk/publications/what-are-health-inequalities

73 Cutler, D.M. and Lleras-Muney, A. (2006) *Education and Health: Evaluating Theories and Evidence*, National Poverty Center Working Paper Series#06-19, Michigan, MI: National Poverty Center, University of Michigan.

74 DfE (Department for Education) (2021) *Statutory Framework for the Early Years Foundation Stage: Setting the Standards for Learning, Development and Care for Children from Birth to Five*, 31 March, https://assets.publishing.service.gov.uk/government/uploads/system/uploads/attachment_data/file/974907/EYFS_framework_-_March_2021.pdf

75 Public Health England (2017) *Health Profile for England: 2017*, Chapter 6: Social Determinants of Health, www.gov.uk/government/publications/health-profile-for-england/chapter-6-social-determinants-of-health#fn:5

76 Marmot, M. (2010) *Fair Society, Healthy Lives (The Marmot Review)*, London: UCL.

77 Marmot, M. (2010) *Fair Society, Healthy Lives (The Marmot Review)*, London: UCL.

78 Williams, E. (2022) 'What are health inequalities?', The King's Fund, 17 June, www.kingsfund.org.uk/publications/what-are-health-inequalities

79 Marmot, M. (2020) *Health Equity in England: The Marmot Review 10 Years On*, London: The Health Foundation, www.health.org.uk/sites/default/files/upload/publications/2020/Health%20Equity%20in%20England_The%20Marmot%20Review%2010%20Years%20On_full%20report.pdf, p 3.

80 Thomas, C., Breeze, P., Cummins, S., et al (2022) 'The health, cost and equity impacts of restrictions on the advertisement of high fat, salt and sugar products across the transport for London network: A health economic modelling study', *The International Journal of Behavioral Nutrition and Physical Activity*, 19(1): 93, https://doi.org/10.1186/s12966-022-01331-y

81 Yau, A., Berger, N., Law, C., et al (2022) 'Changes in household food and drink purchases following restrictions on the advertisement of high fat, salt, and sugar products across the Transport for London network: A controlled interrupted time series analysis', *PLOS Medicine*, 19(2): e1003915, https://journals.plos.org/plosmedicine/article?id=10.1371/journal.pmed.1003915

82 Marmot, M. (2020) *Health Equity in England: The Marmot Review 10 Years On*, London: The Health Foundation, www.health.org.uk/sites/default/files/upload/publications/2020/Health%20Equity%20in%20England_The%20Marmot%20Review%2010%20Years%20On_full%20report.pdf, p 3.

Chapter 8

1 Quoted in Porter, H. (2014) 'The internet revolution versus the House of Lords', *The Guardian*, 18 January, www.theguardian.com/commentisfree/2014/jan/18/house-of-lords-debate-world-wide-web

2 BBC News (2022) 'Molly Russell inquest: Online life was "the bleakest of worlds"', 21 September, www.bbc.co.uk/news/uk-england-london-62981964

3 BBC News (2022) 'Molly Russell inquest: Father makes social media plea', 30 September, www.bbc.co.uk/news/uk-england-london-63073489

4 Internet Matters (no date) 'What age can my child start social networking?', www.internetmatters.org/resources/what-age-can-my-child-start-social-networking

5 Pinterest (no date) 'Terms of service', https://policy.pinterest.com/en/terms-of-service, Section 9.

6 BBC News (2022) 'Molly Russell inquest: Pinterest executive admits site was not safe', 22 September, www.bbc.co.uk/news/uk-england-london-62991510

7 Griffiths, S. and Shipman, T. (2019) '"Suicidal generation": Tragic toll of teens doubles in 8 years', *The Sunday Times*, 3 February, www.thetimes.

co.uk/article/suicidal-generation-tragic-toll-of-teens-doubles-in-8-years-zlkqzsd2b

8   UNICEF (United Nations Children's Fund) (no date) *Child Rights in the Digital Age*, www.unicef-irc.org/research/child-rights-in-the-digital-age

9   ONS (Office for National Statistics) (2021) 'Children's online behaviour in England and Wales: Year ending March 2020', 9 February, www.ons.gov.uk/peoplepopulationandcommunity/crimeandjustice/bulletins/childrensonlinebehaviourinenglandandwales/yearendingmarch2020

10 Ben-Hassine, W. (no date) 'Government policy for the internet must be rights-based and user-centred', UN Chronicle, www.un.org/en/chronicle/article/government-policy-internet-must-be-rights-based-and-user-centred

11 Negreiro, M. (2021) 'Curbing the surge in online child abuse: The dual role of digital technology in fighting and facilitating its proliferation', European Parliamentary Research Service, Briefing, www.europarl.europa.eu/RegData/etudes/BRIE/2020/659360/EPRS_BRI(2020)659360_EN.pdf

12 Lasota, M. (2018) 'Growing up in a digital world: Benefits and risks', *The Lancet Child & Adolescent Health*, 2(2): 79, https://gdc.unicef.org/resource/growing-digital-world-benefits-and-risks

13 ONS (Office for National Statistics) (2021) 'Children's online behaviour in England and Wales: Year ending March 2020', 9 February, www.ons.gov.uk/peoplepopulationandcommunity/crimeandjustice/bulletins/childrensonlinebehaviourinenglandandwales/yearendingmarch2020

14 Stoilova, M., Livingstone, S. and Khazbak, R. (2021) *Investigating Risks and Opportunities for Children in a Digital World: A Rapid Review of the Evidence on Children's Internet Use and Outcomes*, Innocenti Discussion Paper, Florence: UNICEF Office of Research – Innocenti.

15 Kardefelt-Winther, D. (2017) *How Does the Time Children Spend Using Digital Technology Impact Their Mental Well-being, Social Relationships and Physical Activity? An Evidence-Focused Literature Review*, Innocenti Discussion Paper, Florence: UNICEF Office of Research – Innocenti.

16 UK Government (2017) 'Making Britain the safest place in the world to be online', 11 October, www.gov.uk/government/news/making-britain-the-safest-place-in-the-world-to-be-online

17 ONS (Office for National Statistics) (2020) 'Dataset internet access – Households and individuals. 2020', 7 August, www.ons.gov.uk/peoplepopulationandcommunity/householdcharacteristics/homeinternetandsocialmediausage/datasets/internetaccesshouseholdsandindividualsreferencetables

18 Children's Commissioner (2020) 'Children without internet access during lockdown', 18 August, www.childrenscommissioner.gov.uk/2020/08/18/children-without-internet-access-during-lockdown

19 BBC News (2019) 'General election 2019: Labour pledges free broadband for all', 15 November, www.bbc.co.uk/news/election-2019-50427369

20 Patrick, C. (no date) 'Top 20 countries with free Wifi: Stay connected to your online world on the go!', Travel Triangle blog, https://traveltriangle.com/blog/countries-with-free-wifi

21 Wheeler, T. (2020) '5 steps to get the internet to all Americans: COVID-19 and the importance of universal broadband', Brookings, 27 May, www.brookings.edu/research/5-steps-to-get-the-internet-to-all-americans

22 Ames, M. (2019) *The Charisma Machine: The Life, Death, and Legacy of One Laptop Per Child*, Cambridge, MA: MIT Press.

23 Kraemer, K.L., Sharma, P. and Dedrick, J. (2009) 'One Laptop Per Child: Vision vs reality', *Communications of the ACM*, 52(6): 66–73.

24 Robertson, A. (2018) 'OLPC's $100 laptop was going to change the world – then it all went wrong', The Verge, 16 April, www.theverge.com/2018/4/16/17233946/olpcs-100-laptop-education-where-is-it-now

25 UK Parliament POST (2020) 'Autism', POSTNOTE Number 612, January, https://researchbriefings.files.parliament.uk/documents/POST-PN-0612/POST-PN-0612.pdf

26 Creer, S., Enderby, P., Judge, S., et al (2016) 'Prevalence of people who could benefit from augmentative and alternative communication (AAC) in the UK: Determining the need', *International Journal of Language and Communication Disorders*, 51(6): 639–53.

27 NHS England (2016) *Guidance for Commissioning AAC Services and Equipment*, www.england.nhs.uk/commissioning/wp-content/uploads/sites/12/2016/03/guid-comms-aac.pdf

28 DWP (Department for Work and Pensions) (2022) 'Family Resources Survey: Financial year 2020 to 2021', 31 March, www.gov.uk/government/statistics/family-resources-survey-financial-year-2020-to-2021

29 KPMG (2018) *Leading from the Front: Disability and the Role of the Board*, May, https://assets.kpmg/content/dam/kpmg/uk/pdf/2018/05/leading-from-the-front-disability-and-the-role-of-the-board.pdf

30 DWP (Department for Work and Pensions) (2020) 'Family Resources Survey 2018/19', https://assets.publishing.service.gov.uk/government/uploads/system/uploads/attachment_data/file/874507/family-resources-survey-2018-19.pdf

31 ONS (Office for National Statistics) (2021) 'Coronavirus related deaths by disability status, England and Wales: 2 March to 14 July 2020', www.ons.gov.uk/peoplepopulationandcommunity/birthsdeathsandmarriages/deaths/articles/coronaviruscovid19relateddeathsbydisabilitystatusenglandandwales/2marchto14july2020

32 Williams, R. and Brownlow, S. (2020) *The Click-Away Pound Report 2019*, Brighton: Freeney Williams Limited, www.clickawaypound.com/downloads/cap19final0502.pdf

33 Paraskevopoulos, D. (2021) 'Estonia – A European and global leader in the digitalisation of public services', e-Estonia, 15 November, https://e-estonia.com/estonia-a-european-and-global-leader-in-the-digitalisation-of-public-services

34 e-Estonia (2022) 'This is the story of the world's most advanced digital society', https://e-estonia.com/story

35 Education Estonia (2021) 'Services & products', www.educationestonia.org/services-and-products

36 Toome, E. (2023) *Smart Solutions for Education Innovation*, Education Estonia, www.educationestonia.org

37 Edmond, C. (2020) 'These are the countries where children are most satisfied with their lives', World Economic Forum, 4 September, www.weforum.org/agenda/2020/09/child-well-being-health-happiness-unicef-report

38 In 2018, 75% of Year 6 students (10- and 11-year-olds) in England reached the expected standard in their SATs reading test. See DfE (Department for Education) (2018) 'National Curriculum assessments at Key Stage 2 in England, 2018 (revised)', https://assets.publishing.service.gov.uk/government/uploads/system/uploads/attachment_data/file/774446/KS2_Revised_2018_text_MATS_20190130.pdf#page=5

39 Morrisroe, J. (2014) *Literacy Changes Lives 2014: A New Perspective on Health, Employment and Crime*, London: National Literacy Trust.

40 Kothari, B. and Bandyopadhyay, T. (2014) 'Same language subtitling of Bollywood film songs on TV: Effects on literacy', *Information Technologies & International Development*, 10(4): 31.

41 Turn On The Subtitles (2022) 'Research into same-language subtitling', www.turnonthesubtitles.org/research

42 Frey, N. and Fisher, D. (2010) 'Reading and the brain: What early childhood educators need to know', *Early Childhood Education Journal*, 38(2): 103–10.

43 MITx Videos (2019) 'Science of learning: Interview with John Gabrieli', www.youtube.com/watch?v=cdHlYWdnU04&t=380s

44 Koskinen, P.S., Wilson, R.M., Gambrell, L.B., Jensema, C.J. (1986) 'Using closed captioned television to enhance reading skills of learning disabled students', *National Reading Conference Yearbook*, 35: 61–5.

45 Koskinen, P.S., Wilson, R.M. and Jensema, C.J. (1985) 'Closed-captioned television: A new tool for reading instruction', *Reading World*, 24(4): 1–7.

46 OECD (Organisation for Economic Co-operation and Development) (2021) *Children in the Digital Environment: Revised Typology of Risks*, OECD Digital Economy Papers, No 302, Paris: OECD.

47 Hern, A. (2021) 'UK children's digital privacy code comes into effect', *The Guardian*, 2 September, www.theguardian.com/technology/2021/sep/02/uk-childrens-digital-privacy-code-comes-into-effect

48 Hern, A. (2021) 'Social media giants increase global child safety after UK regulations introduced', *The Guardian*, 5 September, www.theguardian.com/media/2021/sep/05/social-media-giants-increase-global-child-safety-after-uk-regulations-introduced

49 Hern, A. (2021) 'UK children's digital privacy code comes into effect', *The Guardian*, 2 September, www.theguardian.com/technology/2021/sep/02/uk-childrens-digital-privacy-code-comes-into-effect

50 Hern, A. (2021) 'TikTok acts on teen safety with "bedtime" block on app alerts', *The Guardian*, 12 August, www.theguardian.com/technology/2021/aug/12/tiktok-acts-on-teen-safety-with-bedtime-block-on-app-alerts

51 Hatmaker, T. (2023) 'Instagram and Facebook introduce more limits on targeting teens with ads', TechCrunch, 10 January, https://techcrunch.

com/2023/01/10/instagram-and-facebook-introduce-more-limits-on-targeting-teens-with-ads

[52] Cohen, D. (2021) 'YouTube, YouTube Kids add safety measures for users under 18', *Adweek*, 10 August, www.adweek.com/media/youtube-youtube-kids-add-safety-measures-for-users-under-18

[53] Brooks, M. (2021) 'Giving kids and teens a safer experience online', The Keyword, 10 August, https://blog.google/technology/families/giving-kids-and-teens-safer-experience-online

[54] Hern, A. (2021) 'UK children's digital privacy code comes into effect', *The Guardian*, 2 September, www.theguardian.com/technology/2021/sep/02/uk-childrens-digital-privacy-code-comes-into-effect

[55] 5Rights Foundation (2021) *But How Do They Know It Is a Child? Age Assurance in the Digital World*, London: 5Rights Foundation, October, https://5rightsfoundation.com/uploads/But_How_Do_They_Know_It_is_a_Child.pdf

[56] Internet Matters (no date) 'What age can my child start social networking?', www.internetmatters.org/resources/what-age-can-my-child-start-social-networking

[57] 5Rights Foundation (2021) *But How Do They Know It Is a Child? Age Assurance in the Digital World*, London: 5Rights Foundation, October, https://5rightsfoundation.com/uploads/But_How_Do_They_Know_It_is_a_Child.pdf

[58] Lievens, E. (no date) 'The United Nations Convention on the Rights of the Child and what it means for online services', Information Commissioner's Office, https://ico.org.uk/for-organisations/childrens-code-hub/how-to-use-our-guidance-for-standard-one-best-interests-of-the-child/the-united-nations-convention-on-the-rights-of-the-child

[59] Information Commissioner's Office (2020) 'Age appropriate design: A code of practice for online services', https://ico.org.uk/for-organisations/guide-to-data-protection/ico-codes-of-practice/age-appropriate-design-a-code-of-practice-for-online-services

[60] Information Commissioner's Office (2020) 'Age appropriate design: A code of practice for online services', https://ico.org.uk/for-organisations/guide-to-data-protection/ico-codes-of-practice/age-appropriate-design-a-code-of-practice-for-online-services

[61] IEEE Standards Association (2021) 'IEEE standard for an age appropriate digital services framework based on the 5Rights Principles for Children', https://standards.ieee.org/ieee/2089/7633

[62] OHCHR (Office of the United Nations High Commissioner for Human Rights) (2021) 'General Comment No 25 (2021) on children's rights in relation to the digital environment', 2 March, www.ohchr.org/en/documents/general-comments-and-recommendations/general-comment-no-25-2021-childrens-rights-relation

[63] Department for Digital, Culture, Media & Sport (2021) *Draft Online Safety Bill*, www.gov.uk/government/publications/draft-online-safety-bill

64 This is defined in the Draft Online Safety Bill as 'an internet service by means of which content that is generated by a user of the service or uploaded to or shared on the service by a user of the service, may be read, viewed, heard or otherwise experienced ("encountered") by another user, or other users. Content includes written material or messages, oral communications, photographs, videos, visual images, music and data of any description.' See Department for Digital, Culture, Media & Sport (2021) *Draft Online Safety Bill*, www.gov.uk/government/publications/draft-online-safety-bill

65 Lewis, R. (2022) 'Prince William makes online plea after the suicide of Molly Russell', *Cambridge News*, 1 October, www.cambridge-news.co.uk/news/uk-world-news/prince-william-makes-online-plea-25153127

Chapter 9

1 Brown, G. (2018) 'Government must abandon roll-out of Universal Credit says Gordon Brown', The Office of Gordon and Sarah Brown, 10 October, https://gordonandsarahbrown.com/2018/10/child-poverty-crisis-government-must-abandon-roll-out-of-universal-credit-says-gordon-brown

2 All-Party Parliamentary Group for Ending Homelessness (2017) *Homelessness Prevention for Care Leavers, Prison Leavers and Survivors of Domestic Violence*, July, www.crisis.org.uk/media/237534/appg_for_ending_homelessness_report_2017_pdf.pdf

3 Ribeiro-Addy, B. (2021) 'The care-to-prison pipeline shows our failure of looked-after children', *The Independent*, 25 November, www.independent.co.uk/voices/children-in-care-prison-social-care-b1964142.html

4 Smith, N. (2017) *Neglected Minds: A Report on Mental Health Support for Young People Leaving Care*, Ilford: Barnardo's www.barnardos.org.uk/sites/default/files/uploads/neglected-minds.pdf

5 The Children's Society (no date) 'Children missing from home', www.childrenssociety.org.uk/what-we-do/our-work/children-missing-home

6 ACEs are potentially traumatic events that occur in childhood. For more information, see: CDC (Centers for Disease Control and Prevention) (2019) *Preventing Adverse Childhood Experiences (ACEs): Leveraging the Best Available Evidence*, National Center for Injury Prevention and Control.

7 CDC (Centers for Disease Control and Prevention) (2022) 'Risk and protective factors', www.cdc.gov/violenceprevention/childabuseandneglect/riskprotectivefactors.html

8 Centre for Social Justice (2020) *Facing the Facts: Ethnicity and Disadvantage in Britain*, London: Centre for Social Justice, www.centreforsocialjustice.org.uk/library/facing-the-facts-ethnicity-and-disadvantage-in-britain

9 MacAlister, J. (2022) 'Executive Summary', in *The Independent Review of Children's Social Care*, https://childrenssocialcare.independent-review.uk/wp-content/uploads/2022/05/Executive-summary.pdf, p 8.

10 *Community Care* (2022) 'Two-thirds of social workers experiencing deteriorating mental health because of work, finds survey', 26 January, www.communitycare.co.uk/2022/01/26/two-thirds-of-social-workers-experiencing-deteriorating-mental-health-because-of-work-finds-survey

11 BASW (British Association of Social Workers) (no date) 'Support the BASW England 80-20 pledge', www.basw.co.uk/support-basw-england-80-20-pledge

12 Quoted in Unison (2019) 'Social work at breaking point', www.unison.org.uk/content/uploads/2019/06/Social-work-at-breaking-point.pdf

13 Quoted in BASW (British Association of Social Workers) (2022) *The BASW Annual Survey of Social Workers and Social Work: 2021 – A Summary Report*, Birmingham.

14 Johnson, C., Coburn, S., Sanders, A., et al (2019) *Longitudinal Study of Local Authority Child and Family Social Workers (Wave 1)*, Research report, August, GSR (Government Social Research), https://assets.publishing.service.gov.uk/government/uploads/system/uploads/attachment_data/file/906780/Longitudinal_study_of_local_authority_child_and_family_social_workers_Wave_1.pdf

15 Preston, R. (2021) 'Growing majority of children's social workers feeling stressed and overworked, finds DfE study', *Community Care*, 26 July, www.communitycare.co.uk/2021/07/26/growing-majority-childrens-social-workers-feeling-stressed-overworked-finds-dfe-study

16 Preston, R. (2022) 'Social workers felt uninvolved in "inadequate" council's attempts to improve, says commissioner', *Community Care*, 11 February, www.communitycare.co.uk/2022/02/11/social-workers-felt-uninvolved-in-inadequate-councils-attempts-to-improve-says-commissioner

17 Walker, S. (2022) *Report on the Options for Children's Services in the City of Bradford Metropolitan District Council*, January, https://assets.publishing.service.gov.uk/government/uploads/system/uploads/attachment_data/file/1053781/Bradford_Commissioners_Report.pdf

18 Walker, S. (2022) *Report on the Options for Children's Services in the City of Bradford Metropolitan District Council*, January, https://assets.publishing.service.gov.uk/government/uploads/system/uploads/attachment_data/file/1053781/Bradford_Commissioners_Report.pdf

19 Pierro, L. and Preston, R. (2022) 'Two thirds of social workers experiencing deteriorating mental health because of work, finds survey', *Community Care*, 26 January, www.communitycare.co.uk/2022/01/26/two-thirds-of-social-workers-experiencing-deteriorating-mental-health-because-of-work-finds-survey

20 Quoted in Pierro, L. and Preston, R. (2022) 'Two thirds of social workers experiencing deteriorating mental health because of work, finds survey', *Community Care*, 26 January, www.communitycare.co.uk/2022/01/26/two-thirds-of-social-workers-experiencing-deteriorating-mental-health-because-of-work-finds-survey

21 *File on 4* (2022) 'Children's homes – Profit before care', BBC Radio 4, https://downloads.bbc.co.uk/rmhttp/fileon4/PAJ_4562_PG08_Childrens_Homes.pdf

22 *File on 4* (2022) 'Children's homes – Profit before care', BBC Radio 4, https://downloads.bbc.co.uk/rmhttp/fileon4/PAJ_4562_PG08_Childrens_Homes.pdf

23 *File on 4* (2022) 'Children's homes – Profit before care', BBC Radio 4, https://downloads.bbc.co.uk/rmhttp/fileon4/PAJ_4562_PG08_Childrens_Homes.pdf

24 Titerhadge, N. (2022) 'Children's homes close after BBC reveals failures', BBC News, 18 August, www.bbc.co.uk/news/uk-62144399

25 MacAlister, J. (2022) *The Independent Review of Children's Social Care: Executive Summary*, https://assets.publishing.service.gov.uk/government/uploads/system/uploads/attachment_data/file/1141532/Independent_review_of_children_s_social_care_-_Final_report.pdf

26 MacAlister, J. (2022) *The Independent Review of Children's Social Care: Executive Summary*, https://assets.publishing.service.gov.uk/government/uploads/system/uploads/attachment_data/file/1141532/Independent_review_of_children_s_social_care_-_Final_report.pdf

27 Rapaport, J. (2011) 'Forty years since Seebohm', Professional Social Work, February, BASW, www.basw.co.uk/system/files/resources/basw_104828-4_0.pdf

28 MacAlister, J. (2022) *The Independent Review of Children's Social Care*, www.gov.uk/government/publications/independent-review-of-childrens-social-care-final-report

29 UNESCO (United Nations Educational, Scientific and Cultural Organization) (1994) *The Salamanca Statement and Framework for Action on Special Educational Needs*, https://unesdoc.unesco.org/ark:/48223/pf0000098427

30 UNESCO (United Nations Educational, Scientific and Cultural Organization) (1994) *The Salamanca Statement and Framework for Action on Special Educational Needs*, https://unesdoc.unesco.org/ark:/48223/pf0000098427, p ix.

31 Ainscow, M., Slee, R. and Best, M. (2019) 'The *Salamanca Statement*: 25 years on', *International Journal of Inclusive Education*, 23(7–8): 671–6.

32 DfE (Department for Education) (2021) 'Special educational needs in England: January 2021', National statistics, www.gov.uk/government/statistics/special-educational-needs-in-england-january-2021

33 House of Commons Education Select Committee (2019) *Special Educational Needs and Disabilities: First Report of Session 2019*, https://publications.parliament.uk/pa/cm201919/cmselect/cmeduc/20/20.pdf

34 National Statistics (2022) 'Reporting year 2022: Education, health and care plans', https://explore-education-statistics.service.gov.uk/find-statistics/education-health-and-care-plans

35 National Statistics (2022) 'Reporting year 2022: Education, health and care plans', https://explore-education-statistics.service.gov.uk/find-statistics/education-health-and-care-plans

36 Ambitious about Autism (2019) '95% of parents prevailing over local authorities at special educational needs tribunals', News, 26 October, www.ambitiousaboutautism.org.uk/about-us/media-centre/news/95-parents-prevailing-over-local-authorities-special-educational-needs

37 Hutchinson, J. (2021) *Identifying Pupils with Special Educational Needs and Disabilities*, London: Education Policy Institute.

38 National Education Union (no date) 'SEND crisis', https://neu.org.uk/funding/send-crisis

39 House of Commons Education Select Committee (2019) *Special Educational Needs and Disabilities: First Report of Session 2019*, https://publications.parliament.uk/pa/cm201919/cmselect/cmeduc/20/20.pdf

40 D'Alessio, S. (2012) *Inclusive Education in Italy*, Vol 10, Springer Science & Business Media.

41 Contardi, A. and Gherardini, P. (2003) 'Together at school: Mainstream school in Italy, from kindergarten to high school', *Down Syndrome News and Update*, 3(1): 11–15.

42 DfE (Department for Education) (2022) *Summary of the SEND Review: Right Support, Right Place, Right Time*, www.gov.uk/government/publications/send-and-ap-green-paper-responding-to-the-consultation/summary-of-the-send-review-right-support-right-place-right-time#a-single-national-send-and-alternative-provision-system

43 DfE (Department for Education) (2022) *Summary of the SEND Review: Right Support, Right Place, Right Time*, www.gov.uk/government/publications/send-and-ap-green-paper-responding-to-the-consultation/summary-of-the-send-review-right-support-right-place-right-time#a-single-national-send-and-alternative-provision-system

44 UNHCR (United Nations High Commissioner for Refugees) (no date) 'Refugee statistics', www.unrefugees.org/refugee-facts/statistics

45 OHCHR (Office of the United Nations High Commissioner for Human Rights) (2020) 'OHCHR and the right to a nationality', 12 June, www.ohchr.org/en/nationality-and-statelessness

46 UNHCR UK (United Nations High Commissioner for Refugees) (no date) 'Children', www.unhcr.org/uk/children.html

47 GOV.UK (no date) 'How many people do we grant protection to?', www.gov.uk/government/statistics/immigration-system-statistics-year-ending-december-2022/how-many-people-do-we-grant-protection-to#about-the-statistics

48 GOV.UK (no date) 'How many people do we grant protection to?', www.gov.uk/government/statistics/immigration-system-statistics-year-ending-december-2022/how-many-people-do-we-grant-protection-to#about-the-statistics

49 Home Office (2022) 'Statistics on Ukrainians in the UK, Table 3: Demographic (age/sex) breakdown for those arriving on Ukraine Schemes as of 30 June 2022', National statistics, www.gov.uk/government/statistics/immigration-statistics-year-ending-june-2022/statistics-on-ukrainians-in-the-uk

50 Legrain, P. (2016) 'Refugees are not a burden but an opportunity', OECD, www.oecd.org/migration/refugees-are-not-a-burden-but-an-opportunity.htm

51 The LEGO Foundation (2018) *Learning through Play: Strengthening Learning through Play in Early Childhood Education Programmes*, New York: UNICEF, www.unicef.org/sites/default/files/2018-12/UNICEF-Lego-Foundation-Learning-through-Play.pdf

52 National Scientific Council on the Developing Child (2007) *The Science of Early Childhood Development: Closing the Gap Between What We Know and What We Do*, Cambridge, MA: Center on the Developing Child, Harvard University, www.developingchild.harvard.edu

53 Nores, M. and Barnett, S.W. (2010) 'Benefits of early childhood interventions across the world: (Under) Investing in the very young', *Economics of Education Review*, 29(2): 271–82.

54 Children's Commissioner (2021) 'Child poverty: The crisis we can't keep ignoring', 21 January, www.childrenscommissioner.gov.uk/report/child-poverty

55 *The Guardian* Datablog (no date) 'UK GDP since 1955', www.theguardian.com/news/datablog/2009/nov/25/gdp-uk-1948-growth-economy#data

56 CPAG (Child Poverty Action Group) (2022) *Child Poverty Facts and Figures*, https://cpag.org.uk/child-poverty/child-poverty-facts-and-figures

57 Full Fact (2019) 'Poverty in the UK: A guide to the facts and figures', 27 September, https://fullfact.org/economy/poverty-uk-guide-facts-and-figures

58 Commission on Young Lives (2022) *Hidden in Plain Sight: A National Plan of Action to Support Vulnerable Teenagers to Succeed and to Protect Them from Adversity, Exploitation, and Harm*, November, http://files.localgov.co.uk/sure.pdf

59 Crawford, R. and Emmerson, C. (2020) 'Coming of age: Labour's Child Trust Funds', IFS Comment, 31 August, https://ifs.org.uk/articles/coming-age-labours-child-trust-funds

60 Blair, T. (no date) 'We need a national plan to eradicate child poverty', Children's Commissioner, www.childrenscommissioner.gov.uk/reports/child-poverty/we-need-a-national-plan-to-eradicate-child-poverty

61 Butler, P. (2017) 'Universal credit cuts hits families with children hardest, study finds', *The Guardian*, 1 March, www.theguardian.com/society/2017/mar/01/universal-credit-hits-families-with-children-hardest-study-finds

62 Elliot, L. (2018) 'Halt universal credit or face summer of discontent, Gordon Brown tells PM', *The Guardian*, 10 October, www.theguardian.com/society/2018/oct/10/gordon-brown-halt-universal-credit-rollout

63 Richardson, H. (2018) 'Get in debt or turn down job? Universal Credit's "stark choice"', BBC News Online, 23 December, www.bbc.co.uk/news/education-46649160

64 BBC News Online (2017) 'Universal credit: MPs urge government to cut waiting time', 26 October, www.bbc.co.uk/news/uk-politics-41754280

65 Richardson, H. (2018) 'Universal credit "could cost more than current benefits system"', BBC News Online, 15 June, www.bbc.co.uk/news/education-44468437

66 Morris, S. and Adams, R. (2021) 'Children's commissioners urge UK government to scrap two-child limit for benefits', *The Guardian*, 26 October, www.theguardian.com/uk-news/2021/may/26/childrens-commissioners-urge-uk-government-to-scrap-two-child-limit-for-benefits

67 Butler, P. (2020) 'Two-child benefit cap influencing women's decisions on abortion, says BPAS', *The Guardian*, 3 December, www.theguardian.com/society/2020/dec/03/two-child-limit-on-benefits-a-key-factor-in-many-abortion-decisions-says-charity

68 Butler, P. (2019) 'Two-child benefit limit pushes families further into poverty – study', *The Guardian*, 26 June, www.theguardian.com/society/2019/jun/26/two-child-benefit-limit-pushes-families-further-into-poverty-study

Chapter 10

1 Thunberg, G. (2019) '"You did not act in time": Greta Thunberg's full speech to MPs', *The Guardian*, 23 April, www.theguardian.com/environment/2019/apr/23/greta-thunberg-full-speech-to-mps-you-did-not-act-in-time

2 BBC News (2016) 'EU Referendum: Results', www.bbc.com/news/politics/eu_referendum/results

3 ONS (Office for National Statistics) (2016) 'Overview of the UK population: February 2016', www.ons.gov.uk/peoplepopulationandcommunity/populationandmigration/populationestimates/articles/overviewoftheukpopulation/february2016

4 Curtice, J. (2014) 'So how many 16 and 17 year olds voted?', What Scotland Thinks, 16 December, https://whatscotlandthinks.org/2014/12/many-16-17-year-olds-voted

5 *The Guardian* (2019) '*The Guardian* view on 16-year-old soldiers: Armies are for adults', 21 August, www.theguardian.com/commentisfree/2019/aug/21/the-guardian-view-on-16-year-old-soldiers-armies-are-for-adults

6 ONS (Office for National Statistics) (2020) 'Marriages of 16 and 17 year old grooms and brides by age difference, England and Wales, 2016', www.ons.gov.uk/peoplepopulationandcommunity/birthsdeathsandmarriages/marriagecohabitationandcivilpartnerships/adhocs/11461marriagesof16and17yearoldgroomsandbridesbyagedifferenceenglandandwales2016

7 Quoted in Moorhead, J. (2018) 'Should we give children the vote? We ask nine kids what they think', *The Guardian*, 23 December, www.theguardian.com/global/2018/dec/23/should-we-give-children-the-vote-voting-at-age-6-politics-interviews

8 BBC News (2019) 'Cameron Kasky: How being a student gun control activist took its toll', 13 February, www.bbc.co.uk/news/stories-47217467

9 Weaver, M. (2018) 'Lower voting age to six to tackle bias against young, says academic', *The Guardian*, 6 December, www.theguardian.com/politics/2018/dec/06/give-six-year-olds-the-vote-says-cambridge-university-academic

10 Foa, R.S., Klassen, A., Wenger, D., Rand, A. and Slade, M. (2020) *Youth and Satisfaction with Democracy: Reversing the Democratic Disconnect?*, Cambridge:

Centre for the Future of Democracy, www.bennettinstitute.cam.ac.uk/publications/youth-and-satisfaction-democracy

11 UNICEF (United Nations Children's Fund) (2021) *The Climate Crisis is a Child Rights Crisis: Introducing the Children's Climate Risk Index*, New York: UNICEF, www.unicef.org/reports/climate-crisis-child-rights-crisis

12 UNICEF (United Nations Children's Fund) (2021) 'One billion children at "extremely high risk" of the impacts of the climate crisis', Press release, 19 August, www.unicef.org/press-releases/one-billion-children-extremely-high-risk-impacts-climate-crisis-unicef

13 Parker, L., Mestre, J., Jodoin, S. and Wewerinke-Singh, M. (2022) 'When the kids put climate change on trial: Youth-focused rights-based climate litigation around the world', *Journal of Human Rights and the Environment*, 13(1): 64–89.

14 BBC News (2019) 'Sisters petition McDonald's and Burger King for plastic toy ban', 22 July, www.bbc.co.uk/news/uk-england-hampshire-49069522

15 Billen, A. (2020) 'Burger King, McDonald's and two girls' stand on free plastic toys', *The Times*, 4 April, www.thetimes.co.uk/article/burger-king-mcdonalds-and-two-girls-stand-on-free-plastic-toys-vx608jsqv

16 Wood, Z. (2014) 'Tesco chairman pledges to turn around ailing supermarket group', *The Guardian*, 27 June, www.theguardian.com/business/2014/jun/27/tesco-chairman-pledgres-turnaround

17 Fridays For Future (no date) 'Who we are', https://fridaysforfuture.org/what-we-do/who-we-are

18 BBC News (2019) 'School strike for climate: Protests staged around the world', 24 May, www.bbc.co.uk/news/world-48392551

19 Fridays For Future (no date) 'Strike statistics', https://fridaysforfuture.org/what-we-do/strike-statistics

20 Friends of the Earth (2020) 'Over two-thirds of young people experience eco-anxiety as Friends of the Earth launch campaign to turn anxiety into action', Press release, 21 January, https://friendsoftheearth.uk/climate/over-twothirds-young-people-experience-ecoanxiety-friends-earth-launch-campaign-turn

21 Zero Hour (2020) *Climate & Ecology Bill*, www.zerohour.uk/bill

22 *Wakefield Express* (2018) 'Parts of Wakefield among the most deprived in the UK', 28 February, www.wakefieldexpress.co.uk/news/parts-of-wakefield-among-the-most-deprived-in-the-uk-286698

23 The Wildlife Trusts (no date) 'The natural world is the foundation of our health, wellbeing and prosperity', www.wildlifetrusts.org/nature-health-and-wild-wellbeing

24 Costanza, R., d'Arge, R., de Groot, R., et al (1997) 'The value of the world's ecosystem services and natural capital', *Nature*, 387: 253–60.

25 Costanza, R., d'Arge, R., de Groot, R., et al (1997) 'The value of the world's ecosystem services and natural capital', *Nature*, 387: 253–60.

26 Xu, C., Kohler, T.A., Lenton, T.M., Svenning, J.-C. and Scheffer, M. (2020) 'Future of the human climate niche', *Proceedings of the National Academy of Sciences of the United States of America*, 17(21): 11350–5.

[27] Global Climate Change (2022) 'Vital signs: Carbon dioxide', https://climate.nasa.gov/vital-signs/carbon-dioxide

[28] Farese, N.R. (2021) *Potential Space: A Serious Look at Child's Play*, New York: MW Editions.

[29] The UN Refugee Agency (no date) 'Refugee statistics', www.unrefugees.org/refugee-facts/statistics

[30] Haidt, J. and Lukianoff, G. (2018) 'How to play our way to a better democracy', *The New York Times*, 1 September, www.nytimes.com/2018/09/01/opinion/sunday/democracy-play-mccain.html

[31] Horwitz, S. (2015) 'Cooperation over coercion: The importance of unsupervised childhood play for democracy and liberalism', SSRN, https://papers.ssrn.com/sol3/papers.cfm?abstract_id=2621848

[32] Free-Range Kids (2015) 'The Free-Range Kids & Parents Bill of Rights', 10 February, www.freerangekids.com/the-free-range-kids-parents-bill-of-rights

[33] UNGA (United Nations General Assembly) (1989) 'Convention on the Rights of the Child', *United Nations Treaty Series*, 1577(3): 1–23, www.ohchr.org/en/instruments-mechanisms/instruments/convention-rights-child

[34] The New School (no date) 'Our principles', www.thenewschool.org.uk/principles

[35] Cracknell, R., Tunnicliffe, R., Barton, C. and Audickas, L. (2022) 'Social background of Members of Parliament 1979–2019', House of Commons Library Research Briefing, 15 February, https://commonslibrary.parliament.uk/research-briefings/cbp-7483

[36] Taylor, R. and Aguilar Garcia, C. (2019) 'Commons people: How diverse are MPs – and do they reflect the UK?', Sky News, 12 November, https://news.sky.com/story/commons-people-how-diverse-are-mps-and-do-they-reflect-the-uk-11829868

[37] Turkie, A. (2009) 'More than Crumbs from the Table: A Critique of Youth Parliaments as Models of Representation for Marginalised Young People', in B. Percy-Smith and N.P. Thomas (eds) *A Handbook of Children and Young People's Participation*, Abingdon: Routledge, pp 284–91.

[38] Children and Young People's Assembly on Biodiversity Loss (no date) Home page, https://cyp-biodiversity.ie

[39] Laughland, O. (2021) 'Claudettte Colvin – the woman who refused to give up her bus seat nine months before Rosa Parks', *The Guardian*, 25 February, www.theguardian.com/society/2021/feb/25/claudette-colvin-the-woman-who-refused-to-give-up-her-bus-seat-nine-months-before-rosa-parks

[40] Johnstone, N. and Uberoi, E. (2022) 'Voter ID', House of Commons Library Research Briefing, 10 March, https://commonslibrary.parliament.uk/research-briefings/cbp-9187

[41] Garland, J. (2022) 'Voter ID list gives few options for younger voters', Electoral Reform Society, 11 November, www.electoral-reform.org.uk/voter-id-list-gives-few-options-for-younger-voters

[42] All voters can apply to their local council for a Voter Card free of charge if they don't possess one of the approved photo identifications. See DLUCH

(Department for Levelling Up, Communities and Housing) (2022) 'Protecting the integrity of our elections: Voter identification at polling stations and the new Voter Card, Annex A: List of identity documents that will be accepted', www.gov.uk/government/publications/voter-identification-at-polling-stations-and-the-new-voter-card/protecting-the-integrity-of-our-elections-voter-identification-at-polling-stations-and-the-new-voter-card#annex-a-list-of-identity-documents-that-will-be-accepted

43 EHRC (Equality and Human Rights Commission) (no date) 'Your rights under the Equality Act 2010', www.equalityhumanrights.com/en/advice-and-guidance/your-rights-under-equality-act-2010

44 Children's Rights Alliance for England (no date) 'Making the most of the Equality Act 2010', https://crae.org.uk/sites/default/files/uploads/CRAE-Equality-Act-2010-guide.pdf

45 Daly, A., Stern, R.T. and Leviner, P. (2022) 'UN Convention on the Rights of the Child, Article 2 and discrimination on the basis of childhood: The CRC paradox?', *Nordic Journal of International Law*, 91(3): 419–52.

46 Young Equals (2009) *Making the Case: Why Children Should Be Protected from Age Discrimination and How It Can Be Done. Proposals for the Equality Bill*, London: Young Equals, https://archive.crin.org/en/docs/Making_case_3.pdf

47 UK Parliament (2022) *Wellbeing of Future Generations Bill [HL]*, https://bills.parliament.uk/bills/3315

48 UK Government (no date) 'The Office of the Children's Commissioner', www.gov.uk/government/organisations/office-of-the-children-s-commissioner

49 Children's Commissioner (2020) *Report to the United Nations Committee on the Rights of the Child*, 10 December, www.childrenscommissioner.gov.uk/report/report-to-the-united-nations-committee-on-the-rights-of-the-child

50 UNICEF (United Nations Children's Fund) (1989) *The United Nations Convention on the Rights of the Child*, www.unicef.org.uk/wp-content/uploads/2010/05/UNCRC_united_nations_convention_on_the_rights_of_the_child.pdf

51 UNICEF (United Nations Children's Fund) (no date) 'How we protect children's rights with the UN Convention on the Rights of the Child', www.unicef.org.uk/what-we-do/un-convention-child-rights

52 UN (United Nations) (no date) 'Introduction to the Committee', www.ohchr.org/en/treaty-bodies/crc/introduction-committee

53 Sandland, R. (2017) 'Lessons for Children's Rights from Disability Rights?', in E. Brems, E. Desmet and W. Vandenhole (eds) *Children's Rights Law in the Global Human Rights Landscape. Isolation, Inspiration, Integration?*, Abingdon: Routledge, pp 109–28, p 124.

54 ECPAT (Every Child Protected Against Trafficking) (no date) 'Important wins for child rights as the House of Lords pushes back on Priti Patel's Nationality and Borders Bill with five major changes at report stage', Press release, www.ecpat.org.uk/news/important-wins-for-child-rights-as-the-

house-of-lords-pushes-back-on-priti-patels-nationality-and-borders-bill-with-five-major-changes-at-report-stage

55 *R (SC) v Secretary of State for Work and Pensions* and *R (AB) v Secretary of State for Justice.*

56 *R (SC) v Secretary of State for Work and Pensions* and *R (AB) v Secretary of State for Justice*, para 162.

57 Our focus on Scotland is not to diminish moves made by other devolved administrations to embed the UNCRC into decision making, such as children's rights impact assessments in Wales and Northern Ireland's efforts to incorporate the Convention into policy and legislative vehicles.

58 While an October 2021 UK Supreme Court judgment ruled that certain provisions concerning duties on public authorities were beyond the Scottish Parliament's legislative competence, at the time of writing work is still ongoing to reach a compromise and ensure that incorporation to the maximum extent possible is carried out.

59 Scottish Government (2019) *United Nations Convention on the Rights of the Child: Consultation Analysis*, www.gov.scot/publications/uncrc-consultation-analysis-report/pages/5

60 UN Committee on the Rights of the Child (2021) 'List of issues prior to submission of the combined sixth and seventh reports of the United Kingdom of Great Britain and Northern Ireland', CRC/C/GBR/QPR/6-7, https://digitallibrary.un.org/record/3905476

61 UCL News (2021) 'Smacking young children has lasting effects', 13 January, www.ucl.ac.uk/news/2021/jan/smacking-young-children-has-long-lasting-effects

62 Children's Commissioner (2020) *'Are We There Yet?' Our Rights, Our Say*, A report for the UN Committee on the Rights of the Child, www.childrenscommissioner.gov.uk/wp-content/uploads/2020/12/cco-are-we-there-yet.pdf

63 UNICEF UK (no date) 'Rights Respecting Schools', www.unicef.org.uk/rights-respecting-schools

64 Kohn, A. (1993) *Choices for Children: Why and How to Let Students Decide*, www.alfiekohn.org/article/choices-children/?print=print

Chapter 11

1 Yousafzai, M. (2013) '16th birthday speech at the United Nations', https://malala.org/newsroom/malala-un-speech

2 WHO (World Health Organization) (2023) 'WHO Coronavirus (COVID-19) Dashboard', https://covid19.who.int

3 UNICEF (United Nations Children's Fund) (no date) 'Child poverty', www.unicef.org/social-policy/child-poverty

4 Kennedy, R.F. (1966) 'Day of Affirmation Address, University of Cape Town, Cape Town, South Africa, June 6 1966', www.jfklibrary.org/learn/about-jfk/the-kennedy-family/robert-f-kennedy/robert-f-kennedy-speeches/day-of-affirmation-address-news-release-version-university-of-capetown-capetown-south-africa-june-6, p 119.

5   Quoted in Kennedy, K., Adams, E. and Richardson, N. (2001) *Speak Truth To Power: Human Rights Defenders Who Are Changing Our World*, New York: Random House International, p 119.

6   Quoted in Kennedy, K., Adams, E. and Richardson, N. (2001) *Speak Truth To Power: Human Rights Defenders Who Are Changing Our World*, New York: Random House International, p 61.

7   Quoted in Kennedy, K., Adams, E. and Richardson, N. (2001) *Speak Truth To Power: Human Rights Defenders Who Are Changing Our World*, New York: Random House International, p 193.

8   Quoted in Kennedy, K., Adams, E. and Richardson, N. (2001) *Speak Truth To Power: Human Rights Defenders Who Are Changing Our World*, New York: Random House International, p 15.

9   Siddiqui, N. (2021) *Speak Truth to Power. Human Rights Education Programme in UK Schools. Programme Delivery and Impact*, RFK Human Rights UK www.rfkhumanrights.uk/_files/ugd/f87030_55bf00d990db4929936e1213 6c637cc2.pdf

Chapter 12

1   Kennedy, J.F. (1963) 'Televised address to the nation on civil rights, 11 June 1963', www.jfklibrary.org/learn/about-jfk/historic-speeches/televised-address-to-the-nation-on-civil-rights

2   Yates, J. (2021) *Fractured: Why Our Societies Are Coming Apart and How We Put Them Back Together Again*, Manchester: HarperNorth.

3   UNICEF (United Nations Children's Fund) (2020) *World of Influence: Understanding What Shapes Child Well-being in Rich Countries*, Innocenti Report Card 16, Florence: UNICEF Office of Research – Innocenti, www. unicef-irc.org/publications/pdf/Report-Card-16-Worlds-of-Influence-child-wellbeing.pdf

4   OECD (Organisation for Economic Co-operation and Development) (2018) *A Broken Social Elevator? How to Promote Social Mobility*, Paris: OECD, www.oecd.org/social/broken-elevator-how-to-promote-social-mobility-9789264301085-en.htm

5   Wolf, S. and Bruhn, J. (1998) *The Power of Clan: Influence of Human Relationships on Heart Disease*, Abingdon: Routledge.

6   Page-Gould, E., Mendoza-Denton, R. and Tropp, L.R. (2008) 'With a little help from my cross-group friend: Reducing anxiety in intergroup contexts through cross-group friendship', *Journal of Personality and Social Psychology*, 95(5): 1080–94.

7   Chetty, R., Hendren, N., Kline, P. and Saez, E. (2014) 'Where is the land of opportunity? The geography of intergenerational mobility in the United States', *The Quarterly Journal of Economics*, 129(4): 1553–623.

8   Shepherd, J. (2011) 'Academies and free schools get right to reserve places for poorer pupils', *The Guardian*, 27 May, www.theguardian.com/education/2011/may/27/academies-free-schools-poorer-pupils

9   Moreno, M., Mulford, B. and Hargreaves, A. (2007) *Trusting Leadership: From Standards to Social Capital*, Nottingham: National College for School Leadership.

10 Groves, M. and West-Burnham, J. (2013) *Schools of Tomorrow: Towards a New Understanding of Outstanding schools*, Peterborough: The Beauchamp Group.

11 Nuthall, G. (2007) *The Hidden Lives of Learners*, Wellington, New Zealand: NZCER Press.

Chapter 13

1   Jefferson, T. et al (1776) *Declaration of Independence*, 4th July, www.archives. gov/founding-docs/declaration

2   Davis, T. (2019) 'What is well-being? Definition, types, and well-being skills', *Psychology Today*, 2 January, www.psychologytoday.com/us/blog/ click-here-happiness/201901/what-is-well-being-definition-types-and-well-being-skills

3   MacAlister, J. (2022) *The Independent Review of Children's Social Care*, www. gov.uk/government/groups/independent-review-of-childrens-social-care

4   UNICEF (United Nations Children's Fund) (2019) 'Child health experts warn air pollution is damaging children's health', Press release, www.unicef. org.uk/press-releases/child-health-experts-warn-air-pollution-is-damaging-childrens-health

5   Bite Back 2030 (no date) 'About us', www.biteback2030.com/about-us

6   Save the Children (2022) 'Spring statement 2022', Twitter, https://twitter. com/savechildrenuk/status/1506579916267180032?s=20&t=WHpjusrt2w 217GPe2vfTIA

7   ONS (Office for National Statistics) (2022) 'Families and households in the UK: 2021', 9 March, www.ons.gov.uk/peoplepopulationandcommunity/ birthsdeathsandmarriages/families/bulletins/familiesandhouseholds/latest

8   Resolution Foundation (2022) 'Inflation nation: Putting Spring Statement 2022 in context', 24 March, www.resolutionfoundation.org/publications/ inflation-nation

9   Kirkup, J. (2020) 'Why does Labour "welcome" school closures?', *The Spectator*, www.spectator.co.uk/article/why-does-rebecca-long-bailey-welcome-school-closures-

10 Hughes, R.C., Absoud, M. and Bhopal, S.S. (2022) 'Is the UK's covid inquiry at risk of forgetting about children and young people?', *BMJ*, 376.

11 Schleicher, A. (2019) *PISA 2018: Insights and Interpretations*, Paris: OECD Publishing.

12 The Gregson Family Foundation (no date) Home page, https:// gregsonfoundation.org.uk

13 The Gregson Family Foundation (2020) 'PISA 2018: Analysis of implications for the UK', March, https://img1.wsimg.com/blobby/go/4971bc14-d459-4e68-b6c3-e9d9f7a014e5/downloads/PISA%202018%20-%20Analysis%20 of%20implications%20for%20the%20U.pdf?ver=1606327004812

14 Acosta, R.M. and Hutchison, M. (2017) *The Happiest Kids in the World: Bringing Up Children the Dutch Way*, New York: Random House.

[15] Youth Monitor (no date) Home page, https://jeugdmonitor.cbs.nl/en/home-en

[16] DutchNews.nl (2020) 'Dutch press ahead with easing covid-19 rules and ramping up testing', 19 May, www.dutchnews.nl/news/2020/05/dutch-press-ahead-with-easing-covid-19-rules-and-ramping-up-testing

[17] Youth Sport Trust (2021) 'Parents want well-being prioritised in schools as pandemic hits home', www.youthsporttrust.org/news-insight/news/parents-want-wellbeing-prioritised-in-schools-as-pandemic-hits-home

[18] Times Education Commission (2022) '"A lack of preparation for the world of work": The business view on education', 26 January, www.thetimes.co.uk/article/times-education-commission-the-business-view-on-education-mvqc2sjqd

Chapter 14

[1] UNGA (United Nations General Assembly) (1989) 'Convention on the Rights of the Child', *United Nations Treaty Series*, 1577(3): 1–23, www.ohchr.org/en/instruments-mechanisms/instruments/convention-rights-child

[2] HM Treasury (2021) 'Second UK Green Gilt raises further £6 billion for green projects', News story, 21 October, www.gov.uk/government/news/second-uk-green-gilt-raises-further-6-billion-for-green-projects

[3] Cabinet Office (2022) 'Social Impact Bonds and the Life Chances Fund', www.gov.uk/guidance/social-impact-bonds

[4] In 2022 the Labour Party, in opposition, pledged to establish an £8 billion Green National Wealth Fund as part of its manifesto commitment at the next general election. See Devlin, K. (2022) 'Labour pledges new "wealth fund" to give taxpayers stake in green British industries', *The Independent*, 26 September, www.independent.co.uk/news/uk/politics/rachel-reeves-labour-wealth-fund-industry-b2174891.html

[5] Nordic Council of Ministers (2016) *Children and Young People in the Nordic: Region – A Cross-Sectoral Strategy for the Nordic Council of Ministers 2016–2022*, www.norden.org/en/publication/children-and-young-people-nordic-region

[6] Aho, E., Pitkanen, K. and Sahlberg, P. (2006) *Policy Development and Reform Principles of Basic and Secondary Education in Finland Since 1968*, Education, Working Paper Series Number 2, https://pasisahlberg.com/wp-content/uploads/2013/01/Education-in-Finland-2006.pdf

[7] Mandela, N. (1995) 'Address by President Nelson Mandela at the dedication of Qunu and Nkalane Schools', www.mandela.gov.za/mandela_speeches/1995/950603_qunu.htm

Index